A GUIDE FOR
NEW
TESTAMENT
STUDY

A GUIDE FOR
NEW
TESTAMENT
STUDY

William W. Stevens

BROADMAN PRESS
Nashville, Tennessee

4213-60
ISBN: 0-8054-1360-X

All Scripture quotations are taken
from the American Standard Version.

Dewey Decimal Classification: 225.07
Subject Headings: BIBLE, NEW TESTAMENT—STUDY

Library of Congress Catalog Card Number: 76-62920
Printed in the United States of America

To my three sons
William,
David,
and
John.

CONTENTS

PART FOUR
The Acts of the Apostles:
Holy Spirit Extending the Church

PART FIVE
The Epistles:
Conflicts Confronting the Church

PART SIX
The Apocalypse:
God Fulfilling the Church

Charts, Photographs, and Maps

Photographic Credits

We are grateful to the Foreign Mission Board, Southern Baptist Convention, Richmond, Virginia, for the use of photographs appearing on pages 132, 137, 146, 167, 177, 206, 224, 229, 245, 258, 261, 269, 309, 342, 347, 352, 373, 380, 382, 386; also to the Israel Government Tourist Office for photographs on pages 188 and 316.

PART ONE

The Christian Background: Pagan and Jewish

1.
Historical Summary

1. The New Testament in the Light of the Old

To the casual reader of the Bible it is very obvious that there is a definite relationship between the Old Testament and the New Testament. The Old Testament looks forward and anticipates the New, while the New looks back and builds upon the Old. The New not only supplements the Old; it complements it as well. The Old anticipates; the New presupposes. The leaders and writers of the New Testament were well aware that they were heirs of a very rich spiritual heritage and that what they had heard and seen and beheld (1 John 1:1) was a fulfillment of Old Testament anticipation.

Jesus himself recognized that he was the realization of that which Abraham, Moses, and the prophets had envisioned. To the Jews he declared, "Your father Abraham rejoiced to see my day: and he saw it, and was glad" (John 8:56). In connection with Jesus' unique interview with the two disciples on the road to Emmaus, Luke revealed, "And beginning from Moses and from all the prophets, he interpreted to them in all the scriptures the things concerning himself" (Luke 24:27).

Bible history is salvation history or faith history, the history of the mighty acts of God performed here on earth as he revealed himself to his people. This revelation reached a climax in Christ, the apex of it all. What God initiated at creation and continued at Calvary will be consummated some great day when all the loose ends of history will be tied together. Both the Old and New Testaments have vital roles in conveying this redemption history. The New Testament becomes much richer in meaning when it is studied in the light of the Old Testament. There is truly a unity in the Bible, a unity that stems from the central theme of redemptive love.

2. The Old Testament Era and Hebrew History

Due to the importance of the Old Testament in New Testament interpretation, it is appropriate to consider a brief summary of Hebrew history.

(1) The Beginnings The first eleven chapters of the book of Genesis

deal with many "beginnings": of the world, of man, of the home, of the sabbath, and of sin. This section contains the account of the temptation and fall of man, with his consequent punishment. There is the slaying of Abel and the birth of Seth. There is the account of the flood, the building of the ark, and the new start after the flood. The tower of Babel and the confusion of tongues are also depicted.

(2)   Patriarchal Age   The twelfth chapter of Genesis starts the history of Abraham, and thus the history of the Hebrews as a nation. This was about 1900 B.C. There is the call of Abraham in Mesopotamia and the ensuing career of the forefather of the Hebrew race. This is followed by the career of Isaac, the very dramatic fortune of Jacob and his twelve sons, and the changes of life encountered by Joseph. Genesis continues with the journey of Jacob and his sons to Egypt and ends with the death of Joseph in the land of the Nile.

(3)   From Slavery to Freedom   Starting with the book of Exodus there is the story of the bondage of the Israelites by the Egyptians and the very dramatic deliverance of God's peculiar people to the land of Canaan, a work of epic nature performed by Moses about 1250 B.C. The events of the book of Exodus are continued in Leviticus, Numbers, and Deuteronomy. Moses, born and reared in Egypt by the daughter of pharaoh as her own son, was the towering figure in this era. Fleeing to the land of the Midianites in the Sinaitic peninsula, he lived a nomadic life for forty years. There he was called of God to return to Egypt to deliver the Hebrews from their degrading bondage.

With much fortitude and amid extreme difficulty, he led God's people forth to Mt. Sinai. Here they received the covenant, with its accompanying law, and then proceeded to Kadesh. Due to their sin of lack of faith to enter the land of Canaan and to capture its inhabitants, they were forced to wander nearly forty years. After many trials and hardships Moses led them to the land east of the Jordan, where they conquered the occupants of that territory. Then he relinquished his leadership to Joshua just prior to his mysterious death and burial on Mount Nebo.

(4)   Conquest and Occupation   The books of Joshua and Judges tell of the conquest of the land of Canaan by the very able general Joshua. This was the land of their forefathers: Abraham, Isaac, and Jacob. Subsequent to the so-called conquest the land was divided among the twelve tribes. After the death of Joshua there ensued what is called the period of the judges, an age of denying the spiritual and of moral decay, sometimes called the "dark ages" of Hebrew history. The last and greatest leader of this period, one who became the transition between the period of the judges

and the monarchy, was Samuel.

(5) **The Hebrew Kingdom**   This period may be divided into two sections: the undivided kingdom and the divided kingdom. The former consisted of the reigns of Saul, David, and Solomon, forty years each. Saul, son of Kish, was the only king in his dynasty, for David was the son of Jesse of the tribe of Judah. Under David the monarchy grew into an empire of vast proportions, with the years of David and Solomon becoming known as the "golden age" of Israel's history. But the unwise policies of Solomon shattered the extensive empire. The resultant divided kingdom consisted of the kingdom of Israel in the north, ending in the fall of Samaria in 722–721 B.C., and the kingdom of Judah in the south, ending in the fall of Jerusalem in 587–586 B.C.

Israel fell to Assyrian might and Judah fell to Babylonian might. Israel was ruled by nineteen kings in all, consisting of nine dynasties; Judah was also under the sovereignty of nineteen kings, but there was only one dynasty. This was the Davidic dynasty established by David, son of Jesse, and is the line of kings found in the genealogy of Joseph in Matthew 1:2–16. Just before and after the fall of Jerusalem about 50,000 people of Judah were taken captive to Babylonia.

(6) **The Babylonian Exile and Restoration**   The Hebrews remained in Babylonian captivity for about seventy years, not as slaves but as colonists. They were restricted only in that they could not return to Jerusalem and Judah. Just as there had been three deportations to Babylonia, there were also three returns to their homeland, the latter due to the lenient policy of Cyrus, king of Persia. Under the leadership of Zerubbabel the Temple was rebuilt; under the guidance of Ezra the people were instructed in the law; and under the supervision of Nehemiah the walls of Jerusalem were restored and the reform instituted under Ezra was continued. Still subjects of Persian sovereignty, the Jews were at least in their beloved homeland. With this status the Old Testament closes about 400 B.C.

3. The Interbiblical Period

The period of time extending from the close of the Old Testament era and ending with the birth of Christ is termed the interbiblical, or intertestamental, period. It was an era of defeat and triumph, sorrow and joy, tribulation and victory for the Jews in Palestine. Knowledge of this period is essential for understanding the meaning and message of the New Testament. Far-reaching changes took place in the political, social, economic, and religious life of the Jews. From the end of Malachi to the beginning of

Matthew the reader finds himself in a new environment, a different life indeed.

Since neither the Old Testament nor the New Testament provides knowledge concerning this period, to what historical records do we turn for information? There are primarily three sources. First, there are the writings of Flavius Josephus, the Jewish historian and military commander living from about A.D. 37 to about 100. Although his major works are four in number, the one that reveals much of the events concerning the Jews during the interbiblical period is *The Antiquities,* consisting of several volumes written in A.D. 93–94. It is a history of the Hebrew nation from creation to A.D. 66, the date of the start of the Jewish war with Rome. Were it not for his literary endeavors, we would know little of the Jews from about 333 B.C. to A.D. 100.

The second source of information of the interbiblical period is the Apocrypha, Jewish books written between 200 B.C. and A.D. 100 that are both historical and religious in nature. *Apocrypha* is a Greek term meaning "hidden" or "secret." There are fourteen books in all: 1 Esdras, 2 Esdras, Tobit, Judith, the Rest of Esther, Wisdom of Solomon, Ecclesiasticus, Baruch, Song of the Three Holy Children, Susanna, Bel and the Dragon, Prayer of Manasseh, 1 Maccabees, 2 Maccabees. The Greek-speaking Jews regarded these books as inspired of God, while the Aramaic-speaking Jews of Palestine did not regard them as God-given oracles.

Since Protestants follow the Hebrew Old Testament canon derived from Palestine, they do not accept the Aprocrypha as being inspired. However, Roman Catholics follow the Greek Alexandrian canon of the Old Testament; therefore, they consider the Apocrypha as inspired. Even though Protestants do not consider the fourteen books as divinely given, they do regard them as profitable sources of Jewish historical information, especially in the interbiblical era. First and Second Maccabees are very helpful in this respect.

The third source, though definitely the least in importance, is the work of secular historians. The brief allusions made by Roman and other historians to the Jews and their life in Palestine during the few centuries prior to the Christian era do not add significantly to the knowledge offered by Josephus and the Apocrypha. Yet these writings do constitute a primary historical source.

4. Divisions of the Interbiblical Period

Since the Jews were under four distinct governmental authorities during the time between the Old and New Testaments, it is usual to divide the period into four sections: Persian sovereignty from 538 to 332 B.C.; Greek control from 332 to 167 B.C.; Hebrew independence (Maccabean dynasty) from 167 to 63 B.C.; Roman domination from 63 B.C. to A.D. 70 (the destruction of Jerusalem). Since the interbiblical period goes from c. 400 B.C. to 4 or 5 B.C., it is discerned that the dates given for the four divisions overlap the actual period, per se. They were under Persian control when it started and under Roman control when it terminated with the birth of our Lord.

5. Persian Mastery

Assyrian conquest grew under Tiglath-pileser until Assyria, with its capital at Nineveh on the Tigris, was master of all Mesopotamia and vast areas beyond. The Hebrew kingdom of Israel came under its sway with the fall of Samaria in 722 B.C., with Israel becoming one of its satellite nations. But Assyrian aggression was to succumb to Babylonian militarism; for Nebuchadnezzar enlarged that empire, with its capital at Babylon on the Euphrates, to encompass all that Assyria had and more. Due to waning Assyrian strength Nineveh finally fell in 612 B.C. to the Babylonians. The Hebrew kingdom of Judah, unable to cope with the surging power of such a formidable nation, finally surrendered with the fall of Jerusalem in 587 B.C.; and about 50,000 Hebrews were marched in chains to the territory of the Euphrates.

Yet, a new and mightier foe was gathering its forces in the northeast. This was Persia, under Cyrus the Great. One of the most remarkable of ancient kings, Cyrus built an empire embracing far more territory than anyone prior to his time. He first emerged as a man of royal blood, thirty years of age in the province of Anshan in Media, where he revolted and took as prisoner the Median king. Marching south, he captured Persia and formed the Medo-Persian kingdom. Wisely bypassing Babylon at this time, he marched against northern Mesopotamia and Armenia, then on into Asia Minor.

Within twenty years his domain encompassed most of the land from the Indus River in the east to the Aegean Sea in the west. Then he besieged Babylon in 539 B.C., capturing it the next year with a masterful plan. The Euphrates flowed through the middle of the city; Cyrus diverted the waters so they no longer went through it. Then his armies marched down the river bed and under the gates, forcing a surrender almost without a fight. Cyrus was at last master of the entire Middle East.

6. Lenient Policy of Cyrus

Cyrus the Great had keen insight in administering the affairs of his gigantic realm. Conquered people prior to his time were treated ruthlessly, being moved far from their homelands to distant realms. Many times other peoples were moved into the subjected territory to intermarry with the remaining residents. Such had been the policy of the Assyrians and Babylonians. Cyrus reversed that plan with a general proclamation that all displaced people in his empire could return to their fatherlands, where they might worship their gods in their own sanctuaries. The proclamation to the Jews came in 538 B.C., two copies being found in the book of Ezra (1:2–4; 6:3–5).

Anyone reading Cyrus' decree might be led to think that he was a devotee of Jehovah, the God of Israel; but a study of various other inscriptions of Cyrus show him to have been a polytheist, one desiring the favor of all of his gods. Yet Cyrus became God's providential agent in accomplishing the divine purpose for Israel. In Isaiah 44:28 he is termed God's shepherd, and in Isaiah 45:1 he is called God's anointed.

Due to the famous decree three migrations returned to Jerusalem: one under Zerubbabel, one under Ezra, and one under Nehemiah. Scholars estimate that a total of 60,000 people returned, not a large number, indeed. Babylonian culture was too enticing, and Cyrus' tolerant policy was too comforting. Many of the Jews had not only intermarried but had become well settled in business ventures, and their knowledge of their remote homeland was only secondhand. Many lacked the faith necessary to leave an economically secure life to face the hazardous journey home to the bleak hills of Judah and to a devastated Jerusalem.

The rebuilding of the Temple under Zerubbabel, the reforms executed by Ezra as he endeavored to emphasize the importance of the Mosaic law, and the discouragements and triumphs of Nehemiah as he rebuilt the wall of Jerusalem and led in needed reforms are vividly described in the books of Ezra, Nehemiah, Haggai, and Zechariah. At this time the Jews were in a state of servitude under Persia; for though Persia was benevolent in many ways, Persian might was still supreme. Authority emanated from Susa, the capital, to all corners of the domain, of which Palestine was merely one small segment. Yet apparently there was no outspoken resentment on the part of the Jews toward their overlords. When the Old Testament period came to a close the Jews were still vassals of Persia, a condition that prevailed to 332 B.C.

7. Greek Sovereignty

The Greek nation was to affect mightily the course of ancient history, for the Greek way of life, which is called *Hellenism*, was indeed remarkable.

They excelled in every phase of life and every area of human activity. The name *Athens* is synonymous with intellectual and philosophical achievement. All the arts flourished lavishly. Philosophy, sculpture, architecture, literature, dramatics, physical games, rhetoric, debate, language—all played parts which made the Greeks the greatest contributor to culture in the history of mankind. Prominent Greek names are immediately recalled—Socrates, Plato, Aristotle, Diogenes, Xenophon, Demosthenes, Zeno, and many others. Greek culture was so enticing that it was carried by devotees into far distant parts, there to affect mankind mightily for centuries. There was truly a diffusion of the Greek spirit permeating both the East and the West.

However, the military superiority of the Greeks should never be underestimated. Philip II was king of Macedonia, a Greek state just north of Achaia. Having an aggressive military spirit, he built in Macedonia a strong military state; but he also was successful in leading the small Greek city-states into a Hellenic league, thus making Macedonia strong and united, the first real nation in European history. He prepared the way for his brilliant son, Alexander III, born in 356 B.C. at Pella, the capital of Macedonia. The youth's mother was Olympias.

Alexander truly deserved the title "the Great." He was handsome, athletic, and loved hunting and riding. When fourteen years of age he was personally tutored by the famous philosopher Aristotle, who influenced him tremendously, especially in a love for literature and for the Greek way of life. Logic, science, and drama were specialties for the great philosopher, so these must have been part of the curriculum Aristotle imposed upon his young student. Alexander is said to have memorized Homer's *Iliad*, a story of the deeds of Achilles, his constant model in all things.

8. Conquests of Alexander the Great

At the death of his father Alexander took over as king, being twenty years of age at the time. He soon had to quell a revolt by the city of Thebes, which he defeated and plundered as a punishment. Crossing the Hellespont into Asia Minor with an army of 35,000 men in 334 B.C., he turned his attention to conquering Persia. He met the Persians at the river Granicus and defeated them.

Proceeding further, he conquered King Darius III of Persia at Issus. Then he marched on through Syria to Phoenicia and captured Tyre, sometimes considered his greatest victory. Since Tyre was on an island he built a causeway out to it, making it submit after a seven-month siege. Then he captured Gaza after a three-month siege and marched on into Egypt. The Egyptians welcomed him, for they hated their harsh Persian overlords. At the mouth of the Nile on the island of Pharos he built the city Alexandria, destined to become a center of world commerce and learning.

With Syria and Egypt under his control, Alexander turned eastward with an enormous army in 331 B.C. and met the Persians on a vast plain at Arbela, east of the Tigris River. Again Alexander routed Darius and his army, this battle being considered by some one of the fifteen decisive battles of history. Babylon soon succumbed to his might; then Susa and Persepolis, capitals of Persia, also fell.

The next few years were interspersed with further battles; and in 327 he entered India, sailing down to the mouth of the Indus River. Then he turned back west to organize and administer his huge realm. His aim was to combine Asia and Europe, thus bringing together the best of the East and the West. He encouraged both intermarriage and the spread of Greek culture into Asia. He chose Babylon as the site of his new capital and planned for an invasion of Arabia.

But Alexander, though able to conquer vast hordes of people and extensive territory, could not master himself. He drank to excess and in 323 B.C. died of malarial fever in Babylon, a little over eleven years after crossing the Hellespont and starting his dramatic military career. He had introduced Hellenism to the East, but the East had made its imprint on him. The luxuries and revelry of the Orient had weakened him. He had become vain and suspicious, taking on many of the characteristics of an Oriental despot. After having made an indelible imprint upon history, his career came to a close at the young age of thirty-two years.

9. The Division of an Empire

When Alexander's meteoric conquests suddenly terminated, there was no one appointed to succeed him. He had left no heirs old enough to take the throne, so his vast domain was divided four ways, each of his four major generals receiving a portion. Ptolemy acquired Egypt and southern Syria; Cassander acquired Greece and Macedonia; Antigonus received western Babylonia and northern Syria; Lysimachus claimed western Asia Minor and Thrace.

A little later Seleucus I took over the territory held by Antigonus, and the territory held by Lysimachus was also absorbed by the Seleucid kings. This left the Ptolemaic kingdom of Egypt and the Seleucid kingdom of Syria, with the Jews sandwiched in between and desired by each one. The armies of the two nations marched up and down the coastal plain of Palestine, with the country falling under the dominion of one power, then the other. The high priesthood and most of the people were in favor of the Seleucids, while some of the people favored the Ptolemies; so even the Jews were divided in their loyalties.

10. The Ptolemies of Egypt

When Alexander died in 323 B.C., the Jews found themselves under the Ptolemies; but this did not last, for Jerusalem changed hands many times during the next quarter of a century. However, nominally speaking the Jews were ruled by the Ptolemies from 323 to 198 B.C. Whenever the Jews were subject to these Egyptians kings, they experienced peace and security; for these rulers had generally a lenient attitude toward their subjugated people.

11. The Septuagint

The greatest event, as far as the Jews were concerned, occurring during the reign of the Ptolemies was the translation of the Hebrew Scriptures into the Greek language. The Jews living in Alexandria, as well as in many other places outside of Palestine, had ceased to speak in their native tongue and had turned to Greek. So the Alexandrian Jews translated the Hebrew Scriptures into Greek, a version that became known as the *Septuagint*, meaning seventy, since seventy men are supposed to have produced it. (Actually seventy-two men made the translation.) It is often designated by the symbol LXX, from the Roman numerals for seventy.

This version was not only used exclusively by the Jews of the Dispersion (Jews outside of Palestine) but by the writers of the New Testament as well. When one of them wanted to quote an Old Testament passage in his Greek writing, he would quote from the Septuagint rather than make his own translation from the Hebrew. The Septuagint was the Bible of the early Greek-speaking Christians. It was known to well-educated Gentiles throughout the Greco-Roman world; and it is an aid to present Bible study, for it throws light on the meaning of many of the Greek words used in the New Testament.

The Jews of Alexandria accepted the Septuagint as their official Bible or canon, but they added to that canon the fourteen books known as the Apocrypha. (See the section in this chapter entitled "The Interbiblical Period.")

The Jewish historian Josephus and philosopher Philo never quoted from the Apocrypha; nor did any New Testament writer quote directly from it. Jesus himself never referred to those books. The Jewish Council of Jamnia, meeting in A.D. 90, upheld the Hebrew list of books and did not include the

Apocrypha in the canon. The books are still valuable for information concerning the Jews in the interbiblical period, especially 1 and 2 Maccabees.

12. The Seleucids of Syria

The tranquil life of the Jews under the Ptolemies came abruptly to an end in 198 B.C. when Antiochus III or Antiochus the Great was able to defeat the Ptolemaic powers and wrest Palestine from them. He even wanted to take over Egypt itself but was unable to do so. At any rate, Palestine came under Seleucid control (198–167 B.C.), with the capital of the Seleucid kingdom at Antioch, a city on the Orontes River. The king who followed Antiochus III was Seleucus IV, who was in turn followed by Antiochus IV, grandson of Antiochus the Great. Antiochus IV had two nicknames: to some he was Epiphanes, "manifest god," and to others he was Epimanes, "madman." In various ways he was brilliant, and in other ways he was senseless. Since he was extremely devoted to Hellenism and wanted to see it deeply embedded in the culture of all his subjects, the Jews were destined for a very critical experience.

Antiochus endeavored to invade Egypt in 169 B.C. but was prevented from doing so by Roman interference. Returning disgruntled, he fanatically determined to bring the Jews under control. He treated Jerusalem as though it had been the cause of his military failure. He sacked the city, burned it, and slaughtered many of the citizens. Some were imprisoned, others sold as slaves. Many devout Jews were massacred in the synagogues as they worshiped on the sabbath.

His main target was those who were loyal to the laws of Moses, especially the Hasidim ("pious ones"). The Temple was plundered of its precious treasures and made into a shrine for the Greek god Zeus, an image of the god being set up in the Temple area. He even sacrificed a sow on the altar of burnt offering, an animal considered unclean by the Jews and therefore not to be sacrificed or eaten, and poured the broth throughout the building. Not only were heathen shrines set up in all parts of the country; heathen festival observance was made compulsory. Crimes punishable by death were observing the sabbath, performing the rite of circumcision, observing the Jewish festivals, and possessing copies of the Hebrew Scriptures. Copies of the Torah were to be destroyed. The royal edicts were enforced relentlessly. Truly it was a bitter religious persecution!

13. The Maccabean Revolt

The persecution was intolerable; conflict was inevitable; resistance burst into flame. Antiochus was unable to estimate the devotion of the Hadisim (also called Hasideans). A new spirit arose to replace the passive one of meekly submitting to being slaughtered. In the village of Modein (or Modin) west of Jerusalem, near the Philistine border, an aged priest named Mattathias lived with his five sons: John, Simon, Judas, Eleazer, and Jonathan. They were of the Hasmon family and were therefore known also as Hasmoneans.

In 167 B.C. a dramatic event set off a veritable revolution. An officer of Antiochus appeared at the village of Modein, built an altar to Zeus, and offered a reward to Mattathias if he would set the example by offering a heathen sacrifice to Zeus. The aged priest very ardently refused. When a younger, less conscientious Jew stepped forward to comply with the request, Mattathias killed him at the altar, then turned and killed the king's agent and destroyed the altar.

Mattathias and his sons fled to the wilderness and the hill country of Judea, where they enlisted a considerable following of fanatically devout Jews. In a program of armed resistance they ranged up and down the Judean hills, destroying pagan altars and encouraging the people to observe the Mosaic law. Many attacks were made at night. Mattathias died in 166 B.C., after about a year of such strenuous activity, but not before encouraging his sons to continue in their zeal for the law. Prior to his death he appointed Judas, his third son, to replace him as leader. Judas was nicknamed Maccabeus, "the Hammerer."

Time verified his choice as a wise one; Judas was bold and courageous, an intrepid general and a skilled strategist. He was familiar with every nook and ravine of the Judean countryside, a prime requisite for conducting guerrilla warfar against the Syrians in that rugged setting. By avoiding pitched battles Judas won victory after victory, most of the time over numerically superior forces and with only crude weapons. Seleucid generals would march against Judas with forces numbering 50,000 to 60,000 and be defeated by much smaller bands of rebel Jews. More than once he almost annihilated the Syrian forces as they proceeded down a valley or through a mountain pass. After Lysias, commander-in-chief for Antiochus, and a large force of Syrians were defeated by Judas just north of Hebron, a compromise was reached resulting in the withdrawal of Lysias and his army.

14. Rededication of the Temple

Judas and his forces entered Jerusalem, cleansed the Temple, destroyed the pagan altars and heathen gods, repaired the building, and replaced the altar to Jehovah. On December 25, 165 B.C., the Temple was rededicated to the worship of God. This resulted in the annual Feast of Dedication called Hanukkah, from the Hebrew word for dedication. (It is sometimes spelled Chanukah.) In John 10:22 it is termed "feast of dedication," but it sometimes goes under the name Feast of Lights.

15. Political Independence

Judas proceeded to war against all the neighboring peoples who had befriended the Syrians: Idumeans, Philistines, Ammonites, and Gentile forces in Galilee and Gilead. Judas did this in spite of many of the Hasidim, who wanted to withdraw now that they had the Temple and their orthodox worship restored to them. Not only did the Syrians still have fortifications remaining in Jerusalem; there was yet a small segment of Jews who favored Hellenization.

What was begun as a struggle for religious liberty was continued as a revolution for political freedom. Antiochus IV soon died, still breathing hatred for the Jews. Lysias came against Judas with a tremendous force, even besieging Judas and his army walled up in Jerusalem. Finally he withdrew to Antioch, due to trouble there, and lifted the siege. When Judas was killed on the battlefield, his brother Jonathan took his place. He in turn was murdered by a Syrian general, Trypho; and Simon, last remaining son of Mattathias, replaced Jonathan as leader of the Jewish forces. This was in 142 B.C. Simon did well militarily and even recaptured Acra, the Syrian fortress in Jerusalem. Because Demetrius II, king of Syria, wanted Simon's favor, he recognized him as ruler. Although not a member of the high priestly family, Simon was appointed high priest. In 142 B.C. Demetrius granted Simon and the Jews political freedom and release from the payment of all taxes. Coins were struck with Simon's name upon them. The victory of the Maccabees over the Syrians terminated all influence of the Seleucids in Palestine and gave the Jews an autonomous nation, a freedom that lasted until the Roman conquest in 63 B.C. This period of freedom, lasting almost eighty years, was the only freedom the Jews knew between 587–586 B.C. and the middle of the twentieth century.

16. Under the Hasmoneans

The Hasmonean dynasty in Palestinian history lasted from 142 B.C., the beginning of the rule of Simon, to 37 B.C., the beginning of the rule of Antipater (the start of the Herodian dynasty). Simon's reign (142–135) was a prosperous one; a treaty was even negotiated with Rome, who recognized the independence of the Jewish state. When the Syrians broke their pact of friendship, Judah and Jonathan, Simon's two sons, were able to defeat them in battle and to remove the danger. Simon, along with two of his sons, was murdered by Ptolemy, his son-in-law. Simon's remaining son, John Hyrcanus, took over as ruler (135–104) and was able to overcome Ptolemy, who soon fled to Egypt. John Hyrcanus, an able ruler, was successful in conquering surrounding territory, thus restoring the country to much of the status it had during the time of David. He beautified Jerusalem and issued Jewish coins. He finally identified himself with the Sadducees, a party of Jews opposed to the Pharisees.

Judah Aristobulus, John's son, lasted about a year as leader of the nation and then died (104–103). Alexander Janneus, another son of John, then became ruler (103–76) and continued to expand the boundaries of the kingdom, as his father had done before him. His reign was a period of turmoil and civil strife, however. He even attacked fellow Jews who opposed his territorial expansion. He put some of the Jewish leaders to death. Some of the religious aims that initiated the Maccabean revolt were obliterated. He was severe in his treatment of the Pharisees, for he was a Sadducee.

His widow, Salome Alexandra, ruling after his death (76–67), was highly in favor of the Pharisees and merciless in her treatment of the Sadducees. After her death there was strife and general turmoil in the nation. Her two sons, Aristobulus II and Hyrcanus II, vied with each other for power. Aristobulus acquired the throne (67–63) and deposed Hyrcanus from the priesthood. Due to the turmoil in Palestine Rome intervened, attacked the city of Jerusalem, and was able to conquer it in 63 B.C. with the aid of Hyrcanus. Aristobulus II and his family were taken to Rome as captives, and Hyrcanus II was appointed king by the Romans (63–40). In 49 B.C. Caesar also recognized him as king. His minister was Antipater, father of a later ruler, Herod the Great. Later, the Parthians attacked Jerusalem, carried off Hyrcanus, and appointed Antigonus, son of Aristobulus, as king in 40 B.C. Three years later with Roman aid, Herod took over Jerusalem and executed Antigonus.

Thus ended the Hasmonean line, one that in its later years (63–37 B.C.) was dominated by Roman imperialism. These Maccabeans were not so competent as rulers as they were as revolutionaries, for many times they were as cruel and domineering as the Seleucids they had replaced. Yet they did create a Jewish state, one in which the leader many times combined both political and religious authority. He was king and high priest at the same time. The Hasmoneans fostered Jewish nationalism and a study of Jewish traditions.

17. Roman Domination

A small city sprang up on the banks of the Tiber in Italy in 753 B.C., a community that was later to become the center of the mighty Roman Empire stretching from the British Isles, across Europe through the entire Mediterranean basin and eastward to the Euphrates and the Black Sea. The Sahara would compose its southern border. Unification and growth proceeded, and about 500 B.C. Rome had a republican form of government. There were further alliances, plus successful wars in the north against the Etruscans and the conquering of wealthy Greek communities in the southern part. Other tribes fell to the advancing Roman armies, till by 265 B.C. Rome was in control of the entire Italian peninsula. Mighty Carthage, across the Mediterranean on the African coast, was the chief maritime power of the region. From 264 to 146 B.C. Rome was in a prolonged struggle with Carthage, for evidently there was not room for both powers in the same territory.

Carthage finally fell in 146 B.C. and was razed to the ground; North Africa, Spain, and southern France came under Roman might. Also, in 146 B.C. Corinth fell, with Achaia (Greece) coming under the Roman banner. Illyria (modern Yugoslavia) was added. Asia Minor, as far as the Taurus mountains, was annexed. Syria and Egypt were the last two great powers remaining.

In 64 B.C. Pompey conquered Syria and made it a Roman province. Also in 63 B.C. he added Judea, and the Jews came under Roman rule. In 58–57 B.C. Julius Caesar conquered Gaul, thus adding it to the vast stretches under Roman sway. Caesar returned a hero in 49 B.C. and conquered Pompey in 48 B.C. He then aligned himself with Egypt's young queen, Cleopatra, thus virtually bringing the land of the Nile into Rome's fold. When Caesar was murdered in 44 B.C. Octavius, later named Augustus by the senate, assumed command. At the famous naval battle of Actium in 31 B.C. the combined fleets of Mark Antony and Cleopatra suffered a crushing defeat. After the two lovers committed suicide in Egypt, Augustus took over as sole ruler. The republic died, giving birth to the mightiest and most extensive empire the world had yet known.

The Roman rulers who were contemporaries of the advent and growth of Christianity were:

Augustus	27 B.C. to A.D. 14
Tiberius	A.D. 14–37
Caligula	A.D. 37–41
Claudius	A.D. 41–54
Nero	A.D. 54–68
Galba	A.D. 68
Otho	A.D. 69

Vitellius	A.D. 69
Vespasian	A.D. 69–79
Titus	A.D. 79–81
Domitian	A.D. 81–96
Nerva	A.D. 96–98
Trajan	A.D. 98–117

Augustus ruled wisely, for under his leadership the empire was thoroughly established. He organized and built well. He cleared the pirates from the seas, thus making the Mediterranean safe for commerce. He strengthened the borders of the empire by defensive outposts. His boast was that he found Rome brick and left it marble. He established a *Pax Romana,* peace of Rome, although the peace was one due to fear of invincible Roman might. He very wisely combined the old republic and the new dictatorship; he retained the senate but had the right of calling the meetings and introducing the first topics. His powers were not despotic and arbitrarily seized, but he manipulated things to the point that great rights were conferred upon him. He wanted to be considered the first among equals, and he lived a simple life, fostering morality among the people. He endeavored to increase the morale of his subjects. In many places he was worshiped as *Dominus et Deus* (Lord and God); but, unlike Domitian later on, he did not demand the worship due one holding such a title. Peace and prosperity characterized his forty-one-year reign. This was the man who headed the empire when Jesus was born (Luke 2:1).

Though the Greeks had endeavored to Hellenize their subjects in the East, Rome made no attempt to Romanize them but continued mainly the policies laid down by the Greeks. Local governments were allowed to continue their past procedures, and local courts were permitted to decide their own cases. Rome wanted law and order to prevail and the taxes to flow into the coffers by the Tiber. Yet the Jews felt that their freedom was a thing of the past and that they were subjects of Rome's representative in Syria.

Even before Pompey entered Jerusalem he found that there was a bitter rivalry there between two brothers, Aristobulus II and Hyrcanus II. After capturing the city (63 B.C.) the Roman general deposed Aristobulus, took him to Rome, and set up Hyrcanus as ruler and high priest. The able but ambitious minister to Hyrcanus was Antipater, an Idumean (Edomite in the Old Testament). When Pompey also placed a heavy tribute on the Jews to be paid annually, Jewish independence was at an end.

18. Herod the Great

Pompey had made Antipater the minister to Hyrcanus. When Pompey was defeated by Julius Caesar in 48 B.C., Antipater had to shift his loyalty to Caesar, which he successfully did. Caesar made him Procurator of Judea, thus placing him above Hyrcanus rather than below him. The Jews hated him, for he was a descendant of their ancient bitter enemy, the Edomites. He had two sons, Phasael and Herod. The latter became known as Herod the Great and reigned from 74–4 B.C. Antipater was poisoned, and Julius Caesar murdered soon afterward. Herod was successful in getting himself appointed king by Antony and Octavius in 40 B.C. and strengthened himself by marrying Mariamne, a Hasmanean and grand-daughter of Hyrcanus, a very beautiful woman. Even though he was ruler of both Judea and Samaria, he needed three years to force the Judeans to accept him. He finally overcame Antigonus, his rival claimant to the throne, and with the help of Roman forces captured Jerusalem in 37 B.C. Then he began his actual reign at the age of 22 years. Rulership in name became rulership in fact. Augustus Caesar confirmed his kingship in 30 B.C. Even though a puppet ruler, he was a capable one and therefore received the title Herod the Great.

Herod very wisely built a superstructure on the foundation laid by his father, Antipater. He constructed military installations and fortifications to save Palestine from being harassed by its neighbors. Trade and economy flourished. There was peace and prosperity. He wished to aid Augustus in his desire to spread a common Greco-Roman culture throughout the whole Roman Empire. Consequently he built temples in the cities of Palestine honoring Augustus. He rebuilt many old cities and Hellenized them by constructing gymnasia, stadia, and theaters.

But he never succeeded in winning the Jews to his side; for his Idumean blood posed too great an obstacle, and his heathen cults were in opposition to all that Judaism affirmed. His greatest service to the Jews was in rebuilding their Temple on a grand scale. The Temple area was increased to twice its size, and the Temple itself was adorned with enormous carved masonry (Mark 13:1). This reconstruction was begun in 20 B.C. and was not completed till decades after his death. But even this great gesture on Herod's part seemingly failed to conciliate the Jews.

Herod was ambitious, vain, and distrustful, dealing harshly both with members of his family and with political opponents who might pose threats in any way. He killed two of his ten wives, including Mariamne, his favorite, at least three of his sons, and many others of his own family. Conspiracy and intrigue marked his entire reign. Being plagued with cancer of the intestines and with dropsy, he finally passed away amid great suffering in 4 B.C. From a study of his life and his despicable and jealous nature it is not surprising that, after the visit of the Magi from the East, he

HEROD THE GREAT
37-4 B.C.
MATT. 2:1-19
LUKE 1:5

BY DORIS   BY MARIAMNE (GRANDDAUGHTER OF JOHN HYRCANUS)

ANTIPATER   ARISTOBULUS   ALEXANDER

BY MARIAMNE (DAUGHTER OF HIGH PRIEST SIMON)

HEROD PHILIP (FIRST HUSBAND OF HERODIAS)
MARK 6:17

BY CLEOPATRA (OF JERUSALEM)

HEROD PHILIP, TETRARCH OF ITUREA, TRACHONITIS,
GAULANITIS, AURANITIS, AND BATANEA
4 B.C. TO A.D. 34
LUKE 3:1

BY MALTHACE (THE SAMARITAN)

HEROD ANTIPAS, TETRARCH OF GALILEE AND PEREA
4 B.C. TO A.D. 39
LUKE 3:1; 13:31,32; 23:8-12
MARK 6:14-29   MATT. 14:1-12

ARCHELAUS, ETHNARCH OF JUDEA, SAMARIA,
AND IDUMEA
4 B.C. TO A.D. 34
MATT. 2:22

HEROD OF CHALCIS

HEROD AGRIPPA I, KING OF JUDEA
A.D. 37-44
ACTS 12:1-23

HERODIAS

BY HEROD PHILIP

SALOME
MATT. 14:6-11

BERNICE, (CONSORT OF HER BROTHER, HEROD AGRIPPA II)
ACTS 25:13-26:32

HEROD AGRIPPA II, TETRARCH OF CHALIS AND THE NORTHEAST TERRITORY,
AND FINALLY GALILEE AND PEREA
ACTS 25:13-26:32

DRUSILLA (WIFE OF M. ANTONIUS FELIX,
PROCURATOR OF JUDEA)
AROUND A.D. 52-59
ACTS 24:24

should have so cruelly ordered the massacre of all the boy babies in and around Bethlehem (Matt. 2:16–18). Such a deed is in complete conformity to his entire despotic reign.

19. Herod's Successors

According to Herod's last will, his kingdom was to go to his son Archelaus, who proceeded to Rome to effect his appointment. He left his brother Philip in charge. According to Herod's second will a third son, Antipas, was to receive his kingdom, who in turn went to Rome to make his claim. But the Jews also sent a delegation to Rome asking that none of the sons be appointed but that the Jews be granted the right of self-government. Augustus finally settled the cases by giving each son a section, or territory, of Palestine. Archelaus received Judea, Samaria, and Idumea, with the title of *ethnarch* (4 B.C. to A.D. 6); Herod Antipas received Galilee and Perea, with the title of *tetrarch* (4 B.C. to A.D. 39); Philip was granted the territory northeast of the Sea of Galilee, composed of Iturea, Trachonitis, Batanea, Auranitis, Gaulanitis, and Panias (a city) with the title of *tetrarch*. ("Ethnarch" means ruler of a nation, while "tetrarch" means ruler of a fourth part.)

Archelaus was an incompetent ruler, very cruel and tryannical. After nine years of suffering, a group of Jews and Samaritans went to Rome to complain to Augustus and were successful in getting Archelaus deposed and sent to Gaul in A.D. 6. Matthew told us that after the death of Herod the Great, Joseph was warned not to take Mary and Jesus back to the territory of Archelaus; so he took them to Galilee instead (Matt. 2:22). Rome next instituted a succession of Roman procurators to rule Judea and Smaria, the most famous being Pontius Pilate (A.D. 26–36), who condemned Jesus to death.

Herod Antipas, very prominent in the four Gospels, is called by Jesus "that fox" (Luke 13:32), thus alluding to his craftiness. He built a new capital, Tiberias, on the southwest shore of the Sea of Galilee. He had a half brother, Herod Philip I (Matt. 14:3), not to be confused with Philip the tetrarch in northwest Palestine. When Herod Antipas visited Herod Philip in Rome, he became enamored with Herodias, Herod Philip's wife. He divorced his own wife, the daughter of the Arabian king Aretas, and married Herodias. This is the Herod Antipas and the Herodias who took the life of John the Baptist at Machaerus in Perea.

Jesus appeared before Herod Antipas between his two appearances before Pilate. Herod Antipas was pleased with the prospect of seeing Jesus, for he thought that Jesus might possibly perform a miracle before him;

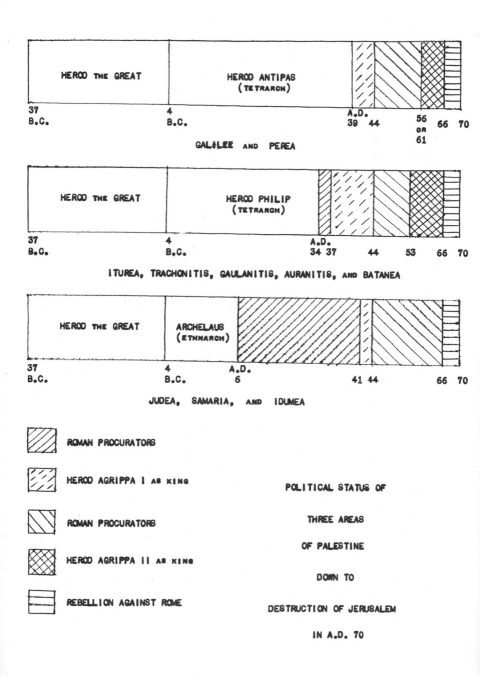

GALILEE AND PEREA

37 B.C. — HEROD THE GREAT — 4 B.C. — HEROD ANTIPAS (TETRARCH) — A.D. 39 44 — 56 OR 61 — 66 70

ITUREA, TRACHONITIS, GAULANITIS, AURANITIS, AND BATANEA

37 B.C. — HEROD THE GREAT — 4 B.C. — HEROD PHILIP (TETRARCH) — A.D. 34 37 — 44 — 53 — 66 70

JUDEA, SAMARIA, AND IDUMEA

37 B.C. — HEROD THE GREAT — 4 B.C. — ARCHELAUS (ETHNARCH) — A.D. 6 — 41 44 — 66 70

ROMAN PROCURATORS

HEROD AGRIPPA I AS KING

ROMAN PROCURATORS

HEROD AGRIPPA II AS KING

REBELLION AGAINST ROME

POLITICAL STATUS OF

THREE AREAS

OF PALESTINE

DOWN TO

DESTRUCTION OF JERUSALEM

IN A.D. 70

Jesus did not do so, however. Herod and his men treated Jesus with mockery. Herod Antipas' marriage to Herodias finally cost him his crown; for he was banished, and Herod Agrippa I received his territory.

Philip the tetrarch's territory extended almost to Damascus in the north and to the Decapolis in the south. It was mainly Syrian and Greek, interspersed with a small element of Jews. As far as the Herods were concerned, Philip was very exceptional, for he was fair and considerate. He rebuilt the ancient city of Panias near the springs of the Jordan and named it Caesarea in honor of Caesar. It is usually called Caesarea Philippi or Caesarea of Philip and is mentioned in Matthew 16:13. Philip also built Bethsaida Julias on the northwest shore of the Sea of Galilee. He married Salome, daughter of Herodias.

Herod Agrippa I (A.D. 37–44) was the son of Aristobulus, son of Herod the Great. Herod the Great had Aristobulus killed in 7 B.C. for plotting his death. In A.D. 37 he was given the territory previously held by Philip the tetrarch. In A.D. 39 Herod Antipas was banished, and Herod Agrippa I received Galilee and Perea. In A.D. 41 he received Judea and Samaria, thus finally obtaining all the territory previously held by Herod the Great (all Palestine). He was a devotee of Judaism, worshiping regularly at the Temple. He became one of the first persecutors of Christianity, executing James the son of Zebedee and having Peter placed in prison. An angel miraculously released Peter, after which the king had the guards put to death (Acts 12:1–19). His own death, a sudden one, is dramatically told by Luke (Acts 12:20–23).

Herod Agrippa II (A.D. 50–100) was only seventeen years of age when his father died. Claudius, emperor at Rome, placed Palestine under Roman governors, making it a Roman province. Finally, in A.D. 53 Herod Agrippa II was given the old tetrarchy of Philip. Then between A.D. 56 and 61 (a disputed date) he was granted Galilee and Perea, the old tetrarchy of Herod Antipas. He never did acquire Judea and Samaria, which remained under a Roman governor. Therefore his kingdom never was expanded to equal that of his father. While Herod Agrippa II and his sister Bernice were visiting the governor Festus at Caesarea, Paul pleaded to them for himself and Christianity (Acts 25:13 to 26:32).

The revolt against Rome, starting in A.D. 66, led to the overthrow of Jerusalem in A.D. 70. Herod Agrippa II sided with the Romans in the revolution, even against his own countrymen. He joined with Titus in the triumph, after which his kingdom was enlarged. Agrippa died in A.D. 100.

2.
Cultural Setting

1. Geographical Areas

The entire territory in which the events of Old Testament history took place involved Mesopotamia (modern Iraq), Persia (modern Iran), Syria, Phoenicia (modern Lebanon), Palestine, and Egypt. During the New Testament period geographical attention shifted, with very little mention of Egypt, Mesopotamia, and Persia, and very much about Palestine, Asia Minor, Greece, various Grecian islands, Macedonia, and Rome. To understand the historical events recorded in the Bible one must have a clear concept of the geography involved. The world of the Bible encircling the Mediterranean, with Palestine at its heart, must be clearly brought into view.

(1) Palestine There are four geographical divisions in Palestine, all running north and south.

A. Next to the Mediterranean Sea, called the Great Sea in the Bible, is the *Maritime Plain*, which in turn is divided into three parts: the plain of Acre and Tyre in the north, the plain of Sharon in the middle, and the plain of Philistia in the south. The coastal plain is low, sandy, and fertile, noted for grain and fruits. At the north it is sometimes only a mile wide, while at the southern end it is as much as thirty miles in width.

B. Parallel to the Maritime Plain is the second division, the *Western Highlands,* a long ridge of mountains varying in height from 1,000 to 2,500 feet. It begins in the Lebanon mountains in the north and extends to the desert country, the Negeb, in the south. It is also divided into three parts: Galilee in the north, Samaria in the center, and Judah (or Judea) in the south. Between Galilee in the north and Samaria in the middle is a geographical break in the form of a very lush and fertile valley, the valley of Jezreel (or plain of Esdraelon). Due to its strategic location, great armies have often wrestled for its control. In Judah is located Jerusalem, the most famous city in all Palestine.

C. Parallel to the Western Highlands is the *Jordan River Valley,* a

33

THE GREAT SEA

SYRIA

Damascus

Sidon

MT. HERMON

PHOENICIA

Tyre

Caesarea Philippi

ITURAEA

Capernaum   Bethsaida
GALILEE   Sea of Galilee
Cana
Tiberias
Nazareth   MT. TABOR
PLAIN OF ESDRAELON
Nain   Gadara
DECAPOLIS

SAMARIA
Samaria   MT. EBAL
MT. GERIZIM   Sychar

PEREA

Jordan River

Joppa

Bethel
Jericho
JUDEA
Jerusalem   Bethany
Bethlehem
WILDERNESS OF JUDAH
Dead Sea
Machaerus

Hebron

IDUMEA

ARABIA

Beersheba

NEGEB

N

0   10   20   30
SCALE OF MILES

Palestine in the Time of Christ

ravine varying from one to fourteen miles in width. Having its inception in the north, near Mount Hermon, the Jordan flows down to the Waters of Merom, then on to the Lake of Galilee, and then to the Dead Sea. North of the Lake of Galilee it is called Upper Jordan, and from Galilee to the Dead Sea it is called Lower Jordan. The Waters of Merom, about seven feet above the level of the Mediterranean, was the scene of one of Joshua's battles. It figures very little in the New Testament. Called Lake Chinneroth in the Old Testament (Josh. 12:3), the Lake of Galilee also goes by the name of Gennesaret (Luke 5:1) and by the name of Tiberias (John 6:1). It lies about 685 feet below the level of the Mediterranean and attains a depth of 150 feet. It is 13 miles long and 8 miles wide. Situated on the northern shore of the lake was Capernaum, the hub of the Galilean fishing industry and the center of Jesus' ministry while he was in that region.

In the Bible the Dead Sea is called by such names as Salt Sea, Sea of the Arabah, and Sea of the Plain. It is about 1,292 feet below the level of the Mediterranean and is the lowest spot on the surface of the globe; it goes to a depth of 1,319 feet. Its length is 48 miles and its width 11 miles. Since about 6.5 million tons of water enter into it daily, and since the only exit for the water is an extraordinary evaporation, there is a rich mineral deposit contained in its waters. Hot springs beneath pour chemicals constantly into its depths. There is a 25 percent solid substance, of which 7 percent is salt. It is readily apparent why the river is called Jordan, which means "Descender."

D. Parallel to the Jordan River are the *Eastern Highlands,* now called Transjordania or simply Transjordan. It is noted in the Bible as an agricultural and pastoral country. In the Old Testament period the northern part was known as Bashan and the central part as Gilead. In New Testament times this central part was known as the "Decapolis," meaning ten cities. Prior to the time of Christ, large and prosperous Greek and Roman cities were located in this region, for the successors of Alexander the Great established a federation of Greek communities. East of the Decapolis and the other inhabited lands east of the Jordan was arid Arabian desert country.

(2) Asia Minor Asia Minor, known today as Turkey, is a large peninsula forming a land bridge between southwest Asia and southeast Europe. Along the north and the south are mountain ranges, with a plateau in between. Toward the west there are plains and lush river valleys, with many cities that are mentioned in the New Testament. The chief cities in Asia Minor during New Testament times were Ephesus, on the western coast, and Tarsus, home of Paul, at the southeast corner. Asia Minor was

divided into several Roman provinces, one of which extended on over into the territory previously known as Syria, just north of Palestine. The chief city here was Antioch, capital of the old Seleucid kingdom and center of the New Testament missionary movement. Paul traveled extensively throughout Asia Minor, using Antioch as his base.

(3) Macedonia and Greece   Greece proper is known in the New Testament as Achaia. Just north of Achaia was Macedonia, the home of Philip of Macedon and his more illustrious son, Alexander the Great. Thessalonica was the chief city in Macedonia. For a while Achaia and Macedonia constituted one Roman province; but just before Paul's activities it was divided into two provinces, with the seats of government at Thessalonica and at Corinth. Some of Paul's greatest work was performed in this region.

(4) Rome   Rome, the large and pagan capital of the vast Roman Empire, was situated on the Tiber River in Italy. In 265 B.C. Rome gained complete control of Italy and thus was able to enter the struggle for world power along with the successors of Alexander the Great. Roman power increased and expanded till Augustus Caesar, the real founder of the Roman Empire, reigned supreme. Even after his time additional territories were added as new provinces.

In Rome the apostle Paul was imprisoned for his Christian faith and Christian proclamation. Here he wrote several of his famous epistles, and here he suffered martyrdom for his beliefs. Even prior to his arrival in the metropolis on the Tiber, he wrote to the church there what we call the epistle to the Romans.

Rome became the scourge for first-century Christians, as much as did Babylon for the Hebrews during the Old Testament period. Therefore, the term *Babylon* in the book of Revelation is the code name for Rome (Rev. 17:1 to 19:10). She is called "the great harlot" (17:1). Even though she is pictured as very wealthy, she is also portrayed as a prostitute calling the world to the worship of the emperor.

2. Governmental State

The political scene in Palestine during the New Testament period was one of Roman domination, and it had been so since Pompey captured Jerusalem in 63 B.C. Native rulers were permitted to rule until 40 B.C., when an Idumean named Herod was appointed king. Since it required three more years for him to force the people of Judea to accept his actual rule, 37 B.C. is generally placed as the date of the beginning of his authority. Since he died in 4 B.C. he was the ruler at the time of Jesus' birth in

Bethlehem and was the one who gave the order for slaughtering all the boy babies in and around Bethlehem (Matt. 2:16).

Though a puppet ruler of imperial Rome, Herod so successfully governed that he was given the title Herod the Great. Before his death his realm included all Palestine—Judea, Samaria, Perea, Galilee, Idumea, and the territory northeast of Galilee. Thus a new dynasty began in Israel, the house of Herod. He restored a great degree of law and order to Palestine and made it somewhat of a buffer state between Roman authority and the Arab states. However, the Jews hated him. For one thing, he was an Idumean. Second, he tried to Hellenize the kingdom. Augustus, one of Rome's greatest emperors, was reigning in the imperial city; he was one who had hopes of establishing a common Greco-Roman culture throughout the empire. Herod also endeavored to foster this culture throughout Palestine.

Since the Romans acclaimed Augustus as a divine savior-king, Herod built temples in his honor in various cities of his realm. One of these was at Sebaste (Greek for Augustus), a city built on the old ruins of Samaria. The white columns of this temple could be seen from Caesarea, a coastal city built by Herod and named for Augustus Caesar. Augustus had given Herod an old Phoenician coastal fortress, that Herod used as the nucleus of the new city, Caesarea—which rivaled Jerusalem in importance and exceeded it in artistic grandeur. Founded in 22 B.C. and dedicated in 12 B.C., it became the seat of government for Roman rule in Palestine.

Here Herod built many public buildings, two aqueducts for bringing fresh water into the city, and a great harbor with buildings and statues at the entrance, not to mention a huge breakwater constructed in twenty fathoms of water. Since the city increased in Roman population, it became a source of friction between Jews and Romans. From here Titus marched in A.D. 70 to sack Jerusalem, and here both Jews and Christians were slaughtered by Roman command. This mighty city built at the edge of the plain of Sharon thus became a symbol of Roman domination in Palestine during the New Testament period.

An abridged genealogy of the Herodian family is included to manifest the deep penetration of this dynasty into New Testament history. Herod himself was cruel and despotic, hated by the Jews. He killed two of his ten wives and at least three of his sons, not to mention a brother-in-law and a grandfather of one of his wives. Since he knew that no one would mourn *due to* his death he arranged a scheme whereby they would mourn *at* his death. He planned for the leading Jews to be shut up in the arena at Jericho and be put to death at the time he passed away. However, when he did die, these prisoners were released and his plan foiled. Thus, the killing of the boy babies in Bethlehem is merely one of a long line of inhumane acts.

He did endeavor to bring some measure of conciliation to the Jews by rebuilding their Temple. The Temple of Zerubbabel, erected by the returnees from the Babylonian captivity, was far removed in grandeur from its predecessor, Solomon's Temple. Herod began an extensive reconstruction process that extended over many years. The old area was increased to twice its size, and much carved masonry was added (Mark 13:1). This construction was continued long after Herod's death; at a certain point in Jesus' ministry it had been in process forty-six years (John 2:20), and it had many more years to go. It was finally completed sometime in the A.D. sixties, only to be demolished in A.D. 70. The Jews have had no Temple since that very tragic day.

After the death of Herod the Great in 4 B.C. his realm was divided among his three sons. Archelaus was so evil he had to be deposed in A.D. 6, after which Roman procurators (governors) ruled until A.D. 41. The most famous of these governors was Pontius Pilate. Herod Antipas was made tetrarch of Galilee and Perea and ruled till A.D. 39. Most of Jesus' boyhood was spent in this territory. Philip, made tetrarch of Northeast Palestine, ruled till A.D. 34, but he figures only incidentally in the New Testament story.

3. Economic Conditions

During the days of the early church the Roman empire occupied the lands surrounding the Mediterranean sea. Here fruits, grains, and vegetables were grown in abundance. Archaeology has revealed that North Africa, though largely desert today, in New Testament times abounded in large farms, where cattle grazed and where fruits and grains flourished.

Since machine tools were practically unknown and goods had to be hand-produced, manufacturing was not so prevalent as today. What few factories existed were privately owned and maintained by slave labor. There were a few small shops. Certain areas were noted for certain things: dye from Tyre; copper products from Campania; paper from Egypt; and so on. Furniture and household goods were produced locally. Gold, ivory, rare woods, jewels, furs, and other luxurious articles were imported. Shipping was accomplished by means of rivers and, in the summer months, by sea lanes.

The standard coins in the empire were the silver *denarius* and the gold *aureus,* or pound. Forty denarii equaled one aureus. The denarius is mentioned several times in the New Testament, where it is translated "penny" (King James) or "shilling" (American Standard) or "denarius" (Revised Standard and Amplified Bible) or "the usual day's wage" (The New English Bible) or "$20 a day" (The Living Bible). It appears to have been a usual day's wage for a laboring man in Palestine during the New Testament era (Matt. 20:2). Not only did many cities have a right to mint their own coins; Rome did not require that local coins in the conquered nations be withdrawn from circulation. Banking was carried on, though it seems that the banks were privately endowed. Moneylending was a thriving business (Matt. 25:15).

Rome had an excellent system of roads throughout the provinces, the best that the world had seen till those of modern times. They made cuts through the hills and built viaducts over streams and valleys; thus the roads were comparatively straight. They were so superbly constructed that some are in use today. The Appian Way ran from Rome to the south, and the Via Flaminia ran from Rome to the north. In Palestine the most famous road was the Via Maris, or Way of the Sea. Starting in Egypt, it went to Gaza, to Ashkalon, to Megiddo, and finally to Damascus. Other roads in Palestine were the Waterparting Route, the Red Sea Route, the King's Highway, and the Pilgrim's Road.

However, most commercial transportation was by water—sea, river, and canal. The Mediterranean had many good ports. Where the Phoenicians of Tyre and Sidon were dominant in Mediterranean waters in Old Testament times, Alexandria was the chief port in New Testament times, mainly due to a needed outlet for the Egyptian grain crop. Alexandrian merchant ships were the largest and the finest; Pual used Alexandrian ships in his travels (Acts 27:6;28:11). Long plundered by pirates, the Mediterranean was freed from this menace by Roman warships. These warships were faster than the merchantmen, being manned by oars pulled by galley slaves. Some ships had two, three, and five banks of oars.

4. Social Environment

In the pagan world of the first century the social aspect was much as it is today. Rich and poor, good and bad, educated and uneducated lived side by side. The various strata of society were easily differentiated, however. In fact, there were four main levels. The first was the aristocracy. Due to the civil wars of Rome the old free landholding population of Italy had disappeared, replaced by a new aristocracy who controlled public lands due to their influence and who bought private lands cheaply from those financially bereft due to war and other causes. This same aristocracy was also on hand to exploit the newly conquered provinces.

Second, there was the middle class, one that was almost crushed out of the empire due to the rise of an extremely large slave population. These slaves were mainly the victims of wars and military campaigns, the very wars that had required the lives of many of the middle-class Romans. Others of the middle class were not able to compete against slave labor, so they lost their farms and homes and became part of the mobs filling the great cities. They thus became dependent upon the state for food and homes.

Third, the plebs, or the poor people, were very numerous and piteous. In many ways their plight was worse than the slaves, since the latter at least had something to eat and to wear. The plebians did not have steady employment and, therefore, were an easy prey to anyone who offered to feed and to amuse them. They were people who had been born free, however.

Fourth, there were the slaves, those constituting a large part of the population of the empire. Tacitus, the Roman historian, states that in the time of Augustus and Tiberius almost half the population was made up of slaves. Tacitus tells of an incident that happened in A.D. 61 when Pedanius Secundus was murdered by one of his slaves. The law for such an offense was put into effect; not only was the offender killed, but all his kinsmen and some 400 innocent men, women, and children also were executed. However, not all were so inhumanely treated; there are also records of very humane treatment of slaves.

Generally speaking, the daily lot of the slave was very difficult. They were considered things, not human beings—*res*, not *personae*. They were bought, sold, and mated with little more respect than animals and were completely at the mercy of their masters. They could be scourged, beheaded, crucified, and mutilated at the whims of their owners. A runaway slave, captured again, was marked with an *F* (Fugitive) on his forehead. Self-respect was almost impossible if one were a slave, for his law was obedience to every whim of his master. Flattery and trickery were the best devices employed by the slave to secure what he desired. War, debts, and births helped to swell the ranks of the slaves so that their number was extremely large. A respectable Roman family was expected to have at least ten slaves. Prominent families would have from 100 to 200. Some had many, many more than this. Slave markets in the streets of Rome were common sights.

Some slaves were refined and educated people, being merely the victims of a militant age. Many were physicians, teachers, artisans, accountants, and philosophers, Epictetus, the great Stoic philosopher, was one of them.

Some slaves labored in a friendly relationship, not in fear at all. Some were able to secure enough property from tips and gifts to buy their freedom, while others were freed by their masters either during the lifetime of the latter or at his death. These freedmen, becoming either middle-class citizens or plebs, took their places in the life of the empire, some even attaining prominence.

The New Testament speaks of slavery frequently, but nowhere in its pages is the institution of slavery either defended or attacked. Paul's letters reveal that there were both Christian slaves and Christian masters. Ephesians 6:5–9 presents Paul's advice for the proper attitude of the slave for his master and vice versa. However, the power of the gospel and of Christian love is discerned in the fact that the institution of slavery has so weakened that it has virtually disappeared.

5. Languages

The two most prominent languages of the Roman world were Latin and Greek. Latin was the official language, the language of the conquerors, the language of the Roman courts and Roman literature. It was spoken widely in the western section of the empire: Italy, Spain, Gaul, Britain, and North Africa. It was learned by the conquered peoples, probably flavored by their own dialect. Latin was used by the Roman soldiers and the Roman governors wherever they were stationed in the empire. When Jesus was brought before Pilate, an interpreter was probably used, although the common people knew everyday Latin words for *centurion, praetorium, denarius, legion, province, colony.*

Greek, the cultural language of the empire, was spoken from Rome eastward; but all well-educated people spoke Greek. The Greek of the first century A.D. is called *koiné* Greek or common Greek since it was common to the Mediterranean world. It was spoken in Palestine and was probably used by Jesus and his disciples in their dealings with Gentile people. To the north of Palestine, Greek was widely spoken, for this territory was known as "Galilee of the Gentiles." The widespread use of Greek in the eastern half of the empire was a result of the Hellenizing influence of the successors of Alexander the Greek. They attempted to Hellenize (Hellas means Greece in the Greek language) all their conquered people. The use of the Greek language was a part of the whole cultural change expected of the subjugated ones. The providence of God can be discerned in that the world then possessed a common language in which the New Testament could be penned.

There were two local or provincial languages found in Palestine at the time of Christ. These were Hebrew and Aramaic. Hebrew was the language of the Old Testament period—more specifically, that of Abraham and the patriarchs, of Saul, David, and Solomon, and of the entire period of the divided kingdom. The Hebrew Scriptures, as the term implies, were written in the Hebrew language; therefore, Hebrew continued to be the sacred language of the Jewish people. Copies of the Scriptures for use in the Temple and in the synagogues were written in Hebrew. It is also the language selected as the vernacular tongue of the new state of Israel established in 1948. The title Pilate placed on the cross relative to Jesus, "Jesus of Nazareth, the King of the Jews," was "written in Hebrew, and in Latin, and in Greek" (John 19:20).

Aramaic was the second provincial language used during the time of Christ, being the language of the street, the marketplace, and the home. When the Hebrew people were carried captive to Babylonia, they encountered a new medium of conversation in Mesopotamia: Aramaic. It was kin to the Hebrew, for both were Semitic in origin; yet it was different from Hebrew. The returnees who migrated back to Israel under Zerubbabel, Ezra, and Nehemiah brought the Aramaic with them; they had lived in Babylonia for two or three generations. The Aramaic replaced the Hebrew in Jerusalem, Judea, and elsewhere. This language, the predominant tongue in the Near East, was firmly entrenched in Palestine by the time of Christ.

Hebrew, though well known by the rabbis and scribes, had become a dead language for the majority. The Hebrew Scriptures were read in the synagogues of Palestine and of Babylon in the original Hebrew, but they were also read in an Aramaic paraphrase, called Targum. The dialect of Aramaic in Galilee was different from that in Jerusalem (Matt. 26:73). A trace of Aramaic can be seen in some religious phrases used in the New Testament, such as "Abba" (Rom. 8:15) and "Maranatha" (1 Cor. 16:22), which leads us to believe that some of the earliest Christians spoke Aramaic.

What language or languages did Jesus use? In all probability he grew up at his home in Nazareth speaking Aramaic, but later in life acquired a knowledge of Greek and Hebrew. All of his teaching and preaching to the common people would have been in Aramaic, but his discussions with the learned scribes, priests, and rabbis would have been in Hebrew. In the synagogue at Nazareth they delivered to him the roll of the prophet Isaiah, from which he immediately read and commented. This roll was undoubtedly written in Hebrew, but his comments were probably in Aramaic (Luke 4:16–22). When Jesus spoke to one such as the Syrophoenician woman, who would be non-Jewish, he probably spoke Greek, the common language. More than likely he used the same language in talking to the Roman centurion.

6. Morality

Some historians have painted a very degrading picture of the moral conditions of the Roman empire as a whole. It may not have been quite so low as they have depicted, but it was certainly lower than that of today. There were some good people, and there were some fine families involved in wholesome living; but generally speaking, the desolate picture that Paul has handed down in Romans 1:18 to 3:20 is a very accurate one. Other literary sources attest to this fact. The prevailing tendency in the society of that day was an embracing of immorality, indulgence, and lawlessness. Murder, suicide, and infanticide were very common. One writer said that baby skeletons could be taken from the bottom of the Tiber by the cartloads. Another, in writing to his wife, advised her to let live any boy baby that she might have but to expose to death any girl baby.

Human life seems to have been cheap. Divorce, being easily obtained, multiplied rapidly, thus laying the foundation for the eventual decay of family life. Even a pagan writer such as Seneca, Nero's tutor, while advising lofty ways of living, remarked, "Vice no longer hides itself; it stalks forth before all eyes. Innocence is no longer rare; it has ceased to exist." However, even Seneca did not exemplify what he counseled. The paganism of that age possessed no power to lift itself to a higher level; and, as a result, pessimism set in. The keynote in pleasure was licentiousness, and the prevailing mood in politics was corruption. Superstition flourished everywhere.

7. Education

Education in the Roman empire was limited largely to the upper class and some of the middle class. There was no program for all the people, for our modern system of free education by the state to all under eighteen was unknown in that day. By the time of Vespasian the rulers began to think about public education. A Roman child was trained in the home by a *paidogogos,* an educated slave who not only instructed the boy himself but led him to and from a private school in his city. The boy stayed with his paidogogos till he became a young man with adult responsibilities. What schools there were were drab and unattractive, held in halls where the markets and shops were found.

Modern methods of educational psychology were not employed, but repetition and stern discipline were the rule. There were no chalkboards, charts, and decorations as are used today. Reading, writing, and arithmetic were the usual subjects. As the student progressed he studied the Greek and Latin poets, probably memorizing long passages which he then recited with the proper eloquence. Later he would study oratory, with the wealthy youth being sent abroad to the Greek universities at Athens, Rhodes, Tarsus, Pergamum, and Alexandria. At various times traveling philosophers were available to lecture and to expound as they went from city to city.

Therefore the Greco-Roman world of the first century had a high state of intellectual growth, but it was mainly for the upper class and those with the necessary wealth to obtain it. The Latin works of Cicero, Virgil, and Horace were available for study. The works of Euclid and other great Alexandrian mathematicians were also available. Medicine, pharmacy, sculpturing, painting, architecture, law, oratory, astronomy—all were subjects at hand for the inquisitive Roman youth. Professional scribes produced manuscripts for those who could purchase them.

The Jewish boy learned to read and to write with the Hebrew Scriptures as his guide. This was done at first in the home and then at the synagogue. Here he learned not only from the Scriptures but from the traditions of the fathers as well. He became well versed in the ritual required by the Judaism of his day. Jewish boys outside of Palestine (Jews of the Dispersion) would also be taught the Greek language.

8. Religions

The Roman pantheon (a Greek word meaning all gods) was based on the Greek pantheon, for Roman militarism brought a contact with Greek civilization. Jupiter, god of the sky, was the same as Zeus; Juno, his wife, was the same as Hera; Neptune, god of the sea, was Poseidon; Mercury, messenger of the gods, was Hermes; Pluto, god of the underworld, was identified with Hades; Venus, goddess of love, was identified with Aphrodite; Diana, goddess of the hunt, was the same as Artemis; Mars, god of war, was the same as Ares; Bacchus, god of wine, was the same as Dionysus, and so on. Homer's entire list of deities was transferred to Latin counterparts.

During the days of Augustus, when considerable building was in progress, new temples were constructed in honor of the various gods. Even new priesthoods were founded. Many times in Greece a city or city-state would have a god or goddess as a patron of that city, a custom that even persisted over into the Roman era. Artemis, or Diana, was the patron goddess of Ephesus. Paul ran counter to the fanatical worship of Diana during his work in this great city of Asia Minor. The large image of Diana, reputedly fallen from heaven, was contained in the Temple of Diana, one of the seven wonders of the ancient world. The shrieking mob forced Paul to abandon his work at Ephesus (Acts 19:23–41).

However, these gods and goddesses were only magnified men and women, with all the immoralities, the jealousies, the connivings, and the deception of humanity. They were open to satire and to ridicule, especially by the philosophers. As a result, the worship of the gods and goddesses of classical mythology declined more and more, especially from the time of Christ. Plato, much earlier than Christ, in his *Republic* wanted their worship excluded in his ideal state; he maintained that such worship would corrupt the youth. So the philosophers scorned the worship of them. Just prior to the time of Plato, Euripides and Aristophanes ridiculed in their plays the antics of the Olympian deities.

As the foundations for belief in the old pantheon of gods began to crumble, some turned to agnosticism; others turned in the opposite direction to superstition and astrology. The occult began to have as great a pull upon the people of that day as it has on many today. Horoscopes, omens, amulets, charms, exorcisms—all had their part in replacing the vacuum created by the passing of the Olympian deities. There was a regard on the part of the masses for the powers supposedly inherent in the universe. The world was inhabited by spirits and demons who could be commanded to perform one's desires if only the correct formula were known. Belief in magic was widespread throughout the empire, and this affected both Jews and Gentiles. Philip converted Simon, a magician, while working in Samaria (Acts 8:9–13). Peter and John had to reprove this same Simon for an erroneous concept (Acts 8:14–24). After Paul's effective work at Ephesus the inhabitants of the city burned their books of magic in a bonfire (Acts 19:19). The spread of Christianity did not, however, completely squelch superstition; astrology, originating in Babylonia, spread throughout the empire.

Some even turned to a new cult, emperor worship. The very fact that the emperor had vested in himself powers representing the Roman state, and that he was able to use those powers for the good of the empire, seemed to suggest that he was more than human—perhaps divine. There was a gradual but steady increase in the superhuman powers and honors that were attributed to the emperor. After his death Julius Caesar was called Divus Julius. From the time of Augustus Caesar's reign (27 B.C. to A.D. 14) on, the senate voted deification to each emperor at his death. Caligula (A.D. 37–41) ordered his statue to be set up in the Temple at Jerusalem, but his death canceled the necessity for this order to be put into effect.

Domitian (A.D. 81–96) was the first reigning head of the empire to command that his subjects worship him. Not only did he order that sacrifices be offered to his image; he demanded that he be addressed as "Lord and God." The Christians' refusal to participate in such a pagan ritual was the factor that caused widespread and violent persecution. For the polytheistic Roman, adding one more god to his list of deities offered no problem whatsoever; while the Christians' refusal to do so offered to Domitian the savor of an unpatriotic attitude. The book of Revelation reveals the hostility on the part of Christians toward worshiping the state or its head.

As the worship of the Olympian deities passed away and emperor worship emerged, other religions also sprang up. The imperial cult was a religion too collective, too ritualistic, and not personal enough; there was no strength in time of spiritual need. The exotic mystery religions from the East fulfilled the needs of the people to a greater extent. There was the cult of Cybele, the Great Mother, from Asia; there was the cult of Isis and Osiris (or Serapis) from Egypt; and there was the cult of Mithraism, from Persia. The remains of temples and meeting places of adherents of these religions have been uncovered by archaeologists in all lands of the Roman empire except within Judea. Each of these religions had a god who died and was resuscitated, and in each form of worship there was a secret and dramatic representation of the experience of that god. Each inductee was initiated into that experience (received the mystery, so to speak), and was therefore made a candidate for immortality. After being initiated into the mystery the inductee became part of the brotherhood. Personal and emotional elements not felt in the imperial cult were found in the mystery religions.

9. Philosophies

Ignorant superstition and a nonsatisfying ritualism do not fully meet the needs of thoughtful people. The thinker desires a rational answer to his problems. The universe presents mysteries that call for satisfying interpretations. This was the situation in the Greco-Roman world from Alexander the Great to Augustus Caesar. Uncertainties arose due to the passing away of shopworn ideas and beliefs. The time was ripe for philosophies and world views that could fill the moral and religious vacuum many people felt.

A philosophy is a world view, an endeavor to take all existing knowledge of the universe and human experience and correlate it into some form or system of thought. In the Greco-Roman world there were numerous systems of philosophies.

(1) Platonism Platonism derived its name from the great Athenian pupil of Socrates who lived in the fourth century B.C. and who founded the Academy. Plato (427–347 B.C.) believed that the only real world is the world of ideas back of the material world. The true and perfect realities exist eternally and are not dependent on the world that can be seen, felt, or heard. The present world is a feeble reflection of the true world, the world of ideas. Therefore man should seek, by reflection and meditation, to escape from this unreal world to the real. Plato's thoughts were so modified by his successors that, by the time of Christ, Platonism could hardly be recognized.

(2) Epicureanism Epicureanism was named for Epicurus (342–270 B.C.), who lived many decades later than Plato. He gathered about him in a garden at Athens a brotherhood of followers known as Epicureans. He taught that the world was made by chance collisions of atoms. Therefore there is no purpose or design in the universe; neither is there absolute good. The highest good is pleasure, or the absence of pain. Contrary to what most people think, Epicureanism, then and at present, does not advocate sensual indulgence but a higher type of pleasure, that which gives the longest and most satisfying enjoyment to an individual. Pure dissipation is frowned upon. Epicureanism is atheistic and antireligious, for Epicurus could very well be termed a practical atheist.

(3) Stoicism Stoicism, founded by Zeno (340–265 B.C.), a native of Cyprus, became the most influential philosophy in the Hellenistic period. In Athens Zeno did not address his pupils in a lecture hall but in the painted porch (*stoa*), a colonnade with elaborate paintings connected with the *agora* (marketplace). Stoicism fosters the development of moral and religious character. The whole material universe is permeated by divine reason or Logos. Man has within him at birth a spark of this Logos or divinity and is, therefore, well equipped to reason about the world in which he lives. The chief end of man is to live in harmony with nature. He is to be indifferent to pain, poverty, or misfortune; the emotions are to be denied. Some of the great Stoics were Seneca, Epictetus, and the emperor Marcus Aurelius, who lived a century and a half after Christ.

(4) Other Philosophies Other philosophies also prevailed. Aristotelianism was named after Aristotle, the great pupil of Plato and personal teacher of Alexander the Great. He dealt mainly with physics and metaphysics, whereas his master had dealt with the ethical. Gnosticism derived its name from the Greek word for knowledge, *gnosis*. It promised man salvation by knowledge and affirmed the materialistic world to be

inherently evil. Neo-Platonism, founded by Plotinus, was a combination of Platonism and ideas from Persia. Cynicism grew out of the teaching of Socrates, the great teacher of Plato. It taught the independence of all desires. Man should have no wants whatsoever. Skepticism taught that there is no final standard, for every man's experience differs from that of his associates. All judgments are relative.

All of these variant philosophies shared a certain degree of popularity, but they failed to satisfy the ordinary man. They were too abstract. Besides, they tended to lack the final and certain answer that the soul craves. Thus the world was ripe for the only true answer, that found in the Word become flesh.

3.
Jewish Religion

1. Judaism

The religion of the Jews during the first century was one of many found in the Roman Empire, but it was distinctive in many ways. First, it was monotheistic, demanding the worship of one God and him alone. Other religions might emphasize the worship of one God, but the Jew would not even admit the existence of any other god. Second, it was highly moral, containing a system of ethics deeply embedded in its structure and based on the nature of God as holy and righteous. Ethical living was demanded of every adherent. Third, it was based on a revelation from God himself, the witness of that revelation being found in the Hebrew Scriptures. It was not based on mystic intuition or human ingenuity. Fourth, it was built around one Temple dear to the heart of every Jew, a temple with no images (or icons), and a temple with a sacrificial system deeply enmeshed in its theological beliefs.

The descendants of Jacob (or Israel, as he was also named) were known as Hebrews or Israelites. The term *Jew* was not current until the sixth century B.C.; it is a religious term denoting a religious commitment. A Jew was one who had Judaism as his religion; and Judaism, *per se,* with all its legalistic exactions and formal demands, did not originate until the years of the captivity. The returnees from the Babylonian captivity had greatly altered their religious practices and were termed Jews (since they originally came from Judah) by the people of Jerusalem, who witnessed their migration back home. Once settled in Jerusalem and Judea, Judaism continued its development, moving on in its legalistic requirements for making the Torah (or law) the rule of life in all personal conduct.

The return of Ezra to Jerusalem in 458 B.C. was a highly significant event, for he exerted a tremendous influence in drawing the people to a study of the Torah. He is called "a ready scribe in the law of Moses" (Ezra 7:6). After Ezra's death the scribes, as expounders and interpreters of the Torah, came to the religious forefront. Their interpretations grew into the oral law, which was later written down for future generations. Thus Judaism expanded till it became unwieldy and led to formalism and hypocrisy.

2. The Dispersion of the Jews

During the time of the Roman Empire there were far more Jews living outside Palestine than within. These Jews, participants in the Diaspora or Dispersion, were located in almost all the major cities of the Mediterranean world and beyond. This spreading had its inception with the capture of the Northern Kingdom, Israel, and the deportation of its citizens to Assyria in 722 B.C. These events were followed later by the capture of Judah in 587 B.C. and the moving of the Southern Kingdom citizens to Babylonia. Only a remnant of the Hebrews returned from Babylon three or four generations later, for many stayed due to business prosperity and other factors. The conquests of Alexander the Great in the fourth century B.C. furthered the migration of the Jews, for the followers of Alexander offered citizenship and tax exemption to those who would move out to cities in the Hellenistic world.

Alexandria had one large section devoted to Jews, where it is estimated that there were 2,000,000 of them—the largest single concentration in any one city. Pompey brought many Jews back to Rome as prisoners of war. These were finally freed and settled on the west bank of the Tiber. It is estimated that at the time of the birth of Christ Rome had 8,000 Jews. Mesopotamia, Egypt, Syria, and Asia Minor had millions of Jews. Acts 2:9-11 lists many foreign countries from which Jews had come to attend Pentecost at Jerusalem, Jews who no longer spoke the language of the streets and homes of their fatherland. They spoke only the languages of their places of residence.

Many of these dispersed Jews departed from the customs, teachings, and religion of their forefathers; but the majority remained faithful to their Judaism. They were true to their monotheism and their Torah, traveling from distant places to Jerusalem to attend the prominent festivals and to worship at the Temple. They continued to pay the annual tax of half a shekel demanded to support the Temple. They observed sabbath regulations and worshiped regularly in their native synagogues.

By the time of Christ Palestinian Judaism and Diaspora Judaism were somewhat dissimilar. Palestinian Judaism relied upon the Hebrew Scriptures as its word of authority, while Diaspora Judaism relied upon the Septuagint, the Greek translation of the Hebrew, as its source of religious truth. Since the Septuagint contained the Apocrypha, the Jews of the

Dispersion had fourteen books in their sacred writings that the Jews of Palestine did not have. These Jews tended to absorb the forms of Greco-Roman culture except where their religious faith was concerned. They spoke either Greek or the language of their resident country and adopted the customs of those around them.

3. The Temple

The first Temple, built by Solomon about a thousand years prior to the Christian era (1 Kings 6:1), became the center point of the Hebrews' worship of God. It was destroyed in 587 B.C. when Nebuchadnezzar sacked and burned Jerusalem, taking the people in chains to Babylon. The second Temple, authorized by Cyrus the Great of Persia (Ezra 6:2–5), was built by Zerubbabel and those returning with him in 538 B.C. This Temple was begun in 537 B.C. and finally, after the persuasive preaching of Haggai and Zechariah, was completed in 516 B.C. Since it was far less magnificent than the previous Temple, Herod the Great endeavored to increase his favor with the Jews by progressively rebuilding it on a more grandiose scale, an operation that was commenced in 20–19 B.C. and not completed till long after Herod's death. Though the main part of the building was finished by 9 B.C., the courts, outer buildings, and porticoes were not completed till sometime in the A.D. sixties. The building was made of white marble, much of which was overlaid with gold, thus producing an effect of dazzling splendor.

The whole Temple complex stood within an area of about twenty-six acres called "the court of the Gentiles," a territory open to both Jews and Gentiles. Inside this was a smaller court which housed two others. They were the court of the women and the court of the Israelites. Inside the court of the Israelites was the court of the priests. The sanctuary, elevated above the inner court, was patterned after that of the old tabernacle, containing a holy place and a holy of holies (the most holy place). Inside the holy place was the table of showbread, the seven-branched lampstand, and the altar of incense. Only the priests entered here. The holy of holies had been empty since the ark of the covenant became lost at the destruction of Solomon's temple. The high priest, and the high priest only, entered the holy of holies once a year, on the Day of Atonement.

Outside the sanctuary and within the court of the priests was the great altar of burnt offering, eighteen feet square and fifteen feet high. Here animal sacrifices were consumed in the daily ritual; here the fires burned continually. North of the altar was the place where the animals were slaughtered and prepared for sacrifice.

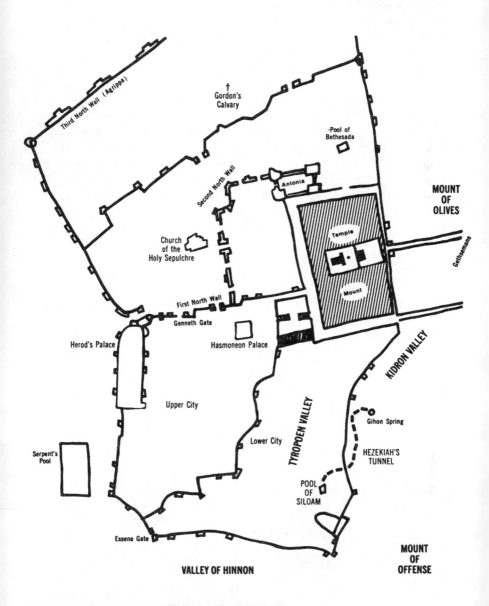

JERUSALEM IN NEW TESTAMENT TIMES

The Romans allowed the Jews to keep a guard or police corps to maintain order in the Temple area, and it was this guard who took charge of Peter and John when they were arrested for their preaching.The guard maintained a watch at the Temple at all times to see that no unauthorized person entered into a forbidden place. The chief officer of the guard was called a *strategos,* or "captain of the temple" (Acts 4:1).

The Temple was the center of Jewish religious life. Every day burnt offerings were presented, each morning about 9:00 A.M. and each evening about 3:00 P.M. These offerings were presented to God on behalf of all the people. To these daily offerings additional sacrifices were offered on feast days and on the sabbath, as well as at very elaborate ceremonies. The Temple was to the Jew a place sanctified by the presence of God himself, especially in regard to the inner courts. The outer courts, open to Gentiles as well, were used for public gatherings. Through the gates, halls, and courts of the Temple passed temple singers, musicians, porters, servants, guards, treasurers, and priests. Probably as many as 20,000 priests served in the Temple in twenty-four different courses. The high priest, head of all the priesthood, enjoyed considerable power and prestige; he was always chosen from the same small group.

4. The Synagogue

Practically all scholars agree that the synagogue had its origin during the Babylonian exile after the destruction of the Temple in 587 B.C., although there is very little information about its beginning. There is no mention of the synagogue in the Old Testament, except maybe a passing reference in Psalm 74:8; nor is there any reference to it in any of the Jewish writings between the Testaments. Probably very religious Jews, with no Temple but with an acute need for prayer and the study of the Scriptures, met in special places to worship, especially on the sabbath. Having no place of sacrifice, they turned to a study of the Torah or law. A scribe such as Ezra, who studied the law and interpreted it, became as important a figure among the people as the priest had been when the Temple was in operation (Ezra 7:1–6). During the days of Jesus the scribes exerted a tremendous influence on Judaism.

As the Jews were further dispersed throughout the empire there was a pressing need for a local center of worship, a need that was fulfilled in the rise of the synagogue. Wherever ten men could be found to form a congregation, a synagogue could be established. The term *synagogue* is from the Greek and means assembly or coming together. When the Temple was reconstructed, the institution of the synagogue persisted alongside; for all the people could not get to the Temple. Here they met on the sabbath for prayer and worship, as did Jesus when a boy and a youth (Luke 4:16).

The synagogue was an institution of laymen for laymen, and they chose one of their members to be their ruler; it served the common man. Not only did the synagogue arise during the Babylonian captivity when there was no temple available, but it was also the synagogue that maintained and fostered Judaism after the destruction of Herod's Temple in A.D. 70.

During the Christian era synagogues were found in almost all the cities and the towns of Palestine and in most of the great centers throughout the Mediterranean world. Large cities had several synagogues; Jerusalem probably had many, although the number 480 that is referred to in the Talmud is probably a great exaggeration. Jerusalem contained foreign synagogues, where Jews from the Dispersion, coming home for the festivals, could associate with other Jews speaking the language of their home province (Acts 6:9).

The importance of the synagogue cannot be overemphasized. It served not only as the educational medium for keeping the law uppermost before the people and for instructing the children; but also as the social center for the inhabitants of a city. Prayer and a study of the law were substituted for sacrifice, and the rabbi took the place of the priest. The ruler or head of the synagogue presided over the services there; Jairus, whose daughter Jesus raised from the dead, was such a one (Mark 5:22). It was the duty of the ruler to see that order was maintained during the service and to have general oversight of the building. There was also an attendant, one who was paid to be the custodian of the building. It was his duty to care for all the property and equipment necessary to the services held at the synagogue.

One of the most important pieces of equipment was the chest or ark containing the roll of the law; but there was also a platform with a reading desk from which the Scripture for the day was read to all the people. When Jesus visited the synagogue at Nazareth, he read part of the roll of Isaiah from the platform (Luke 4:20).

A typical service in a synagogue in New Testament times probably consisted of four parts. The opening part was an invitation to prayer, with the leader saying, "Bless ye the Lord who is to be blessed." The congregation responded with the words "Blessed be the Lord who is to be blessed for ever." Then the *Shema* (meaning hear) was read. "Hear O Israel: The Lord our God is one Lord." The second part consisted of prayers, with one person praying and the people responding with "Amen." These prayers were called the lifting up of hands. The third part was a reading of a lesson from the Mosaic law. The whole Pentateuch was divided into sections so that it was completely read in from three to three and a half years. A lesson from an Old Testament prophet was also read. The fourth part was the closing, consisting of the priestly (Aaronic) benediction read by a priest (Num. 6:24–26). If no priest was present, a layman gave the benediction.

The synagogue played an important part in the preparation of the world for the advent of Christianity. It not only helped to produce a piety in the Jewish family; many Gentiles, dissatisfied with empty paganism and its formal rites, turned to the synagogue for worship and for a stimulus to ethical living. These people, known as God-fearers, were the first Gentiles to embrace Christianity. Thus it is easily discerned that the synagogues became seed plots, so to speak, for the sprouting of early Christianity.

5. The Feasts or Festivals

The feasts of the Jews were interspersed throughout the Jewish year. The Jews had twelve lunar months in their calendar year, adding a month whenever it was necessary to make the lunar year equal the solar year. They had both a civil year and a sacred year, the former beginning in the fall with the month Tishri, and the latter beginning in the spring with the month Nisan. Tishri corresponded to our September-October and Nisan to our March-April. The Jewish New Year, celebrated by Jews even today, occurred on the first day of Tishri and, therefore, started the civil year in autumn. This day was also called the Feast of Trumpets. But due to the fact that the Passover occurred during Nisan (also called Abib), this date was later changed. "This month shall be unto you the beginning of months: it shall be the first month of the year to you" (Ex. 12:2). Therefore Nisan initiated their sacred year.

The Jews of Jesus' day observed several feasts. *First,* there was the Feast of Trumpets, held on the first day of Tishri. During this day trumpets were blown in the Temple from morning till night. This feast, observed in the synagogue as well as in the Temple, was known as Rosh Hashanah. It occurred in our month of September.

Second, there was the Day of Atonement or Yom Kippur, held on the tenth day of Tishri—the day on which the high priest went into the holy of holies to make atonement, first for himself and the priests and then for the people. It occurred in late September. Luke in Acts 27:9 termed this day a fast; it was really more a fast than a feast. Also, the high priest placed his hands upon the head of a live goat and confessed the sins of the people, after which the goat was released into the wilderness. This was a sign that the sins of the people had been taken away forever (Lev. 16: 23,27–32).

This goat was termed the *scapegoat* (from "escape" plus "goat"). Today these two festivals are united by the Jews into days of penitence and heart-searching.

Third, the Feast of Tabernacles, also called the Feast of Booths and the Feast of Ingathering, occurring in late September or early October, symbolized both the gathering of the ripe fruits and the dwelling of the Hebrews in booths during their wilderness wanderings (Lev. 23:43). They were to live temporarily in booths or huts made of branches, much like those of their sojourning forefathers. Lasting seven days, this feast was the most joyous of them all. It was called *Sukkoth,* from the Hebrew for "booth," and is mentioned in John 7:37. All three of these feasts were celebrated during Tishri.

Fourth, the Feast of Dedication or the Feast of Lights, observed for eight days, had its origin during the interbiblical period; therefore, it is not mentioned in the Old Testament. The term is found in John 10:22, however. It occurred in our month of December, almost exactly the same time as Christmas, being first established when Judas Maccabeus cleansed the Temple after it was profaned by Antiochus Epiphanes with swine sacrifice. This rededication of the Temple to the worship of God was in 165 B.C. The feast was called *Hanukkah,* from the Hebrew word *dedication.* Every home was brilliantly lighted during the feast.

Fifth, the Feast of Purim occurred in our month of March and was also termed Feast of Lots, for *purim* is Hebrew for "lots." It was a two-day feast, and the book of Esther was read publicly in the synagogue during this time. The feast commemorated the saving of the Jews by the heroic effort of Esther during the days of the Persian empire. It is not mentioned by name in the New Testament. The Feast of Dedication and the Feast of Purim might be considered minor feasts.

Sixth, the Feast of Passover or the Feast of Unleavened Bread was the most significant of all the feasts, both historically and spiritually. It symbolized the deliverance of the Hebrews from Egyptian bondage by the redemptive hand of God and their beginning as an independent nation. It occurred during the month of Nisan, corresponding mostly to our April, and lasted for seven days. Every male Jew living within fifteen miles of Jerusalem was expected to be in the Holy City for this feast. Pilgrims came from throughout Palestine and from many foreign provinces. It went by the Hebrew name *Pesah.*

Seventh, there was the Feast of Pentecost, which was also called Feast of First Fruits, Feast of Weeks, and Feast of Harvest. Since it occurred fifty days after the Passover meal, it received the name Pentecost from the

Greek word meaning fifty. Since it occurred on the day following seven weeks after the Passover, it received the name Weeks. It was also known by *Shavuoth* (the Hebrew for Pentecost) and was a one-day feast occurring in June. Since it was an expression of gratitude for the grain harvest, two wave loaves of bread were offered to the Lord. The Jews also saw in this feast a commemoration of the Mosaic law given on Mount Sinai. It is important to Christians due to the pouring out of the Holy Spirit upon the disciples of the Lord in the upper room, a very significant event in the inception of the early church.

6. Jewish Sects or Parties

In religion there has always been a tendency to branch off into sectarianism, and Judaism was no exception. All the Jewish sects had one thing in common: allegiance to the law, the Torah. The range went from liberalism to conservatism, from mysticism to political fanaticism. At any rate, there was a party spirit prominent in Jesus' day, with several classes of people evolving.

(1) The Pharisees The largest, most influential, most democratic party of the Jews in Jesus' time was that of the Pharisees. Their name is derived from a Hebrew verb *parash,* meaning to separate. Therefore, they were recognized as the separatists of their day, the Jewish "Puritans." When one considers that there were close to 2,000,000 people in Palestine at that time, with 500,000 to 600,000 of these being Jews, mostly living in Judea—and that the number of Pharisees was just above 6,000—it is clearly seen that the proportion of Pharisees to the total Jewish population was small. Probably most of the Pharisees lived in or near Jerusalem.

It is held by most scholars that they were the successors of the Hasidim (or Hasideans), the "Pious Ones" who arose during the Maccabean uprising (see chap. 1). As the Hasidim were devoted to the Torah, so were the Pharisees. They considered Ezra their founder. Yet their theology and religious beliefs were based on the entire Hebrew Scripture: Torah, Prophets, and Writings. They placed great value on the oral law, the tradition of the elders, a kind of second authority above and beyond the Scriptures themselves. This tradition was composed of very detailed and exact legislation consisting of the verdicts and interpretations of the rabbis on the Pentateuch, the first five books. The Pharisees observed this tradition in great detail. (See Matt. 15:1–20 to observe the disdain with which Jesus viewed the tradition of the elders.)

The Pharisees believed in the existence of angels, demons, and ministering spirits. They also believed in the immortality of the soul, the resurrection of the body, and final judgment. The Pharisees fasted frequently, tithed meticulously, and practiced ritual prayer and ritual washings. They ate only kosher foods. They strictly abstained from any work on the sabbath and avoided all contacts with the Gentiles. They looked down upon the common people because of their ignorance of the law and their apparent apathy in observing it.

Religion to them consisted of conformity to the law, with God's grace being conferred on the doers of the law. Outward formalism seemed to be more significant than the inward condition of the heart; this misplaced emphasis is what produced their clash with Jesus (Matt. 23:1–36). They were very unsympathetic with any people who differed from them, for they considered themselves the guardians of orthodoxy. Josephus, the Jewish historian, observed, "The Pharisees are a group of Jews who have the reputation of excelling the rest of their nation in the observance of religion, and as exact exponents of the laws" (*Jewish War,* I. v. 2). Pharisaism is the only sect of Judaism to persist till the modern day, being the foundation of orthodox Judaism.

It should be added, however, that there were many among the Pharisees who were virtuous and pious men, leaders of their time. Nicodemus, who sought out Jesus during Jesus' ministry, was a Pharisee (John 3:1). Paul declared that he was "a Pharisee, a son of Pharisees" (Acts 23:6). He also avowed that "as touching the righteousness which is in the law, [he was] found blameless" (Phil. 3:6). It is true that the strict observance of the Torah on the part of the Pharisees had a tendency to make them self-righteous and hypocritical, but it must be admitted that their moral and spiritual standards were extremely high.

(2)   The Sadducees   The Sadducees formed the priestly party. The term *Sadducee,* according to tradition, is derived from the term *Zadok,* the name of the priest who officially anointed Solomon and became his high priest (1 Kings 2:35). The priesthood of Aaron (brother of Moses) was given to Zadok and his descendants; in this family line it remained until it became thoroughly confused during the days of the Maccabees. The Sadducees claimed the exclusive right to conduct all sacrifices in the Temple, thus giving to them the legitimate succession of the priestly office. This would give weight to the view that the name Sadducee was derived from the high priest Zadok. (The name Zadok was many times written "Sadduok" in Greek.) Josephus states that the Sadducees were supported by John Hyrcanus (135–104 B.C.) and that the Pharisees broke away from him and from the Hasmoneans. Since the Sadducees left very little of their own literature, any knowledge relative to them is derived from the writings

of their opponents.

During the days of the Hellenizing process of the Seleucids, the Sadducees were much more influenced by the Greek way of life than were the Pharisees. Politically they were liberals, using every opportunity to align themselves with whatever power was dominant so as to maintain political power and prestige. Religiously they were conservatives, believing that the Pentateuch, the first five books of the Old Testament, revealed all the laws and rules required for the priesthood, the Temple, and the sacrificial system. They firmly believed that a faithful and exact fulfillment of the sacrificial worship in the Temple, as prescribed by God in the Torah, was the means of maintaining Israel's covenant with God.

Most of the priests belonged to the Sadducees, as one would imagine, but a few belonged to the Essenes. The wealthy, aristocratic, and priestly families were included in the Sadducee ranks. The landed laymen in and around Jerusalem were also included. Though their total number was relatively small, they exerted a tremendous influence both politically and religiously. They were well educated, holding prominent positions. The masses were not represented in their ranks, for their sympathies were mostly with the Pharisees. For years they held the dominant position in the Sanhedrin, the high priest himself being the presiding officer. Since this body of seventy-one persons controlled the civil and religious life of the Jews, the Sadducees enjoyed extreme power. Due to their dominant role in both Temple and Sanhedrin, they were the official spokesmen in all dealings with Rome. They favored coexistence with the Romans, a fact that tended to decrease their favor with the masses. Their wealth also did not add to their popularity.

They placed supreme value on the Torah and relegated the prophetic writings and other books of the Hebrew Scriptures to a secondary position. They did not believe in angels, demons, evil spirits, resurrection, judgment, and future life. They also rejected the oral law that the Pharisees considered so important. Thus it is easily discerned that there was contention between the Sadducees and the Pharisees. The Sadducees were also bitterly opposed to Jesus; for he, in his ministry and teaching, threatened to undermine their establishment in the Temple. His cleansing of the Temple is a vivid example of his attitude toward their perversion of the Temple cult as God intended it to be (Matt. 21:12–17). When the Romans destroyed the Temple in A.D. 37, the Sadducees' reason for existence ceased. They soon disappeared from the scene, and the triumph of the rival Pharisees was assured.

(3) The Essenes The Essenes constituted the third major party

among the Jews at the time of Christ; they developed during the last two centuries B.C. but are not mentioned in the New Testament. Our information concerning these people up to the time of the discovery of the Dead Sea Scrolls was due to three men: Philo, the Jewish philosopher; Josephus, the Jewish historian; and Pliny, a Roman writer. Some believe that their origin lay back in Maccabean times, as in the case of Pharisees and Sadducees, and that the Essenes also came from the Hasidim. In their case, however, the protest they made took the form of a withdrawal from social and religious associations, making them more truly separatists than the Pharisees. Their total number was small, about 4,000.

They believed in a very simple life, one abstaining from luxury and wealth. Very strict Essenes did not even endorse marriage. After a probationary period of three years one was admitted to their communal way of life, at which time all private property was turned over to the communal treasury. Such a way of life necessitated the sharing of all property as well as responsibility and work. Rigid discipline and submission to the authority of superiors was the order of the day. Ritual meals and ritual washings were practiced, as well as stated periods of prayer, beginning at sunrise. Their meals were very simple. They continually read and studied the Hebrew Scriptures, believing that God's promises for the future as seen by the prophets were being performed in their community. They considered themselves the people of God's future, destined to share in the glory of the end of history.

The Essenes observed the sabbath with the utmost exactitude, probably even more so than the Pharisees. They gave themselves diligently to personal cleanliness, even to the point of wearing white robes as a symbol of inward purity. Since they considered the Temple worship to be polluted, they refrained from participating in the annual sacrifices there. The ascetic brotherhood of the Essenes is comparable in many ways to the monasticism that arose later in early Christianity. It has been debated for years whether or not John the Baptist and Jesus knew or had contact with the Essenes; no evidence conclusively points to such a contact. The strict legalism of the Essenes and the God-given grace of Christianity stand in utter contrast, making any relationship between the two extremely remote.

Tending to avoid large cities, the Essenes were found in colonies in the villages and towns of Judea; but the wilderness area just west of the Dead Sea was a favorite location. In 1947 the famous Dead Sea Scrolls (also known as Qumran Scrolls) were discovered in caves along the cliffs in that area. Two young Bedouin shepherds found in one cave eight large jars containing scrolls. A further search in this cave and in others produced hundreds of manuscripts and many thousands of scroll fragments. The conclusion was that these scrolls had been secreted away in the caves (eleven caves are of major importance) to save them from destruction by an invading army. The dating of the scrolls indicates that they were hidden about the time of the Jewish revolt of A.D. 66–70, when the Romans invaded and destroyed Jerusalem.

In 1951 some ruins near the caves were excavated by archaeologists, and what was once considered the remains of a Roman fort was found to have been the living quarters of a large settlement of people, with dormitories, cisterns, dining hall, and scriptorium. Further study revealed that there were people living there just prior to the destruction of Jerusalem in A.D. 70. This community was called Qumran.

The scrolls, evidently produced by the people who lived at the Qumran settlement, contained most, if not all, of the Old Testament books and some writings that belonged specifically to the sect at Qumran. These were the *Manual of Discipline,* the *Damascus Document,* the *Thanksgiving Hymn,* and the *Order of Warfare.* The striking observation is that not only are the Essenes not mentioned in the New Testament; they are not mentioned in the Qumran Scrolls either. Therefore, who were the people of Qumran? Were they the Essenes mentioned in the Josephus-Philo-Pliny writings? Most of the Jewish and Christian scholars today maintain that the people who wrote the scrolls and who lived at Qumran *were* the Essenes. There were both similarities and differences, but the former are more numerous than the latter.

Josephus says, however, that the Essene communities did not have women and that their members did not marry, while the Qumran community included women. The Essenes did not send sacrifices to the Temple, while the Qumran community did not forbid animal sacrifice. However, the overall evidence points to the fact that the Qumran community *was* an Essene one. Thus, the writings found in the caves, especially the *Manual of Discipline,* throw great light on the customs and beliefs of the Essenes. Of the total number of 4,000 Essenes, only a small group lived at Qumran; but it is highly possible that the entire group would assemble there for a great event—for example, the celebration of one of the great Jewish festivals. It is not known whether or not the Qumran community performed sacrifices there, but they did celebrate the great festivals at their Dead Sea community.

There were people living at Qumran until the siege of Jerusalem; at this time Roman soldiers destroyed the community. Many people were slaughtered, while some escaped. The important thing is that at some time prior to the devastating work of Rome, they had been able to conceal in nearby caves a large library of their religious beliefs.

(4)   The Zealots   Though the sect called Zealots did not appear on the surface till the first century A.D., their roots go back many centuries. They believed in the worship of the one true God of Israel; anyone, or any movement, that opposed this must be ardently condemned. They were devotees of the law given by God to Israel, and in this respect they were like the Pharisees; but in their zeal they were like Mattathias and his sons during the days of the Maccabean revolt. They were fanatical nationalists who advocated violence to rid the nation of any oppressor. To them, paying tribute to a pagan, foreign emperor was an act of treason against God. They were superpatriots, warlike Jewish rebels whose activities were not dominant most of the time; but when oppressive movements arose, they advocated open revolt. The Zealots constituted the fourth of the four philosophies described by Josephus. (The other three have been discussed.)

It is very likely that the Zealots were connected with the assassins mentioned in Acts 21:38; the chief captain asked Paul if he were one of them. One of Jesus' apostles, Simon (not Simon Peter), was a Zealot, as indicated by his name. In Luke 6:15 he is referred to as "Simon who was called the Zealot" in the American Standard Version. In the King James Version he is termed "Simon called Zelotes." (The identical phrase is found in Acts 1:13.) In Matthew 10:4 this same apostle is called the "Cananaean," which is merely a transliteration of the Aramaic word for Zealot. The very fact that Jesus chose a Zealot as one of his inner circle, as well as choosing one who collected taxes for the despised Romans (Matthew), shows his regard for men of diverse cultures and backgrounds. Zealots were also very active in the great revolt against Rome in A.D. 66–70.

(5)   The Herodians   This group, existing in Palestine in the first century A.D., constituted neither a religious sect nor a political party. They seem to have been Jews of influence and prestige who favored the Herodian rule and, therefore, Roman rule, since the Herods received their authority from Rome. In a way these men represented a continuing attitude of acceptance of the Hellenizing process begun by the Seleucids, successors of Alexander the Great. Since most of the Jews were strongly opposed to Roman domination, the Herodians were in the minority. They appear in the Gospels as enemies of Jesus both in Galilee (Mark 3:6) and in Jerusalem (Mark 12:13). In both instances they were lined up with the Pharisees against Jesus.

(6)   The Common People   Over 90 percent of all the Jews of Palestine

were not found in any of the groups or sects just discussed. They were known as the people of the land *('am 'arez)*. In the early books of the Old Testament this term merely differentiated these people from the aristocracy, the ruling class; but after the Jews returned from the Babylonian exile, at which time Judaism was beginning to take definite form, the term referred to those with whom pious Jews were told not to intermarry (Ezra 9:1–2; Neh. 10:30) and with whom they were not to trade and buy on the sabbath (Neh. 10:31). In New Testament times the term referred to all those who ignored the Torah and all its demands, whether this was due to ignorance, lack of motivation, or an overwhelming burden in the secular affairs of the world. In John 7:49 the Pharisees allude to the common people in a derogatory manner. "But this multitude that knoweth not the law are accursed." The contempt of the Pharisees for the ignorant masses would allow no more contact with them than was absolutely necessary; this would discourage eating with them or intermarrying with them.

The fact that Jesus was very friendly with these unfortunate people, outcasts to both Pharisees and Sudducees, led to animosity toward him on the part of the recognized religious leaders of that day. "But when he saw the multitudes, he was moved with compassion for them, because they were distressed and scattered, as sheep not having a shepherd" (Matt. 9:36). When Jesus was eating in the house of Levi, the publican, the Pharisees questioned his disciples in scorn, saying, "Why do ye eat and drink with the publicans and sinners?" (Luke 5:29–32). At the time Jesus was condemned for eating in the house of Zacchaeus, a sinner, he replied, "For the Son of man came to seek and to save that which was lost" (Luke 19:10).

7. The Scribes

The scribes constituted a profession, a vocation, not a religious or political sect. One could be a Pharisee and a scribe at the same time. Throughout the biblical lands the scribes for many centuries had filled a very useful place in society as public secretaries, producing manuscripts from dictation or copying existing manuscripts. They were penmen, copyists, ancient officials who performed clerical duties. Their tools for work were ink, pen, and scrolls.

For Israel, however, conditions arose during the Babylonian exile that called for a distinct class of teachers or interpreters. The Temple, with its ritual and sacrificial cult, had been destroyed. The Torah or law of Moses became the center of religious life, to which the Hebrews gave themselves in utter devotion. The synagogue arose as a place for the study of the

Torah, where the people could gather (synagogue means assembly) for the reading of the Scriptures and for worship. The people dedicated themselves with unremitting zeal to the study of the Torah and its application to ethical daily living.

When they returned home to Jerusalem and Judea under the lenient policy of Cyrus the Great, they brought with them the institution of the synagogue, a very democratic lay movement. The Temple was rebuilt under the wise leadership of Zerubbabel, but a very famous scribe named Ezra dedicated all his efforts to instilling in all Jewish people a desire to know and obey the Torah. Two Old Testament verses depict Ezra's aim: Ezra 7:10; Nehemiah 8:8. He wanted them to understand the true meaning of the Scriptures without being plagued with doubts and questionings.

In time the priests became very heavily involved with the sacrifices, the ritual, and the cult of the second Temple, with the added fact that they became entangled in the political affairs around them. Many of the priests submitted to both the Hellenizing process of the Seleucids and to the political corruption brought on by the presence of Roman overlords. This meant that any scholarly study, with the subsequent training and education of the people, was increasingly laid upon the scribes in the synagogues. Schools were set up in both homes and synagogues, and the work of the scribes passed more and more from mere copyists to that of teachers and interpreters of the law. They attempted to give meaning to the Torah in such a practical way that it could legislate for the everyday problems of everyday life.

The infinite variety of day-to-day decisions presented new problems, calling for new interpretations of the law. These the scribes proceeded to hand down through the years, thus becoming the lawyers of their day. Their verbal comments grew and grew, becoming known as the oral law, or the tradition of the elders (Mark 7:3); this was as binding to the Jew as the written law in the Pentateuch itself. The synagogue was the scribe's domain. He was to study the law, teach the law, and be the legal expert of Israel.

These scribes, religious descendants from Ezra, were called *sopherim,* Hebrew for "scribes." There were probably some priests numbered among them at the time of Jesus, but most were laymen. Though most scribes belonged to the Pharisaic party, there is good reason to believe that there may have been Sadducean scribes also. As the office of priest went out with the destruction of Herod's Temple in A.D. 70, the office of scribe lived on, increasing in importance. The term *rabbi,* meaning "my master," was a title given the scribe to show respect. Another title was *teacher.* The rabbi of today is the spiritual descendant of the scribe of Jesus' day.

8. The Sanhedrin

In Judea there were local courts, each with at least three judges; these tried all minor offenses. There seem to have been one in each of Judea's eleven districts. The great council or Sanhedrin (from the Greek meaning "council") of Jerusalem was composed of seventy members, with the high priest presiding and making seventy-one. Josephus states that the high priest served as head of the Sanhedrin as early as the second century B.C. At the time of Jesus the Sanhedrin had three types of members: the high priests (the acting high priest and all former high priests), the elders (men from the lay aristocracy), and the scribes (lawyers from the Pharisees).

The authority held by the Sanhedrin depended on who happened to be the ruler in Judea at that time. Herod the Great left it very little power; Roman procurators gave it unlimited power in religious matters and freedom in civil matters within the boundaries set by Rome. The death sentence evidently had to be ratified by the procurator (John 18:31). Since the high priest owed his appointment to the Roman overlord, his office became quite a prize, the result of political intrigue and conniving. The law of Moses was supposed to underlie every phase of the work of the Sanhedrin. However, the Jews made no distinction between civil and religious law; so the Sanhedrin had authority over every phase of Jewish life. Rome recognized the Sanhedrin as the official ruling body of the Jews, thus giving this august council great authority. Its jurisdiction was within Judea only, but this limitation did not prevent its influence in being felt throughout the whole of Palestine. It had its own corps of police, with power of arrest (see Mark 14:43).

The Sanhedrin is mentioned several times in the New Testament. It was before this body of Jewish leaders that Jesus was tried (Matt. 26:59). Peter and John were questioned by this council (Acts 4:5–7; 5:27, 34). Stephen was brought before the council (Acts 6:12). Paul also appeared before the council and made his defense (Acts 22:30; 23:15). Later, at Caesarea, Paul appealed to Caesar rather than be sent back to Jerusalem to appear before the council (Acts 25:9–11). Just as in the case of the Sadducees, the Sanhedrin ceased to exist after the destruction of Jerusalem in A.D. 70.

9. Home Life

Jewish life in Jesus' time was centered in the home. It was a simple, pious life, with children considered blessings from God. The more children a family had, the more it was blessed. The home was considered the place

of instruction in the Torah as well as in the great historical events that made
the Hebrews God's chosen people. The family was the key to a continuation of Judaism and to a simple, sincere faith in God. The celebration of the
Passover was a family event of major significance; here the great event of
the release from Egyptian bondage was annually recounted in the family
circle. "And these words, which I command thee this day, shall be upon
thy heart; and thou shalt teach them diligently unto thy children, and shalt
talk of them when thou sittest in thy house, and when thou walkest by the
way, and when thou liest down, and when thou risest up" (Deut. 6:6,7).

The Torah commanded reverence for parents, a duty next in importance
to those that related to God himself. The first four of the Ten Commandments have to do with man's relation to God; the very next commandment
concerns one's relation to his parents. "Honor thy father and thy mother,
that thy days may be long in the land which Jehovah thy God giveth thee"
(Ex. 20:12). To strike a parent was a capital offense. "And he that smiteth
his father, or his mother, shall be surely put to death" (Ex. 21:15). The
Torah likewise jealously guarded the sanctity of marriage; for adultery,
along with murder, was punishable by stoning to death (Lev. 20:10). All of
these and many similar commandments were taught diligently in the home,
thus producing a distinct family piety in the homelife of Israel.

PART TWO

The Christian Records: Manuscripts and Versions

4.
Origin of the New Testament Records

1. Significance of the New Testament

About A.D. 30 there arose in Palestine a community of people previously reared in the atmosphere of the Temple, the synagogue, and the Torah that believed the "new age" had arrived. It was the age that had been promised by the prophets and witnessed in the Hebrew Scriptures, an age that began when God broke into history in the incarnation and atoning act of Jesus of Nazareth. These people firmly believed that they were the nucleus of those instituting the new age, a people destined later to be termed *Christian*. Their convictions were undergirded by the belief that God had raised Jesus from the dead and, in so doing, had exalted him as the One for inaugurating the new age. Peter proclaimed "that God hath made him both Lord and Christ, this Jesus whom ye crucified" (Acts 2:36). One born of an obscure peasant girl in a small village in Judea was none other than the Messiah, the triumphant and reigning Lord and King. This was the one who, more than any other living person, was to affect vitally the course of human history; and his people, the Christian community, knew that they, not historic Israel, were the ones through whom the prophetic promises made to Israel were being fulfilled.

2. Period of Literary Inactivity

Prior to the writing of the books of the New Testament, the Bible of the early Christians was the Septuagint, the Greek translation of the Hebrew Scriptures. This book also included the Apocrypha, the fourteen books written during the interbiblical period. When the early Christians went out to proclaim the gospel, they used texts for their preaching and teaching selected from the Old Testament books. When Philip the evangelist encountered the Ethiopean treasurer on the road to Gaza, he won him to Jesus by reading and interpreting to him the fifty-third chapter of the book of Isaiah (Acts 8:25–40).

Jesus' method in proclaiming the good news of salvation to the two on the road to Emmaus during the interlude between his resurrection and ascension was employed by the apostles and evangelists for many years subsequently; he announced that he, Jesus, was the fulfillment of the Scriptures considered by the Jews the oracles of God. "And beginning from Moses and from all the prophets, he interpreted to them in all the scriptures the things concerning himself" (Luke 24:27). The sermons found in the book of Acts preached by Peter, Stephen, and Paul depended heavily upon the Old Testament as the source of authority.

For at least a quarter of a century after the resurrection of Jesus, there was seemingly nothing written about his ministry or his teachings. What was the reason for this literary inactivity in regard to the atoning work of our Lord? There seem to be at least three reasons. First, the early Christians expected his return to be imminent; his second appearance was to take place within their lifetime. Therefore, with the return of Jesus for judgment so soon in the future, why write books?

Second, there were many people who had been with Jesus after the resurrection, who had seen him, who had heard him teach and preach, and who could witness to his resurrection. An oral tradition about Jesus went from person to person, with continual repetition making it more and more uniform.

Third, the early Christians already had a Bible: the Septuagint. This they read daily to discern how Jesus was the fullfillment of the promises and foretellings recorded throughout its pages. The Christians of Berea received the gospel readily, "examining the scriptures daily, whether these things were so" (Acts 17:11). This custom was probably found throughout all the Christian communities.

3. Need for a Written Record

There was the *gospel,* and English word meaning God-story or good story, a translation of the Greek word *euangelion,* meaning good news. This was the main message of Jesus that was preached, the story of his death and resurrection and the significance of these events for all mankind. This preached message was known as the *kerygma.* To the kerygma was added the sayings, stories, and parables of Jesus, along with accounts of his miraculous works. It was not sufficient to have merely a collection of Jesus' ethical teachings or a series of his sayings. His identity, his person, his aim, his purpose—all was very significant. All combined to form the oral tradition of the early church.

"And every day, in the temple and at home, they ceased not to teach and to preach Jesus as the Christ" (Acts 5:42). Such activity continued for at least a generation before there arose a feeling that the death, resurrection, and ascension of Jesus, as well as his sayings and his miracles, should be recorded. So the oral message preceded the written message. This is possibly what Paul had in mind when he admonished the Thessalonian Christians to hold securely "the traditions which ye were taught" (2 Thess. 2:15). The early missionary movement gave birth to the New Testament documents, not vice versa. The apostles, teachers, and evangelists proclaimed the good news and founded churches throughout the empire. As the churches grew, problems arose. As time passed, the ranks of the eyewitnesses were reduced by death. The expectation of the imminent return of Jesus—for most Christians within their lifetime—became dimmer and dimmer.

The reasons for the writing of the New Testament documents are now very evident. First, the eyewitnesses of all that Jesus said and did were passing from the scene. Those who could authoritatively declare what had transpired were becoming fewer and fewer. An authoritative record was needed to replace an authoritative word of mouth.

Second, there was a growing importance to anything connected with Jesus: his words, his parables, his sayings, his birth, his miracles, his death, his resurrection, his ascension. There was an emerging significance relative to the gospel story, the good news of God's atoning activity realized through the death and resurrection of Jesus. Anything this important needed to be recorded!

Third, there was a growing need to differentiate between Christianity and Judaism. Both held the Hebrew Scriptures to be the Word of God. Both worshiped the same God. The Old foretold the New; the old covenant was replaced by the new covenant. The Hebrew Scriptures had foretold the coming of Jesus the Messiah. From the loins of the religion proclaimed by the prophets came forth the new faith, Christianity. But what a difference there was! This new faith must be expounded and set forth in detailed order.

Fourth, heresies and false beliefs soon began to show their faces. Sects began to arise. There were debates about the nature of Christianity, the form of worship, and the daily practice of Jesus' teachings. There were controversies about Jesus' person and being. The New Testament was a necessity if a pure and unaltered Christian faith was to survive.

4. The Name New Testament

The English Bible is divided into two parts: the Old Testament and the New Testament. The former division has to do with God's dealings with peoples and events prior to the coming of Christ, and especially with the

Hebrews, his special ones. The latter deals with the life, teachings, death, and resurrection of Jesus and with the Christian missionary movement evolving from them. To the believers in Christ the old set of writings foretold, led up to, and were fulfilled in Christ; they were incomplete without the second set. The new writings not only supplemented the old; they complemented them as well. Hence the terms *old* and *new* arose to set them apart.

The word *testament* is not the best term with which to translate the Hebrew and Greek words used by the original writers. The term *covenant* is a much better term, one more closely aligned with the Hebrew and Greek involved. The word *testament* is primarily used today because of the influence of Jerome's Latin Vulgate. He used *testamentum*; and the early English translators employed *testament* to translate Jerome's term, when they should have gone back to the original Hebrew and Greek. It would be much better today to speak of Old Covenant and New Covenant instead of Old Testament and New Testament.

The covenant idea is basic in both the Hebrew Scriptures and in the New Testament documents. At Sinai, immediately after the great deliverance from Egyptian slavery and oppression, God made an agreement or covenant with Israel whereby they became his chosen people, a position that gave them both privileges and responsibilities. However, Israel failed to live up to the covenant and broke the covenant instead. This is revealed in Jeremiah 31:31–34, where the great prophet also declared that God would make a new covenant with his people, an inner and spiritual one, not written on slabs of stone but upon the heart.

Christ established that covenant with his life, death, and resurrection. At the instituting of the Lord's Supper he said of the cup, "This cup is the new covenant in my blood, even that which is poured out for you" (Luke 22:20). The writer of Hebrews quoted Jeremiah's new covenant passage twice as being fulfilled in Christ. All who accept the new covenant which Jesus has effected—the Christians—constitute new Israel, heirs of the promises made to old Israel (Rom. 9:6–8). Christians are Abraham's seed and heirs of the promise (Gal. 3:26–29); they are the people of the covenant, the new covenant fulfilling and superseding the old covenant. The old covenant finds its highest significance and reason for being in the new covenant.

5. Contents of the New Testament

In the Old Testament there are thirty-nine books, and in the New Testament there are twenty-seven books. The New is about one third the

Old in length.

First in the New Testament there are four documents that are termed *Gospels*. These tell of the birth, life, miracles, teachings, death, and resurrection of our Lord Jesus Christ. They are named for the four men that tradition says composed them: Matthew, Mark, Luke, and John. Not one of them contains the name of the author embedded anywhere in the text; very early each man's name was associated with that respective book as the composer and writer. This is why the name appears at the head of the book and not in the book.

Not one of the four is pure biography; each author has other distinct values to contribute rather than just a chronological account of the life of Jesus. Nor does any claim to be a complete account of the earthly life of Jesus; they present only a small part of what hc did and said.

The second group in the New Testament writings, "The Acts of the Apostles," was written by Luke as a sequel to his Gospel. It is a book of history, presenting the growth of the early missionary movement of the church.

Third in order are the thirteen epistles written by the apostle Paul: Romans, 1 and 2 Corinthians, Galatians, Ephesians, Philippians, Colossians, 1 and 2 Thessalonians, 1 and 2 Timothy, Titus, and Philemon. These books range in scope from a very heavy theological work, Romans, to a delightful private letter, Philemon, concerning a runaway slave. They are vital and dynamic documents dealing with the problems and difficulties in the churches of that era, each one intended to deal with some critical situation producing a crisis at that time. These are called the Pauline Epistles.

Fourth, after the Pauline Epistles are found the eight General Epistles or Catholic Epistles. (The term *catholic* as employed here simply means "universal" and is in no way connected with the Roman Catholic Church.) Sometimes they are termed the Non-Pauline Epistles. These books include Hebrews, James, 1 and 2 Peter, 1, 2, and 3 John, and Jude. Most of these books were written during the last part of the first century.

Fifth, after the General Epistles there is a book of visions called Revelation. Sometimes it is termed the *Apocalypse,* which is merely a word derived from the Greek as *revelation* is derived from the Latin. Dealing with the theme of Christian hope amid Roman persecution and death, it is highly apocalyptic in nature and abounds in symbols and hidden meanings.

6. Arrangement of Books of the New Testament

These twenty-seven distinct pieces of writing were composed by many men from about A.D. 50 to about A.D. 100, although some scholars place the last book to be written as late as A.D. 150. There is quite a varied opinion about the dates of composition of the New Testament books; the main thing to remember is that the inspirational quality of a book of the Bible does not rise or fall on our knowledge of its date of writing.

Nor are these twenty-seven documents arranged in the New Testament according to the time they were written. There may be a great difference between the date a book was composed and the era with which it deals. To attempt to arrange the books in the order in which they were written would reveal a striking difference between that arrangement and the one now found in the New Testament. Not only is that true, but many others would disagree with the probable order set forth due to the fact that the date of writing of many of the New Testament books is a matter of scholarly dispute. There is simply not enough evidence, either within or without the books, to speak definitely about dates of composition.

Matthew's Gospel was certainly not the first of the New Testament books to be written. John's Gospel has been dated from the middle of the first century all the way to the middle of the second century. All of Paul's epistles, with the exception of the pastoral epistles (1 Timothy, 2 Timothy, and Titus), were written prior to the penning of the four Gospels. Many scholars believe that Revelation was written prior to the Gospel of John and the three epistles of John, while some believe that 2 Peter was written last of all.

Why, then, are the books of the New Testament arranged in the present order in the English Bible? We would certainly expect to see the Gospels first, since they deal with the birth, life, death, and resurrection of our Lord. Although Matthew was probably not the first of the four to be composed, it emphasizes Jesus as the fulfillment of the Old Testament promises concerning the coming of the Messiah. Therefore it is a bridge, so to speak, between the Old Testament and the New Testament and sets the stage for the other three Gospels. The book of Acts tells of the expansion of the early missionary enterprise and the spread of the early church; therefore, the book of Acts is next in sequence to the life and teachings of Jesus as found in the Gospels. Paul's Epistles are next in order, since they deal with the problems and difficulties encountered by the churches. Then come the General Epistles, dealing with additional problems, followed in turn by Revelation. Since the book of Revelation deals with the end of history and the consummation of the kingdom, we would expect it to occupy the final position.

The books of the New Testament may also be classed according to their literary character. There are historical books in the New Testament; these include Matthew, Mark, Luke, John, and Acts, for they each tell a story. Acts is the sequel to Luke. There are also doctrinal books; these would be Romans, 1 and 2 Corinthians, Galatians, Ephesians, Philippians, Colossians, 1 and 2 Thessalonians, Hebrews, James, 1 and 2 Peter, Jude, and 1 John. Most of these are very informal letters dealing with Christian beliefs and Christian ethics. There are also personal books, letters written to individuals rather than to groups. These are 1 and 2 Timothy, Titus, Philemon, and 2 and 3 John, all intended for private counsel. There is one prophetic book, the book of Revelation, dealing both with this life and the next.

7. Writers of the New Testament

All the writers of the New Testament books were Jews with the exception of Luke. Matthew, Peter, and John were among the twelve apostles of Jesus. It is apparent that Mark was highly influenced by Peter. Though Luke and Paul did not personally know Jesus during his ministry, they were well acquainted with those who did. Jude and James must have been active in the early church. Practically all scholars today are of the opinion that Paul did not write Hebrews, but we do not know who wrote the book. Many names—Luke, Barnabas, Silas, Apollos, Clement of Rome, and others—have been submitted. The identity of the author of Hebrews is one of the mysteries connected with the study of the New Testament.

8. Language of the New Testament

The New Testament documents were written in the Greek language, the Greek that was common to the Mediterranean world during the first century A.D. Classical Greek, as taught in many modern universities and colleges, is the Greek that was spoken and written during the Golden Age of Greece, the age of Pericles, Socrates, Plato, Aristotle, and Demosthenes. This was during the fourth and fifth centuries B.C. By the first century A.D. the Greek language had changed considerably, as well as having spread out over a much larger area. This Greek was termed *koiné* Greek, a term meaning common Greek, for it was common to the Mediterranean world.

The successors of Alexander the Great endeavored to Hellenize or "Greekize" all the lands subjugated by their great commander, and the Greek language was one of the factors involved. Their aim was to force all the people to speak Greek; as a result, Greek became a second language to them. It appears as though God was providentially giving to the world a common tongue in which the New Testament could be written for all mankind. *Koiné* Greek, first century A.D. Greek, and New Testament

Greek are one and the same. Modern Greek, as employed in Greece today, is different, however; there has been a tremendous change in the language in the last nineteen centuries.

9. Canon of the Old Testament

The word *canon* is derived from a Greek term, which in turn descended from a Semitic term meaning reed. The reed was a very early instrument used in measuring; therefore, the word reed came to mean rule, standard, or norm. When *canon* was finally applied to the Scriptures, it denoted the books that were considered to be divinely inspired as opposed to those that were not. (There is a canon of the Old Testament, a canon of the New Testament, and an overall canon of the Bible.) The term canon was used as early as the third century A.D., for at that time the renowned scholar and writer Origen employed it to designate the books considered to be the oracles of God. Canonization is the process by which a canon is formed. It is the spiritual measuring of all the writings with a view to determining those spiritually authentic and divinely authoritative.

The Old Testament was canonized by the Jews and considered the final word of God to the Hebrew people; they referred to their sacred writings as the Hebrew Scriptures. There are three sections to the Hebrew Bible: the Torah or Law; the Nebiim or Prophets; and the Kethubim or Writings. The first to be canonized was the Torah, found in the Pentateuch: Genesis, Exodus, Leviticus, Numbers, and Deuteronomy. (The word *Pentateuch* means "five vessels," designating the five books of the law.) These books grew in authority until by 400 B.C. there was very little question about their acceptance as the sacred word of God.

The second section to be canonized was the Nebiim or Prophets. Though the law never lost its primary position as the foundation of Israel's religion, it was only natural that the ethical and social teachings of the prophets were of secondary importance. The demand for moral and ethical living as proclaimed by the Hebrew prophets constituted one of Israel's great gifts to the world. By 200 B.C. this section of the Hebrew Scriptures was solidly in the folds of the canon.

The third section to reach canonical status was the Kethubim or Writings, a number of unrelated books of miscellaneous character. They formed an appendix, more or less, to the law and the prophets, with the Psalms as a nucleus. The Psalter or Psalms was the hymnbook of the Hebrew people. Much of this third section was considered inspired prior to the Christian era, but it was the Council of Jamnia in A.D. 90 that pronounced it canonical—besides confirming the other two sections canonical as well.

The Council did not include the Apocrypha, the fourteen books contained in the Septuagint, in their official canon. The destruction of Jerusalem in A.D. 70 called for the Jews to consolidate and give definite form to their faith. This they did in a formal canonization in A.D. 90. After this date no change was ever made in the Palestinian canon. The Septuagint became the official Scriptures for the Jews of the Dispersion, however; it included the Apocrypha. The two great centers for the Jews of the Dispersion were Babylon and Alexandria, and it was in Alexandria that the Septuagint had originated.

10. Canon of the New Testament

The Bible of the first-century Christians was the Septuagint, which was their canon. With this as their official Bible and with the oral tradition of Jesus being passed by word of mouth, they felt no need for the creation of a distinctly Christian Bible. Yet by the end of the third century there *was* a Christian Bible, the New Testament, canonized and equal in authority to the Old Testament. What was the process by which this occurred?

The New Testament was the result of the missionary movement, not the reverse. The apostles had been preaching, teaching, and founding churches for at least twenty years before Paul wrote 1 Thessalonians, probably the first book in the New Testament to be penned. None of the New Testament writers believed that they were producing a book to be included in a Christian canon; rather, they were writing to fulfill some critical need in a church or group of churches. The New Testament writers did not, in conference, decide to compose the New Testament books and then to march forth to employ them in proclaiming the gospel. They dispersed themselves in a mighty missionary enterprise, only to meet obstacles and difficulties that called for written documents and epistles as weapons of defense. The canonical books were those that the church chose as most representative of its life, its practice, and its beliefs. The New Testament was produced by the church to be used of the church.

There were many Christian documents produced by early church leaders in the century and a half after the birth of Jesus; yet only twenty-seven books are included in the New Testament canon. Some of these writings are even older than a few that are included in the New Testament. We now possess lists of books considered sacred and inspired and drawn up by certain leaders in the church during the second and third centuries, but these lists disagree as to what books should be included. There is no universal agreement whatsoever. As with the Old Testament canon, the books of the New Testament canon were not immediately recognized as inspired.

Paul's epistles other than the pastoral ones (1 Timothy, 2 Timothy, Titus) were the first of the New Testament books to be written, beginning with 1 and 2 Thessalonians about A.D. 50. Yet Paul's letters were not considered sacred and inspired when they first appeared in circulation. The Gospel of Mark entered the scene about A.D. 70, while the Gospels of Matthew and Luke were written about A.D. 85. These three, termed the Synoptic Gospels, do not mention any of Paul's writings. Other books followed; Revelation came about A.D. 95, and the Gospel of John and 1, 2, and 3 John appeared about A.D. 100. These writings show signs of knowledge of Paul's works, so the Pauline epistles must have been well copied and circulated by the end of the first Christian century. Some think Jude and 2 Peter came much later, but these dates are not absolute in any respect.

One passage in the New Testament refers to Christian writings as "scripture"; 2 Peter 3:15–16 mentions the letters of Paul along with "the other scriptures." Many times the word *scripture* or *scriptures* is found in the pages of the New Testament referring to the Old Testament. To the Sadducees Jesus said, "Ye do err, not knowing the scriptures, nor the power of God" (Matt. 22:29). And to the Jews he declared, "Ye search the scriptures, because ye think that in them ye have eternal life; and these are they which bear witness of me; and ye will not come to me, that ye may have life" (John 5:39–40). However, the passage in 2 Peter is the only time that the term *scripture* is used to refer to New Testament writings.

As was the case with the Old Testament canon, not all the writings concerning Jesus, the gospel, and the early church were included in the list declared sacred. When Luke started his Gospel, he informed his readers that many others had "taken in hand to draw up a narrative concerning those matters which have been fulfilled among us," but that he wanted to trace "all things accurately from the first" (Luke 1:1–3). What finally became of the "many" other documents about Jesus referred to by Luke? They seem to have disappeared. Was it because some were fantastical or heretical? Surely some must have been quite valuable. Some of these noncanonical gospels and epistles, having recently been discovered, make a valuable contribution to our knowledge of early church affairs.

In the last of the first century and continuing into the second century, two developments made imperative the formation of a distinct list of Christian sacred writings. One was the appearance of heresies: false beliefs concerning the person of Jesus, his great atoning act, the person of the Holy Spirit, the practice of the Christian faith, and the differentiation between the ethical and the unethical. Docetism, Gnosticism, Marcionism, and Montanism were a few of the unorthodox teachings that were causing trouble. Hence the church needed a basic and authoritative statement of the true Christian faith; the New Testament canon was a vital necessity.

The second development was the appearance of a mass of literature, more or less Christian, shading off from the orthodox into the unorthodox. Some of this vast array of writings was outright false, spurious; some was true. At any rate, an authoritative list of sacred books was needed, a "springboard of orthodoxy," a standard, a norm of authority.

The work of a heretic named Marcion, writing about A.D. 140, hastened the process of canonization. This brilliant but falsely motivated and heretical leader in the early church proceeded to draw up his own list of books worthy in his opinion of the Christian faith. He was highly anti-Jewish, which led him to include only ten of the epistles of Paul and the Gospel of Luke as documents meeting his approval. He rejected the Old Testament completely, made editorial changes in Luke, and ignored the other New Testament writings. Marcion's revolutionary list of books hastened the more conservative leaders to draw up other lists.

Tatian, about A.D. 160, wove the four Gospels we now have in the New Testament into a harmony, a composite gospel. Irenaeus, about A.D. 180, also placed great emphasis upon our present four Gospels, and in the present order: Matthew, Mark, Luke, John. It is striking that no mention of Philemon, 2 Peter, 2 and 3 John, and Jude was made by any of the writers prominent in the very early church; these books seem to have had no status throughout the first and second centuries.

Other lists of canonical books continued to appear on the Christian scene. The earliest list of canonical books that approached what we now have in the New Testament is that contained in the Muratorian Fragment, about A.D. 195, probably drawn up by Victor, bishop of Rome. It reveals what the church at Rome at the last of the second century considered inspired.

The first list of books set forth as canonical that agrees exactly with our list today was one made in A.D. 367 by Athanasius of Alexandria. This renowned scholar wished to distinguish between the twenty-seven canonical books and the apocryphal ones. Of the twenty-seven he said, "In these alone is proclaimed the good news of the teaching of true religion. Let no one add to them nor remove anything from them." Therefore the date of A.D. 367 should probably be used as the date of canonization of the New Testament. An important church council, the Council of Carthage, meeting in A.D. 397, drew up exactly the same list. After that date all debate concerning the inclusion or exclusion of any book in the New Testament canon virtually ceased.

Two factors actually determined what books should be included in and excluded from the canon. Some books were used over and over in the worship services of the early church, right along with the Old Testament. They were read repeatedly; many copies were produced and dispersed; the books grew in popularity. They fulfilled the spiritual needs of the people and "proved themselves worthy." Common usage placed them on a scriptural plane. The second factor of selection was the ratification by bishops, presbyters, and church councils; but these church groups did not select the books or formulate the canon. They merely recognized the books that had proved themselves by prominent usage in the churches and in the homes, thus giving to the selected books church authority and weight.

5.
Spread of the New Testament Records

1. Writing Materials and Scribes

The invention of the printing press by Johann Gutenberg in the middle of the fifteenth century so revolutionized the production and circulation of books that the common man could possess them. Prior to that time all books were written by hand, and other copies were produced by scribes. The scribes constituted a professional class, at least down to the sixth century. From that time on the manuscripts were mainly produced by the monks in the monasteries. It is obvious that the Christian scribe (or monk) carried a tremendous responsibility, that of reproducing the text with accuracy. A study of the various manuscripts reveals that the monks did their work relatively accurately.

The Old Testament text was written on scrolls or rolls. Using parchment, the monks glued together the skins to make an extended length of writing surface. This in turn was rolled up to make a roll or a book. Also used was a paper made from the papyrus plant growing plentifully in the marshland of the East, especially Egypt. The plant stem was cut into lengths about a foot long, then cut into thin strips. These fiber strips were placed beside each other to form a sheet; then more strips were placed upon these at right angles to make another layer. Then the layers were pressed firmly together to produce a sheet, which in turn was dried and polished. The finished pieces of papyrus paper were glued together to form a continuous writing surface, which was wound around a stick to produce a roll. Papyrus paper was used in Egypt for stationery as early as 3000 B.C.

The New Testament documents were at first written in scroll form on papyrus paper with a reed pen and ink. The writing followed the direction of the fiber strips, so it was done on the side of the paper on which the strips went horizontally. Separation of words and punctuation marks were not included. Sometimes the writer wanted to indicate a change in thought. If so, he would show the change by a short horizontal line in the margin, the origin of our word paragraph. (*Paragraph* is from a Greek word meaning

written alongside.) The title of the book was placed at the end; the
document was then rolled up and put in a cylinder.

About the third century A.D. the Christians began to use a form that had
great advantage over the roll. This was the *codex* form (plural, *codices*) or
leaf form. The sheets of paper were not glued end on end to make a roll;
they were folded in the middle and then sewed together at the fold. This
type of structure could be opened at any desired place with ease, which was
not always the case with a scroll. Also, could it be that the early Christians
wanted a form for their sacred writings that would differentiate church
usage from synagogue usage? All the writings in the synagogues were on
scrolls.

During the fourth century another change began to take place in manuscript development. Vellum was on the way to replacing papyrus paper,
partly due to the decrease in the availability of papyrus and partly due to the
greater practicality of vellum. Scribes could write on both sides of a sheet
of vellum but only on one side of papyrus paper. Vellum was stronger and
easier to bind into book form. Vellum, since it was derived from the skin of
the young of the flock, had a finer texture than the parchment of that day.

2. The Greek Manuscripts

An original writing produced by Paul, John, or Peter is called an
autograph, derived from two Greek words meaning writing itself. We have
no autographs of the New Testament documents in our possession today.
However, we have manuscript copies and copies of copies made by scribes
to fulfill the demands of the early Christian community. The term *manuscript* is derived from two Latin terms meaning hand written, a very apt
term. They were truly hand written, a very slow and laborious task.

Not only do we not possess any autographs of the New Testament
documents; we possess no papyrus scrolls of these writings either. There is
a possibility that at some later date one or more may be discovered. Till
that time we must be content with some fragments of papyrus manuscripts
from the third century and with some vellum manuscripts from the fourth
century on. We now possess some 2,500 manuscripts of the Bible, varying
in length from the complete Bible down to a few verses from a single book.

Most of the Greek manuscripts down to the eighth century were written
in large, square, capital letters and were called *uncials,* from the Latin
word for inch. The later manuscripts, from the ninth century on, were
written in a cursive or running style, with flowing strokes. They were
called *minuscules,* or *cursives.* Some of the early manuscripts had as many
as four columns to the page; as time passed the number of columns was

reduced. By the seventh century most manuscripts were of the one-column variety. Even at this late date the words were still not separated, with the result that the scholars and translators of today have the added task of dividing the words accurately. Generally this is not too difficult.

3. Uncial Manuscripts

The uncial manuscripts that we now possess are all of the codex or book-form variety. Some fragments of New Testament manuscripts written on papyrus paper have been discovered that are older and nearer the original writings than some of the great vellum manuscripts of the fourth century and later. These fragments are called *papyri,* from the plural of the word *papyrus.* The Rylands Fragment is a small piece of papyrus, about an inch and a half square, from a page of the Gospel of John. This piece of writing might have been written as close as fifty years to the original, the autograph. The Bodmer Papyrus of John was written sometime in the third century, as also were the most famous of all the papyri, the Beatty Papyri, discovered by A. Chester Beatty in Egypt in 1931 and consisting of twelve fragments. The date of writing for most of the Beatty fragments is about A.D. 250, but some scholars believe a portion could have been written a hundred years earlier. Originally they probably contained the Gospels, Acts, the epistles of Paul, and Revelation.

It is the longer and more extensive uncial manuscripts of the fourth century and later, written on vellum, that most aid scholars in their study of the old Greek texts. These manuscripts are very valuable, for some contain almost all of the Bible. There are five or six very significant ones.

(1) Codex Vaticanus, or *B,* is an uncial manuscript produced during the early part of the third century. Written on vellum, it has three columns to the page and contains 759 leaves. As the name implies, it is in the Vatican Library, having been there since 1481. It contains almost all of the Old Testament and most of the New Testament and is the most valuable of all the vellum manuscripts.

(2) Codex Sinaiticus, or *Aleph,* was written on vellum in uncial letters during the latter half of the fourth century. There are four columns to the page, and it contains 347 leaves. A renowned Greek scholar, Count L. F. K. Tischendorf, discovered the manuscript in the library of the monastery of St. Catherine in the remote area of Mt. Sinai in 1859. The Czar later purchased it and brought it to St. Petersburg, where it was kept until the Soviets took over. Then it was purchased by Great Britain for a half million dollars and placed in the British Museum. It is the only uncial manuscript with a complete New Testament as well as a complete Old

Testament. Tischendorf used Aleph, the first letter of the Hebrew alphabet, with which to designate this manuscript, because *A* had already been designated for another uncial manuscript.

(3)   Codex Alexandrinus, or *A,* is the third most important manuscript. The name is derived from the fact that it was in the library of Alexandria until 1621. At this date the Patriarch of Alexandria gave it to James I of England. It was written sometime early in the fifth century and is also, as is Codex Aleph, in the British Museum. It includes most of the Old and New Testaments.

(4)   Codex Ephraemi Syri, or *C,* was also produced in the fifth century, at which time it contained the whole Bible in Greek. In the twelfth century a scribe partially erased the Greek text and over and between the lines wrote in Syriac thirty-eight sermons of Ephraem. With the aid of chemicals the Greek text has been read and edited. The manuscript, written in the fifth century, is now in the National Library in Paris. It is called a *palimpsest,* from a Greek word meaning scraped again.

(5)   Codex Bezae, or *D,* was written in Greek on the left-hand page and Latin on the right-hand page. For years it was believed to have come from the sixth century, but recent scholarship places it from the fifth century. There is great probability that it was written in France, since the people of that area spoke Latin in that era. The Latin is not a direct translation of the Greek, although it is based on the Greek. The manuscript was named for Theodore Beza, a Protestant reformer at Geneva, Switzerland. He obtained the manuscript from the Monastery of St. Irenaeus at Lyons, France, in 1562, giving it to the University of Cambridge in 1581. It has one column to the page, and the Gospels and Acts are not complete.

(6)   The Washington Codex, or *W,* in the Freer Art Gallery in Washington, D.C., is the most significant manuscript in the United States. It was purchased in Egypt in 1906 by C. L. Freer of Detroit. It is a fifth-century work having the Gospels in the order of Matthew, John, Luke, and Mark. It is sometimes called the Freer Manuscript.

4. Minuscule Manuscripts

The minuscules or cursives are not as important as the uncials for a study of the Greek text. This is because of their time distance from the autographs. They date from the ninth to the fifteenth centuries. Instead of being indicated by capital letters, as in the case of the uncials, they are indicated by numbers.

Minuscule 33, of the ninth or tenth century, contains the entire New Testament except for Revelation. Some of the most famous of the cursives are 13, 69, 124, 230, 346, 543, 788, 826, 983, 1689, and 1709. Minuscule 2400 is the Rockefeller-McCormick New Testament of the thirteenth century. It has seventy-four colored illustrations and was discovered by Edgar J. Goodspeed in an antique shop in Paris in 1927.

5. Early Versions

A version of the Bible is a translation from the Hebrew Old Testament or from the Greek New Testament into another language. The first version of the Old Testament, the Septuagint, a translation from the Hebrew into the Greek, was made before the New Testament was even written. We are primarily concerned here, however, with translations of the Greek New Testament into other languages. The very first versions, sometimes called primary versions, were necessitated due to the spread of the church into new areas, far-flung provinces of the empire where Greek was not spoken.

(1) Latin Versions The church in western Europe, centered in Rome, was known as the Western Church or Latin Church. North Africa had Latin as the official language, not Greek. Carthage, a city of North Africa across the Mediterranean from Rome, was a city of great commercial and cultural prominence. The language here was Latin. The well-educated people in Rome spoke and read Greek, but the lower social strata in the capital city used Latin. Therefore a Latin version of the Bible, of both the Old and New Testaments, was demanded at an early age of the church. We know there was a Latin version of the Bible as early as A.D. 150.

After this date many Latin versions were produced, varying somewhat one from another. These Latin manuscripts, designated today by small letters of the alphabet (such as *a, e, h, k, q*), continued on down to the seventh century, some even later. There were almost as many versions as there were individual manuscripts. The confusion of Latin texts became so great that Pope Damasus of Rome commissioned Jerome, his secretary, to make a new standard Latin translation. This Jerome began in A.D. 382, starting with the Old Testament. He moved to Bethlehem shortly, where he did most of his work. He lived and worked in the famous city for twenty-five years, using Hebrew and Greek manuscripts, as well as an old Latin text, for his revision. Jerome's scholarly contribution was not universally accepted at the time it came out, but it gained favor in the ninth century. At the Council of Trent in 1546, it was officially adopted by the Roman Catholic Church, at which time it received the title *Vulgate,* from the Latin word for common.

(2) Syriac Versions The gospel spread not only westward into Latin-speaking territories but also eastward into areas where Syriac was

spoken. Edessa, a city in Mesopotamia, became the center of Christianity in an area where a Syriac version would be in demand. Since Syriac is closely related to Aramaic, the reader of a Syriac version would be using practically the same language spoken by Jesus himself.

It seems that the first Syriac version came out about 170; this was the *Diatessaron* (meaning "by four") of Tatian, who did his work first in Greek and then translated it into Syriac. This was a combination of the four gospels into one continuous account, eliminating duplicating stories and events. For about two and a half centuries this work held sway as the popular Syriac version by the people of Edessa and Assyria. The Old Syriac version came out about 200. The *Peshitta* (meaning "simple") version, coming out in 435, became the standard for the Assyrian church.

(3) Egyptian Versions   The spread of the gospel into Egypt required a version in the native language of Egypt. Alexandrians spoke Greek, but in the remote areas of Egypt the usage of native dialects caused a need for more than one version. In the third century the Sahidic version, also known as the Thebaic version, came out in Upper Egypt. The Bahairic version came out in the region of the Nile delta. Also called the Coptic version and the Memphitic version, it became the official text of the Coptic church.

The Latin, Syriac, and Egyptian versions are what are known as primary versions. Secondary versions appeared later. They are Gothic, Armenian, Ethiopic (or Abyssinian), Georgian, and Arabic.

6. Anglo-Saxon Versions

The Anglo-Saxon period in English history spanned the years from about 450 to 1066, the date of the Norman invasion. The culture of this era was due to the mixture of several peoples: the old Britons, the Romans, the Angles, the Saxons, and the Jutes, the last three arriving in the fifth century. In 596 there was a great missionary movement in England conducted by the Roman Catholic Church, and thousands of converts were claimed. Due to the powerful influence of Rome, Latin was the official language, with Jerome's Latin Vulgate being introduced as the Bible for the churches and for all religious instruction.

However, the only ones who could read it were the clergy, the monks and nuns in the monasteries, and the nobility. The commoners were not versed in Latin; nor were they encouraged to learn it. The same held true for the Anglo-Saxon or Old English, the vernacular of the home, the marketplace, and the street. The commoner could neither read nor write the everyday language of his homeland, a factor that discouraged all translations of the Holy Scriptures. However, in spite of the extreme lack of learning in the six centuries of the Anglo-Saxon period, there were a few

attempts at translating the Latin into Old English. These were more paraphrases than they were translations, for they expressed the translator's idea
of the contents of a passage in his own words, a very free rendering.

Caedmon, an illiterate Saxon of Northumbria, was the forerunner in the
attempt at an Anglo-Saxon production of the Scriptures. Since Caedmon
was unable to read, the abbot and the monks in the monastery at Whitby
translated from Latin into his native tongue the various Bible stories. These
he immediately put into paraphrases to be sung to the accompaniment of
musical instruments, thus becoming quite a popular figure with the common people. Caedmon died about 680. Aldheim, bishop of Sherborne,
who died about 709, translated the Psalms into Anglo-Saxon; and Bishop
Egbert translated the Gospels into the native language also.

The Venerable Bede (673–735), the first scholarly man to attempt an
Old English translation, is referred to as the father of English church
history; his *Ecclesiastical History of England* is a classic of its age. This
extraordinary man made translations relating to more than twenty-five
books of the Old Testament and practically all the books of the New
Testament. Alfred the Great (849–890), the most outstanding of the
Anglo-Saxon rulers, also did some translating into the native tongue. He
did the Ten Commandments (known as Alfred's Dooms), the Lord's
Prayer, and some of the Psalms. About 950 there appeared what became
known as the Lindisfarne Gospels, an interlinear attempt, with Latin
(Jerome's Vulgate) on one line and an Anglo-Saxon translation on the next
line. About the year 1000, Anglo-Saxon Gospels (with the Latin) appeared,
the work of an abbot named Aelfric, one who later was made Archbishop
of Canterbury. He also produced translations of the first seven books of the
Old Testament, as well as Esther, Job, and a part of Kings.

This effort on the part of the Aelfric was on the threshold of the Norman
invasion by William the Conqueror, with his victory at the battle of
Hastings in 1066. There were three and a half centuries between Caedmon
and William, duke of Normandy, conqueror of England; in this period, as
is easily discerned, there was only a meager attempt at Bible translation.
Even then, since the common people were extremely limited in educational
pursuits, there was very little circulation of the Bible among their ranks.
Added to this disadvantage was the presence of many dialects throughout
the country. When William the Conqueror started his rule he outlawed the
use of the Anglo-Saxon language, requiring Norman French to be spoken
instead. The result was that the two languages ran along side by side for a
time, later to be merged, along with Latin, into one language, the English.
As a result there was no Bible translation from Aelfric until the day of John
Wycliffe, a span of over three and a half centuries.

7. English Versions

(1) Wycliffe Bible   Because he gave the people of England the Bible in their own tongue, John Wycliffe was dubbed "John Wicked-Believe" by his enemies. He served as parish priest at Lutterworth but was in time declared a heretic by the Roman Catholic Church. He was a courageous reformer and openly fought abuses of the common people by the church or by the crown. Wycliffe, who has been termed the "flower of Oxford scholarship" and the "morning star of the Reformation," produced an English Bible in 1382. He had a following of wandering preachers named Lollards, poor priests who went about proclaiming a gospel of simplicity and purity, free from Church control. Wycliffe and the Lollards helped significantly in speeding the Reformation in England, but his greatest gift to the people was the Bible in their own language, which was produced in 1382. "The jewel of the clergy" at last became "the toy of the laity." Since this English Bible was produced sixty-eight years before the invention of the printing press, it was written by hand and copied by hand. It was the first Bible to mark off chapter divisions and also include the Apocrypha. Since Wycliffe translated directly from the Latin, his book was a translation of a translation. Those manuscripts that exist today, of which there are about 170, were done on illuminated vellum. John Wycliffe died a natural death; but the Church in 1428 had his bones removed from the grave, burned, and cast upon the Swift River. This was in 1428. Wycliffe holds an honored spot among English Bible translators.

(2) Tyndale Bible   William Tyndale's version did not appear until 1525, 143 years after Wycliffe's version. This man was a master in seven languages, so his translation used Hebrew and Greek manuscripts as well as the Latin. The Renaissance, standing between Wycliffe and Tyndale, produced a great interest in all language study, including Hebrew and Greek, which worked in Tyndale's favor over Wycliffe. Therefore, his work is the first English translation made directly from the Hebrew and the Greek, a monumental step in English Bible translation.

The Reformation, strong on the continent, had not yet touched England; the Roman Church was still opposed to the translation of the Bible into English. Tyndale could not work without the approval of the Church, and his appeal to Bishop Tunstall of London brought only scorn. Fleeing England, Tyndale went to Hamburg, Cologne, and Worms (in Germany), where he finished his New Testament and had it printed. Six thousand copies, secretly shipped to England, were confiscated and burned. However, some money was gained, which was in turn used to produce and ship more copies to England. Tyndale started his translation of the Old Testament but completed only through Chronicles before his death. However, in 1534 and in 1535 he produced revisions of his New Testament version.

The opposition to Tyndale increased; on October 6, 1536, he was strangled and then burned at the stake. As he died he said, "Lord, open the King of England's eyes," a prayer that in time was answered. Scholars say that 80 percent of the King James Version has Tyndale's phraseology. Tyndale remarked to a churchman who had criticized him, "If God spare my life, ere many years I shall cause a boy that driveth the plough shall know more of the Scriptures than thou dost." This desire on the part of the great scholar was also later fulfilled. What Martin Luther's German translation did for the German-speaking people of the continent, Tyndale's English translation did for the people with the English vernacular.

(3) Coverdale Bible Although the years between Wycliffe's Bible (1382) and Tyndale's Bible (1525) add up to over one and a third centuries, the English Bibles that appeared between Tyndale's and the King James of 1611 came in rapid order. They were mainly revisions, however, of Tyndale's monumental work. Miles Coverdale's translation of 1535, the next in line, had the distinction of being the first complete English Bible to make its appearance. For the books of the Old Testament that Tyndale did not get to translate, Coverdale used Jerome's Latin, Luther's German, Zwingli's Zurich Bible, and Pagninus' Latin. He also included the books of the Apocrypha, but he did not consider them as canonical and inspired.

Coverdale's mild manner and moderate dealings with others aided him in being able to get his Bible completed and accepted; he even dedicated the 1535 edition to the king, while his 1537 edition had the king's approval. It is ironical that just one year after the martyrdom of Tyndale (1536), a Bible that, from all practical standpoints, was Tyndale's, appeared under the approval of the crown.

(4) Matthew's Bible In the same year as Coverdale's revision, Matthew's Bible appeared, the work of John Rogers, a man who had been associated with Tyndale and had secured some of Tyndale's manuscripts. Evidently Thomas Matthew was his pen name, probably used because there was still some feeling against Tyndale. Roger's work, mainly a revision of Tyndale and Coverdale's versions, was dedicated to the king and queen. Matthew's Bible and Coverdale's Bible were both licensed by royal decree. However, when Mary Tudor came to the throne, Rogers was declared a heretic and burned at the stake.

(5) Taverner's Bible In 1539 Richard Taverner, a lawyer and Greek scholar, produced a version that was very significant; it contained changes

in the New Testament that were carried over into subsequent translations.

(6)   The Great Bible   In 1539 a translation appeared that, due to its size, was called the Great Bible. Sir Thomas Cromwell commissioned Miles Coverdale to revise Matthew's Bible, which he began in Paris and completed in London. This was during the reign of Henry VIII. Yet in a sense, this Bible was really Tyndale's translation, for Matthew's Bible was based on Tyndale's work.

The King James Bible (1611) has been known for centuries as the Authorized Version; though sponsored by King James it was never officially authorized by either the king or anyone under him. However, the Great Bible was the first and only English translation to be officially authorized, for Sir Thomas Cromwell authorized Coverdale to produce it. The title page of the 1540 edition carried the words: "This is the Bible appointed to the use of the churches." Since Archbishop Cranmer wrote a preface to the second edition of the Great Bible, it has at times been referred to as Cranmer's Bible.

(7)   The Geneva Bible   After the days of Henry VIII there were unsettled political conditions in England. Edward VI continued the Protestantism of his father, so the Great Bible continued in favor. During the reign of Mary Tudor, known as Bloody Mary, there was a return to Catholicism; hundreds of Protestants were executed, and death was the punishment meted out to any who read the Bible. Coverdale fled to the continent.

Many prominent Protestant scholars went to Geneva, Switzerland, and it was there that the Geneva Bible was both translated and printed, coming out in 1560. (The New Testament had appeared in 1557, three years previously.) The Old Testament was mainly the work of Anthony Gilby, and the New Testament was mainly the work of William Whittingham. Dedicated to Queen Elizabeth, the Geneva Bible became the most popular one of that period, being the family Bible throughout England and Scotland. The early Puritans used it. There were at least eight editions made even after the King James appeared. Since Genesis 3:7 included the words "sewed fig leaves together and made themselves breeches," this Bible became known as the Breeches Bible.

It contained a number of firsts. It was the first Bible to arrange the text in verses, with each sentence as a separate unit; it was the first English version not to include the Apocrypha; it was the first English translation to employ italics for the English words for which there were no Hebrew and Greek terms in the original texts; it was the first to omit Paul's name in the heading for the book of Hebrews; and it was the first to use Roman type rather than Old English type in the printing operation.

(8)   The Bishop's Bible   The Bishop's Bible came out in 1568. The Bible to be read in the churches was the Great Bible; but the Geneva Bible was more popular and, at the same time, denoted higher scholarship. When those high in the church decided that they wanted their own translation, one to supplant earlier translations, they appointed the Archbishop of Canterbury, Matthew Parker, to see that it was done. Since his committee was composed mainly of bishops in the Church of England, the Bible was named the Bishop's Bible. To a certain extent it replaced the Great Bible but not the popular Geneva Bible.

(9)   The Rheims-Douay Bible   This version, which came out in 1610, was a Bible for English-speaking Catholics. Just as Protestants fled from Mary Tudor to the continent and produced the Geneva Bible, Catholics fleeing to the continent from Elizabeth produced the Rheims-Douay Bible. Evidently the Catholics thought that they had to do something to offset the gaining popularity of the Bibles of the Protestants and the advantages gained by the Protestant churches in their use of them. The Catholic New Testament appeared in 1582, having been started at Douai in France and finished in Rheims, France. The Catholic Old Testament appeared in 1609 and 1610 at Douai. Based on Jerome's Latin Vulgate, it was the work of one named Gregory Martin. It included, of course, the Apocrypha, and was revised in 1750.

(10)   The King James Version   The King James Bible or Authorized Version appeared in 1611, having been started in 1607. King James I, successor to Elizabeth, heartily favored a new translation; so he appointed a committee of fifty-four men to accomplish the work, although only forty-seven men actually participated in it. This committee included Anglicans and Puritans, both clergy and laymen; it was the first large group ever to undertake a translation of an English Bible. The committee was requested to follow mainly the Bishop's Bible, but also to consult the Hebrew, the Greek, the Vulgate, and the many other translations, both in English and other languages. A chain of influence is readily apparent in Bible translations: from Tyndale, to Matthew, to Great, to Bishop, to King James. Tyndale's imprint is still indelibly felt as one reads the King James today.

The first revision came in 1613 with about 300 changes. There were revisions in 1629, 1638, 1762, and 1769. This fifth revision (1769) is the one bought in bookstores today. The Apocrypha was included in the 1611 edition but, since it is noncanonical, was later dropped. After the first appearance of the King James there was to be no other English translation for 274 years, or until 1885, the date of the release of the English Revised Version. In those years the King James increased in popularity until it became the Bible for the English-speaking Protestants, the only Bible for some people. It does have a beauty of language and simplicity of expression that is hard to excel. It is one of the great monuments of the English-speaking world. Some scholars believe that the popularity of the King James Version will, over an extended period, lose its force; but this is very doubtful.

(11) The English Revised Version   With no rival in the field for two and three-quarter centuries, the King James Version became more and more entrenched in the hearts of the people. However, during that time certain developments took place, especially during the nineteenth century, that were eventually to call forth another and more accurate translation. For one thing, the English language itself underwent many changes. More than 250 words had lost their original meaning, and many new words had been added. Second, scholarship in the original languages, Hebrew and Greek, had increased, with the accompanying desire to translate the Hebrew and Greek manuscripts more exactly. Third, many ancient manuscripts had been discovered, some going back very near to the originals. Not one of the uncial manuscripts discussed in previous pages of this book were available for use in any of the translations up through the King James.

The English Revised New Testament came out in 1881 and the English Revised Old Testament in 1884; both came out in 1885 as the English Revised Version. The Anglican Church led in its production, though Christian scholars from many denominations helped to produce it. It represented the highest point in English Bible translation, even though the public did not show too much enthusiasm at its appearance.

(12) The American Standard Version   This translation was offered to the public in 1901. Since the suggestions of the American scholars who had helped the larger English committee in producing the English Revised Version had been ignored, it was only natural that the Americans would desire to issue an American counterpart to the English work. They pledged the English to do nothing in this regard for at least fourteen years, however. When this time had elapsed the American Standard Version appeared, exactly sixteen years later than the English one. Therefore, in a sense, the American Standard Version is merely a variant of the English Revised Version. The same sincere effort that went into the latter work went into the former also.

(13) The Revised Standard Version   Many new discoveries in the twentieth century of materials relative to Bible study called forth other

efforts at Bible translation. In 1937 a large group of scholars began work on a new version, part of them working on the Old Testament and part working on the New Testament. The New Testament was released in 1946 and the complete Bible in 1952; the new version was termed the Revised Standard Version. Twenty-two scholars composed the translation committee, a committee that was formed in 1930 and had as its aims readability and accuracy, the preservation of the literary value of the King James, and the incorporation of the advances made in recent textual and biblical scholarship. These aims were fulfilled quite well. The Revised Standard Version is a church-sponsored Bible, one in a direct descent from Tyndale's.

(14) Recent Translations Since the appearance of the American Standard Version in 1901, many and varied translations have hit the market. Some of these are private translations, the accomplishment of one person; some constitute the work of small groups. Weymouth's *The New Testament in Modern Speech* came out in 1903. Moffatt's *The Bible: A New Translation* appeared in 1913. Goodspeed's *The New Testament: an American Translation* made its appearance in 1923, coming closer to the actual American vernacular than any other. Mrs. Montgomery's *Centenary Translation of the New Testament* is dated 1924. William's *The New Testament, a Translation in the Language of the People* was placed on the market in 1957. Phillips' *The New Testament in Modern English* (1958) is a skillful rendering of the original Greek for the modern English reader.

Two very popular publications have appeared on the scene. The American Bible Society produced Today's English Version: *Good News for Modern Man* (1966, 1971), a New Testament translation intended for English readers with a limited vocabulary. However, this version became extremely popular, selling millions of copies. The *Good News Bible* (1976) is composed of both Old and New Testaments in Today's English Version. *The Living Bible, Paraphrased* made its appearance in 1971 and has also had phenomenal sales. It is composed of both the Old and New Testaments and is distinctly a paraphrase, not a literal translation.

PART THREE

The Gospels:
Christ Founding the Church

6.
Our Knowledge of Jesus Christ

1. Outside the New Testament

The sources of our knowledge of Jesus Christ from outside the New Testament, though very meager, are not to be discounted or ignored. These sources are Roman, Jewish, and noncanonical Christian writings.

(1) Roman Sources

a. Pliny Due to the bad state of affairs in the province of Bithynia, Trajan, the emperor at Rome, sent Pliny the Younger to be its governor and to straighten things out. He ruled in this north central province of Asia Minor from 111 to 115. Since some of his problems had to do with the Christians, he wrote a letter to Trajan concerning them (Pliny, *Letters,* XCVII) in which he asked the emperor's advice of what to do when they were tried before him. He termed Christianity an "absurd and extravagant superstition." He stated that on a certain day the Christians would assemble before daylight and address a prayer to Christ as they would to a god. His letter reveals that Christianity was present in Bithynia at that time and that it presented conflicts with the Roman authorities. However, it does not give much information about Christ himself.

b. Tacitus was a Roman historian who had at one time been a governor over a Roman province. In his *Annals,* covering the years 14–68, he gives information concerning the fire that raged in Rome in 64. He states that Nero, having been accused of starting the fire, blamed it on the Christians and had them tortured. He says the Christians were termed so by the crowds and that Christus suffered extreme penalty by Pontius Pilate, one of the procurators. He terms Christianity a "deadly superstition," checked for awhile only to break out later, both in Judea and in Rome. Evidently Tacitus secured his information concerning the Christians from a non-Christian source. Tacitus' word is genuine evidence from a nonbiblical source that Christ existed; not only that, it confirms information that we have in Christian sources, the New Testament.

c. Suetonius was a young friend of Pliny who, in about 120, published his *The Lives of the Twelve Caesars.* He was a biographer and a reporter more than a true historian and one who mentioned Christianity twice: once in his section on Nero and once in his section on Claudius. In the former reference to the Christians, he stated that punishment was inflicted on the ''new and wicked superstition.'' In the latter reference he told of Claudius' expulsion of the Jews from Rome. (His spelling ''Chrestus'' creates a problem, since Tacitus' spelling is ''Christus.'') None of these three Roman writers offered any information about the life or teaching of Jesus that is not contained in the Christian writings.

(2) Jewish Sources

a. Flavius Josephus was the Jewish historian born about 37 or 38, who referred to Jesus twice in his *Antiquities* (XVIII:3,3 and XX:9,1). The former reads as follows:

Now there was about this time Jesus, a wise man, if it be lawful to call him a man; for he was a doer of wonderful works, a teacher of such men as receive the truth with pleasure. He drew over to him both many of the Jews and many of the Gentiles. He was the Christ. And when Pilate, at the suggestion of the principal men amongst us, had condemned him to the cross, those that loved him at the first did not forsake him; for he appeared to them alive again the third day; as the divine prophets had foretold these and ten thousand other wonderful things concerning him. And the tribe of Christians, so named for him, are not extinct at this day.

The later passage is as follows:

So he [Ananus] assembled the sanhedrin of judges, and brought before them the brothers of Jesus, who was called Christ, whose name was James, and some others . . . . He delivered them to be stoned.

Because the Jews considered Josephus a renegade to Judaism, the Jewish scribes did not wish to perpetuate his writings. So Christian scribes did so. It is debated even today about whether these Christian scribes changed the longer passage so it would have a Christian flavor. Josephus himself remained a Jew and did not accept Jesus as the Christ, and the longer passage appears to have come from the hand of a believing author. At any rate, Josephus is the earliest non-Christian writer to make a statement verifying the historicity of Jesus Christ.

b. The Talmud There were two Talmuds: the Babylonian Talmud and the Palestinian Talmud. The former is the one that bears witness to the historical fact of Jesus' life and ministry. The Talmud consists of a vast collection of Jewish traditions brought together and considered authoritative in supplementing the Hebrew Scriptures. These interpretations of the Mosaic law cover a span of time from Ezra down to the sixth century of the

Christian era. The Babylonian version contains at least a half-dozen references to Jesus, mostly of a slanderous and vindictive nature. However, in spite of the animosity toward Jesus expressed in the book, the Talmud does at least affirm his existence. It also refers to his ability to perform miracles and to his claim to be the Son of God.

(3) Noncanonical Christian Sources There were several gospels written concerning Jesus and his work, both before and after the four canonical Gospels, that furnish information about him not contained in the New Testament. These are known as apocryphal gospels, some of which we have today and many of which are extinct and known only through quotations from other writings. The names of some of these gospels are often included in lists of books put out by early church writers. It was in the age following the life span of the apostles that these gospels really flourished. Luke referred to them in the opening lines to his Gospel: "Forasmuch as many have taken in hand to draw up a narrative concerning those matters which have been fulfilled among us, even as they delivered them unto us, who from the beginning were eyewitnesses and ministers of the word, it seemed good to me also" (1:1–3). We know the titles of about forty of these gospels; we have all or part of about a dozen of them.

Some of the apocryphal gospels, lost for ages, have been recently discovered. One of the greatest of the discoveries was made at Nag Hammadi in Upper Egypt in 1946, where several lost gospels were uncovered. Thirteen Coptic manuscripts in book form (codices), containing nearly 800 pages, were made available to scholars. These manuscripts, probably based on originals written in Greek, date as early as the third century. After the manuscripts were carefully studied for a number of years, it was discovered that they were once the possession of a church or monastery whose ruins were very near the place of manuscript discovery. The writings are Gnostic in nature and were preserved by Gnostics.

One of the manuscripts discovered at Nag Hammadi is the gospel of Thomas, a very old gospel probably dating from the middle of the second century A.D. It contains over 100 sayings attributed to Jesus, many of which are quite similar to those found in the four documents of the New Testament and many of which are very different. These sayings are called *logia* (one of which is a *logion*). One of the logia from this gospel reads, "He said to them, Give the things of Caesar to Caesar, give the things of God to God, and give me what is mine." Matthew 22:21 reads, "Render therefore unto Caesar the things which are Caesar's; and unto God the things that are God's." This presents quite a similarity; other logia are different from anything attributed to the lips of Jesus found in the New

Testament Gospels.

It is easily apparent that the apocryphal gospels do not compare with the four canonical ones. Some were written to further certain religious viewpoints, while others were written to teach doctrines that are definitely known to be false. Some of the sayings attributed to Jesus may actually have been declared by him and may therefore be true; other sayings may not be of this category. Especially did the people of the early church became curious about what Jesus did and said between the age of forty days (the time of his infancy presentation in the Temple), the age of twelve years (the time of his youthful appearance in the Temple), and between the ages of twelve and the age of thirty years (the start of his active ministry). Many times when historical information was lacking, questionable stories about Jesus began to circulate. More and more stories developed, all of which spread rapidly. One example will suffice. There is the account that when Jesus was five, he was making mud pies with some playmates on the sabbath. He fashioned twelve sparrows from soft clay, clapped his hands, and gave command for the clay birds to take flight. This they did, even with audible chirping. This story is found in one of the gospels.

These apocryphal gospels seem to imply that the writers knew and possessed the canonical Gospels. Sometimes they are known as the "excluded gospels"; but this is not a good term, for they were not excluded. They merely did not possess the characteristics of truly inspired writings, qualities required for them to be included in the canon of the New Testament.

Besides the gospel of Thomas, already mentioned, some of the titles are as follows: Gospel According to the Hebrews (c. A.D. 125), Gospel According to the Egyptians (c. A.D. 130), Gospel of Peter (c. A.D. 130), Gospel of Basilides, Gospel of Truth, and Gospel of Philip. There are also the Infancy Story of Thomas, the Acts of Paul, the Acts of John, and the Protoevangelium of James.

2. Within the New Testament

The very fact that the four Gospels contained in our New Testament received canonization would indicate that they present the greatest source of knowledge concerning Jesus. These are the books that were copied and recopied, read and reread, by the early Christians. They tell of his birth, his ministry, his teaching, his preaching, his death, and his resurrection.

Jesus himself left no writing, no book, no manuscript. There is recorded the fact that he wrote once with his finger on the ground (John 8:6), but we have no idea of what he wrote even then. He taught and he preached, and men remembered quite vividly what he declared. This is not something at which we marvel; for the gospel (good news) that he proclaimed, the kingdom that he announced, and the hope that he promised were so strikingly unique that men had to remember. His message became indelibly inscribed in the memory of his followers.

(1)   The Oral Gospel   For a quarter of a century, more or less, the good news of the coming of Jesus remained in an oral form. There was no felt need to record the incidents of his work and his message, even that of his sorrowful death and his joyous resurrection. Thousands of eyewitnesses were at hand to tell of the wondrous story, and this they did, willingly. The minds of his followers constituted a memory bank, so to speak, of his sayings and his miracles. Besides, there was a sincere conviction that he would come again soon for judgment, which would only turn permanent records into useless trivia. (And did not the Christians already possess a Bible, the Septuagint, which they read and studied regularly? This was the Hebrew Scriptures in a Greek translation, and the early Christians interpreted Jesus as the fulfillment of all that God had begun to accomplish in a previous age. "But now apart from the law a righteousness of God hath been manifested, being witnessed by the law and the prophets" (Rom. 3:21).)

(2)   The Canonical Gospels   As the years passed the followers of Jesus perceived the advisability of drawing up fixed written records of the life and teachings of their Master. Therefore they drew heavily on the oral tradition in writing permanent accounts concerning the miraculous things that had happened among them. The urgency for such writings was apparent. The eyewitnesses were passing away one by one. The second coming of Jesus seemed to be more remote with the passing of the years. Heresies and false concepts had arisen that needed to be downed, a victory that would be much easier with written and authentic records. Christianity needed to be clearly differentiated and set apart as a faith in its own right, not merely viewed as a sect of Judaism.

Out of the many attempts to produce accounts of the life and teachings of Jesus in written form, four were finally selected and set apart as the authoritative oracles of God: Matthew, Mark, Luke, and John. Even a cursory comparison of the four will reveal that the first three have much in common and that they stand apart from the fourth. Since, in general, the first three present the life and teaching of Jesus from the same point of view, they are called *Synoptic,* a term from the Greek meaning "seeing together." They present a chronological account of Jesus' life and ministry. All three give prominence to his early ministry in Galilee, while John gives special attention to his early Judean ministry. The only great event (prior to the betrayal, arrest, trial, death, and resurrection of Jesus) which all four dwell upon is the feeding of the five thousand. Very few of the events of Jesus' life that are found in the Synoptics are found in John. The style and language of Jesus' message in the Synoptics is somewhat different from that in John. In the Synoptics Jesus' teaching is mainly about the kingdom, while in John Jesus' teaching is mainly concerning himself, who and what he was. John contains none of Jesus' parables of the type found in the Synoptics. John's Gospel, many times called the Fourth Gospel, is an interpretive Gospel; by this is meant that the author interprets for his reader much of what Jesus said and did. For instance, where the Synoptics say that Jesus healed a blind man, John's Gospel tells of Jesus' saying, "When I am in the world, I am the light of the world" and then healing a man born blind.

It should always be remembered that the four Gospels are religious literature, written from a religious viewpoint. There were penned by believers, those who had accepted Jesus as Lord and Christ. They believed that what God had promised and set forth in the Hebrew Scriptures was being fulfilled in Jesus of Nazareth and in the church founded by him. Therefore they wrote from the Christian perspective, with the aim that every reader should also experience what they had experienced. The writer of the Fourth Gospel very frankly gives this evangelistic aim as the purpose of his writing: "These are written, that ye may believe that Jesus is the Christ, the Son of God; and that believing ye may have life in his name" (John 20:31). The writer of the Gospel was concerned with what Jesus did, where he went, and what he said; but he was more concerned with these words and events as they revealed *who* Jesus was. He was the Logos, the Son of God, the Lamb of God, the Christ, Rabbi. Even though the Synoptics do not state their purpose so openly, their reason for writing is very obvious: Jesus is the Savior sent into the world for the atonement of mankind.

(3) The Synoptic Gospels It is the opinion of most scholars that Mark, Matthew, and Luke were written prior to John. Therefore John's Gospel is the Fourth Gospel both in the order in the New Testament and in the order of writing. Mark, Matthew, and Luke are built on a common arrangement, and even through their differences this common order of events can be discerned. When the three Synoptic Gospels are placed in parallel columns this common agreement becomes very obvious. Such an arrangement in parallel columns is what is termed a harmony of the Gospels.

Mark has 661 verses. Of the 661 verses, 606 appear in Matthew and 350 appear in Luke. Also, in Matthew and in Luke there are 235 verses that are identical but which are not found in Mark. The view of most scholars is that Mark was written prior to the other two, that both Matthew and Luke had copies of Mark and used them in their writing in arranging the events in Jesus' life, and that Matthew and Luke had a common source of information that is now lost. This source is represented by the letter Q, standing for the German word *Quelle,* meaning source. This would be shown by a diagram as follows:

This is known as the two-source theory, that Matthew and Luke had two sources in writing their Gospels: Mark and Q.

However, there are about 300 verses in Matthew that are not in any other Gospel, and there are 520 verses in Luke that are in no other Gospel. The verses special to Matthew are designated by the letter M, and the verses unique to Luke are designated by the letter L. The parables of the prodigal son (Luke 15:11–32), the good Samaritan (Luke 10:29–37), the Pharisee and the publican (Luke 18:9–14), and the story of the rich man and Lazarus (Luke 16:19–31) are contained in Luke's Gospel alone. The parables of the weeds (Matt. 13:24–30), the hidden treasure (Matt. 13:44), the pearl (Matt. 13:45–46), and the last judgment (Matt. 25:31–46) are contained in Matthew's Gospel alone. It is apparent that Matthew and Luke had access to independent sources, but of what nature were the sources? Were there two written sources that were more or less equivalent to M and L? If so, Matthew and Luke had four sources, which leads to what has been known as the four-source theory. It would be shown by a diagram as follows:

There is widespread acceptance of the two-source theory, but in recent years there is a lot of questioning concerning the four-source theory. Much of what is in M might have come from Q, a part that Luke did not use, and much of that is in L might also have come from Q, a part that Matthew did not use. Both Matthew and Luke could have secured most or all of M and L

from the oral tradition. At any rate, *M* and *L* have come to designate the material peculiar to Matthew and Luke, respectively, with less and less reference to the character of the sources. The best attitude toward the sources of the three Synoptic Gospels is that each author had at his disposal several sources, both written and oral, and that he used these in writing his own Gospel, with his own special purposes and aims in mind.

All of this discussion about the sources of information used by the authors of the Synoptic Gospels does not negate God's hand in the spread and transmission of Christian truth. The four Gospels are the inspired word of God, for God worked in many and varied ways to bring together, collect, and record the marvelous story of his Son and his redeeming love. God's hand was in the oral transmission period as well as in the written. The very fact that these four Gospels were the ones read and reread, were copied and recopied, and were finally selected as the canonical Gospels attests to the fact that they were grounded in God's great revealing act through our incarnate Lord. *Inspired* means breathed into, and this is exactly what happened in regard to the canonical Gospels. God truly breathed into them, and his Spirit aided the four writers in their significant work of transmission. They were the books that passed the usage test, fulfilling the spiritual needs of the people, and the eccesiastical test, being the ones formally accepted by the councils and leaders of the church. These books radiated the fact that they were the oracles of God.

(4) The Epistles of Paul   Paul's letters are the earliest New Testament writings to tell us about Jesus; for most of them, if not all, were written prior to the composing of our four canonical Gospels. The earliest of his writings was penned about 50, with the last up in the sixties. The information about the earthly life of Jesus in these epistles is not plentiful, and it is scattered and piecemeal when it does occur. He often mentioned Jesus' death and resurrection, but he did not have in mind the writing of a Gospel. His primary aim was to declare the power of the risen Christ who had so marvelously changed him on the Damascus road and commissioned him as a proclaimer of the Christian way of life. He seemed to have presupposed the presence of the oral gospel and to have built upon it, rather than recording it; this he left for others to do. However, the few references that Paul did include concerning the birth and earthly life of Jesus confirm the viewpoint of the Gospels that Jesus was an actual historical figure.

Paul was a contemporary of Jesus, but we do not know whether he knew Jesus in the flesh. The chances are that he did not and therefore he was not an eyewitness of Jesus' ministry, death, and resurrection. But after his dramatic conversion he came in contact with many of those who had witnessed these exciting events firsthand: Peter, John, and James, the brother of Jesus (Gal. 2:9).

Paul stated that Jesus was born of a woman and was subject to the law (Gal. 4:4) and that he was an Israelite of Davidic descent (Rom. 1:3; 9:4). Paul mentioned Jesus' brothers (1 Cor. 9:5) and spoke of James as Jesus' brother also (Gal. 1:19). When he stated what Jesus said at the institution of the Lord's Supper, he implied that Jesus had a following with whom he ate the Last Supper (1 Cor. 11:23–26). Paul mentioned Jesus' crucifixion and his being alive again (2 Cor. 13:4). He stated that Jesus was killed by the Jews (1 Thess. 2:14–15), that he died, was buried, and was raised on the third day (1 Cor. 15:4).

Paul several times alluded to the teaching of Jesus, the most important having to do with the Lord's Supper (1 Cor. 11:23–25) and with the resurrection (1 Cor. 15:3–8). Paul told of the institution of the Lord's Supper and gave Jesus' words as he initiated this great right (1 Cor. 11:23–25). Concerning Jesus' resurrection, Paul spoke of "all that which also I received" (1 Cor. 15:3). In one place he stated, "Even so did the Lord ordain that they that proclaim the gospel should live of the gospel" (1 Cor. 9:14), a statement of our Lord not found in any of the four Gospels. It is very obvious from reading the Pauline epistles that the great apostle assumed that his readers were aware of other incidents in the life of Jesus. Even though he felt no need to report them, a knowledge of them is quite necessary to understand his writings. "O foolish Galatians, who did bewitch you, before whose eyes Jesus Christ was openly set forth crucified?" (Gal. 3:1). Only a thorough knowledge of the crucifixion, as set forth in the gospel story, makes such a statement meaningful.

(5) Later New Testament Writings The New Testament books written at a later period give a few facts concerning the earthly life of Jesus; these writers also presuppose a knowledge of Jesus' life on the part of possible readers. The book of Hebrews contains a number of statements concerning Jesus' earthly life. It speaks of the revelation that comes through his incarnate life (1:2) and of the fact that his message had been passed along by those who had received his teaching (2:3). It speaks of the sufferings and temptations of Jesus (2:18; 4:15; 5:8). Second Peter mentions the transfiguration of Jesus (1:16–18). Revelation also alludes to a few facts in the life of Jesus. By his death we are saved from our sins (1:5), and by his shed blood we are redeemed (5:9). The crucifixion is again mentioned (11:8), as well as his being dead and living again (1:18). He is a descendant of David (5:5).

It is very apparent that the New Testament books apart from the four canonical Gospels do not reveal a great deal of information about the historical Jesus. The significant fact is that these writers presuppose that there is much information about Jesus that is already known to the believers; therefore, they start from this vantage point and build their writings accordingly. The meager knowledge they offer serves to verify the historicity of Jesus as presented by Matthew, Mark, Luke, and John and to confirm some of the events of his life recorded in the four canonical Gospels. No serious study of the life of Jesus could be undertaken on the basis of the scanty material found in the New Testament apart from the four Gospels. Therefore, to the four Gospels we must turn for the wondrous story of the life, death, and resurrection of our Lord.

7.
A View of the Four Gospels

The aim of the Gospel writers was not to produce a purely objective, historical account of the life and teaching of Jesus. They were believers, Christians who had accepted Jesus as Savior and Lord and who believed that he was the long-awaited Messiah promised in the Hebrew Scriptures. They believed that with his coming the new age had begun. Something miraculous had happened, and the miracle was proven by Jesus' resurrection from the dead. Therefore the Gospels were penned with this Christian perspective clearly in mind.

1. Mark

Of the four canonical Gospels, Mark was the first to be written, a fact supported by many evidences. Matthew and Luke used Mark as one of their important written sources. Matthew used about 90 percent of Mark in his and Luke used about 50 percent in his. When a passage of Mark is not found in Matthew or is not found in Luke, there is a great possibility that it is found in the other Gospel; this would show that Mark did not write later than Matthew and simply reduce Matthew's Gospel down to his. Also, the order of events in Jesus' life found in Mark generally occurs in Matthew and Luke. If either departs from Mark's order at any time, the other writer retains it.

(1) Authorship How did Mark's name become attached to this Gospel, since his name, unlike Paul's epistles, is not found embedded in the text itself? In fact, all four Gospels are in a sense anonymous, since the name of no writer is in the body of his respective document. Each name is depicted as the writer in a superscription at the beginning.

An early tradition attributes to Mark the authorship of this book. Papias, an early bishop of Hierapolis, declared John Mark the author. Irenaeus, bishop of Lyons, affirmed the same thing a little later. There is really no reason to say that Mark did not write the Gospel credited to his name. There is no reason to reject the statements of early Christian writers that this Gospel was composed by John Mark of Jerusalem.

John Mark's mother opened her house in Jerusalem for a meeting place for the church of that city (Acts 12:12). Mark also went with Paul and Barnabas on the initial part of their first missionary journey, withdrawing from them at Perga to return home to Jerusalem (Acts 13:13). However, later, becoming reconciled with Paul, he became a Christian worker in Rome (Col. 4:10; 2 Tim. 4:11; Philem. 24). He was a cousin of Barnabas (Col. 4:10). The writer of 1 Peter calls him "Mark my son" (5:13) and associates him with Rome (even though "Babylon," the symbolical name for Rome, is used in the passage). Not only is he called "Mark my son" in 1 Peter; Papias (c. 115), Bishop of Hierapolis, calls him Peter's "interpreter" and states that he recorded what he recalled of Peter's preaching. Eusebius (375), the early church historian, quotes Papias as saying:

Mark became Peter's interpreter and wrote accurately all that he remembered, not, indeed, in order, of the things said or done by the Lord. For he had not heard the Lord, nor had he followed him, but later on, as I said, followed Peter, who used to give teaching as necessity demanded but not making, as it were, an arrangement of the Lord's oracles, so that Mark did nothing wrong in thus writing down single points as he remembered them. For to one thing he gave attention, to leave out nothing of what he heard and to make no false statements on them (*Ecclesiastical History,* III, 39, 14).

Eusebius also quotes Clement of Alexandria (c. 180) as saying that the ones who heard Peter preach asked Mark to leave some written record of the doctrine that Peter preached concerning Jesus, and that Peter even authorized this work to be read in the churches (*Ecclesiastical History,* II, 15). Origen, who followed Clement of Alexandria as leader of the church in that city, also is quoted as saying that Mark wrote his Gospel as Peter explained things to him (*Ecclesiastical History,* VI, 25). Irenaeus indicates that "after the death of Peter and Paul, Mark delivered to us in writing things preached by Peter" (*Against Heresies,* III, i, 1). These early writers agree on two things: that John Mark wrote the Gospel and that he drew heavily from the preaching of Peter. The weight of evidence seems to rest on the view that John Mark is the author of the Gospel that bears his name.

(2) Date of Writing Clement and Origen indicate that it was written during Peter's lifetime, while Irenaeus indicates that it was written after Peter's death. The Gospel could hardly have been written later than 70. Most scholars place the date of writing between 65 and 70, although some have placed it as early as 50. 70 seems the most likely date. The Jewish War of 66–73 seemed to be imminent or in progress at the time of the writing (see Mark 13). The siege of Jerusalem by the Romans was 67–70,

begun by Vespasian and finished by Titus; in the siege the Temple was destroyed. Most scholars believe that the "holy place" (Mark 13:14) that was desecrated was the Jerusalem Temple, for the parallel passage in Matthew (24:15) clearly states it as such. The vividness with which Mark describes the event would lead one to believe that the event in chapter 13 was not far off.

Mark did not feel it was necessary to date the time of the writing of his Gospel. None of the New Testament writers felt so inclined; there was no compulsion on their part to give the exact time of their writings. The urge to date documents—letters, deeds, receipts, historical data, religious treatises—is a modern scribal imperative. The biblical writers felt the dating of their writings to be a trivial matter; the content was the all-important factor. It would certainly simplify scholarship today if they had felt inclined to date their works, but they were certainly not prone to do so.

(3) Place of Writing Tradition says that Mark's Gospel was written in Rome, but nothing in the Gospel itself suggests that it was penned there. Some scholars point to what are termed *Latinisms* in Mark, such as *modius* for bushel, *census* for tribute, and *praetorium* for Pilate's palace. Apparently he used these instead of the Greek equivalents because they were more common. It is true that there is little in the Gospel on Jewish law and custom, but this would not prove a Roman origin. It has been said that, since Mark was not an apostle, his Gospel was accepted into the canon because of its connection with Rome. But would not its connection with Peter be a greater weight in such logic? Some think that the Gospel was written in Antioch of Syria, while others select Alexandria as the place of writing. All in all, Rome may have the greatest weight of evidence. At least the gospel was written for Gentile readers.

(4) Distinguishing Characteristics The author is more concerned with what Jesus *did* than what he *said*. In this Gospel Jesus is more a doer than a sayer. It is an action-packed Gospel, full of many events in Jesus' life. He collects disciples, he heals, he travels, he disputes with adversaries, and he overpowers demons. It is the oldest and the shortest of the four Gospels. The word "immediately" or "straightway" occurs forty-two times in the sixteen chapters.

There is very little of Jesus' teaching found here, as is richly abundant in Matthew and John. There are very few of Jesus' parables. There are two clear-cut divisions, approximately equal in length. One is his Galilean ministry, 1:14 to 8:26; the other is his Jerusalem ministry, 11:1 to 16:8. Between these two are found Peter's great confession at Caesarea Philippi, the transfiguration, and the journey to Jerusalem. There is great stress placed on the humanity of Jesus. He asks questions, displays human emotions, sleeps, experiences hunger, becomes weary, weeps, dies. Yet at the same time the very opening lines declare him the Son of God, a theme that is recurrent throughout the entire Gospel. The demoniac, the centurian, the voice from heaven—all declare his divine sonship.

There is no prologue in Mark, and direct quotations from the Old Testament for prophetic interpretation are very few. There are, however, many quotations and allusions from the Old Testament. Proportionate to its size, Mark gives great space to the miracles of Jesus, more than any other Gospel. This would be in line with the fact that the author was more interested in deeds than interpretation or speculation. His purpose is an evangelistic one, to bring the work of Christ before people in such a manner that it will be seen as a new message with a new hope for mankind.

Mark is a very vivid Gospel. It is full of reactions against what Jesus says or does. Those that see and hear Jesus are "amazed" or "astonished," or they become afraid or hostile. The book is not mainly a study in character, though many personalities are present in its pages. The writer is more interested in action, the progress of the story, than in character analyses. It is not primarily a biography of Jesus, for it does not give his parentage, his birth, his early life, or any particular phase of his youth. It presents a series of episodes in his ministry with special emphases upon the events in the last week of his life on earth, all seemingly in chronological order. The writer offers very little comment but lets the narrative speak for itself. Yet the total impression derived from the reading of the episodes in Jesus' life give us a good picture of who he was and of what he accomplished.

2. Matthew

Mark is presented first in this series of four pictures because it was written first. Matthew used Mark as his principle source of information, for he reproduced in his Gospel 90 percent of Mark. In a sense, his Gospel is a revised and enlarged second edition of Mark. Yet he did not slavishly follow Mark, for he used the earlier Gospel in a manner to show forth his own purpose. His Gospel is truly distinct.

(1) Authorship Tradition says that this Gospel was written by a converted tax collector or publican by the name of Matthew, also called Levi. Practically nothing is known of him except his name and occupation and that he became an obscure member of the band of twelve apostles (Matt. 9:9–13). After being included in the list of the twelve in Acts 1:13 he is not mentioned thereafter in Scripture. His name is not embedded in

the text of the Gospel itself.

Again we go to Papias, Bishop of Hierapolis, for a statement of Matthew's authorship. Eusebius, in his *Ecclesiastical History* (III, 39, 16), quotes Papias: "Matthew collected the oracles in the Hebrew language, and each interpreted them as best he could." By "oracles" does he mean sayings, and by "interpreted" does he mean translated? Similar statements are made by Irenaeus of Lyons, Origen of Alexandria, and Jerome of Bethlehem. Irenaeus' remark is that "Matthew also issued a written Gospel among the Hebrews in their own dialect, while Peter and Paul were preaching at Rome and laying the foundations of the church" (*Against Heresies*, III, 1, 1). Do these writers mean by "Hebrew" the Aramaic language, the spoken language of the home, the street, and the marketplace of the Jews at the time of Christ? There is a great possibility that they do.

Since so many of the early leaders of the church say that Matthew wrote it, there must have been great weight for this view. And would not his position as a publican give him the literary ability that he would need for the task? Even though Matthew originally wrote the sayings of Jesus, or perhaps even the whole Gospel, in the native language of the people, this would not rule out the possibility that he later produced a Greek edition of his work to supersede the original.

There are some scholars today, however, who believe that this Gospel was written by someone a generation removed from the apostles, that his native tongue was Greek even though he was of the Hebrew race, and that he secured his knowledge of Jesus not from personal remembrances but from oral and written traditions of Jesus that were in circulation at that time. They believe that an apostle would not have depended heavily upon the writing of one not an apostle, such as John Mark. They point to the fact that many Jewish authors wrote under the names of past notables. However, the weight of evidence seems to rest upon the fact that Matthew the apostle was the author of this Gospel.

(2) Date of Writing We do not know exactly when the Gospel was written. The first early writer to mention it in his own works was Ignatius of Antioch, who died as a Christian martyr in the last years of Trajan, 110–117. Since Ignatius regarded the Gospel as authoritative, it must have been written sufficiently prior to 115 for it to be considered so; and since the author quotes Mark's Gospel, it must have been written after Mark, or after 70. It seems that in Matthew 22:7 there is a reference to the conquest and burning of Jerusalem, which occurred in the year 70. Therefore the date that seems most reasonable is 85–90.

(3) Place of Writing Most scholars believe that the Gospel of

Matthew was written in Antioch of Syria, or at least somewhere in Syria, a supposition supported by the fact that Ignatius, Bishop of Antioch, was the first prominent person to mention it. The author used Greek sources and made most of his Old Testament quotations from the Septuagint, a Greek translation of the Hebrew Scriptures that was popular among the Jews of the Dispersion. Therefore it is very likely that the Gospel was composed in some locality of Greek-speaking Christians who were surrounded by a strong Hebrew influence. Antioch would fit this category. Even though Alexandria and Caesarea have been mentioned as possible sites of composition, Antioch is still the preferred place.

(4) Distinguishing Characteristics This Gospel was written to convince Jewish readers that Jesus of Nazareth, whom they had seen and heard, was their long-awaited Messiah foretold in the Hebrew Scriptures. Jesus is presented as the Messiah of David's line, one who fulfills Old Testament prophecy. Many times the author uses the phrase "that it might be fulfilled" and then, after each use, states what some Old Testament prophet or psalmist predicted. He either quotes directly or alludes to the Old Testament about 130 times, something we would expect him to do according to his purpose in writing. He quotes the Old Testament far more than any other Gospel writer.

Matthew began with a genealogy tracing Jesus' ancestry from Abraham, considered by the Jews as the "founder" of the Hebrew race, down through David and the succeeding kings of Judah. David's hometown is Bethlehem, and it is here that Jesus was born (Matt. 2:1). Wise Men from the East come to pay homage to one "born King of the Jews" (2:2). Matthew cites many people who testify to Jesus' Davidic lineage. Two blind men address him, "thou son of David" (9:27). The multitude questions, "Can this be the son of David?" (12:23). A Canaanite woman cries out, "Have mercy on me, O Lord, thou son of David" (15:22). The crowds viewing his royal entry into Jerusalem (21:9) and the children in the Temple (21:15) call him "son of David." Matthew declares Jesus King over a kingdom prepared from the foundation of the world (25:34). In Matthew's point of view Jesus' kingdom rests on the Old Testament Davidic kingdom. He is not only the anticipated Messiah; he is King of Israel as well.

The fulfillment of Hebrew prophecy is, therefore, a dominant theme in Matthew. The author mentions many messianic titles for Jesus, tracing each one of them back to an Old Testament passage. The Son of David and King of Israel titles have already been mentioned. He is the fulfillment of the Immanuel passage of Isaiah 7:14 as well as the Bethlehem-birth passage of Micah 5:2. He is also the Suffering Servant of Isaiah 53 and Psalms 22 and 40. He is the King of humility in Zechariah 9:9 and the Son of man of Daniel 7:13. Matthew probably traced these titles back to the Hebrew Scriptures in order to strengthen the Christian community in any controversies they might have with Judaism, as well as to aid them in the evangelization of the Hebrew people.

Not only did Matthew trace the many titles for Jesus back to the Old Testament; he depicted various other Old Testament prophecies as being fulfilled in Jesus as well. Some of these are the virgin birth (1:22–23), the return from Egypt (2:15), the crying over the slain boy babies in and around Bethlehem (2:17–18), Jesus' being reared in Nazareth (2:23), his preaching in Galilee (4:14–16), his bearing of man's infirmities (8:17), his desire to have healing miracles kept silent (12:17–21), his habit of teaching in parables (13:35), and the buying of the potter's field (27:9–10). Matthew endeavored to show that Jesus' entire ministry was one prearranged according to a plan found in the Hebrew Scriptures.

This Gospel abounds in the miraculous, with God's power shining forth in event after event. Jesus' supernatural birth, the guiding of the Magi by the star, God's will revealed through dreams, many healings (one even at a distance), the feeding of the five thousand and of the four thousand, the resurrection of the saints at his death, his own resurrection—these and other supernatural events attest to divine power being released.

Mark does not contain much of Jesus' teaching; it is mainly action-packed. Matthew, using the same chronology as Mark, interspersed his Gospel with five distinct blocks of teaching. These are as follows:

Sermon on the Mount	5:1 to 7:29
Instructions to disciples	9:35 to 11:1
Parables of the kingdom	13:1–53
Instructions on sin and forgiveness	18:1 to 19:2
Characteristics of the end of the age	24:1 to 26:2

Was the author thinking of the fivefold divisions of the Torah or Mosaic law? Each section of teaching ends with a phrase such as "when Jesus had finished all these words." Matthew divided the genealogy of Jesus into three sections of fourteen names each. The teaching arrangement and the genealogical arrangement reveal Matthew's fondness for structure. At any rate, the Gospel is rich in the sayings and teachings of our Lord. Some scholars go so far as to maintain that it was written mainly as a teaching manual for the leaders in the early church, but only a part of the Gospel would fit into such a category. Its purpose was wider than a mere manual of general Christian instruction.

Matthew's Gospel shows a fondness for threes. There are three sections to the genealogy, three gifts brought by the Wise Men, three temptations, three illustrations of righteousness (6:1–18), three prohibitions (6:19 to 7:6), three commands (7:7), three miracles of healing (8:1–15), three miracles showing divine power (8:23 to 9:8), three reasons why his disciples did not fast (9:14–17), three "fear nots" (10:26, 28, 31), three sayings about "these little ones" (18:6, 10, 14), three questions asked of Jesus (22:15–40), three parables of warning regarding stewardship (24:45 to 25:30), three prayers of Jesus in Gethsemane (26:36–46), three denials by Peter (26:69–75), and three wonders at the crucifixion (27:51–53). Some of these groups of threes are found in the other Gospels, but most are found only in Matthew.

Matthew included almost all of Mark and much more. His book is very conveniently arranged, with a very pleasing style of writing. Writers of the second century quoted it more than any other Gospel. Finally, when all four Gospels began to circulate in combination, Matthew was placed first of the four. It never lost this position.

3. Luke

The third of the Synoptic Gospels, those that "see together," is the Gospel of Luke.

(1) Authorship Tradition says that the third Gospel was written by Luke, the physician who accompanied Paul on his travels. Papias, the early writer already referred to in connection with Mark and Matthew, does not mention Luke by name. Irenaeus, however, in his book *Against Heresies* (III, 13, 3) says that Luke, who was an attendant of Paul, wrote Acts. Evidence from the Roman church late in the second century confirms this view. However, the name of Luke is not embedded in the text of the Gospel itself; nor is there anything in the style and language of the Gospel to indicate that it was written by a physician. Therefore, the identity of the writer of the Gospel rests upon the relationship between the Gospel and the book of Acts.

Both the Gospel and Acts are addressed to the same person, one called Theophilus. Also, the book of Acts mentions "the former treatise," a work which concerns "all that Jesus began both to do and to teach" (Acts 1:1). This undoubtedly refers to the Gospel of Luke. There is great stress placed upon the resurrection of Jesus in Acts, which agrees well with the stress on the resurrection in Luke 24. In both the Gospel and Acts there is great significance placed upon the work of the Holy Spirit. The vocabulary and style of writing of the two works are similar. Therefore we can safely assume that Luke, the author of Acts, also wrote the Gospel that bears his name. From late in the second century it was widely quoted as being from Luke.

(2) Date of Writing The Gospel was written sometime between 70 and 90. Mark was written about 70, and Luke used 50 percent of Mark. Also, Acts was written about 90; so the Gospel must have been written prior to this date, since Acts is the sequel to the Gospel of Luke. Luke made no use of Matthew, and Matthew made no use of Luke. Luke also showed little if any knowledge of Paul's epistles, which were well circulated after 100. Therefore, the best guess for the date of composition of Luke is about that of Matthew, or 85–90.

(3) Place of Writing The place of composition of the Gospel is unknown. Many guesses have been made: Greece, Asia Minor, Palestine, Rome, Caesarea, Alexandria. No evidence is given in the Gospel itself that would indicate where it was written, and there is no reliable early writing that would show where it originated. All we know is that it was written somewhere in the Hellenistic world by someone who knew and understood Gentiles.

(4) Distinguishing Characteristics The order of events in Luke follows the same sequence, generally, of that found in Mark and Matthew. Yet there are many accounts and events in the life of Christ that are found in this Gospel alone. Much detail is given to the birth of John the Baptist. There is a genealogy of Jesus, but it follows a different line from the genealogy found in Matthew's Gospel. The birth and childhood account of Jesus is also different from that in Matthew. Matthew presented the adoration of the magi from the east and the jealousy and vengeance of Herod the Great, while Luke gave the story of the angelic chorus from heaven and the coming of the shepherds from the fields of Bethlehem the very night of Jesus' birth. Luke alone told of Jesus' preaching at Nazareth (4:16–30) and the special call that Peter received at the time of the miraculous catch of fish (5:1–11). Luke presented several miracles and many parables that are not found in any of the other Gospels. The story of Zacchaeus and the sycamore tree (19:1–10) and the details of the conversation with the two on the road to Emmaus after his resurrection (24:13–35) are unique to this Gospel.

This Gospel, the longest of all four, is also the most literary of all four. The stories Luke gave are beautifully recounted, all with a vocabulary and style of writing rich and expressive. This Gospel has been called "the most beautiful book in the world." Luke wanted to present Christianity in such a way that cultured readers like Theophilus, to whom the work is dedicated

(1:3–4), would embrace it and become followers of Jesus. He presented four songs or poems having to do with Jesus' birth and infancy that are now hymns sung in the church. The *Magnificat* (1:46–55) is the song of Mary on her visit with Elizabeth; the *Benedictus* (1:67–79) is the song of Zacharias when John the Baptist is born; the *Gloria in Excelsis Deo* (2:14) is the song of the heavenly chorus at the birth of Jesus; and the *Nunc Dimittis* (2:28–32) is the prayer of Simeon at the dedication of Jesus in the Temple when Jesus was forty days old.

Luke seemed to have Gentile readers in mind more than Jewish ones. There are few quotations from the Old Testament, a characteristic quite unlike Matthew's Gospel. The Old Testament would have been quite an unknown book to non-Jewish readers. To present Jesus as an answer to prophecy would not be a major concern for Luke. Instead of using the Jewish word *rabbi* for Jesus, a word meaning "my master," Luke employed a Greek term for master. Jesus is presented as one who is concerned for all races and all classes of people. His message is a universal one, presenting a universal gospel. Whereas Matthew, being a Hebrew, traced the genealogy of Jesus back to Abraham, Luke carried it back to Adam, the first man. In tracing it back to God's original creation, Luke emphasized Jesus' connection with all humanity, not just the Hebrew people. In Simeon's prayer at Jesus' dedication in the Temple (2:29–32) the salvation which God sends through Jesus is "prepared in the presence of all peoples" and is to be "a light for revelation to the Gentiles." Luke was the only Gospel writer who recorded that Jesus commended Samaritans (10:30–37;17:11–19), a race despised by the Jews. The Jesus presented in this gospel is the Savior of all mankind: the poor, the sick, harlots, lepers, Samaritans, shepherds, publicans, outcasts, sinners, Gentiles, Jews, fishermen, and women.

Luke gave more attention to women and to their place as followers of Jesus than did Mark and Matthew. There is the story of Jesus' anointing by a sinful woman in the house of a Pharisee (7:36–50); several women are mentioned in one incident in the Gospel, women who were healed and who ministered to Jesus and the twelve (8:2–3); Martha and Mary ministered to Jesus in their home in Bethany (10:38–42). Luke recounted how the women observed the tomb where Jesus was buried, went away, prepared spices, and then returned early on the first day of the week to find that he had arisen (23:55 to 24:11).

Luke also presented Jesus as one deeply humanitarian. Jesus has great sympathy for the poor, the outcast, the downtrodden, the oppressed. Luke's account of the Sermon on the Mount, shorter than Matthew's, ends with the words "Be ye merciful, even as your Father is merciful" (6:36). Luke alone quoted Jesus as saying, "But woe unto you that are rich! for ye have received your consolation. Woe unto you, ye that are full now! for ye shall hunger. Woe unto you, ye that laugh now! for ye shall mourn and weep. Woe unto you, when all men shall speak well of you! for in the same manner did their fathers to the false prophets" (6:24–26). Luke alone stated that Jesus recommends giving a dinner and inviting the poor, the maimed, the lame, and the blind, rather than those who are kin or who are rich, and who will issue an invitation in return (14:12–14).

Another characteristic of Luke's Gospel is the great emphasis upon the work of the Holy Spirit. Everyone having to do with the supernatural birth of Jesus is "filled with the Holy Spirit": John the Baptist (1:15); Mary (1:35); Elizabeth, mother of John the Baptist (1:41); Zacharias, father of John the Baptist (1:67); John the Baptist (1:80); and Simeon (2:25). Jesus was led by the Spirit into the wilderness where he was tempted by the devil (4:1) and was in turn led out of the wilderness by the Spirit (4:14). He declared that his ministry was inaugurated by "the Spirit of the Lord" (4:18). On one occasion he "rejoiced in the Holy Spirit" (10:21). The same emphasis upon the Holy Spirit found in this Gospel is continued in the book of Acts, Luke's sequel. Due to the purpose of Acts, there is even more stress upon the work of the Spirit than in the Gospel.

Luke is the only Gospel to contain a formal preface (1:1–4). In these few introductory lines the author stated his purpose in writing, his method of study and research, and his dedication of his work to one called Theophilus, a name meaning lover of God. In his sequel, Acts, Luke mentioned Theophilus again and referred to his "former treatise," his Gospel. He wanted Theophilus to "know the certainty concerning the things wherein thou wast instructed." Both works express the same concerns and use the same vocabulary.

4. John

The Gospel of John is not numbered among the Synoptics; it stands apart in many ways. The style of writing is very distinct. The contents differ considerably from the contents of the Synoptics. There is a different approach in the teaching aspects of the gospel.

(1) Authorship By the latter half of the second century A.D., almost all writers ascribed the book to John, brother of James and son of Zebedee. This would make the writer an apostle, one of the original twelve. Therefore, even though this Gospel, like the other three, does not have the name of the author embedded in the text, it has the weight of tradition concerning

the one who penned it.

The first writer to mention John as the author was Theophilus of Antioch, about 181. The most important early writer to verify John as the author was Irenaeus, writing at about the same time. As a boy Irenaeus lived in Ephesus. He heard Polycarp, later Bishop of Smyrna. In his elderly years he recalled that Polycarp said that John wrote his Gospel while he lived in Ephesus. "Afterwards, John, the disciple of the Lord, who also learned upon his breast, did himself publish a Gospel during his residence at Ephesus in Asia" (*Against Heresies,* III, i, l). Here we have a chain of evidence from Theophilus of Antioch to Polycarp to Irenaeus. At the same time, however, other early writers, such as Ignatius, Polycarp, and Justin Martyr, do not mention John as the author. But an argument from silence proves nothing.

Is there any evidence within the Gospel that John wrote it, even though his name does not appear there as the author? Some scholars believe that there is and that the author is the disciple "whom Jesus loved" (13:23; 19:26; 20:2; 21:7,20,24). According to Mark 9:2 and 14:33 there were three disciples who were very close to Jesus during his ministry: Peter, James, and John. James was killed as a martyr by Herod Agrippa I, and Peter is differentiated in the Gospel of John from the disciple "whom Jesus loved." This line of reasoning would leave only John to be identified as the one "whom Jesus loved." But there remains the puzzling question as to why John would refer to himself as the one "whom Jesus loved." Along with such reasoning goes the added fact that John the apostle is never mentioned by name throughout the entire Gospel. If he were the author, why would he purposely omit his name throughout his work? The difficulty in answering such questions lies in the lack of sufficient evidence.

(2) Date of Writing   It is hard to determine the date of the writing of this Gospel. Scholars have estimated the date anywhere between 40 and 140. The date 40 is much too early; and the discovery of the Rylands Fragments, three papyrus fragments dated about 130–150 and containing parts of John 18:31–33,37–38, make any date later than the middle of the second century impossible. This discovery would show conclusively that the Gospel was in use during the first half of this same century. The author probably knew and used Mark and Luke when he was writing his own work, for there are various factors within the Gospel that would lead to such a conclusion. The most likely date seems to be somewhere near the close of the first century.

(3) Place of Writing   There are three cities that have been suggested as the possible site of writing for the Gospel: Ephesus, Antioch of Syria, and

Alexandria. Those who advocate a certain city give reasons for doing so. However, the city that is the favored of these three is Ephesus, capital of the province of Asia in Asia Minor. This city was the seat of a large Jewish community as well as the center for many aspects of Grecian culture and thinking. The Gospel was evidently written in a predominantly Gentile surrounding, since the author felt a need to explain certain Jewish feasts and customs (2:13; 4:9; 19:31).

(4)   Distinguishing Characteristics   There are three main sections to John. There is a prologue (1:1–18), an epilogue (21), and a main narrative (1:19 to 20:31). The main section is divided into two parts, one having to do with Jesus' public ministry (1:19 to 12:50) and another dealing with his instruction of the twelve, his trial and crucifixion, and his resurrection (13:1 to 20:31).

This Gospel presents to the reader a paradox in that it is at the same time the simplest Gospel and the most profound Gospel. The Greek John used is the simplest in the New Testament. His vocabulary was the least extensive of any of the four Gospel writers, and his sentence structure was very plain and simple. Beginning New Testament Greek students are generally started on their reading in the New Testament with the task of translating this simple but very impressive book. John uses characteristic words like *love, truth, light, darkness, life, judgment, sin, world, flesh, hour, glory, witness,* and *believe* that are repeated constantly, all of which creates a very forceful effect. The discourses of Jesus found here are very profound and theologically impressive, each with a particular theme.

Many times in these discourses Jesus is interrupted by questions from his hearers, questions that often reveal an objection to what he is declaring and teaching. This does not occur in the Synoptic Gospels. This book of the New Testament is truly a Gospel, since it presents Jesus' ministry, his teachings, many of his miracles, and his death-resurrection experience. Yet at the same time it is an *interpretive* Gospel, for the author interprets for his readers various activities and sayings of Jesus. It is not sufficient that we should know that Jesus *did* something; we must also know *why* he did so. It is no wonder that Clement of Alexandria termed this Gospel "the Spiritual Gospel."

The chronology differs here from that found in the Synoptics. The Synoptics mention only one Passover, while John mentions three Passovers, with a possibility of even a fourth one. (John 5:1 uses the phrase "a feast of the Jews," which most scholars believe refers to a Passover. This cannot be stated in an absolute sense, however.) If there happened to be only one Passover in Jesus' ministry, that ministry would have been about a year in duration. If there were three Passovers, it would have been little more than two years, and if four Passovers, a little more than three years. The three definite Passovers in this Gospel are mentioned in 2:13; 2:23; 6:4; and 12:1. John 5:1 is the fourth possibility.

Counting the number of Passovers in Jesus' ministry is our only evidence relative to the length of his ministry. Therefore, this is a very significant factor in a study of the life of our Lord. In the Synoptic Gospels the cleansing of the Temple is found in the late part of Jesus' ministry. In this Gospel it evidently comes early in his ministry, thereby posing the decision as to whether there was one cleansing or two. At any rate, John seems to have been guided by more of a theological or interpretive interest than he was by a chronological presentation of Jesus' activities on a week-by-week or month-by-month basis. His arrangement is more topical than it is chronological. His interest is more in the meaning of history than history itself.

At the end of the twentieth chapter John stated very graphically his purpose in writing: "Many other signs therefore did Jesus in the presence of the disciples, which are not written in this book: but these are written, that ye may believe that Jesus is the Christ, the Son of God; and that believing ye may have life in his name" (20:30–31). The term *signs* is John's designation for miracles. There are seven of these, all selected to illustrate various phases of the power of Jesus and to bear witness to his deity, the central doctrine of the Gospel. They are as follows:

Changing of water into wine	2:1–11
Healing of the nobleman's son	4:46–54
Healing of the impotent man	5:1–9
Feeding of the five thousand	6:1–14
Walking on the water	6:16–21
Healing of the blind man	9:1–12
Raising of Lazarus	11:1–46

These signs, all performed in areas where man is incapable of rising above the natural order, manifest Jesus' ability to perform the supernatural. Their purpose is to move the reader to belief, that he may partake of the spiritual life offered by Jesus alone. Through the revelation of the glory of God man is able to experience the sum total of all God has prepared for him.

Just as John recorded seven miracles or signs to emphasize the deity of Jesus, he employed eight witnesses to strengthen the same concept. These witnesses are brought forth one by one, each adding weight in the declaration of Jesus' sonship. They are as follows:

John the Baptist	1:6,7,15,32,34

The Father	5:32,37; 8:18
Jesus' works	5:36; 10:25,38
The Scriptures	5:39–40
Jesus the Son	8:14,18
The Comforter (Holy Spirit)	15:26
The disciples	15:27
The writer himself	19:35; 21:24

One statement from John the Baptist will illustrate. "And I have seen, and have borne witness that this is the Son of God" (1:34).

John also used a third means to bring emphasis upon the deity of Jesus, the "I am" sayings. These are claims of Jesus set forth by the simple phrase "I am." The seven sayings are as follows:

I am the bread of life.	6:35
I am the light of the world.	8:12; 9:5
I am the door.	10:7
I am the good shepherd.	10:11,14
I am the resurrection and the life.	11:25
I am the way, the truth, and the life.	14:6
I am the true vine.	15:1

The Synoptics contain no statements of Jesus just like these.

Therefore, the central doctrine in this Gospel is Jesus' divine nature. Yet, at the same time, the writer emphasized highly Jesus' humanity; no other Gospel portrays his humanity any more clearly than John. Just as there are words like "The Word was God" (1:1), there are also statements that show Jesus was weary (4:6), was thirsty (4:7), was disappointed in people (6:26), longed for something (6:67), wept (11:35), and was troubled (12:27). To those who met and knew him he was "that man that is called Jesus" (9:11), and to those who were constantly by him he was recognized as "the Holy One of God" (6:69). This strange combination of divinity and humanity in the nature of Jesus is what is termed the *incarnation*. John very skillfully revealed this important doctrine, a necessary element in Jesus' saving activity.

Many divine terms for Jesus are used in the first chapter: the *Word* (Logos), *God, Rabbi* (Teacher), *Messiah* (Christ), *King of Israel*, and *Son of man*. In this Gospel Jesus is recognized by those around him as the divine Son from the very beginning. In the Synoptics there seems to be a gradual unfolding in the minds of his disciples and close followers that he was truly divine as well as human. Peter's declaration at Caesarea Philippi seems to be the turning point (Matt. 16:16) in the Synoptic story. The term Logos, as used by John, would have an appeal to those who were philosophical in nature. The term Son of God would be a familiar term to any reader. The terms Rabbi, Messiah, King of Israel, and Son of man were distinctly Jewish terms. It is at once clear that John was presenting Jesus as a universal figure, not merely a Jewish one.

It is very possible that John wrote to supplement the accounts of Jesus' life and ministry as found in the Synoptics, although this cannot be stated dogmatically. There are certain things that seem to indicate that he knew his readers had copies of the other Gospels. There is almost a complete omission of the Galilean ministry as found in the Synoptics, as well as a general absence of parables. Yet at the same time, some of the historical incidents that John gives fit well chronologically with those found in Matthew, Mark, and Luke. On the surface it would appear that he did not wish merely to repeat what they have given but to add fresh information of his own. Whereas Matthew and Luke presented the story of the virgin birth, John went back prior to the birth and presented the preexistence of Jesus (1:1).

8.

The Birth and Early Life of Jesus

Mark began his gospel with the ministry of Jesus at the age of thirty. John, after briefly mentioning the preexistence of Jesus, began with the ministry also. It is to Matthew and Luke that we turn for an account of Jesus' birth and childhood.

1. The Christian Calendar

In the Greco-Roman world several methods of measuring years were employed. The Romans themselves used a calendar that counted the years from the founding of Rome. This was termed A.U.C., standing for *ab urbe condita,* meaning "from the founded city." (Some authorities believe the three letters stand for *anno urbis conditae,* meaning "year of the city being founded.") This calendar was used for over five centuries after the time of Christ, for during the first half of the sixth century a Scythian monk named Dionysius Exiguus proposed a Christian way of reckoning time. This man, held in high respect as a theologian, mathematician, and astronomer, suggested using the birth of Christ as the starting point for a Christian calendar. All dates are to be computed *anno Domini,* "in the year of the Lord." This is symbolized by A.D., with everything before the birth of Christ as B.C.

The Christians welcomed his idea, but others were slower to accept it. It was introduced into southern Europe very early, but it was not introduced into England until late in the seventh century. By the time of Charlemagne (800) it had gained considerable acceptance, but it was not until the fifteenth century that it was popular throughout the world. However, there is no year 0. From 1 B.C. to A.D. 1 is only one year, not two. Form 3 B.C. to A.D. 3 is five years. Also, Dionysius made an error in his calculations as he shifted from the A.U.C. calendar to the B.C.—A.D. calendar, an error of from four to six years. He used A.U.C. 754 as the pivotal year when he should have used a year prior to A.U.C. 750, the death of Herod the Great. By the time the mistake was detected, it was too late to go back and change all the dated documents.

123

2. The Date of Jesus' Birth

The New Testament does not offer definite information about the year, the month, or the day of Jesus' birth, although there are several events mentioned that throw some light on the year of the nativity. The three most important ones are the death of Herod the Great, the entrance of John the Baptist on his ministry, and the building of the Temple by Herod. As a result of study and calculation, it appears that Jesus was born between 6 B.C. and 4 B.C.

Herod the Great was the king who conversed with the Magi from the east and who later gave the order to kill the boy babies in and around Bethlehem. Matthew gave several events that occurred between the birth of Jesus (2:1) and the death of Herod (2:19). This time could not have been less than two or three months and could have been as much as two years (Matt. 2:16). Josephus, the Jewish historian, tells us that Herod died in A.U.C. 750 on or before the Passover. This would be on or before April 4, 4 B.C. This would throw the birth of Jesus with great probability in 5 B.C. or possibly in 6 B.C.

Luke told us that ''in the fifteenth year of the reign of Tiberius Caesar'' John the Baptist began his preaching ministry (Luke 3:1–3). When Caesar Augustus died in A.D. 14, Tiberius replaced him as emperor. However, Tiberius started helping Augustus with his reign two years before he died, an associate reign that began in A.D. 12. Does Luke have in mind the A.D. 12 date or the A.D. 14 date? If the earlier date is used, Jesus began his ministry about A.D. 26 or 27. John the Baptist began his ministry not long before Jesus began his, and Jesus began his at ''about thirty years of age'' (Luke 3:23). Counting back would bring up the date 5 or 4 B.C. for Jesus' birth.

Herod the Great began the work of reconstructing the Temple complex for the Jews about 20 or 19 B.C. (in the eighteenth year of his reign). At the Passover season not long after Jesus' baptism, the Jews stated that this process of reconstruction had been going on for 46 years (John 2:20), which would make the year of their remark A.D. 27 or 28. Counting back from this date and using thirty years of age as the start of his ministry (Luke 3:23), we would derive the date 5 or 4 B.C. for the year of Jesus' birth. This would agree approximately with the two previous calculations.

It was not until the fourth century that the custom of observing December 25 as the birthday of Jesus arose. Before observing this day in December there was a similar custom of celebrating January 6 as the time the Wise Men made their visit to the home of the Christ child. Early writers mention other dates besides December 25 and January 6 as being connected with the birth of Jesus: March 25, April 18, May 20, and November 17. Lack of agreement existed on this score for hundreds of years. December 17–24 was celebrated in Rome as the pagan Festival of Saturnalia, with the following day, December 25, as Brumhalia, the birthday of the sun. At this time the reckless celebration reached its peak. This day was called *Dies Solis Invicte,* "Day of the Invincible Sun." The pagans noticed that the days were getting longer and that the sun was winning its fight against the forces of darkness. Although it cannot be proved, the early church may have chosen this date to celebrate the birth of Jesus in order to provide Christians with an alternative celebration to offset the pagan celebration. This would be the birthday of the *eternal Son* as over against that of the *created sun.*

3. Matthew and Luke the Sources

Most of the New Testament writings do not place much emphasis upon the birth and infancy of Jesus. To the early Christians the most significant events in his ministry were the cross and resurrection. Calvary and the open tomb proclaimed to them the remarkable nature of his life and work. Because of these crowning events, they knew him to be Lord, the Word of God, the Messiah, the Son of God. "Let all the house of Israel therefore know assuredly, that God hath made him both Lord and Christ, this Jesus whom ye crucified" (Acts 2:36); so said Peter in his great sermon on the day of Pentecost. Yet at the same time, his teachings, his miracles, his birth, his infancy—all these held meaning for the early church. It is Matthew and Luke who presented the infancy narratives dear to the heart of every New Testament reader.

The two accounts are overlapping yet independent. Both record that Jesus was born in Bethlehem during the reign of Herod the Great; that his mother was Mary, at the time of his birth a virgin; that he was conceived through an act of the Holy Spirit; that, due to an angelic command, he was to be named Jesus, meaning Savior, for he would save his people from their sins; that Mary's husband was Joseph, a descendant of David; and that Jesus was brought up in Nazareth of Galilee. After these overlapping accounts Matthew and Luke proceeded to add independent accounts. Matthew told of the visit of the Magi, the hatred and murdering of the infants by Herod, and the flight into Egypt. Luke gave the story of the visit of the shepherds, the angelic chorus, the songs of poetic passages expressed by certain individuals, and an account of the conception and birth of John the Baptist.

4. The Genealogies

Matthew gave his genealogy of Jesus at the very start of his gospel (1:1–17); Luke presented his as he began to tell of Jesus' ministry (3:23–38). Both genealogies rest upon the anticipation that the Messiah would be of Davidic descent. However, a close look at the two lines of descent makes it very apparent that the family trees are quite different. Matthew listed forty-six names and proceeded from Abraham, the forefather of the Hebrew people, down to Jesus. Luke used seventy-seven names and proceeded from Jesus back to Adam, forefather of all men. Would the fact that Matthew was a Jew and Luke a Gentile have anything to do with how far back the line was traced, whether to Abraham or to Adam? Probably so. It is from David down that the genealogies take different paths, after which they cross again and then part again. Matthew divided his list into three sections of fourteen names each.

Both Matthew and Luke gave the virgin birth of Jesus and traced the ancestry of Jesus down to Joseph. However, Jesus was conceived of the Holy Spirit and not of Joseph. Therefore, why, we ask, is the genealogy brought down to Joseph? The reason is evidently to show a Davidic descent through Joseph.

The differences in the genealogies were noted early in the history of the church, being discussed from Julius Africanus in the third century on down to today. As a result, over the centuries several explanations have evolved. One is that Matthew gave the genealogy of Joseph, and Luke gave that of Mary. Roman Catholics prefer this explanation. Joseph was of Davidic descent (Matt. 1:20; Luke 1:27), but nothing is said of Mary. In fact, she was kin to Elizabeth of the tribe of Levi. Another explanation is that Matthew gave Jesus' legal descent and Luke the natural one. Some scholars hold to this view. But would not both writers look with favor on the legal descent, since both state a supernatural birth for Jesus? A third explanation is that the two reports represent traditions arising from different sections of the early church. Though this view is favored by some scholars, it too has its difficulties. To issue any positive statement about the difference in the two lines and about their purpose of inclusion in the narratives is almost impossible.

5. The Virgin Birth

Matthew and Luke recounted two important things about the birth of Jesus: one, he was born of a virgin, and two, he was conceived of the Holy Spirit (Matt. 1:18–25; Luke 1:26–38). One of these realities would not necessarily include the other; both are required to complete the picture of

Jesus' birth. "Now the birth of Jesus Christ was on this wise: When his mother Mary had been betrothed to Joseph, before they came together she was found with child of the Holy Spirit" (Matt. 1:18). Joseph, thinking Mary had been untrue to him, was going to give her a bill of divorcement and very quietly put her out of his house. However, God revealed to him through an angel in a dream that she had conceived through the Holy Spirit and that, when the child was born, he should be called Jesus, "for it is he that shall save his people from their sins" (Matt. 1:21). The name Jesus is the Greek for the Hebrew name Joshua, meaning "Jehovah is salvation." Therefore, his name is a symbol of his great mission: "For the Son of man came to seek and to save that which was lost" (Luke 19:10).

Luke was as definite as Matthew relative to Mary's virginity at the time of the nativity. After stating that Joseph was betrothed to a virgin named Mary (1:27), he added that the angel informed her, "The Holy Spirit shall come upon thee, and the power of the Most High shall overshadow thee: wherefore also the holy thing which is begotten shall be called the Son of God" (1:35).

In Matthew's account Joseph is a very significant figure, for the writer seems to unfold the narrative from Joseph's point of view. The annunciation of the birth of Jesus is made to Joseph in a dream, at which time even the child's designated name, Jesus, is revealed to him. Matthew gave Joseph's reaction when he thinks at first that Mary has been untrue to him, with the resultant desire to "put her away." Luke seemed to unfold the narrative from Mary's point of view. The annunciation is to Mary while she is awake, not in a dream. Joseph's reaction to Mary's expecting a child is not told by Luke. In fact, this writer informed us of very little of Joseph's part in the story.

Matthew, in his desire to depict the gospel story as much as possible as a fulfillment of Old Testament prophecy, stated that the virgin birth of Jesus was an unfolding of a passage from the prophet Isaiah. "Now all this is come to pass, that it might be fulfilled which was spoken by the Lord through the prophet, saying, Behold, the virgin shall be with child, and shall bring forth a son, And they shall call his name Immanuel; which is, being interpreted, God with us" (Matt. 1:22–23). Matthew evidently quoted the Isaiah 7:14 passage directly from the Septuagint, the Greek translation of the Hebrew Scriptures. In this translation the Greek word *parthenos,* meaning virgin, was selected by the translators.

From the first century the historicity of the virgin birth has been debated, probably more than any other Christian issue. Though there are some scholars who reject the reality of it, the vast majority of Christians accept it as true. All the great creeds of the early church include an article about belief in the virgin birth of Jesus. Most scholars who reject this doctrine maintain that to do so does not alter their faith in Christ. They point out that the majority of the New Testament writers do not mention the ancestry, birth, and infancy narratives of Jesus, that Matthew and Luke were the only ones who stated the doctrine.

But to reject a doctrine because many of the New Testament writers do not mention it is to argue from the negative, a method that in reality proves nothing. Paul did not mention the Sermon on the Mount, but this does not prove he did not accept it. Mark began his Gospel with the public ministry of Jesus and, therefore, would not be expected to depict the account of his birth. John went back beyond the birth to the preexistence of Jesus. We would be relatively safe in assuming that both Mark and John implied the virgin birth, an implication stemming from all the other things that these two writers told of Jesus. It is also to be noted that no other writer of the New Testament contradicted Matthew and Luke by challenging their virgin birth accounts; none took a stand against the doctrine.

Many of those who do not accept the virgin birth account believe that it grew out of the theology and doctrine of the church about the close of the first century and was read into the birth stories of our Lord. Therefore, they reason, to a life climaxed by the resurrection, the miraculous birth narratives make a suitable "theological preface," so to speak. From the conviction that Jesus was the Son of God (Mark 1:1,11) came the resultant conviction that he must have been supernaturally born. Such was the case with Matthew and Luke. To this line of thinking they add that, for John, Paul, and Mark, Jesus was the Son of God in the sense that God chose him to fulfill the important role of redeeming mankind. All such reasoning is not only weak, but it brings discredit upon the reliability and spiritual insight of Matthew and Luke, thus making their writings appear as untrustworthy documents.

6. The Preexistence of Jesus

Jesus as Son of God did not have his beginning with his birth in a stable in Bethlehem; this was merely the inception of his life upon earth in the form of man. He had no beginning, for he is, and was, God. There is no time that he was not. Since God is eternal Jesus is eternal, for Jesus is God. We read, "In the beginning was the Word, and the Word was with God, and the Word was God. All things were made through him; and without him was not anything made that hath been made. In him was life; and the life was the light of men" (John 1:1–4). Jesus preexisted in heaven before his descent to earth in the form of man, for his birth in Bethlehem was merely his advent into flesh. There was no time in the dim recesses of eternity past that the Son of God did not exist.

John the Baptist declared of Jesus, "This was he of whom I said, He that cometh after me is become before me: for he was before me" (John 1:15). Jesus told the Jews, "Before Abraham was born, I am" (John 8:58). Jesus prayed, "And now, Father, glorify thou me with thine own self with the glory which I had with thee before the world was" (John 17:5). Paul expressed the same thing in Philippians 2:5–11.

This preexistence was a reality, not a fantasy. Some scholars have endeavored to make us think that it was an "ideal preexistence," that the Son preexisted only as an idea in the mind of God, an idea that came into fulfillment the moment Jesus was born on earth of the virgin Mary. The real preexistence of Christ is thus changed into a preexistence in the mind of God, which is a concept that is not found in Scripture. Jesus prayed that the Father restore unto him the glory which he experienced in his preexistent state (John 17:5). An idea cannot experience glory, for only a real person is able to experience such. Jesus' preexistence was actual and not merely imaginary.

7. The Annunciation

The story of the advent of Jesus in the form of flesh is known as the *incarnation,* a term denoting that God has entered flesh. This story begins with three announcements: one made by the angel Gabriel to Zacharias the priest, one made by the angel Gabriel to Mary, and one made by an angel to Joseph, fiancé of Mary. The first two are recorded by Luke and the last by Matthew. These announcements are heralds to the great events following.

Luke told us (1:8–24) that the aged priest Zacharias was performing his duty in the Temple as an incense burner when there appeared to him on the right side of the altar of incense an angel of the Lord. Quieting the priest's fears, the angel announced to him that he and his wife, though well advanced in years, would be the parents of an extraordinary son. He even informed him, in a general way, of what this son would do for Israel. Due to Zacharias' nonbelief the angel added that Zacharias would be silent and unable to speak until the child was born. Thus God was to take away the barrenness of Elizabeth and abolish her "reproach among men." Not to have children was considered almost a tragedy by Hebrew women of that day. The people in the Temple wondered why Zacharias delayed in emerging from the Holy Place. The aged priest returned to his home in "a city of

Judah,'' after which Elizabeth conceived. All this occurred about 6 B.C.

Luke also related (1:26–38) that Gabriel appeared about six months later to Mary, a young woman living in Nazareth, and announced to her that she was to become the mother of a son to be called Jesus, one who was to be "the Son of the Most High." She was a "virgin betrothed to a man whose name was Joseph" (v. 27). She also registered surprise since, even though they were betrothed, she and Joseph had not experienced a husband-wife relationship. The angel announced to her that conception would take place through the Holy Spirit and that the child born to her would be the Son of God. Luke has recorded the vision in beautiful and delicate words.

Since the angel also informed Mary that Elizabeth, who was in some way related to her, was also expecting a child, Mary went to visit her at her home in Judea, staying there three months before returning to her own home in Nazareth. Mary was so elated over the God-given promise that she would be the mother of the Messiah that she broke forth in song, a poem of praise now called the *Magnificat* (1:46–55). This is the first of four poems given by Luke, each of which became known by the first word, or words, in its Latin translation. (All four are in the first two chapters of Luke.) These two devout women probably had much to discuss during their three-month sojourn together, thus deriving mutual help. Mary evidently stayed with Elizabeth until John the Baptist was born.

Matthew told of the third announcement, one made to Joseph in a dream (1:18–25). "Now the birth of Jesus Christ was on this wise: When his mother Mary had been betrothed to Joseph, before they came together she was found with child of the Holy Spirit. And Joseph her husband, being a righteous man, and not willing to make her a public example, was minded to put her away privily" (vv. 18–19). "Betrothed" with the Jewish people was a much more serious state than is "engagement" in modern social usage. Mary belonged to Joseph, though she was not yet legally his wife. Joseph's first reaction was to think the worst of Mary, all of which necessitated a divine proclamation to him that would reveal the true nature of the event. The message was from the angel of the Lord: "Joseph, thou son of David, fear not to take unto thee Mary thy wife: for that which is conceived in her is of the Holy Spirit" (Matt. 1:20). He was even informed that the child was to be named Jesus; "for it is he that shall save his people from their sins." The name Jesus means "Savior," just as its Old Testament counterpart, Joshua, means "Jehovah is salvation." "And Joseph arose from his sleep, and did as the angel of the Lord commanded him, and took unto him his wife; and knew her not till she had brought forth a son: and he called his name Jesus" (Matt. 1:24–25).

8. The Birth of John the Baptist

When Elizabeth gave birth to a son, all her neighbors and kinfolk rejoiced with her. On the eighth day, the day for circumcision and for naming, they wanted to call the boy Zacharias after his father; but Elizabeth insisted that his name was to be John. When they inquired of the father what the child should be called, he asked for a writing tablet and wrote, "His name is John." Immediately he regained the power of speech, having lost it for nine months. "And fear came on all that dwelt round about them: and all these sayings were noised abroad throughout all the hill country of Judea. And all that heard them laid them up in their heart, saying, What then shall this child be? For the hand of the Lord was with him" (Luke 1:65–66). Zacharias then broke forth into praise, the second of Luke's four songs, or poems. This one is named the *Benedictus* (vv. 68–79).

Luke gave one verse about the child's youth. "And the child grew, and waxed strong in spirit, and was in the deserts till the day of his showing unto Israel" (v. 80). How long Zacharias and Elizabeth lived we do not know. Since they were advanced in years, it is not probable that they lived to see him reach manhood. We can well imagine that John grew strong in the desert country and that there he developed spiritually for the rigorous ministry of being the Forerunner to Jesus. Whether or not John at some time or other lived with the Essenes has been much debated. Nothing in this regard has been firmly established, however.

9. The Birth of Jesus

Both Matthew and Luke declared that Jesus was born in Bethlehem. Luke told of a Roman census: "Now it came to pass in those days, there went out a decree from Caesar Augustus, that all the world should be enrolled. This was the first enrollment made when Quirinius was governor of Syria. And all went to enrol themselves, every one to his own city" (2:1–3). According to the decree, every male citizen was required to go back to his ancestral home to be enrolled for the purpose of taxation. Therefore, Joseph had to leave Nazareth, his home at the time, and return to the original territory of his tribe. Since he was of the tribe of Judah he departed from Nazareth, crossed the fertile plain of Esdraelon, then traversed Samaria, and then traveled on to the historic city of Bethlehem. Micah the prophet had predicted years before that a ruler would come forth from Bethlehem. "But thou, Bethlehem Ephrathah, which art little to be among the thousands of Judah, out of thee shall one come forth unto me that is to be ruler in Israel" (5:2).

Bethlehem, from the Church of the Nativity

According to law Mary was not required to accompany Joseph to Bethlehem; but, evidently because she was "great with child" and the birth was near at hand, she made the trip with him, probably riding upon a donkey, the common beast of burden. While she was in Bethlehem the time came for her to deliver. "And she brought forth her firstborn son; and she wrapped him in swaddling clothes, and laid him in a manger, because there was no room for them in the inn" (Luke 2:7). One wonders if the innkeeper ever discovered the identity of the famous guests that he relegated to the stable on that momentous day! At any rate, Mary wrapped the baby in long bands of white cloth, according to the custom of that day, and placed him in a manger.

From the earliest centuries of Christianity a certain cave has been indicated by the local people as the grotto connected with the inn to which Joseph and Mary went for a place to stay, the grotto where tradition says Jesus was born and then placed in a stone manger used for feeding the animals. Today a great star marks the spot in the stone floor. A magnificent church was built over this cave in 330 by Constantine, the first Christian emperor. This church still stands. Today the group of churches and monasteries erected over and around the rocky cave or grotto is known as the Church of the Nativity. One enters a low doorway and descends a stairway to the grotto, directly situated beneath the altar above. This may or may not be the authentic spot where Jesus was born.

10. Homage to the King

Even though the Christ child was born of a peasant girl in a remote corner of the earth, there were certain very unusual occurrences at the time of his birth—shepherds, Magi, and a star. Luke told of the shepherds (2:8–20) and Matthew of the Magi and the star (2:1–18). An angel of the Lord appeared to the shepherds, bringing to them the joyful news of the birth of "a Saviour, who is Christ the Lord." Besides the angel there was a "heavenly host" praising God and singing what was later to be known as the *Gloria in Excelsis Deo* (2:14), the third of the four poems, or songs, found in this section of Luke. Leaving their fields, the shepherds made their way to Bethlehem to visit the little child "lying in a manger." After making known to Mary the miraculous happenings out in the field and the revelation they experienced there, they returned to their work, "glorifying and praising God."

Matthew recounted the story of the Magi, or Wise Men, coming "from the east" to Jerusalem, evidently following a star that they saw at their home. "The east" could have been anywhere in Mesopotamia or east of there, Persia. When they arrived in Jerusalem many days had elapsed since they started their journey. They asked of Herod the Great, ''Where is he that is born King of the Jews?'' (2:2). Such a question caused consternation not only for Herod but for ''all Jerusalem with him.'' When he inquired of knowledgeable people where such a one would be born, they cited the famous passage from Micah that Bethlehem was the favored spot (Micah 5:2). Then he requested of the Magi that they search out the child and return and inform him of his whereabouts, that he ''also may come and worship him'' (2:8). Evidently his worship was to be with the assassin's knife. One who had murdered some of his wives and his own sons would not stop at murdering a possible rival to his throne.

The star led the Magi directly to Bethlehem, for ''it came and stood over where the young child was'' (2:9). By this time, probably months since the shepherds made their joyous visit on the night of Jesus' birth, Joseph and Mary had secured a home; the Magi ''came into the house and saw the young child with Mary his mother'' (2:11). They not only lay prostrate before the child and worshiped him, but presented to him three costly gifts: gold, frankincense, and myrrh. Then they were warned by God to take an indirect path home, skirting around Jerusalem and the home of jealous King Herod. ''They departed into their own country another way'' (2:12).

11. Erroneous Concepts

The popular mind is many times filled with details about Jesus' birth that are not warranted in Holy Scripture. One is that he was born in a crude wooden stable on December 25 in the year A.D. 1. It was probably in a stable consisting of a rock grotto or cave; the custom in that day was to use caves for sheep due to their warmth in winter and coolness in summer. An outer corral could then be built adjoining the cave. The day of his birth was probably not on December 25, as has already been discussed. The time of pasturage in Judea was between March and November, so shepherds would not have been out in the fields at night in December, one of the winter months. Also, it would have been hard for Mary to have made the long trek from Nazareth to Bethlehem in her condition during the winter. Herod the Great, who conversed with the Wise Men, died in 4 B.C., so Jesus' birth must have been in 5 or 6 B.C., maybe even earlier.

Another erroneous concept, as displayed on Christmas greeting cards, is that the shepherds and Magi visited the infant Jesus at the same time. These two events are recorded by different writers of separate New Testament documents. The shepherds came from the fields outside Bethlehem, probably two or three miles away, while the Magi made a journey requiring an extensive time.

Another false concept is that the Magi were kings, that there were three of them, that their names were Gaspar (white), Melchior (light), and Balthasar (lord of the treasury), and that the three expensive gifts symbolized three aspects of Jesus' future ministry to mankind. The Bible does not state that there were three; this idea probably arose from the fact that they offered to the infant Jesus three gifts. There probably were more than three men, since caravans moving from the east down to the territory of Judah would comprise many people. Three men alone would have offered an easy prey to the numerous robbers frequenting the way.

Henry Van Dyke's famous story "The Other Wise Man" has contributed much to perpetuate the "three concept," as well as modern Christmas greeting cards. The hymn that begins "We three kings of Orient are" has furthered both the three idea and the king idea. However, we do know that these men had some unusual knowledge of the star that guided them to the home of the infant Jesus. These and other familiar declarations are the result of pious imaginations who wish to add vivid details to the birth stories of Jesus, details not warranted by the historical sources of that era.

These unfounded declarations are revealed among the thinking of many people today; they constitute the false thinking of the popular mind. Many scholars, those who have devoted long hours to the study of the Bible, have also put forth certain heretical ideas about the origin and birth of Jesus. The fact that some scholars deny his virgin birth and that some deny his real preexistence have already been mentioned. We might add to these a third heretical idea: Jesus was born in Nazareth, not Bethlehem, an idea that seems to be gaining ground in recent years. The strongest argument used by those who advocate such thinking is that the story of the Bethlehem nativity provided Jesus with the proper credentials, since Micah had prophesied that the Messiah would come from Bethlehem. Therefore, the belief that he was born in "the city of David" was read into the birth narratives by the early church. This is the same argument used by those who want to discount the virgin birth story. They believe that all the birth accounts of Jesus played no part in his public ministry but arose after he was acknowledged as the Messiah. All three of these "scholarly heresies" should be set aside as unwarranted.

12. The Incarnation

The virgin birth of Jesus brought into reality what is called the *incarnation:* the miracle of the coming of God in the form of a human being. Jesus was both God and man, being truly God and truly man. Neither of these was negated or watered down in any respect. He was the eternal Son of God and also one who lived a truly human life.

Jesus was not God masquerading as a man, for he entered the world as a real human being subject to all the laws of human development. He grew, he learned, he became weary, he hungered, he thirsted, he suffered pain, and he died. He was not simply half God, half man, for both natures were complete. He was not God *and* man, nor God *in* man. He was the God-man. He was not a good man that God raised to the level of divinity, for he was the Word become flesh (John 1:14). The incarnation was the union of the divine and the human in a manner that challenges human understanding. Men have for centuries tried to probe this mystery, but it is beyond finite mind to do so. Jesus Christ was one "who, existing in the form of God, counted not the being on an equality with God a thing to be grasped, but emptied himself, taking the form of a servant, being made in the likeness of men" (Phil. 2:6–7).

To say that Jesus was all divine and not human or to say that he was all human and not divine would be to deny the incarnation. To alter or to water down either the divine or the human would be to misunderstand the incarnation. All four attempts have been expressed throughout church history by heretical believers here and there. In the one person Jesus Christ there were two natures, a divine and a human, each complete, yet united in such a way that no third nature was formed thereby. This is a mystery incapable of psychological explanation. It was a mystery to Paul, the apostle of Tarsus, for he talked of "the mystery of God, even Christ, in whom are all the treasures of wisdom and knowledge hidden" (Col. 2:2–3).

13. Occurrences After the Shepherds' Visit

The first announcement of Jesus' birth was made to shepherds, people generally despised by orthodox Jews because their work prevented them from observing the strict requirements the Jews had heaped upon the Mosaic law. They were poor, unlearned, and rudely dressed individuals, most of the time smelling like sheep. They had no gifts to bring to Jesus except adoration.

Soon after "the night of wonder," Mary and Joseph complied with all the requirements of Mosaic law in connection with the birth of a son. There were three things that were done. First, the child was circumcised on the eighth day after birth, making him a party to the covenant that God made with Abraham relative to all the descendants of the great patriarch (Gen. 17:10–14). Luke informed us, "And when eight days were fulfilled for

Bethlehem, place of the Nativity

circumcising him, his name was called Jesus, which was so called by the angel before he was conceived in the womb" (2:21). Luke, however, subordinated the requirement of the law to something of a deeper significance, that his name was Jesus, denoting his saving intent.

The second thing that was performed had to do with the firstborn male, for the firstborn male child belonged to God and had to be redeemed or bought back by a gift of money (Ex. 13:11–16). "Thou shalt set apart unto Jehovah all that openeth the womb . . . and all the first-born of man among thy sons shalt thou redeem" (vv. 12–13). Luke said, "They brought him up to Jerusalem, to present him to the Lord" (2:22), all in accordance with the Mosaic demand.

The third event was simultaneous with the second, the purification of Mary. After childbirth the mother was considered to be in spiritual uncleanness; therefore, a sacrifice had to be made to remove it (Lev. 12:6–8). If she had a male child she was considered in a state of impurity for forty days, after which the sacrifice was to be offered. "And when the days of their purification according to the law of Moses were fulfilled, they brought him up to Jerusalem to present him to the Lord" (Luke 2:22). They also offered "a sacrifice according to that which is said in the law of the Lord, a pair of turtledoves, or two young pigeons" (2:24). The law called for a lamb and a pigeon or turtledove or, if the family happened to be of meager means, two pigeons or two turtledoves. Mary and Joseph were not rich, so the two birds were offered. Jesus was forty days old when he was brought to the Temple for these two ceremonies.

During the ceremonial visit to the Temple the family of three met and conversed with two aged people, Simeon and Anna (Luke 2:25–38). Simeon, righteous and devout, was looking for the "consolation of Israel." "And it had been revealed unto him by the Holy Spirit, that he should not see death, before he had seen the Lord's Christ" (Luke 2:26). As soon as he saw Jesus, he received him unto his arms and gave blessing to God. He sang a song or poem called the *Nunc Dimittis* (Luke 2:29–32), · fourth of the four songs in this section of the Gospel of Luke. Simeon expressed the significance of the advent of Jesus, that he had come for both Gentiles and Israel. To Mary he gave words of warning. "Behold, this child is set for the falling and the rising of many in Israel . . . and a sword shall pierce through thine own soul" (Luke 2:34–35). Anna, a prophetess waiting there in the Temple, immediately recognized Jesus as the Christ child (vv. 36–39). She had been a widow for 84 years and had lived with her husband seven years prior to that; so she must have been between 105 and 110 years of age. Giving thanks to God, she spoke of Jesus "to all them that were looking for the redemption of Israel.''

14. Occurrences After the Magi's Visit

The Magi, after visiting the infant Jesus, were warned in a dream to depart to their own country ''another way'' and not to return to Herod in Jerusalem (Matt. 2:12). An angel appeared to Joseph in a dream and instructed him to take the young child and his mother into Egypt until further word, ''for Herod will seek the young child to destroy him.'' They departed by night for Egypt, remaining there till Herod the Great had died (2:13–15). Matthew quoted a passage from the prophet Hosea: ''Out of Egypt did I call my son'' (Hosea 11:1). Hosea was originally referring to the exodus of Israel from Egypt under Moses, but Matthew viewed Jesus as a second Moses, a greater Moses. To Matthew the return of the family of three out of Egypt (Matt. 2:13–23) was a later counterpart of the great Mosaic exodus.

Herod, already troubled by the news of a newly born King of the Jews brought to him by the visitors from the east, became ''exceeding wroth'' when he realized that his request of the Wise Men had been ignored. Therefore, he ordered that all male children in and around Bethlehem two years old and under be killed (Matt. 2:16). This mass murder of the infants in and near the birthplace of Jesus seems very cruel to the casual reader of the New Testament, who does not know that Herod had already ordered several of his own family put to death, some of whom might possibly have been future claimants to his throne. In his last days he was exceedingly cruel and jealous, suspecting even those who should have been very dear to him. After he was mocked by the Wise Men, his anger knew no bounds; so he issued his despotic order. Matthew mentioned Rachel's weeping for the slain children; Rachel was buried near Bethlehem, having died there when she gave birth to Benjamin (Gen. 35:19–20).

After Herod was dead (4 B.C.), an angel of the Lord informed Joseph to return with Mary and the baby Jesus to Israel, which he did. Archelaus, the son of Herod, was ruling in Judea in Herod's stead (4 B.C.—A.D. 6), so the situation was hardly improved. Joseph was warned of God in a dream to go into Galilee. There he dwelled in Nazareth, and there it was that Jesus was reared.

Nazareth, situated in southern Galilee, was in one of the most beautiful parts of Palestine. It not only overlooked the luxurious plain of Esdraelon but was situated at the crossroads of the ancient highways running across Galilee. The famous Via Maris road, running from Damascus to the coast, passed through Nazareth. Roman armies marched across the town on their way to distant parts. It was a cosmopolitan city in every respect. There it was that Jesus grew up and was "in all points tempted like as we are, yet without sin" (Heb. 4:15). There it was that Joseph had his carpenter's shop and where he and Mary reared a family of several children. Jesus had four half brothers—James, Joses, Judas, and Simon—and two or more half sisters.

15. The Jerusalem Visit at Twelve

Luke gave one verse for the activities of Jesus from the age of forty days till twelve years. "And the child grew, and waxed strong, filled with wisdom: and the grace of God was upon him" (2:40). Then he recorded an incident that happened when Jesus was twelve, a visit to Jerusalem and to the Temple at the Passover season. This is very typical of what might happen in Jewish family life in Palestine during the first century A.D. during a trip to Jerusalem for the greatest festival of the Jewish year. It was in the Jewish month of Nisan, and Jesus accompanied his parents to the holy city for the celebration. When the caravan started home, Jesus was not only absent among the travelers; he was not even missed until the caravan had gone "a day's journey." Hunting diligently, his parents could not find him. He was later discovered in the Temple, "sitting in the midst of the teachers, both hearing them, and asking them questions: and all that heard him were amazed at his understanding and his answers" (Luke 2:46–47).

Mary and Joseph were astonished at the whole event and questioned Jesus concerning it, stating that they had sought him in sorrow. His reply was in the form of a question; "How is it that ye sought me? knew ye not that I must be in my Father's house?" (v. 49). This is a free rendering; the Greek actually says, "about the things of my Father." Joseph and Mary did not understand the meaning of his words, the first recorded ones for our Lord; but this statement reveals that at a very young age Jesus had a deep consciousness of his high mission. Even then he sensed the unique relationship he had with his Father and the great work that was soon to develop from it. But when the family returned to Nazareth "he was subject unto them" (v. 51).

Luke then made a remark for the succeeding eighteen years of Jesus' life. "And Jesus advanced in wisdom and stature, and in favor with God and men" (v. 52). Joseph is not mentioned after the Jerusalem incident, when Jesus was twelve years of age. It is generally assumed that Joseph died sometime prior to the entrance of Jesus upon his ministry, but such a supposition cannot be proved. Apparently Jesus took up the carpenter's trade, becoming known as "the carpenter" (Mark 6:3). In doing so he added dignity to the toil and labor of workmen everywhere.

9.

The Beginning of Jesus' Ministry

After Jesus' visit to the Temple at the age of twelve, eighteen years elapsed before he began to proclaim his message of redemption (cf. Luke 3:23).

1. A Forerunner

All four Gospels present John the Baptist as the herald of Jesus' beginning his ministry. For centuries the voice of a prophet had not been heard in Israel. Nathan, Elijah, Micah, Amos, Isaiah, Jeremiah—all these and many more had made a great impact upon God's people. Malachi, a prophet who proclaimed his message late in Israel's history, prophesied, "Behold, I will send you Elijah the prophet before the great and terrible day of Jehovah come" (Mal. 4:5). This coming herald was to be an antitype of Elijah, the great antagonist of Baal worship during the days of Ahab and Jezebel. The angel announced to Zacharias, the father of John the Baptist, that his son would be like Elijah (cf. Luke 1:17).

About thirty years after the angel's message, John received his special call from God to preach. It was "in the fifteenth year of the reign of Tiberius Caesar" that "the word of God came unto John the son of Zacharias in the wilderness" (Luke 3:1–2). Luke told us that John "was in the deserts till the day of his showing unto Israel" (1:80). Here he received the command from God to preach; to obey that command he went "into all the region round about the Jordan" (3:3). In 25 or 26 John broke the silence with prophetic thunder and stirred the hearts of the people.

2. John the Baptist and Elijah

John the Baptist and Elijah of old had much in common. For one thing, their outward appearance was similar; both were striking figures. They wore the same kind of rough clothing (see 2 Kings 1:8 and Matt. 3:4). Also, their messages were similar; both were stern and demanded repentance. Elijah fearlessly denounced Ahab to his face, and John the Baptist denounced Herod Antipas in the same manner (see 1 Kings 21:20–21; Matt. 14:4).

John's message was that of a true prophet. Herod Antipas would have put John to death, but "he feared the multitude, because they counted him as a prophet" (Matt. 14:5). Though John's message was filled with rebuke and stern denunciation, crowds came to hear him and to be baptized by him (Luke 3:5–7). His words stirred them deeply. Probably thousands, including the religious leaders of Jerusalem, heard John preach.

All three of the Synoptic Gospels present John the Baptist as the fulfillment of Old Testament prophecies concerning a Forerunner. Mark quoted from Malachi 3:1 and Isaiah 40:3–5, while Matthew and Luke quoted only from the Isaiah passage. The passage in Isaiah depicts the ancient custom of sending forth men to build or repair a road over which some dignitary would travel; it seems to refer in this case to the return of the Jews from the Babylonian captivity. The Gospel writers saw "the voice" mentioned in the Isaiah passage as being fulfilled in John's voice as he heralded the approach of the Messiah.

The Jews believed that Elijah would return to announce the coming of the Messiah, an opinion based mainly upon a Malachi passage: "Behold, I will send Elijah the prophet before the great and terrible day of Jehovah come" (4:5). Even though John the Baptist denied being Elijah (John 1:21), Jesus, on being questioned about John, said, "And if ye are willing to receive it, this is Elijah, that is to come" (Matt. 11:14).

Peter, James, and John, having seen Moses and Elijah talking with Jesus on the mountain where Jesus was transfigured, asked their Master, "Why then say the scribes that Elijah must first come?" To this question Jesus replied that Elijah had already come, and "they knew him not . . . . Then understood the disciples that he spake unto them of John the Baptist" (Matt. 17:10, 12–13). Jesus saw John the Baptist as fulfilling the Malachi passage, for John came in the same fearless spirit of prophecy that characterized Elijah.

3. John's Message

John's message, along with a dominant personality, was the secret of his power. He preached on sin, repentance, and judgment to come. "Repent ye; for the kingdom of heaven is at hand" (Matt. 3:2). The word translated "repent" means to change one's mind. Therefore, repentance involves a radical change of attitude to the point of a complete reversal in life's direction. The "kingdom of heaven" as found in Matthew is the same as the "kingdom of God" as found in Mark and Luke. It connotes the rule of

God in the minds and hearts of his people. What John the Baptist was advocating for the crowds of that day was that they reverse the direction of their entire living, for the kingdom was at hand.

According to Luke, John preached to the multitudes, "Ye offspring of vipers, who warned you to flee from the wrath to come? Bring forth therefore fruits worthy of repentance" (3:7–8). The "wrath to come" refers to judgment and to the justice to be meted out. All evildoers will reap the reward of their sins; therefore, a real repentance, issuing in a change of conduct, is necessary. All that is good and fine will last; all that is evil and worthless will be destroyed by fire. He declared, "And even now the axe also lieth at the root of the trees" (3:9). The "now" refers to the coming of the Messiah, the agent in the crisis that is soon to appear. John was trying to prepare the people, by their repentance and change in their life-style, for the advent of the Messiah.

We know the ethical slant of John's preaching by his answers to questions posed by three groups who confronted him (Luke 3:10–14). People are to overcome the temptation of greed by sharing food and clothing to those who desperately need it. They are to refrain from all extortion, or the obtaining of money or promises by threat or force. They are to refrain from wrong accusations and are to be content with what they possess. He does not ask his hearers to leave their professions for some other calling; he merely suggests a stricter adherence to the requirements and demands of the one in which they are already involved.

4. Not the Messiah

During the first century A.D. there arose in Christian circles what became known as a John-the-Baptist sect or party. These people had difficulty deciding whether Jesus of Nazareth or John the Baptist from the wilderness of Judea was the Messiah. They were therefore reluctant to pull away from John and to follow Jesus, as did Andrew and his unnamed friend (John 1:35–40).

As John continued his persuasive preaching, people heard him, repented, and were baptized. Probably many of his listeners searched their Scriptures for passages concerning the Messiah. Could this strange, fearless proclaimer of repentance possibly be the Messiah? Could this man who was causing such a spiritual upheaval along the Jordan be the long-awaited deliverer of the Hebrew people? It was true that "all men reasoned in their hearts concerning John, whether haply he were the Christ" (Luke 3:15). John asserted repeatedly that he was not the Messiah. When the Jews sent priests and Levites to ask his identity, he replied, "I am not the Christ. I am the voice of one crying in the wilderness, Make straight the way of the Lord, as said Isaiah the prophet'' (John 1:20, 23).

John added that one was coming after him of whom he was not worthy to unloose the latchet of his shoe (v. 27). He testified of Jesus, ''He that cometh after me is become before me: for he was before me'' (John 1:15). He also declared of Jesus, ''He must increase, but I must decrease'' (John 3:30). On one occasion, seeing Jesus, he said, ''Behold, the Lamb of God, that taketh away the sin of the world!'' (John 1:29). The Gospel writers made it very evident that John the Baptist was *not* the Messiah, but merely his Forerunner.

5. Baptism of Jesus

Josephus, the Jewish historian, mentioned the preaching of John in his *Antiquities* (XVIII, V, 2); but he implied that John's message was merely ethical, concerning only what man is to do. Yet John's message was distinct in its messianic nature, for it contained the strong hope of a coming Messiah.

As an outward symbol of their inward change due to repentance, John baptized in the Jordan all who would receive his message. The Jews had the custom of baptizing proselytes, Gentiles wishing to enter Judaism. However, John was baptizing Jews, and in this respect his baptism was unique. He told the Jews that their blood descent from Abraham was not enough. ''Think not to say within yourselves, We have Abraham to our father: for I say unto you, that God is able of these stones to raise up children unto Abraham'' (Matt. 3:9). What was required was genuine repentance, followed by baptism as a symbol of that repentance (Mark 1:4; Luke 3:3).

Suddenly there appeared at the Jordan one who needed neither repentance nor baptism, for he was without sin (2 Cor. 5:21; Heb. 4:15). Jesus was thirty years of age (Luke 3:23) when he came to John with the simple request that John baptize him. Up to this time Jesus had evidently been in the carpenter's shop at Nazareth.

Why he requested baptism is something that has puzzled New Testament scholars for centuries; even John the Baptist was at a loss to understand Jesus' request (cf. Matt. 3:14). Why should a sinless one submit to a rite that was a symbol for repentance and the cleansing from sin? Men through the ages have given varied explanations for Jesus' request. Matthew quoted one simple statement, Jesus' reply to John. ''Suffer it now: for thus it becometh us to fulfil all righteousness'' (3:15). The word *suffer* is used in the sense of allow or permit; so Jesus was asking the prophet of the Jordan to execute his request "to fulfil all righteousness." Within this phrase lies the key to Jesus' thinking; but personal penitence is not a possibility.

Several explanations concerning Jesus' baptism have been offered. *One,* it denoted the beginning of Jesus' public ministry. It was his announce-ment, so to speak, that the time had arrived for him to devote himself completely to the special work for which he had come to earth, the accomplishment of man's redemption. It was an official dedication to the great atoning work of the ages. *Two,* it was a chosen act of self-identification with the sinful humanity he had come to redeem. He became one with sinful people, took upon himself their sins, and received in their behalf the baptism of repentance. *Three,* it was Jesus' stamp of approval upon everything that John was doing. It was his acceptance of John's work as the Forerunner of his own very significant ministry. However, these attempts at explanation do not completely satisfy our thinking on the matter.

As Jesus was baptized a miraculous thing occurred; "the heavens were opened unto him, and he saw the Spirit of God descending as a dove, and coming upon him; and lo, a voice out of the heavens, saying, This is my beloved Son, in whom I am well pleased" (Matt. 3:16). This constituted Jesus' "anointing" at his baptism as the Messiah, an anointing that took place through the activity of the Holy Spirit. It is the one place in the Scriptures where all three persons of the Trinity are seen functioning at one and the same time. The Father was speaking from heaven; the incarnate Son was being baptized; and the Holy Spirit was descending as a dove. (See also Matt. 17:5 and John 12:28.)

What does the *term* "as a dove" connote? Matthew implied that the Spirit descended in the same manner in which a dove would descend. Luke, however, stated that the Spirit descended "in a bodily form, as a dove" (Luke 3:22). These words imply much more than manner; they refer to form. It is almost as though the Spirit came objectively, materialistic-ally. It is hard to state in an absolute way just *how* the Spirit did descend upon Jesus, but we can say that something miraculous happened as he *did* descend.

The Hebrew term *Messiah* and the Greek term *Christ* have an identical meaning, "anointed." In the Old Testament, prophets, priests, and kings were actually anointed with oil, the underlying idea being that they were thus qualified for their office. Thus the term *anointed* came to denote, in a symbolical sense, those who were set apart for some particular work. Saul, David, and Solomon were anointed with oil, the first two by Samuel and the last by Zadok. The term *Jesus Christ* means Jesus the anointed. At his

Jordan River

baptism the Spirit descended upon Jesus, thus anointing him for the great work he was soon to accomplish. There was an anointing that constituted a solemn consecration to his work as the Messiah. In the synagogue at Nazareth Jesus interpreted Isaiah's words as being fulfilled in him, "The Spirit of the Lord is upon me, Because he anointed me to preach good tidings to the poor" (Luke 4:16–18).

Peter preached of "Jesus of Nazareth, how God anointed him with the Holy Spirit" (Acts 10:38). In one of the great messianic passages of the Old Testament, Isaiah predicted of the Messiah that "the Spirit of Jehovah shall rest upon him" (Isa. 11:2); this was fulfilled at Jesus' baptism with the descent of the Holy Spirit as a dove. This does not mean that Jesus did not possess the Spirit prior to his baptism; it merely denotes that the Spirit came in a special way to anoint him with extraordinary power and guidance.

John's Gospel does not give the narrative of the baptism of Jesus, but it does refer to the descent of the Holy Spirit "as a dove out of heaven." In fact, John the Baptist indicated that the descent of the dove was God's sign to him of the certainty of Jesus' divine sonship (John 1:32–34).

6. The Temptations of Jesus

Right after his baptism, Jesus experienced a period of testing generally known as the temptations; all three of the Synoptics tell us that the Spirit led him into the wilderness for forty days, where he was tempted by Satan (Matt. 4:1–11; Mark 1:12–13; Luke 4:1–13). Mark has the shortest version: "And straightway the Spirit driveth him forth into the wilderness. And he was in the wilderness forty days tempted of Satan; and he was with the wild beasts; and the angels ministered unto him" (1:12–13).

There seems to be a relationship between Jesus' baptism and the temptations. At the baptism he was declared to be the beloved Son of God; for forty days afterward he wrestled with all the implications involved in such a divine status. What was required in his ministry of redeeming mankind? What was involved in his messiahship? Would the path of the atonement be easy, or would it be costly? At any rate, tradition says that this spiritual struggle took place at Mt. Quarautania in Judea, a place west of Jericho and about 1500 feet above the Jordan valley.

According to Matthew, the first temptation concerned the physical needs of man. The devil said, "If thou art the Son of God, command that these stones become bread." Jesus' answer was a quotation from the book of Deuteronomy. "Man doth not live by bread only, but by everything that proceedeth out of the mouth of Jehovah" (Deut. 8:3). The temptation was to make his ministry primarily concerned with the physical requirements of men.

The people of Jesus' day thought that the new age brought in by the Messiah would be characterized by an abundance of material things. The hungry people very much wanted a kingdom built on bread (John 6:31–34), and Palestine had an abundance of rocks to be converted into bread. If Jesus produced bread, this would seem to the people a sign of the Messiah's coming. If Jesus were to use his power to satisfy the bodily needs of mankind, he would gain their love and confidence. But he rejected such an idea, for he would not buy their affection with a display of better conditions. Man's life depends on more than bread; it is derived from obedience to God's Word.

The second temptation in Matthew's account is the third in Luke's account; it concerns the use of his messianic power to produce a spectacular display. Satan took Jesus to Jerusalem, set him upon the pinnacle of the Temple, and said to him, "If thou art the Son of God, cast thyself down: for it is written, He shall give his angels charge concerning thee: and On their hands they shall bear thee up, Lest haply thou dash thy foot against a stone." Again Jesus answered by means of a quotation from Deuteronomy, "Ye shalt not tempt Jehovah your God" (Deut. 6:16).

Jesus did not want to use his messiahship to win the loyalty of his followers through a spectacular show of power. According to a Jewish tradition, when the Messiah came he would appear on the pinnacle of the Temple and announce deliverance for the Jews; but there was no belief that he would cast himself down from the Temple. The devil quoted Psalm 91:11–12, but misinterpreted that which he quoted. He was trying to make Jesus court disaster in order to test the reliability of God's promised protection. Jesus was not willing to thrust himself into peril for such a superficial reason.

The third temptation does not begin with the words "If thou art the Son of God," as do the other two. Taking Jesus to a very high mountain, the devil displayed to him the kingdoms of the world in all their glory and then said, "All these things will I give thee, if thou wilt fall down and worship me." Jesus replied with a terse command: "Get thee hence, Satan." Then for the third time he quoted the book of Deuteronomy. "Thou shalt fear Jehovah thy God; and him shalt thou serve" (Deut. 6:13). Luke's account adds a little more of what the devil said to Jesus. "To thee will I give all this authority, and the glory of them: for it hath been delivered unto me; and to whomsoever I will I give it" (Luke 4:6). Satan's claim was parallel to the Jewish view; for most Jews believed that the devil controlled the world, using it as he saw fit.

The Jews hoped that when the Messiah appeared he would lead his people against Rome and restore the golden era of David and Solomon. In a sense, much of the "gold" of that age was tarnished, but that was evidently forgotten by the Jews. Such a messianic idea confronted Jesus in the third temptation. Had Jesus identified himself with such a cause, he probably would have secured a large following. Virtually, this would have meant to compromise with world power and domination, thus securing world kingship in a cheap and quick manner. It was the temptation to acquire secular power by submitting to the forces of evil.

Jesus' answer to Satan was firm and final. He would not accept a shortcut to his kingship; for he would not bypass the suffering, the rejection, and the shame, but would take the way of sorrow and death instead. Not only was Satan's offer not the type of kingship he came to institute; to submit to Satan would be to deny his very sonship, for his supreme loyalty was to his Father in heaven.

When the devil failed to entice Jesus to lower his standards of messiahship, he departed. Luke added, "And when the devil had completed every temptation, he departed from him for a season. And Jesus returned in the power of the Spirit into Galilee" (4:13–14). The phrase "for a season" should be noted, for this did not put an end to temptations during the earthly life of our Lord. The writer of Hebrews revealed that he was "one that hath been in all points tempted like as we are, yet without sin" (4:15). For this very reason he is able to feel with us greatly as we undergo temptation.

7. The Significance of the Temptations

In short, the three temptations were satanic attempts to lure Jesus to manifest his messiahship in an improper way. The first temptation was to submit to materialism and merely supply the physical needs of the people. The second was to submit to sensationalism and win the attention and applause of the multitude through magical feats. The third was to submit to nationalism and lead the Jews to worldwide dominion. All three testings were related to Jesus as the Messiah and the function of his messiahship. They do not inform us of the specific nature of the messiahship; they inform us of that which it was *not* to consist.

The narratives of the temptations rested upon what Jesus told his disciples at a later period. The disciples remembered and retold the story because of the significance of the person and work of Jesus. It was imperative that Jesus decide at the beginning of his ministry the strategy that he would take in his opposition to evil and its devastating hold on man. Jesus needed to wrestle with the problem and to draw up battle lines that would extend throughout his entire ministry. Temptations would occur again and again; therefore, Jesus' resolves, decisions, and concepts must be well fixed in his mind and heart.

After feeding the five thousand, there would be the temptation to accept a kingship. "Jesus therefore perceiving that they were about to come and take him by force, to make him king, withdrew again into the mountain himself alone" (John 6:15). This was the same type of kingship he had refused in the wilderness. Many times he was faced with the possibility of winning a large following by overawing the multitudes with feats of supernatural power. He knew, however, that every miracle was to be performed according to the true nature of his messiahship and for the spiritual enlightenment of man.

When Peter recklessly drew his sword and cut off the ear of Malchus, servant of the high priest, Jesus rebuked him and said, "Or thinkest thou that I cannot beseech my Father, and he shall even now send me more than twelve legions of angels?" (Matt. 26:53). With that help he could have avoided the intense suffering of Calvary he was soon to experience. In the garden of Gethsemane Jesus endured spiritual agony, praying that the cup of suffering might be spared him. "My Father, if it be possible, let this cup pass away from me: nevertheless, not as I will, but as thou wilt" (Matt. 26:39). Again the temptation to accept an easy way to atone for the sins of a depraved humanity was pushed aside.

Jesus' answer to Satan was firm and fixed, so firm that it carried throughout his entire ministry. His obedience and loyalty was to be toward the Father. His messiahship was to be a suffering and agonizing one. All compromise and surrender was to be brushed aside. Death loomed large and foreboding at the very start of his ministry. Jesus ordered Satan to leave, which he did; but the conflict continued due to the decisions Jesus made at the beginning of his ministry. Only with the cross would "the prince of this world be cast out" (John 12:31). The convictions of Jesus demonstrated in the wilderness pervaded his entire ministry with spiritual triumph, a triumph so great that it was really Pilate who was judged by Jesus.

10.

The Early Judean Ministry

1. The Problem of Chronology

The writers of the four Gospels had little interest in an exact arrangement of the events in Jesus' public ministry, and John had less than the other three writers. These four men were more concerned with the *what* and *why* of Jesus' activities than an exact chronology of the episodes. Their purpose in writing was always uppermost in their minds, and this purpose was to a great extent not colored by a time sequence.

We must remember that for a generation or more, most of the events and sayings of Jesus were circulated by word of mouth in separate units here and there. Only rarely would the geographical setting be brought in; nor would the chronology of the various events be given much attention. Therefore, when the writers of the Gospels began their momentous work, they seemed to have little information about *where* or *when* the various occurrences and sayings of Jesus' ministry took place. There is no *definite* step-by-step account in the Gospels of the events and sayings.

Yet the Gospels do present some clear stages in Jesus' ministry. Especially is this so with the Synoptic Gospels. The chronology found in Mark's Gospel is practically the same as that in Matthew and Luke. Therefore, we are able to reconstruct the various stages of Jesus' ministry to a fair degree of accuracy.

In *Our Lord's Earthly Life,* David Smith provides an outline of Jesus' ministry (pp. xiii–xv) that will aid a student in seeing at a glance the various events in the ministry of our Lord. Although widely accepted, it is not presented as perfect. Due to lack of sufficient evidence, some of the events may be out of order. Some of the years and months may not be accurate. But the outline is a useful aid to study.

INTRODUCTION

5 B.C.	Birth of John the Baptist	March
	Birth of our Lord	August

	Flight to Egypt	October
4 B.C.	Return to Nazareth	October
A.D. 7	His first Passover	April 9
A.D. 26	His baptism	January
	Wedding at Cana	Early March

FIRST YEAR OF HIS MINISTRY

A.D. 26	Passover	March 21
	At Bethabara	April and early May
	Arrest of the Baptist	Early in May
	At Sychar	Close of May
	Settlement of Capernaum	Beginning of June
	Inland mission	Close of June till late summer
A.D. 27	In the wheatfield	March

SECOND YEAR OF HIS MINISTRY

A.D. 27	Passover	April 9
	Ordination of the twelve	May
	Mission in southern Galilee	May till early summer
	Mary Magadalene	
	Visit to Nazareth	
	Commission of the twelve	
	At Nain	
	Deputation from the Baptist	
A.D. 28	The Baptist's execution	January
	Retreat to Bethsaida-Julias	February
	Feeding the five thousand	
	Walking on the water	

THIRD YEAR OF HIS MINISTRY

A.D. 28	Passover	March 29
	In Phoenicia	April till June
	In Decapolis	June
	Retreat to Caesarea Philippi	Close of June to mid-August
	Peter's confession	
	First announcement of Passion	
	The transfiguration	
	Healing of epileptic child	

Second announcement of Passion	
Back in Capernaum	Till near close of August
Revisiting inland Galilee	Till mid-September
Passage through Samaria	September 23
At Jericho	September 24
At Bethany	September 25
Arrival at Jerusalem	September 26
Ministry at Jerusalem	Till close of December

A.D. 29

At Bethabara	Probably till close of February
Raising of Lazarus	Close of February
At Ephraim	Till April 10
At Jericho	Over sabbath, April 11
Supper at Bethany	Sunday evening, April 12

THE PASSION WEEK

Triumphal Entry	Monday morning, April 13
Last Supper	Evening of Thursday, April 16
Crucifixion	Friday, April 17
Resurrection	Sunday morning, April 19
Ascension	Thursday, May 29

The length of Jesus' ministry has been discussed. Our only clue in this regard is based upon the number of Passovers in the Gospel of John. Naturally, for this method to be reliable, the Passovers counted would have to be in the framework of one Gospel; one cannot skip from one Gospel to another. Most scholars accept the view that his ministry was a little over three years in length, which is the view taken in David Smith's chart. It is also the view taken in A. T. Robertson's *Harmony of the Gospels,* upon which we will lean heavily in this book for a chronology of the ministry of Jesus.

The early Judean ministry, the substance of this chapter, is found mainly in John's Gospel. It probably lasted between eight and twelve months.

2. Identity of John the Baptist

The Jews sent priests and Levites from Jerusalem to John the Baptist to find out exactly who he was (John 1:19–28). They asked him if he were the Christ, then Elijah, and then "the prophet," to all of which he gave a negative response. He said, "I am the voice of one crying in the wilderness, Make straight the way of the Lord, as said Isaiah the prophet." John's Gospel tells that the priests and Levites had been sent from the Pharisees; but priests and Levites were Sadducees, and the Pharisees and Sadducees were not on friendly terms at all. However, it appears the Pharisees had sent the Sadducees on this embassy to determine just who John the Baptist was. Then the delegation quizzed John about his baptism; but he immediately turned the conversation back to Jesus, declaring that he was not even worthy to unloose the latchet of his Master's shoe. The gap between him and Jesus was greater than that between the slave and his master.

This is one of many remarks concerning the inferiority of John the Baptist to Jesus. The writer of the Fourth Gospel had a reason: the spiritual conquest of a John-the-Baptist sect. There was definitely a group in the first century who revered John the Baptist. Even today there is a group in Iraq, the Mandaeans, who regard John the Baptist as their redeemer. Therefore, when the writer of the Fourth Gospel pointed out the superiority of Jesus over John, he was doubtless addressing a group of "John worshipers" in Asia Minor.

3. John's Identification of Jesus as the Messiah

When John saw Jesus approaching, he exclaimed, "Behold, the Lamb of God, which taketh away the sin of the world!" (John 1:29). Then he added, "After me cometh a man which is become before me: for he was before me" (v. 30), meaning that the one coming after him in his ministry was before him in time. John was referring to the preexistence of Jesus as compared to his own coming into existence at birth. Then John spoke of the sign that God gave him whereby he would recognize the Messiah: "Upon whomsoever thou shalt see the Spirit descending, and abiding upon him, the same is he that baptizeth in the Holy Spirit." John the Baptist is the first of many witnesses in the Fourth Gospel who bear witness to the divinity of Jesus (v. 34).

4. Jesus' First Disciples

A second time John declared of Jesus, "Behold, the Lamb of God!" (John 1:36). Two of John's disciples left him and began following Jesus;

one of these was Andrew, but the other was unnamed. Most scholars believe that the unnamed disciple was John the brother of James; John the apostle is never mentioned by name in the Fourth Gospel. Is the unnamed disciple in this incident (John 1:40) the same as the "disciple whom Jesus loved" (John 20:2; 21:7,20)? Probably so, but nothing conclusive can be stated.

Andrew found his brother, Simon Peter, and said to him, "We have found the Messiah (which is, being interpreted, Christ)" (John 1:41). Upon being brought to Jesus by Andrew, Simon became a disciple also. Jesus said, "Thou art Simon the son of John; thou shalt be called Cephas (which is by interpretation, Peter)" (v. 42). The next day Jesus found Philip of Bethsaida and challenged him to be his disciple also. After he accepted, Philip found Nathanael and invited him to come to see Jesus. When he did so, Jesus also called him as one of his intimate followers (vv. 47–49). Andrew, Simon, Philip, Nathanael, and probably John— these constituted the first selections Jesus made for the small group of twelve with whom he was to be so closely associated for many months.

5. Jesus' First Miracle

Jesus, his mother, and his disciples left Judea and went into Galilee. At Cana they attended a marriage feast. A feast of this nature lasted a week and required much wine. On this occasion it was gone before the festival was to end. When Jesus' mother told him of the crisis, he answered, "Woman, what have I to do with thee? mine hour is not yet come" (John 2:4). The term *hour* did not refer merely to a time of day or an opportunity to do something helpful for the host. It had a deeper meaning, for it pointed to the climax of his ministry, death and resurrection, when God's revelation would be complete. At that hour a greater miracle than changing water into wine occurred. Shame was changed into glory; apparent defeat was changed into triumph; and death was changed into life.

At the marriage Jesus did turn water into wine, providing not only a copious amount but wine of high quality (John 2:1–11). The ruler of the feast complained to the bridegroom about that (v. 10). One might ask, Why did Jesus turn water into wine when a short time previously he had refused to turn stones into bread? The key to John's inclusion of this miracle among the seven contained in his Gospel is located in one statement. "This beginning of his signs did Jesus in Cana of Galilee, and manifested his glory; and his disciples believed on him" (v. 11).

John's term for miracles was *signs* (a better translation of the Greek), and God's glory shines through each sign, giving evidence of Jesus as the incarnate Son of God. The term *glory* is a word rich in meaning in the Fourth Gospel; it represents the supernatural power of God, especially that seen in Christ. "And we beheld his glory, glory as of the only begotten from the Father" (1:14). It is salvation-producing glory, a glory manifested in the signs of Jesus. Beyond the physical miracle John was interested in what it signified.

6. Cleansing of the Temple

Jesus went from Cana to Capernaum, a busy city on the northwest shore of the Sea of Galilee, for a brief time, accompanied by his mother, his brothers, and his disciples (John 2:12).

When it became time for the Passover, Jesus journeyed to Jerusalem (v. 13). This was the greatest of all the religious festivals of the Jews, a time that the Holy City would be crowded with Jews from many countries returning "home" to observe the sacrifices required during the festive occasion. What Jesus saw there displeased him greatly! Gentiles were admitted to the lower and outer court of the Temple. But it had become a marketplace, with all the noises, smells, and wrangling that accompanied such a bustling environment. Here the animals were sold for the sacrifices, and here the money changers set up their tables for the lucrative business of changing all foreign coins into Hebrew coins acceptable in the Temple requirements. A lucrative racket had superceded the holiness that God intended for his holy hill. The Talmud informs us that the Temple markets were controlled by the high-priestly clan; they were termed "the bazaars of the sons of Annas." Jesus' righteous indignation was manifested in open physical expression; he used a whip to drive out the merchants (John 2:14–16). To Jesus the Temple had been profaned; the sacred had been desecrated.

The Jews immediately challenged Jesus' sudden display of authority. "What sign showest thou unto us, seeing that thou doest these things?" (v. 18). The sign he gave them probably seemed very strange, for he replied, "Destroy the temple, and in three days I will raise it up" (v. 19). The Jews of course understood him to refer to their beloved building. He meant the temple of his body and was, therefore, referring to his death, burial, and resurrection after three days. This is one of many misunderstandings found in the Fourth Gospel; several people or groups, from time to time, fail to realize the full import of Jesus' sayings. The Jews replied, "Forty and six years was this temple in building, and wilt thou raise it up in three days?" (v. 20). This statement, made as a defense by

Jesus' opponents, offers a clue as to the year of Jesus' birth (see p. 124).

The problem in connection with the cleansing of the Temple is its date. John's Gospel places the event at the beginning of Jesus' ministry (2:13–22). The Synoptics place it later in Jesus' ministry; Matthew and Luke place it on the day of Jesus' entry into Jerusalem just prior to his crucifixion (Matt 21:12–13; Luke 19:45–46), while Mark places it the day following his entry (Mark 11: 15–17). Does the answer lie in John's topical arrangement, as over against the chronological arrangement in the Synoptics? In this case there was one cleansing, a view taken by many scholars. But other scholars believe there were two cleansings—one early in Jesus' ministry, recorded by John, and another late in his ministry, recorded by the Synoptics. It is difficult to speak definitely when we have so little evidence on which to base an opinion. We can be certain of one thing: Jesus' displeasure, shown in a stern and overt protest against the abuse of the Temple that was evidently a regular practice. He was the true temple, replacing the old one of cult and ritual.

7. Nicodemus and the New Birth

The third chapter of John relates to a conversation between Jesus and Nicodemus, a very distinguished Pharisee and a member of the Sanhedrin (3:1–15). It appears that the author gave his interpretation of the dialogue also (16–21). Nicodemus, a ruler of the Jews, came one night to Jesus with his probing statement. Many guesses have been made as to why he came at night, but nothing can be proven. Surely it was not because of cowardice on his part. There was a saying among the Pharisees of this time that "it is good to study the Torah by night." Maybe this was in his mind, along with the desire to secure a private interview with Jesus when they would not be disturbed. At any rate we may safely surmise that his intention was to seek an interview with one with whom he was deeply impressed.

The theme of the conversation is entrance into the kingdom of God. Nicodemus called Jesus *Rabbi,* a term from the Hebrew meaning "my master" and used here with great respect. "Rabbi, we know that thou art a teacher come from God; for no one can do these signs that thou doest, except God be with him" (John 3:2). Jesus immediately pushed aside this introductory statement of praise and broached the subject of the new birth as the requirement for entering the kingdom. He initiated his reply to Nicodemus with the words "verily, verily," a phrase meaning "truly, truly" and one used when emphasis was to be placed on the statement to follow. "Verily, verily, I say unto thee, Except one be born anew, he cannot see the kingdom of God'' (v. 3). The Greek term translated "anew" could just as well be translated "from above." It is the Greek word *anothen,* one that has a dual meaning.

Nicodemus, as is shown by his answer to Jesus, received the meaning "anew," or "again"; he replied, "How can a man be born when he is old? can he enter a second time into his mother's womb, and be born?'' This is merely another of the numerous cases found in John's Gospel where words or sayings of Jesus were misunderstood, for Jesus evidently meant that it is necessary for one to be born from above. This would be equivalent to saying that God is the source of the new birth. Jesus answered, "Verily, verily, I say unto thee, Except one be born of water and the Spirit, he cannot enter into the kingdom of God. That which is born of the flesh is flesh; and that which is born of the Spirit is spirit'' (vv. 5–6). Jesus was emphasizing that one is born both physically and spiritually and that these are two completely separate processes.

This is the doctrine of regeneration, and this is its most popular presentation in the New Testament. To be born from above is to be born of the Spirit. All men are born physically, but only those who are born of the Spirit enter into the kingdom. This new birth is made possible through the Son of man, who descended from heaven and has ascended back into heaven (v. 13). This Son of man gives eternal life to those who believe (v. 14). Nicodemus probably did not grasp the full meaning of Jesus' words at the time. We hear of him on two more occasions (John 7:50–51; 19:39–40). He was not mentioned in the Synoptics. In the end he proved to be very loyal to Jesus.

John 3:16 is the most famous verse in the entire Bible. "For God so loved the world, that he gave his only begotten Son, that whosoever believeth on him should not perish, but have eternal life." This one verse, more than any other, sums up the mission of our Lord to mankind. Little children in Sunday School are taught this verse from their infancy. After this famous statement John added, "For God sent not the Son into the world to judge the world; but that the world should be saved through him" (v. 17). The Father sent the Son primarily with a saving mission, not a judging one; when Jesus is accepted, he saves the believer. When Jesus is not accepted, he becomes a judge. "He that believeth on him is not judged: he that believeth not hath been judged already, because he hath not believed on the name of the only begotten Son of God" (v. 18).

8. John the Baptist's Praise of Jesus

The Fourth Gospel gives the Baptist's final testimony (3:22–36). Jesus left Jerusalem not long after the Passover season and went "into the land of Judea" (3:22). This was probably the rural section of Judea just south of Samaria. John, not yet cast into prison, was baptizing in this territory because of an abundance of water (v. 23). The account says that Jesus was baptizing also (vv. 22,25), although a reading of John 4:2 leads us to believe that the actual baptizing was done by Jesus' disciples. He baptized "through" them. At any rate, John's disciples remarked to him about Jesus' baptizing; and John defended Jesus by affirming that Jesus would not go beyond what God had commissioned him to do. "A man can receive nothing, except it have been given him from heaven" (3:27). John reaffirmed Jesus' superiority when he said, "He must increase, but I must decrease" (v. 30).

9. The Samaritan Woman and Life-giving Water

Leaving Judea, Jesus traveled north into Samaria to a city called Sychar, "near to the parcel of ground that Jacob gave to his son Joseph: and Jacob's well was there" (John 4:5–6). (Sychar is known as Askar today.) Here he encountered a Samaritan woman, and a memorable conversation ensued (4:4–26). After a long journey Jesus rested at Jacob's well. This well, about a mile south of the village of Sychar and originally about 150 feet deep, supplied water for people during the days of the great patriarch Jacob. Today the well, a shrine for many tourists in the Holy Land, is shallower than it was originally; it is now about 120 feet deep. A large and unfinished church is built near the famous spot.

A Samaritan woman approached the well, and Jesus asked her for a drink. This happened at "the sixth hour." If John used Roman time, this would be at 6:00 P.M. However, he probably used Hebrew time, as elsewhere in the Gospels; this would place the conversation at noon, during the hot midday and at a very unusual time for a woman to come to draw water.

"Jews have no dealings with Samaritans" (v. 9). The Jews and the Samaritans had had an antagonistic feeling toward each other for years, all stemming from the time the Jews returned from the Babylonian captivity under Zerubbabel (537 B.C.) and rebuilt their Temple. When the Samaritans wished to have a part in the rebuilding, the Jews refused them on the grounds that they were no longer full-blooded Hebrews but were a people of mixed blood. When Samaria, the capital city of Israel, fell in 722–1 B.C. to the Assyrians under Sargon II, the Hebrew people of that area were taken captive to territories around the Tigris River. People elsewhere in the Assyrian empire were brought in and placed in and around the destroyed capital of Samaria. These people intermarried with the residue of the Israelites, thus producing a mixed strain.

To the Jews of Jerusalem these people were now Gentiles and not "those of the covenant." The Jews avoided both the Samaritans and their territory. When one wished to go from Judea to Galilee the usual way was to go to Jericho, cross the Jordan, go north through Perea, and then recross the river into Galilee. From Galilee to Judea required the same path. Jesus was vastly different, for he pushed aside the traditional way and took the more direct Samaritan route.

The woman of Samaria was surprised when Jesus requested a drink of water. "Jesus saith unto her, Give me to drink" (John 4:7). She was a woman, a Samaritan, and an immoral character. A good Jew was reluctant to speak to any woman in public. A good Jew did not deal with any Samaritan, man or woman. A good Jew avoided an immoral woman at all times. But Jesus came as Savior of the world, "to seek and to save that which was lost" (Luke 19:10). He threw tradition to the wind in order to help one who was so obviously a sinner. She questioned him, surprised that he, a Jew, would ask a drink of a Samaritan woman.

Jesus answered, "If thou knewest the gift of God, and who it is that saith to thee, Give me to drink; thou wouldest have asked of him, and he would have given thee living water" (John 4:10). The woman, like so many others in the Fourth Gospel, misunderstood; for she said, "Sir, thou hast nothing to draw with, and the well is deep: whence then hast thou that living water?" (v. 11). Jesus was using the term *water* in a spiritual sense. She thought he meant physical water. Jesus added, "Every one that drinketh of this water shall thirst again: but whosoever drinketh of the water that I shall give him shall never thirst; but the water that I shall give him shall become in him a well of water springing up unto eternal life" (vv. 13–14). For the second time the woman showed a misconception of the real intent of Jesus. "Sir, give me this water, that I thirst not, neither come all the way hither to draw" (v. 15).

When Jesus broached the subject of her sin, the many men in her life, she immediately changed the subject to a theological discussion of the nature of worship. She did not wish the sordid details of her private life to be known. She called Jesus a prophet, asking that he solve a problem of long-standing: where should one worship? "Our fathers worshipped in this mountain; and ye say, that in Jerusalem is the place where men ought to worship" (v. 20). "In Jerusalem" meant the Temple of the Jews, Mount Zion. "In this mountain" meant the temple on Mount Gerizim, one of the twin peaks of Samaria. The other peak was Mount Ebal. The ancient city of Shechem, meaning "ridge," was situated on the ridge running between the twin peaks.

The spot was historically prominent; at the base of the two mountains Joshua, the elders, and the children of Israel had ratified the law during the period of Canaanite conquest. Due to the manner of ratification of the law, composed of both blessings and curses, Mount Gerizim became known as the Mount of Blessings, while Mount Ebal became known as the Mount of Curses. Due to the break between the Samaritans and the Jews, the Samaritans built their temple on Mount Gerizim, the Mount of Blessings. From the remark of the woman of Samaria to Jesus, one would surmise that the temple was in existence at the time of her remark; but John Hyrcanus, grandson of Mattathias, had destroyed the temple about a century and a half prior to that time. (Hyrcannus ruled from 134–104 B.C.)

Jesus' reply constitutes the greatest statement about worship found in the entire Scriptures. "But the hour cometh, and now is, when the true worshippers shall worship the Father in spirit and in truth: for such doth the Father seek to be his worshippers. God is a Spirit and they that worship him must worship in spirit and truth" (vv. 23–24). The woman immediately expressed her faith in Jesus as the Messiah, to which Jesus replied, "I that speak unto thee am he" (v. 26). She hurried to Sychar to inform her villagers of the eventful experience at the well and to bring them to Jesus. "Come, see a man, who told me all things that ever I did: can this be the Christ?" (v. 29).

While she was absent the disciples returned from buying food and said, "Rabbi, eat." Jesus said, "I have meat to eat that ye know not." The disciples, like so many others, misunderstood, for they questioned, "Hath any man brought him aught to eat?" (vv. 31–33). When the villagers arrived with the woman, they asked him to tarry with them for two days. "And many more believed because of his word." They rejoiced in having discovered "the Saviour of the world" (vv. 41–42). We see the scope of Jesus' mission; it was not to be merely to some select people. He was to be a Savior for the world.

It is not coincidental that John placed these two remarkable interviews with Jesus so close together. Nicodemus was a high and esteemed Pharisee, a ruler of the Jews. He had prestige and honor, was versed in the Mosaic law, and probably did not lack for the material things of life. The woman at the well was an immoral woman, a Gentile, a social outcast, a sinner of the worst sort. Both needed to come to God the same way, through the grace that came down to man through Jesus of Nazareth.

10. The Arrival in Galilee

After two days Jesus traveled north into Galilee, which would take him and his disciples through the verdant valley of Esdraelon and into the southern hills of Galilee. His ministry in Judea was successful, for "the Galileans received him, having seen all the things that he did in Jerusalem at the feast" (v. 45).

11.
The Galilean Ministry

1. The Province of Galilee

This province of the Roman empire comprised the northern section of the western highlands. It was a mountainous country of about 1,600 square miles, inhabited by people who were simple in their customs and very open in their reception of new ideas. They were hospitable and considerate, presenting quite a contrast to the closed-minded, legalistic Pharisees and the unscrupulous, manipulating Sadducees of Jerusalem. Here Jesus spent his boyhood and youth; for Nazareth, his hometown, was located in the section just north of the fertile plain of Esdraelon. The inhabitants surrounding the Sea of Galilee numbered more than one hundred thousand people, for there were many cities with as many as fifteen thousand people each. Two of the great cities on the Sea of Galilee were Tiberias on the western edge and Capernaum on the northwestern shore. Another city in Galilee that figured in the journeys of Jesus is Cana (not far from Nazareth), where he turned the water into wine.

The whole province was fertile, although the greatest center of activity was the famous body of water that formed the center. The Sea of Galilee was 685 feet below sea level and about thirteen miles long and eight miles wide. On the eastern side towered high and barren hills, while the western side consisted of a gentle slope that ran down to the sea. The plain of Gennesaret to the northeast of the sea and the plain of Esdraelon just south of it were famous for their production of grains and fruits. The water of the lake teemed with fish, and many fishermen with their boats formed a common sight. The great highways from Egypt to Damascus and on to Mesopotamia passed through this region. In this beehive of activity Jesus had his most productive ministry, teaching and preaching. Here the people were responsive to new truth, for they had not closed their minds to new concepts that challenged their customs and beliefs. Some did reject Jesus and his teaching, as at Nazareth; but on the whole the people were very responsive. Here, and not in Judea, he selected his apostles; it is believed that Judas Iscariot was the only one of the twelve selected in Judea, and he betrayed his Master. Judas was from Kerioth in southern Judea.

2. Character of the Galilean Ministry

The length of time involved in this phase of his ministry was about eighteen months, although we cannot speak categorically. Some scholars think it lasted only a year. Capernaum was Jesus' headquarters, for he went from this busy fishing city on various tours of the province.

It was a time of great popularity for Jesus; his fame rang far and wide. Thousands came to hear him preach; great throngs were amazed at his teachings; multitudes came either to be healed or to see someone else miraculously touched and made whole. At one time he fed five thousand men, besides the women and children (Luke 9:10–17). At another time he went into a desert place, probably for prayer; but "the multitudes sought after him, and came unto him, and would have stayed him, that he should not go from them." He informed them that he needed to preach the gospel to other cities also (Luke 4:42–43). On still another occasion he was so thronged by eager listeners that he had to borrow one of Simon Peter's fishing boats and teach the people from his "floating rostrum" (Luke 5:1–3).

The mass surrounding him one day was so great that some men were unable to get their friend before Jesus that he might heal him; they let the man "down through the tiles with his couch into the midst before Jesus," and Jesus healed him (Luke 5:18–26). (Also see Luke 8:40–42; 12:1.) The people were eager to see and to hear him, so they thronged around him.

3. Reasons for Jesus' Popularity

We might seriously ask the reasons for the extreme degree of Jesus' popularity at this time. There were two factors that stood above others. One was his miracles. He had a tender compassion upon all those in physical or spiritual need. Disease was rampant, and there were many cripples. Sin had left its mark upon thousands. Despondency and discouragement were everywhere because of a forlorn political condition: subjugation to Roman tyranny. Extreme Jewish legalism had left no hope spiritually. Into this abject scene walked a person performing miracle after miracle. The news of his extraordinary works of healing were soon spread. All who were sick either came or were carried to him for him to lay his hands upon them. Even the dead were raised (Luke 7:14–15; 7:22; 8:54–55). He traveled throughout all of Galilee "healing all manner of disease and all manner of sickness among the people" (Matt. 4:23).

He even gave to the twelve apostles the power "to heal all manner of disease and all manner of sickness,'' as well as to cast out unclean spirits (Matt. 10:1) and to raise the dead (v. 8). His spiritual claim to forgive sin was so incredible to the Jewish scribes that Jesus used physical healing to manifest his ability to forgive. ''But that ye may know that the Son of man hath authority on earth to forgive sins (he saith to the sick of the palsy), I say unto thee, Arise, take up thy bed, and go unto thy house.'' This the man did (Mark 2:10–12). Jesus was moved with compassion and healed a leper (Mark 1:40–42). Mark also informed us that ''a great multitude, hearing what great things he did, came unto him'' (3:8). This same Gospel writer revealed that Jesus requested his disciples to have a boat conveniently ready, ''for he had healed many'' (3:9–10).

To the hundreds of miraculous healings were added the many miracles of nature, such as the multiplying of the loaves and the fish, the walking on water, the turning of water into wine, the stilling of the storm, and others. At the stilling of the tempest the men remarked, ''What manner of man is this, that even the winds and the sea obey him?'' (Matt. 8:27).

The other factor that drew the crowds to Jesus was the magnificent manner in which he spoke. His preaching and teaching were fresh and challenging. Luke said of Jesus, ''And he taught in their synagogues, being glorified of all'' (4:15). Matthew said, ''And coming into his own country he taught them in their synagogue, insomuch that they were astonished, and said, Whence has this man this wisdom, and these mighty works?'' (13:54). On recording the completion of the Sermon on the Mount, Matthew added, ''And it came to pass, when Jesus had finished these words, the multitudes were astonished at his teaching: for he taught them as one having authority, and not as their scribes'' (7:28–29). This teaching, mainly concerning the kingdom of God, was both simple and profound—simple because all could comprehend, and profound because it plunged to the depths in revealing the nature of God, the purpose of man, and what God expected of man.

Although the words of Jesus that we possess constitute merely a small segment of all that he uttered, they are sufficient to make us understand the overwhelming effect they had on his eager audiences (John 7:46). They reveal the grandeur of his character and of his personality. He spoke boldly, courageously, and with authority. Unlike the scribes, he did not merely quote others; his statements had a ''but-I-say-unto-you'' character. ''For he whom God hath sent speaketh the words of God'' (John 3:34).

4. Preaching of the Kingdom

Mark said, ''Now after John was delivered up, Jesus came into Galilee, preaching the gospel of God, and saying, The time is fulfilled and the kingdom of God is at hand: repent ye, and believe in the gospel'' (1:14–15). The "time is fulfilled" implies that Jesus considered his work equivalent to the fulfillment of God's eternal purpose. He did not come merely to restore the old Davidic throne on a more grandiose scale. His kingdom was to be free from material, racial, and political limitations. This concept as taught by Jesus completely unnerved the Jews; they rebelled at the thought. Even on the day of his ascension, his disciples looked at him and said, "Lord, dost thou at this time restore the kingdom to Israel?" (Acts 1:6). No, he had come to restore Israel to the kingdom—his eternal, spiritual, heavenly kingdom.

5. Healing of a Nobleman's Son

Jesus entered Cana of Galilee, where he had previously turned the water into wine, and healed the son of a nobleman (John 4:46–54). The unusual thing is that the sick boy was in Capernaum, while the father traveled from Capernaum to Cana to see Jesus and make his request. "Sir, come down ere my child die." Jesus' reply was a command to return home, that his son would live. When the man obeyed and returned to Capernaum, he found that the boy had become well at the exact hour that Jesus had uttered his hopeful command. "This is again the second sign that Jesus did, having come out of Judea into Galilee" (v. 54).

The seven miracles or signs in John's Gospel are all very unusual in the "degree of the miraculous." Scholars say they are "heightened" miracles. Jesus not only made wine from water; he made the very best quality of wine. He not only healed the nobleman's son, but did so over a stretch of many miles. He healed a cripple who had been unable to walk for thirty-eight years. He not only fed thousands, using merely five loaves and two fish; they took up baskets of excess food after the meal was over. Not only did he walk on water; there was a tempest at the time. He healed a man who had been blind from birth. He raised Lazarus from the dead, even though his friend from Bethany had been dead four days and bodily decomposition had set in.

6. His Rejection at Nazareth

When Jesus came to Nazareth, his hometown, he entered the synagogue on the sabbath day "as his custom was" (Luke 4:16). When someone handed him a scroll of the prophet Isaiah he read from it, made a comment, and sat down again—all to the amazement of those present (Luke 4:16–22). The sudden wonder of the people was caused by Jesus' applying the passage to himself, a passage found in Isaiah 61:1,2. (See Luke 4:18–19).

Nazareth

Jesus merely unrolled the scroll till he came to this section and then read. He commented, probably in the Aramaic language, and said, "Today hath this scripture been fulfilled in your ears" (4:21), thus declaring that his anointing came from the Holy Spirit. Does not the term *Christ* mean Anointed One? The startled people questioned, "Is not this Joseph's son?" This was to imply that he had grown up there and that they knew him well. How, therefore, could he be the Messiah? Jesus added further comments, which made the people more incensed against him. "And they were all filled with wrath in the synagogue, as they heard these things," and took him to the top of the hill to throw him down from it. However, he escaped and saved himself (4:23–30). His own townspeople had rejected him and his teaching! He had remarked, "No prophet is acceptable in his own country" (v. 24).

7. A New Residence in Capernaum

Jesus left Nazareth and dwelled in Capernaum; as a result, Nazareth never served as his home during his public ministry. He was at Capernaum for a short time during the early Judean ministry (John 2:12). Then he made the city his base of operations during the entire Galilean ministry, departing there about six months or more prior to the crucifixion, never again to minister in Galilee. During the Galilean ministry, however, Jesus left Capernaum from time to time to make journeys throughout the district and surrounding territories.

8. Jesus Calls Four Fishermen

By the Sea of Galilee, near Capernaum, Jesus called four fishermen to leave their nets and to follow him. There were two sets of brothers involved (Mark 1:16–20). To Simon and his brother Andrew, Jesus said, "Come ye after me, and I will make you to become fishers of men." They immediately obeyed. Then he went a little further and likewise called James and John, the sons of Zebedee. They too obeyed without delay. The problem involved is how to reconcile this calling of the first disciples with the calling discussed in the previous chapter under the heading "Jesus' First Disciples" (John 1:35–51). The most plausible answer is that these two pairs of brothers had already become disciples of Jesus on a previous occasion. At this time they were merely leaving their fishing profession to follow Jesus closely in a continuous fashion. James probably became a disciple soon after Simon, Andrew, and John did; and at this incident all four actually followed their new Master. Philip and Andrew had also responded on the previous occasion.

9. A Miraculous Catch of Fish

After teaching the multitudes while sitting in Simon's boat close to shore, Jesus asked Simon to put out into the deep and to let down his nets for fish. Simon objected, saying, "Master, we toiled all night, and took nothing: but at thy word I will let down the nets." The result was a catch of fish so great that the nets were about to break. They asked their partners for help. The boats even began to sink. The incident had a trememdous effect upon Simon Peter, for he must have become vividly aware of his own unholiness. Falling down at Jesus' feet, he cried out, "Depart from me; for I am a sinful man, O Lord." All four of Jesus' new "fishers of men" were amazed at the miracle. Jesus said, "Fear not; from henceforth thou shalt catch men" (Luke 5:1–11).

10. Healing of a Demoniac

On a sabbath day Jesus was teaching in the synagogue in Capernaum. Luke said, "They were astonished at his teaching; for his word was with authority" (4:32). Mark added that it was "not as the scribes" (1:22). Jesus' words and concepts were so strikingly fresh and remarkably vital that the people were astounded. While in the synagogue our Lord performed a work of exorcism, for he rid a man of an unclean spirit, a demon. This may have been the first cure of this variety that Jesus performed. They were all amazed and said, "What is this? a new teaching! with authority he commandeth even the unclean spirits, and they obey him." Soon all Galilee was buzzing with stories of what Jesus had done (Mark 1:21–28).

11. Healing of Simon's Mother-in-Law

Jesus left the synagogue at Capernaum and went to Simon's home, only to find Simon's wife's mother sick with a fever. Jesus "came and took her by the hand, and raised her up; and the fever left her, and she ministered unto them" (Mark 1:29–31). The fact that she was well enough to continue with her household chores shows the completeness of her cure.

At sunset a marvelous scene took place in this home. The people brought so large a group to Jesus to be cured that "all the city was gathered together at the door." And Jesus healed the sick and cast demons out of others (Mark 1:32–34).

12. Jesus' First Tour of Galilee

The next morning, even before daybreak, Jesus arose and went out to a desert place to pray, only to have Simon and others follow to inform him, "All are seeking thee" (Mark 1:35–37). The crowd begged him to stay and not depart from them (Luke 4:42), but Jesus said that he needed to preach "the good tidings of the kingdom of God to the other cities also," that he came to earth for that purpose (v. 43).

Jesus went about all of Galilee, teaching, preaching, and healing. These are the three phases of his ministry, three aspects that are mentioned time and again in the Gospels. As a result his fame increased greatly; for the people came not only from throughout Galilee but from Syria, Decapolis, Jerusalem, Judea, and beyond Jordan. He healed "all manner of disease and all manner of sickness among the people" (Matt. 4:23–25). All three of the Synoptics recount this first tour of the province of Galilee, a tour that may have lasted several months. He went from village to village with both his miraculous healings and his winsome speaking, becoming more popular all the time. What we have recorded in the Scriptures are merely a few of the healings he performed.

13. A Leper Healed

A leper came to Jesus pleading for help. It is hard to determine whether this incident occurred on the tour of Galilee or soon afterward. The unfortunate man said, "If thou wilt, thou canst make me clean." To touch a leper would be to violate the ceremonial law, as found in Leviticus 13:46. Leprosy was not only hideous to look at and painful to bear; it barred all fellowship of the sufferer with his friends and relatives. There could be no worship at the services in the Temple. One had to live off to himself or with other lepers. However, Jesus disregarded the ceremonial law and touched him, saying, "I will; be thou made clean." The motive back of Jesus' act of kindness was compassion, the motive that lay behind most of the healings in the Synoptic Gospels. The man was immediately made clean and whole again (Mark 1:40–42).

Jesus had no hesitation about not observing regulations of the law that stood in the way of his healing a destitute or pitiable person; yet, at the same time, he did not encourage people to become lax in the observance of that law. In this case he went so far as to touch the leper; yet he commanded the healed man to go to the priest and to offer for "cleansing the things which Moses commanded, for a testimony unto them" (Mark 1:44). He also requested the man to say nothing to anyone about his cure, but the man "went out, and began to publish it much" (v. 45). His refusal to adhere to secrecy made Jesus' popularity increase even more. But Jesus "withdrew himself in the deserts, and prayed" (Luke 5:15–16). Evidently there was some sort of a temptation to thwart his true messiahship and use it unworthily.

14. A Paralytic Through the Roof

Jesus returned to Capernaum and was teaching in a house so thronged about with people that one could not even stand at the doorway. They brought a man sick with palsy but were unable to get him into his presence. Going to the roof, they removed tile and let the man down "into the midst before Jesus." Instead of healing the man, Jesus forgave his sins, saying, "Man, thy sins are forgiven thee" (Luke 5:20). Immediately the scribes and Pharisees accused Jesus of blasphemy, for he claimed to forgive sins; and only God can forgive sins. Blasphemy is the act of speaking evil against someone, and in this case they accused Jesus of speaking evil against God. However, Jesus let his power to heal the man demonstrate his power to forgive the man. He healed him, and the man departed for home "glorifying God." The astonishment of the people moved to the extent of actual fear. "We have seen strange things today" (Luke 5:18–26).

15. Calling of Matthew

All three of the Synoptic Gospels tell of the addition of Matthew, also called Levi, to the nucleus of disciples already committed to the cause. Matthew was a publican "sitting at the place of toll" when Jesus said, "Follow me." Matthew immediately obeyed. A publican was a man very unpopular with the Jews, for he collected taxes for the Romans. He was one who secured his livelihood due to a state of subjugation by a foreign power. The Jews would not let a publican in the synagogue. They considered him to be on a very low level of society.

Matthew invited Jesus to his home to a great feast, and not only Jesus but also many other publicans and sinners as well. Such a sight soon brought the censure of the scribes and Pharisees, for the exclusiveness of their Judiasm would not permit such a mingling with people who were ceremonially unclean. They were evidently too timid to mention the subject to Jesus, so they questioned his disciples. Jesus answered, "I came not to call the righteous but sinners" (Mark 2:13–17).

16. The Problem of Fasting

The Pharisees of that day fasted, on the Day of Atonement, at regular public fasts and twice each week. Jesus did not require his followers to fast and was therefore criticized by the Pharisees for neglecting what to them was vitally important. Jesus seldom mentioned fasting; and whenever he did so, it was generally to condemn fasting as a means of self-discipline. Fasting should be done only as an expression of true sorrow and grief. He used three arguments in defending his disciples for not fasting; one is based on a wedding, one on a garment, and one on wineskins (Matt. 9:14–17).

The kingdom of God was many times viewed as a wedding feast. Jesus was the Messiah ushering in the messianic age. Therefore, he declared that those at a wedding feast do not fast as long as the bridegroom is with them; they fast after the bridegroom has departed. As long as they had Jesus with them they would not fast, for the wedding feast of the messianic age had arrived.

The two illustrations that followed showed that Christianity cannot be contained in the old forms of Judaism. Men do not sew a piece of new cloth that has not shrunk on a garment that has been washed many times. It would tear loose. Also, men do not put the fresh juice of the grapes into a wineskin used the previous year. It would crack and spill the wine. Men put new wine in new wineskins. Jesus was attempting to say, "Don't force my teaching back into the molds of Judaism. Let it stand by itself. It cannot be cramped by the narrowness of Jewish tradition."

17. Sabbath Controversies

The Jews considered the sabbath a sacred institution and observed every sabbath requirement imposed by Judaism in a very meticulous manner. It began at sunset on Friday and ended at sunset on Saturday. Its observance had grown into a very burdensome and cumbersome thing. The Mosaic law as found in the Old Testament had placed some restrictions on the sabbath; but the Jews, starting from there, had multiplied these restrictions many, many times. To endeavor to observe all of them was a very complicated matter, almost impossible. As a result, the Jews had defeated the very purpose of the sabbath: rest, relaxation, and worship. Even the rabbis had difficulty in observing the regulations and had, therefore, resorted to deception. By conniving and trickery they kept the letter of the law, but they did so in such a manner that they could do what they selfishly wanted to do at the same time. This amounted to a superficial legalism, something that disgusted Jesus greatly.

Some of the restrictions placed on the sabbath by the Jews were ridiculous. One could not wear false teeth on the sabbath, since this amounts to carrying a burden. One could not pull out a grey hair, since this is work. One could not pick a head of wheat from the stalk, for this is reaping. Jesus honored the restrictions placed on the sabbath by the Scriptures—Exodus, Leviticus, Deuteronomy—but had absolutely no regard for the restrictions placed there by the prominent rabbis of the ages. This man-made "tradition of the elders" had destroyed the very spirit of the sabbath. Jesus said, "The sabbath was made for man, and not man for the sabbath" (Mark 2:27).

Three controversies concerning the sabbath arose at this time, disputes involving Jesus and the Pharisees. One occurred when Jesus healed a lame man at the pool of Bethesda on the sabbath (John 5:1–47). Another occurred when the disciples plucked ears of grain in the fields on the sabbath (Matt. 12:1–8). A third occurred when Jesus healed a man with a withered hand in a synagogue on the sabbath (Matt. 12:9–14).

18. Lame Man at Pool of Bethesda

This dramatic incident found in John 5 seems to fit into the chronology of Jesus' ministry at this juncture. "After these things there was a feast of the Jews; and Jesus went up to Jerusalem" (John 5:1). What was this feast of the Jews? Was, it a Passover or one of the other prominent feasts? This is the controversial feast previously discussed in this book, for it figures prominently in determining the length of Jesus' ministry. (See "John" in chapter 7, "A View of the Four Gospels.") Most scholars believe that this feast was the Passover.

"Now there is in Jerusalem by the sheep gate a pool, which is called in Hebrew Bethesda, having five porches. In these lay a multitude of them that were sick, blind, halt, withered. And a certain man was there, who had been thirty and eight years in his infirmity" (vv. 2–5). Jesus healed the man, saying, "Arise, take up thy bed, and walk." The man willingly obeyed.

Since this cure was performed on the sabbath, a controversy ensued. The Jews criticized the man for carrying his pallet on the sabbath and remonstrated with Jesus for healing on the sabbath. "And for this cause the Jews persecuted Jesus, because he did these things on the sabbath." When Jesus called God his Father, they criticized him for making himself equal with God (John 5:9–18). Jesus then entered into a long discourse in which he refuted the ones censoring him for the so-called sabbath-breaking. Jesus' discourse rested on the firm foundation of the marvelous relationship between the Son and the Father (vv. 19–47), a recurrent theme in John's Gospel.

19. Disciples' Plucking Grain

This sabbath controversy is located in the Synoptic Gospels. It appears that soon after the healing and the dispute at the pool of Bethesda, Jesus returned to Galilee to continue his ministry there. His popularity continued to grow despite the apparent opposition of a few of the Jews.

"At that season Jesus went on the sabbath day through the grainfields; and his disciples were hungry and began to pluck ears and to eat." The Pharisees immediately criticized them for doing so on the sabbath, since this act was considered reaping (Matt. 12:1–2). God had provided six days in which to do work considered labor; stoning was the punishment for those who labored on the sabbath (Ex. 31:14–15; 34:21). The tradition of the elders listed thirty-nine classes of work that were declared illegal when done on the sabbath. Reaping was one of these. Jesus defended himself and the disciples with various arguments, climaxing with the pronouncement, "For the Son of man is lord of the sabbath" (v. 8). It was on this occasion that he remarked, "The sabbath was made for man, and not man for the sabbath" (Mark 2:27). Minute legalistic exactions had defeated the very purpose of God's giving the sabbath.

20. Man with a Withered Hand

The Synoptics record a controversy that took place in a synagogue in Galilee. The scribes and the Pharisees came with an evil intent, that of watching to see whether Jesus would heal a certain man with a withered hand. They asked him, "Is it lawful to heal on the sabbath day?" Jesus answered this query in his usual manner; he never answered categorically, with a yes or no, but with a counter-question or an example. He said that if a sheep falls into a pit on the sabbath, it is lifted out, and that a man is much more valuable than a sheep. Requesting the man to extend the withered hand, he made it whole. This act, however, had a disastrous effect; "the Pharisees went out, and took counsel against him, how they might destroy him" (Matt. 12:9–14). With the people he was becoming more popular all the time, but with the Pharisees and the scribes the exact opposite was occurring. Matthew added that Jesus noticed this attitude on the part of the Pharisees and departed. However, many people followed him and were healed. He charged them not to make him known (vv. 15–16).

21. Selection of the Twelve

The disciples were a very important element in the public ministry of Jesus, and we have already seen the selection of six of them. At this time the Gospels report on the entire twelve chosen from among his many followers (Mark 3:13–19). The reason for their selection is presented by Mark: "that they might be with him, and that he might send them forth to preach" (3:14). Mark used neither the term disciple nor apostle, and Matthew (10:1–4) and Luke (6:12–16) used the term disciple. Besides the three lists in the Synoptics, there is a list in Acts 1:13; but Judas Iscariot is omitted from the Acts account. Peter's name heads each list.

There are two sets of brothers, Simon Peter and Andrew, and James and John (sons of Zebedee). Then come Philip, Bartholomew, Matthew (also called Levi), Thomas, James the son of Alphaeus, Thaddeus (Luke and Acts name him Judas, the son of James), Simon the Cananean (Luke and Acts say "the Zealot"), and Judas Iscariot. Bartholomew is generally understood to be another name for Nathanael, as found in John's list of the first apostles. Peter is a surname given to Simon by Jesus. (*Peter* and *Cephas* are the same; the former is from Greek and the latter from Aramaic.) Thomas is also called Didymus, a name from the Greek meaning *twin*.

Some of those chosen do not play important parts in the Gospels' presentation of the ministry of Jesus; they are little more than names in the lists of apostles. There are three, however, who formed an inner circle, so to speak, in the twelve. They are Peter, James, and John. They were with Jesus on the mount when he was transfigured, and they went deeper into the garden of Gethsemane with him when he prayed on the eve of the cross. These three are the only ones who continued to be prominent after Jesus' death and resurrection, and Peter was the one who was by far the most prominent in the history of the early church.

However, just because Peter was the spokesman for the twelve during Jesus' ministry, he should not be considered the leader of the group during that time. The rivalry and disputes that existed among the twelve show that they considered Jesus to be the leader till after the cross, resurrection, and ascension. The fact that there were twelve must have been based on the twelve tribes of Israel, probably looking forward to the new Israel being created by our Lord through his great atoning work. Under the care and leadership of these men the new Israel would develop.

22. Sermon on the Mount

The longer version of this famous address of Jesus is found in Matthew 5–7; the shorter form is in Luke 6:17–49. Not only did the twelve need instructions as to what Jesus expected of them; all of his disciples of all the ages need to understand what God expects of his children. Therefore, immediately after the selection of the special twelve Jesus "went up into the mountain," sat down, and began to teach. Sitting down was after the custom of Jewish teachers at that time. Luke said he sat "on a level place," which might easily be a level place on a mountain (Matt. 5:1–2; Luke 6:17). Even though Matthew's version of the sermon is longer and more detailed than Luke's, it is not to be considered a complete account of the sermon but merely a summary of it. Jesus probably gave much more that day than what we now possess in Matthew's account; the entire sermon may have required several hours in its presentation.

The sermon is very practical, for in it Jesus makes very clear what is expected of the redeemed. It concerns what man is to *do*, to *believe*, and to *be*. It has to do with human behavior. Portions of it have been quoted by teachers and preachers time and again. The results of the sermon were amazing. "And it came to pass, when Jesus had finished these words, the multitudes were astonished at his teaching: for he taught them as one having authority, and not as their scribes" (Matt. 7:28–29).

A complete discussion of the sermon, so thought-provoking in every detail, is impossible in a book of this nature. Every student is encouraged to read the account as it is found in Matthew's Gospel. A brief analysis of the main points, taken from Robertson's *Harmony of the Gospels,* is as follows:

1. The Introduction (Matt. 5:3–12; Luke 6:20–26). The Beatitudes and the Woes. Privileges of the Messiah's Subjects.
2. The Theme of the Sermon: Christ's Standard of Righteousness in Contrast with that of the Scribes and Pharisees (Matt. 5:13–20).
3. Christ's Ethical Teaching Superior to that of the Scribes in Six Items or Illustrations—Murder, Adultery, Divorce, Oaths, Retaliation, Love of Enemies—(Matt. 5:21–48; Luke 6:27–30; 32–36).
4. The Practice of Real Righteousness Unlike the Ostentatious Hypocrisy of the Pharisees, as in Almsgiving, Prayer, Fasting (Matt. 6:1–18).
5. Single-hearted Devotion to God, as Opposed to Worldly Aims and Anxieties (Matt. 6:19–34).
6. Captious Criticism, or Judging Others (Matt. 7:1–6; Luke 6:37–42).
7. Prayer and the Golden Rule (Matt. 7:7–12; Luke 6:31).
8. The Conclusion of the Sermon. The Lesson of Personal Righteousness Driven Home by Powerful Parables (Matt. 7:13 to 8:1; Luke 6:43–49).

23. Miracles at Capernaum and Nain

When Jesus finished the sermon, he entered Capernaum. A centurion, a Roman officer over a hundred men, came to him, asking that he heal his servant. He said to Jesus, "Lord, I am not worthy that thou shouldest come under my roof: but only say the word, and my servant shall be healed" (Matt. 8:8). Evidently this Roman, this Gentile, knew of the Jewish belief that a Jew's entrance into a heathen home was considered to bring on ceremonial defilement. He also believed that Jesus could heal at a distance. Our Lord praised his faith, stating that he had not seen a faith so strong among the Israelites (v. 10). The young servant "was healed in that hour"

Capernaum, ruins of synagogue

(v. 13). This incident reveals Jesus' attitude toward the Gentiles and toward all persons in need. The faith of the centurion was rewarded (Matt. 8:5–13).

Soon after this event Jesus traveled south to the village of Nain, accompanied by his disciples "and a great multitude." Near the gate of the city the people carried out to Jesus "one that was dead, the only son of his mother," a widow. He said to the mother, "Weep not," and to the body being carried to him, "Young man, I say unto thee, Arise." The boy began speaking. This strange happening became known even throughout all Judea (Luke 7:11–17).

24. A Message from John the Baptist

John the Baptist was still alive when Jesus was performing these things, for John was in prison at Machaerus, east of the Dead Sea. Herod Antipas had placed him there because John had reproved Herod for his unholy marriage to Herodias, former wife of his half brother. The type of ministry Jesus was performing puzzled even John. He sent a note to Jesus asking, "Art thou he that cometh, or look we for another?" (Matt. 11:3). As he languished in prison John evidently expected to hear that Jesus had begun his messianic reign, but the news he anticipated never arrived. News of greatly different activities on the part of Jesus reached his ears.

John's question could not be answered by a mere yes or no. Jesus *was* the Messiah, but a very *different* Messiah from what John expected. Jesus told the messengers to inform John of all they had seen and heard. He wanted the Baptist to realize that he truly was the Messiah and that he was doing the significant things relative to the kingdom after all. John had *not* been the Forerunner to the wrong person.

As the messengers from John were returning with Jesus' answer, Jesus began to praise and to eulogize John to the multitude around him. He termed him "much more than a prophet," saying that "among them that are born of women there hath not arisen a greater than John the Baptist." He said of John, "This is Elijah, which is to come" (Matt. 11:7–15).

On the heels of his praise of John, Jesus denounced the unrepentant cities around the lake that would not receive his teaching (Matt. 11:20). The cities named were Chorazin, Bethsaida, and Capernaum. Tyre and Sidon, with especially bad reputations among the Jews, would have repented, whereas Chorazin and Bethsaida were not moved at his pleas. Sodom, a city destroyed by fire and brimstone because of an unusual degree of wickedness, would have repented and still have existed had it witnessed what Capernaum had seen of the works of Jesus. The final judgment will be worse for Capernaum because of rejected opportunity (Matt. 11:20–24).

It was at this time that Jesus issued that glorious invitation, read and accepted by millions through the ages. "Come unto me, all ye that labor and are heavy laden, and I will give you rest. Take my yoke upon you, and learn of me; for I am meek and lowly in heart: and ye shall find rest unto your souls. For my yoke is easy, and my burden is light" (Matt. 11:28–30).

25. In Simon the Pharisee's Home

Luke alone recorded Jesus' visit to the home of a Pharisee named Simon. Simon, though inviting Jesus for the express purpose of eating a meal, must have thought that some of the usual courtesies could be dispensed with for this carpenter and his followers; no servant washed their feet as they entered the house. In contrast to Simon's lack of giving was the generous gift and outpouring of soul of a sinful woman, who, on learning that Jesus was there, entered with an alabaster cruse of ointment. She wept as "she began to wet his feet with her tears, and wiped them with the hair of her head, and kissed his feet, and anointed them with the ointment" (Luke 7:38). Simon, evidently knowing the reputation of the woman, had mental misgivings that Jesus would so much as let the woman touch him. Simon's training as a Pharisee would not permit such.

Jesus, perceiving Simon's inner feeling of reproach, preached him a sermon contrasting the hospitality and warmth of Simon as set over against the extravagant love, affection, and humility of the socially unacceptable woman. Simon gave so little; she gave so much. Jesus said to Simon, "Wherefore I say unto thee, Her sins, which are many, are forgiven: for she loved much." To the woman he said, "Thy sins are forgiven. . . . Thy faith hath saved thee; go in peace" (Luke 7:36–50).

This anointing was evidently quite distinct from one that happened about a year later at Bethany, near Jerusalem, in the house of Simon the leper. In this instance Mary of Bethany anointed Jesus (Matt. 26:6–13). The sinful woman in the early anointing was not Mary Magdalene; a late tradition arose to that effect, but it had no historical support whatever. Luke did not even introduce Mary Magdalene until a few verses later (8:2), and then he described her as a new figure in the chronology of Jesus' ministry.

26. The Second Tour of Galilee

Luke added, "And it came to pass soon afterwards, that he went about through cities and villages, preaching and bringing the good tidings of the kingdom of God." His disciples, certain women, and many others accompanied him on his travels (8:1–3). Luke did not feel led to give us the exact route of Jesus and his following; the very fact that it was extensive and that the gospel of the kingdom of God was proclaimed were the important elements.

27. A Busy Day

So many events evidently occurred on the first day of this second tour that it has been called "the busy day." It was a day similar to the last day of Jesus' public ministry, the one that took place in the Temple in Jerusalem.

One of the first things Jesus did was to heal a blind and mute demoniac. This miracle produced both amazement on the part of the multitudes and criticism on the part of the Pharisees. Since these archenemies of Jesus could not deny that the miraculous healing had taken place, they declared that the cure was effected through the aid of Beelzebub, the prince of demons. Jesus addressed the challengers in stern terms, showing them how contradictory their remarks really were. A kingdom divided against itself could only come to ruin. If Satan were to cast out Satan, he would be divided against himself and would be destroying his own domain. Jesus affirmed that his casting out of demons was "by the Spirit of God," an evidence that the kingdom of God had come upon them (Matt. 12:22–28).

Jesus then asserted that blasphemy against the Holy Spirit was a grievous sin. To ascribe to Beelzebub, the prince of demons, what the Holy Spirit was doing was to blaspheme the Spirit. Our word *blaspheme* comes from the very Greek word used in the Gospels and means to speak evil against. The accusation of the Pharisees was against the Holy Spirit, not against Jesus; for the Holy Spirit was the one through whom Jesus was performing his miraculous act. That is why Jesus made his famous declaration: "Therefore I say unto you, Every sin and blasphemy shall be forgiven unto men; but the blasphemy against the Spirit shall not be forgiven. And whosoever shall speak a word against the Son of man, it shall be forgiven him; but whosoever shall speak against the Holy Spirit it shall not be forgiven him, neither in this world, nor in that which is to come" (Matt. 12:31–32).

The next event on the schedule of the busy day was the request of certain scribes and Pharisees to see a sign. Their motive was to get Jesus to prove his claim to messiahship by this sign. Jesus refused their request; no sign would be given except a future one, the sign of Jonah. This referred to his future resurrection from the dead. Jonah's three-day sea venture was a symbol of Christ's death, burial, and resurrection from the grave, though his listeners were not able to comprehend Jesus' words at the time. "For as Jonah was three days and three nights in the belly of the whale; so shall the Son of man be three days and three nights in the heart of the earth" (Matt. 12:38–40).

The next incident occurred when someone came to Jesus announcing that his mother and his brothers stood outside requesting to see him. Jesus used the incident not only to teach that spiritual relationships are much deeper and more significant than human relationships, but that the foundation stone of spiritual relationships is the performing of God's will. To be in the spiritual family of God is of paramount importance; doing the will of God is indicative of this significant condition. "For whosoever shall do the will of my Father who is in heaven, he is my brother, and sister, and mother" (Matt. 12:46–50).

28. A Great Group of Parables

Sometime during this eventful day, and somewhere by the Sea of Galilee, Jesus felt constrained to teach the people by means of parables. The crowd was so tremendous that he resorted to entering a boat and pushing off somewhat from the shore; "and he taught them many things in parables" (Mark 4:1–2). Matthew and Mark listed the parable of the sower (better termed the parable of the soils), the parable of the seed growing of itself, the parable of the tares, the parable of the mustard seed, the parable of the leaven, and many such parables. Then Jesus left the multitudes and went into the house with his disciples, where he explained the parable of the tares. Then he told the parable of the hidden treasure, the parable of the pearl of great price, the parable of the net, and the parable of the householder. "And it came to pass, when Jesus had finished these parables, he departed thence" (Matt. 13:1–53). These parables must be read in the Scriptures in order to grasp the full meaning that they convey.

We do not know just how many parables Jesus told on that day. Evidently the use of so many of them was due to the growing hostility of the Pharisees and to the need for the disciples to know how to interpret parables. Truly Jesus was the masterful parable teller, though many before him had employed this method of conveying truth. There are many parables found in the Old Testament, such as Nathan's parable of the little ewe lamb (2 Sam. 12:1–6) and Jotham's parable of the bramble king (Judg. 9:7–15). But Jesus related parables that are masterpieces of literary beauty. They are paradoxically simple and profound at the same time. They are extremely rich in spiritual truth.

The Greek word translated *parable* means something thrown alongside.

Therefore, a parable is a concrete saying or narrative used to depict an abstract spiritual truth. To illustrate the kingdom of God, Jesus spoke of a man sowing seed or of a woman putting leaven in some meal or of a net cast into the sea. A parable has been termed an earthly story with a heavenly meaning, which would certainly be true for the parables employed by our Lord in his amazing teaching. Sometimes Jesus' parables take the form of a story or narrative, like the parable of the good Samaritan (Luke 10:30–37) or the parable of the prodigal son (Luke 15:11–24). Sometimes his parables are not of story form but merely convey a single act or a single concept, as the parable of new cloth on an old garment (Matt. 9:16) or the parable of new wine in old wineskins (Matt. 9:17). These are of one-verse duration. Sometimes his parables are short, pithy sayings, as "Physician, heal thyself" (Luke 4:23). Sometimes they are of a paradoxical nature, as "But many that are first shall be last; and the last first" (Mark 10:31).

Jesus wisely used parables because he knew the mental processes of his hearers. He was well aware that a story attracts attention and is long remembered. He knew that something concrete and tangible is easier to comprehend than something abstract and of a nebulous nature. He knew that a short, pungent saying would command attention and give food for meditation at a later period. And Jesus was aware that an illustration would stimulate inquiry about the truth he was endeavoring to convey, as happened when his disciples said to him, "Explain unto us the parable of the tares in the field" (Matt. 13:36). When the disciples asked Jesus why he spoke to the multitudes in parables, he replied, "Unto you it is given to know the mysteries of the kingdom of heaven, but to them it is not given . . . Therefore speak I to them in parables; because seeing they see not, and hearing they hear not, neither do they understand" (Matt. 13:11, 13). Jesus also explained to the disciples the parable of the sower (Matt. 13:18–23) that he had previously related to the multitudes (Matt. 13:3–9).

Two things should be kept constantly in mind when interpreting the parables. First, Jesus meant to convey one truth alone when he presented a parable to his hearers, not several truths. At times certain men have maintained that every person or object in a parable is a symbol of a truth or an abstract concept. This is not true; Jesus wanted to teach one truth alone. Every detail in the good samaritan story does not convey a truth. The point of the whole parable of the good samaritan is to depict who one's neighbor is. Second, the background of a parable must be studied and understood; if the setting of the parable is not taken into account, the meaning may be lost. The method of putting fresh grape juice into wineskins in order to produce wine must be understood, or the point of that parable will be misunderstood.

29. More Healings

There are still more events on the agenda of the busy day. Jesus and his disciples, probably wanting to get away from the crowds, sailed to the other side of the lake. Jesus was weary and fell asleep in the boat. When a violent storm began to gather its force, the disciples went into panic and woke their Master. Jesus merely spoke, and the storm subsided; "there was a great calm." The men said, "What manner of man is this, that even the winds and the sea obey him?" (Matt 8:23–27).

The other side of the lake bordered the country of the Gerasenes, where they met a man with an unclean spirit, who lived in the tombs. This man, worshiping Jesus, cried out, "What have I to do with thee, Jesus, thou Son of the Most High God? I adjure thee by God, torment me not." Jesus healed the man, ordering the evil spirit to leave him. He said, "Come forth, thou unclean spirit, out of the man" (Mark 5:7–8).

When Jesus questioned the unclean spirit concerning his name, the man answered, "My name is Legion; for we are many." He requested Jesus that the spirits be sent into a herd of swine feeding on the mountainside. Jesus fulfilled the request; and the herd, about 2,000 in number, rushed headlong into the sea. The people of that country asked Jesus to leave their territory, not so much because of the swine, apparently, but because of their fear of his power. Seeing the healed man, clothed and in his right mind, was too much for them. Jesus did leave, asking the fortunate man of Gerasa to go proclaim what had happened to him. This is exactly the opposite of what Jesus had been doing—telling the people *not* to relate the miracles he was performing. The reversal in request here is probably due to the fact that he was outside the territory of Herod Antipas. The very fact that there were swine present shows he was in a Gentile area. The man spread the word all over Decapolis (Mark 5:1–20).

When Jesus returned to the western side of the lake, a ruler of the synagogue, Jairus by name, came to him asking that he heal his daughter. The child was "at the point of death." On the way he was thronged with people, so much so that a certain woman could very easily touch his garment and in so doing be healed. While praising the woman for her great faith, Jesus was told by one coming immediately from Jairus' house that the young girl was dead. Jesus entered the house and proceeded to raise the girl from the dead (Mark 5:21–43). We have already seen that he raised up the widow's son at Nain.

All the healings for that day were not over, however. Jesus healed two blind men and also cast a demon out of one who was unable to talk. He commanded both the family of Jairus and the two men who had formerly been blind not to tell of the miracles, a contrast to his request to the man of Gerasa. Jesus had returned to the territory of Herod Antipas.

30. Another Visit to Nazareth

Jesus returned to Nazareth, the village where he had been reared, for a brief visit prior to his third tour of Galilee. Again he was received in a way that must have grieved him tremendously. As he taught in the synagogue on the sabbath, the people made remarks about his teaching, questioning the source of his wisdom. "Is not this the carpenter, the son of Mary, and brother of James, and Joses, and Judas, and Simon? and are not his sisters here with us?" They were completely bewildered (Mark 6:1-6). "And he did not many mighty works there because of their unbelief" (Matt. 13:58). Jesus' self-imposed condition for his healing ministry was faith on the part of the one with the malady needing to be removed.

31. The Third Tour of Galilee

"And Jesus went about all the cities and the villages, teaching in their synagogues, and preaching the gospel of the kingdom, and healing all manner of disease and all manner of sickness" Matthew added that "he was moved with compassion" for the multitudes, for they were "as sheep not having a shepherd" (Matt. 9:35-36). Jesus could see the desperate physical and spiritual needs of the Galileans as they thronged to witness his miracles and as they grasped his every word. He knew they were not receiving spiritual help from their religious leaders. They were shepherdless, even though there were Pharisees, Sadducees, and scribes in abundance. Jesus felt an urge to retrace his steps through their villages and cities and to preach and teach again the good news of the kingdom. He pictured the multitudes as a harvest field, ripe, ready to be reaped. "The harvest indeed is plenteous, but the laborers are few" (Matt. 9:37). They were to pray for laborers.

32. The Twelve Sent Forth

Jesus felt led to enlarge his ministry by sending the twelve disciples on a preaching and healing mission. Mark said he sent them forth "by two and two." He gave them instructions and endowed them with power to work miracles. They were to cast out unclean spirits, to heal, to cleanse the lepers, and even to raise the dead. They were to depend upon the hospitality of the people. If they were apprehended and required to give an account of their work, they should not be anxious about their words, "for it shall be given you in that hour what ye shall speak. For it is not ye that speak, but the Spirit of your Father that speaketh in you." Jesus knew they were bound to encounter opposition, for he stated they would be brought before councils, scourged in the synagogues, and brought before governors and kings. This persecution would be for his sake; but he advised them to move on to another place when they were presecuted (Matt. 9:35 to 10:23).

Jesus continued his instructions to the twelve in a marvelous discourse. (This is contained in one of the five discourses found in Matthew's Gospel. The large group of parables found in Matthew 13 is another of the five. A discussion of these discourses is located in Chapter 7 under "Matthew.") The discourse included a great paradox, one alive with spiritual truth. "He that findeth his life shall lose it; and he that loseth his life for my sake shall find it." Since the disciples were going out in his name, the one receiving them was in effect receiving Jesus (Matt. 10:24–42).

33. Herod Antipas and John the Baptist

Herod Antipas, son of Herod the Great and ruler of Galilee and Perea, heard of all the amazing things that Jesus and his disciples were doing. He concluded that Jesus was John the Baptist raised from the dead. At the same time, rumors circulated that Jesus was Elijah or one of the prophets. The Scriptures do not state that any surmised that he was the Messiah.

The prison where John was kept was at Machaerus, about seven miles east of the Dead Sea. Fortified by the Maccabeans about 100 B.C., it was destroyed by the Romans. Herod the Great rebuilt it; Herod Antipas controlled it at the time of Christ's ministry, since it was located in the lower end of the Perean section of Herod's divided territory. Archaeologists have discovered two dungeons at the site; over these the palace was constructed. It is very probable that John occupied one of these formidable dungeons.

Herodias evidently hated John, for she devised to kill him but was unable to do so (Mark 6:19). Herod Antipas was afraid to execute John for fear of John's following; they considered John a prophet (Matt. 14:5). The birthday of Herod was the occasion of a sumptuous feast, with all of Herod's courtiers and the notables of Galilee invited. During the meal Salome, daughter of Herodias, danced; "she pleased Herod and them that sat at meat with him" (Mark 6:22). As a result, he promised upon oath to present to her whatever she requested, even to half of his kingdom. At the instigation of her mother, Salome replied, "I will that thou forthwith give me in a platter the head of John the Baptist."

Herod was extremely sorry about his rash vow, but he fulfilled his oath and immediately had John beheaded. They brought the head on a platter and gave it to the girl; she in turn presented it to her mother. Herodias' foul scheme was at last complete! "And when his disciples heard thereof, they came and took up his corpse, and laid it in a tomb" (Mark 6:29). Matthew added, "And they went and told Jesus" (14:12). The rugged personality who had swayed the multitudes up and down the Jordan valley would preach no more. The one who looked on Jesus and declared, "Behold, the Lamb of God" was silenced.

12.

The Withdrawals from Galilee

Jesus halted his public ministry four distinct times over a period of approximately six months following the Galilean ministry, a time when his popularity had reached its peak. At that time no formal, concerted opposition to Jesus had arisen; such would come later. The journeys to territories outside the range of Herod Antipas not only gave Jesus some time for rest and relaxation; they also offered occasion for training the twelve for the work ahead. Approximately one year of Jesus' ministry remained; and this was the year in which opposition to him grew, finally climaxing in his crucifixion on Golgotha.

1. The First Withdrawal—Across the Lake

When the twelve returned from their special mission of preaching, teaching, and healing, they reported to Jesus every detail of the eventful journey. Jesus invited them to come "apart into a desert place" and "to rest awhile" (Mark 6:31). Luke said they went to Bethsaida (9:10), which evidently referred to the eastern Bethsaida, a city in the territory of Philip. Philip had renamed it Bethsaida-Julias. This community would have been on the northeastern shore of the lake and outside the territory of Herod Antipas.

Jesus and his disciples went by boat across the lake, while the multitudes followed on foot around the northern shore. When Jesus arrived, the crowd was there to meet him. "He welcomed them, and spake to them of the kingdom of God, and them that had need of healing he cured" (Luke 9:11). Evidently Jesus had to temporarily set aside his intention of retiring; he ministered to the eager crowd.

(1) Feeding the Five Thousand As the day came to a close, the disciples suggested that Jesus dismiss the people so that they could go to the villages for food. He countered that the disciples should feed the crowd, which Matthew said numbered about five thousand men, besides women and children (14:21). Someone found a boy with a lunch of five

Sea of Galilee

barley loaves and two fish; Jesus took this meager bit, looked up into heaven and blessed and divided the morsels, and then gave the food to the disciples to pass among the people. After all the people had eaten, twelve baskets of remaining food were gathered up (Matt. 14:15–21). This is the only miracle recorded in each of the four Gospels.

The motive that lay back of Jesus' feeding his congregation seems to have been compassion, but the meaning far exceeded merely putting food into hungry bodies. Mark said that the multitudes "understood not concerning the loaves, but their heart was hardened" (6:52). John depicted Jesus as the living Bread (6:1–71) in his Gospel. The ability to provide material bread for physical life was superseded by the greater ability to provide heavenly bread for spiritual life: "I am the living bread which came down out of heaven" (6:51).

(2) Effect of the Feeding The throng which had been fed expressed its belief that Jesus was the fulfillment of the prophet promised by Moses to Israel centuries before (Deut. 18:15). "This is of a truth the prophet that cometh into the world" (John 6:14).

Their minds raced to some wrong conclusions. "Jesus therefore perceiving that they were about to come and take him by force, to make him king, withdrew again into the mountain himself alone" (John 6:15). He desired greatly to be their king; but his kind of kingdom was not what they had in mind. Jesus had settled the whole matter in the temptations in the wilderness; now when the temptation reappeared, he withdrew "into the mountain himself alone."

2. Jesus Walks on the Water

While crossing the Sea of Galilee the disciples encountered a storm, "for the wind was contrary unto them" (Mark 6:48). Perceiving that they were having difficulty in rowing, Jesus walked by them on the water. This happened between 3 and 6 A.M. The disciples thought he was a ghost and cried out in fear. Jesus said to them, "Be of good cheer: it is I; be not afraid" (Mark 6:50). Peter wanted to walk to Jesus on the water; but soon after he tried, he became fearful and began to sink. Jesus rescued him and said, "O thou of little faith, wherefore didst thou doubt?" When Jesus and Peter entered the boat, the wind ceased; and they all worshiped Jesus, exclaiming, "Of a truth thou art the Son of God" (Matt. 14:33). The whole incident, one in which there were virtually three miracles, was a very moving experience for the disciples.

On the western shore the next day the people again thronged Jesus. This was somewhere south of Capernaum. "And wheresoever he entered, into villages, or into cities, or into the country, they laid the sick in the marketplaces, and besought him that they might touch if it were but the border of his garment: and as many as touched him were made whole" (Mark 6:56).

3. Bread of Life Discourse at Capernaum

On the next day the multitude came to Capernaum seeking Jesus. When they found him, he said to them, "Ye seek me, not because ye saw signs, but because ye ate of the loaves, and were filled." He informed them that they should seek the meat that brings eternal life, not the meat that perishes. "For the bread of God is that which cometh down out of heaven, and giveth life unto the world." The crowd, misunderstanding, exclaimed, "Lord, evermore give us this bread." Again we see one of the many misunderstandings recorded in John's Gospel. Jesus replied, "I am the bread of life: he that cometh to me shall not hunger, and he that believeth on me shall never thirst." The multitude who had been fed desired to be fed again, but Jesus was offering them living food (John 6:22–40).

In a great discourse Jesus declared himself to be the Bread of life coming down out of heaven. The Jews remonstrated with him, but he continued to speak. "I am the living bread which came down out of heaven: if any man eat of this bread, he shall live for ever: yea and the bread which I will give is my flesh, for the life of the world" (vv. 41–51). The Jews began arguing among themselves, "How can this man give us his flesh to eat?" Jesus continued to assert himself as the bread coming down out of heaven. The result was that many of his followers became offended and left him (vv. 52–66).

Jesus tested the faith of the twelve by saying, "Would ye also go away?" Impetuous Simon Peter answered for himself and the others, expressing faith in Jesus as the giver of eternal life. "Lord, to whom shall we go? thou hast the words of eternal life. And we have believed and know that thou art the Holy One of God" (vv. 68–69). Perhaps the resolute faith of Peter reminded Jesus of the treachery of Judas, for he immediately alluded to one of the twelve who should betray him, meaning Judas Iscariot.

4. The Pharisees and Hand Washing

The Pharisees meticulously washed their hands before eating; the tradition of the elders dictated a prescribed manner for doing so. Where the Torah said, "Remember the sabbath day, to keep it holy" (Ex. 20:8), the tradition of the elders presented many minute exactions of what could be done and could not be done to maintain its holiness. Hand washing prior to eating, done to conform to ceremonial purity, was found in the tradition, not in the Scriptures. The tradition of the elders was just as obligatory to the good Pharisee of Jesus' day as the Torah found in the Scriptures. But to Jesus it was not; to him the tradition was human in origin and did not require obedience (Matt. 15:2–3,6).

Some of the scribes and the Pharisees, having come to Galilee from Jerusalem, observed that Jesus and his disciples ate with unwashed hands. "For the Pharisees, and all the Jews, except they wash their hands diligently, eat not, holding the tradition of the elders" (Mark 7:1–3). They quizzed Jesus and his disciples about their laxity in this traditional requirement. Jesus called them hypocrites and quoted a passage from the prophet Isaiah (29:13), saying that their deceit fulfilled that Scripture. He countered their questions with one of his own: "Why do ye also transgress the commandment of God, because of your tradition?" He informed them that they were voiding the word of God by their tradition. Speaking eloquently, he told them that a man is defiled by what he says rather than by what he hears. A man's speech has its beginnings in his heart (Matt. 15:1–20).

5. The Second Withdrawal—into the Region of Tyre and Sidon

"And from thence he arose, and went away into the borders of Tyre and Sidon" (Mark 7:24). These cities were in the country of Phoenicia, where Solomon secured help and material from King Hiram to build the Temple and where Elijah found relief from the hatred of Ahab and Jezebel. It is known as Lebanon today; its capital and greatest seaport is Beirut.

Jesus sought seclusion, but he was not able to conceal himself. A Syrophoenician woman (part Syrian, part Phoenician), falling at his feet, asked him to cast out a demon from her daughter. Commending the woman for her faith, Jesus healed the child; when the mother returned home the demon had left. This incident was another healing at a distance (Matt. 15:21–28).

6. The Third Withdrawal—North Through Phoenicia, East Toward Hermon, South into Decapolis

Jesus purposely avoided the territory of Herod Antipas. Much of this area belonged to the tetrarch Philip, who governed the districts that were east of the lake and east of the upper Jordan. He would have had no occasion to entertain a feeling of antipathy toward Jesus. His territory was highly Gentile, as were Phoenicia and Decapolis. "And again he [Jesus] went out from the borders of Tyre, and came through Sidon unto the Sea of Galilee, through the midst of the borders of Decapolis" (Mark 7:31).

(1) Many Healed Mark recorded Jesus' healing a man who was deaf

and who also had difficulty in speaking. "And his ears were opened, and the bond of his tongue was loosed, and he spake plain." Jesus requested the multitude not to tell of the miracle, "but the more he charged them, so much the more a great deal they published it." And again the people were astonished "beyond measure" (Mark 7:32–37).

Matthew told of "great multitudes" coming to Jesus at this time, bringing the lame, the blind, the mute, the crippled, and many others to Jesus for healing. When Jesus performed spectacular deeds of restoration, the crowd wondered and "glorified the God of Israel" (Matt. 15:30–31).

(2)   Feeding the Four Thousand   Jesus fed this multitude miraculously, for his compassion for them would not permit him to send them away faint and hungry. He received from his disciples seven loaves and a few small fish. Asking the crowd to sit on the ground, he took the food, gave thanks, divided it, and handed it to the disciples to distribute among the crowd. Everyone there ate all he wanted; yet seven baskets of remaining fragments were gathered up. "And they that did eat were four thousand men, besides women and children" (Matt. 15:38); the women and children probably greatly outnumbered the men. There is no reason to debate about whether there were two feedings or merely one. Mark and Matthew told of both feedings, and these two writers quoted Jesus as referring to both incidents in one statement (Mark 8:19–20; Matt. 16:9–10).

(3)   Request for a Sign   Jesus went into the territory of Magadan (Magdala in the King James), where the Pharisees and Sadducees approached him and requested a sign from heaven as proof of the authority of his claims. In this case the Pharisees and Sadducees, normally at sword points with each other, were combined in their attack against Jesus, their common enemy. Jesus informed them that although they were able to read the signs in the sky and predict the impending weather, they were not able to read the signs he had already displayed before them. "Ye know how to discern the face of the heavens; but ye cannot discern the signs of the times." The signs of the times referred to the wonders and miracles he had performed day after day in their very midst and to the fact that his very presence among them was the most significant event in the history of mankind. He added that no sign would be given to that "evil and adulterous generation" except "the sign of Jonah." In this cryptic phrase he was referring to his death, burial, and resurrection at a later point in his ministry (Matt. 15: 39 to 16:4).

7. The Fourth Withdrawal—Northeast to Bethsaida

Bethsaida was on the northern shore of the Sea of Galilee, east of the

Jordan, and in the territory of Philip. (Some maps record the name as Bethsaida-Julius, and others as Bethsaida-Julias.) At this time Jesus stopped there on his way to Caesarea Philippi. During each of the four retirements he entered territories that were inhabited by Gentiles, who knew little or nothing of Judaism and the Mosaic law. The Greek way of life prevailed, and the Greek language predominated.

Mark said, "And he left them, and again entering into the boat departed to the other side" (8:13). The term *them* refers to the Pharisees and Sadducees just reproached by Jesus. The disciples had forgotten to take bread, having only one loaf in the boat. Jesus used the occasion to teach a lesson, saying, "Take heed and beware of the leaven of the Pharisees and Sadducees." At first they did not comprehend; then they realized that he was referring to the teachings of the Pharisees and Sadducees (Matt. 16:5–12).

(1) A Blind Man Restored Before he arrived at Bethsaida, Jesus healed a blind man by spitting on the man's eyes and putting his (Jesus') hands on the man. After the healing, he requested that the man return to his home by a way other than the village (Mark 8:22–26).

(2) Peter's Declaration at Caesarea Philippi All three of the Synoptic Gospels record a very significant conversation between Jesus and his disciples, culminating in what has been termed Peter's great declaration or great confession. When Jesus left Bethsaida he traveled north to the villages surrounding Caesarea Philippi, a city situated at the foot of Mount Hermon and about twenty-five miles north of the Sea of Galilee. Here the famous Jordan River has its beginning. Jesus talked to his disciples about who he was. He wanted to know about the interpretation his disciples and others had placed on his ministry and on who he really was.

"Now when Jesus came into the parts of Caesarea Philippi, he asked his disciples, saying. Who do men say that the Son of man is? And they said, Some say John the Baptist; some, Elijah; and others, Jeremiah, or one of the prophets. He saith unto them, But who say ye that I am? And Simon Peter answered and said, Thou art the Christ, the Son of the living God. And Jesus answered and said unto him, Blessed art thou, Simon Bar-Jonah: for flesh and blood hath not revealed it unto thee, but my Father who is in heaven" (Matt. 16:13–17).

This striking dialogue between the Master and his disciples has been termed the watershed of the Gospels as well as the fulcrum of the Gospels. It marked a turning point in Jesus' ministry in many ways. For one thing, Jesus' popularity, so marked and so tremendous for many months, began to wane. Those who had pressed him, wishing to make him king, began to sound another note. The swelling tide of public favor began to subside and to be replaced by the signs of a coming storm. Second, prior to this time Jesus' teaching was mainly to the multitudes who thronged him, as is clearly shown by his numerous parables. From this incident on his teaching was directed mostly to the twelve so that they could adequately carry on the responsibility and work that he placed upon them. Third, after Peter's declaration of faith in Jesus as the awaited Messiah, Jesus began to tell openly of his approaching death and resurrection.

As soon as Peter made his confession of faith Jesus voiced his approval of his statement, declaring that the apostle had not received his insight from man but from God himself. (The phrase "Bar-Jonah" means son of Jonah.) This reaction to his question was exactly what Jesus wanted—for Peter and his other followers to "catch" from his works, his miracles, his preaching, his teaching ,and his personality, the true identity of his being. Peter, evidently voicing the opinion of the twelve, revealed by his reply to Jesus that this was exactly what had taken place.

(3) Further Teaching of Jesus   After blessing Peter for his wise answer, Jesus added some very pertinent concepts. "And I also say unto thee, that thou art Peter [*petros*], and upon this rock [*petra*] I will build my church; and the gates of Hades shall not prevail against it. I will give unto thee the keys of the kingdom of heaven: and whatsoever thou shalt bind on earth shall be bound in heaven; and whatsoever thou shalt loose on earth shall be loosed in heaven" (Matt. 16:18–19).

The name Jesus bestowed upon Simon was *Peter,* from the Greek word meaning rock. (In the Aramaic this is *Cephas,* a term found occasionally in the Scriptures.) Simon was certainly not a rock during the three denials, but he became quite steadfast during the days of the early church.

Petros denotes a small rock, such as might be used in a sling, while *petra* denotes bedrock. Thus Jesus used a play on words with which to convey a spiritual truth. To what did Jesus refer by the term *petra*? Three interpretations have been prominent through the years. One is that it refers to Peter himself, thereby designating him as the authoritative leader of the church. This has been the Roman Catholic view. Another interpretation is that it refers to the faith demonstrated in Peter's reply to Jesus' query. A third view is that it refers to Jesus himself. This corresponds to the greatest extent with the remaining sections of the Bible, where Jesus is referred to as "the rock" (1 Cor. 10:4; 1 Pet. 2:6–8). Jesus is not only the cornerstone of the church; he is even more, the bedrock upon which it is built. This third view seems the most plausible one.

The term *church* is found only twice in all the four Gospels; both of these are in Matthew (16:18; 18:17). Throughout the Synoptic Gospels Jesus spoke more of the kingdom than of the church, and he did not use the terms *church* and *kingdom* as synonymous.

The term *Hades* is a correct translation of the Greek in the original, not *hell* as in the King James (v. 18). Hades is synonymous with Sheol, mentioned repeatedly in the Hebrew Scriptures. Jesus was saying that death will not swallow up the church; it will always exist. The Revised Standard Version says that "the powers of death shall not prevail against it." This is a very close rendering of the meaning Jesus apparently wished to convey to the disciples concerning his church.

The phrase *keys of the kingdom* refers to the gospel, the story of redemption as centered in Christ, not to a legalistic authority bestowed upon Peter and handed down through apostolic succession to those following him. The disciples were being pressed with the urgency of proclaiming this message to the world, thus opening the doors of the kingdom that all might enter. To do so is to loose on earth; not to do so is to bind on earth.

(4) A Suffering Messiah From that time on Jesus began to teach clearly and openly that he must be rejected, must suffer, must be killed, and the third day be raised up. This would all take place in Jerusalem (Mark 8:31–32). Not being able to accept what Jesus was saying to them, Peter began to rebuke him for his statement concerning his future death. Jesus responded firmly: "Get thee behind me, Satan; for thou mindest not the things of God, but the things of men" (Mark 8:33). Evidently Peter's concept of messiahship did not accord with that of his Lord.

To Peter Jesus *was* the Messiah, the Christ; but the apostle could not conceive of a suffering and dying Christ. The mighty Deliverer, long awaited, would live forever. Peter merely voiced the popular concept of the messiahship anticipated by the Jewish people, that of a conquering and militant one who would overturn all the enemies of the Jews, including Rome, and restore the golden era of David and Solomon. How could a dying Messiah fit in with such a picture? To Jesus the way to the crown was by the way of the cross; therefore, the temptation confronting Jesus by Peter's rebuke was the same temptation proposed by Satan in the wilderness at the beginning of Jesus' public ministry. This is why Jesus called Peter Satan and declared that his thinking was along human lines rather than along God's lines.

To this startling announcement concerning a suffering Messiah, Jesus added a further surprising note: All of his followers must suffer also. Self-denial would be the mark of their lives, and each would have his own cross to bear. To both the multitudes and the disciples he declared, "If any man would come after me, let him deny himself, and take up his cross, and follow me" (Mark 8:34). To this concept Jesus added the paradox that one who tries to save his life shall lose it and that one who loses his life by submerging it in Jesus' cause shall save it. This is what Paul referred to as "the fellowship of his sufferings" (Phil. 3:10); for the sake of Christ he "suffered the loss of all things" (v. 8). The gratification of personal desire must constantly be subordinated to that of service to God. Luke even added that this self-denial must be a daily concern (9:23).

(5) *The Transfiguration* Six days after Peter's great statement of faith, Jesus, accompanied by Peter, James, and John, climbed a high mountain. Luke said that the purpose was to pray. There Jesus "was transfigured before them; and his face did shine as the sun, and his garments became white as the light" (Matt. 17:1–2). This incident is recorded by all three of the Synoptic Gospels, but not one of them tells the name of the mountain. Scholars have been divided in their viewpoints on the matter. Some think that Mount Tabor, midway between Nazareth and the Jordan, was the one; others believe that Mount Hermon, north of Caesarea Philippi and outside of Galilee, was the site of the incident. This second view is the favored one.

As Jesus prayed the change occurred (Luke 9:29); he was glorified. Two men, Moses and Elijah, appeared and began talking with Jesus "of his decease which he was to accomplish at Jerusalem" (v. 31). The word translated *decease* is *exodus* in the original Greek, the same term used in the Old Testament for the exodus of the Hebrew people out of Egypt. As Moses led the children of Israel to a land of freedom, so Jesus would deliver his people, by his death and resurrection, out of the "power of darkness" and "into the kingdom of the Son of his love" (Col. 1:13). The first exodus was a physical deliverance from a mundane slavery of the brick kilns; the second exodus would be a spiritual deliverance "out of darkness into his marvellous light" (1 Pet. 2:9).

Impulsive Peter was the first to speak following the striking change in the appearance of his Lord. He said to Jesus, "Master, it is good for us to be here: and let us make three tabernacles; one for thee, and one for Moses, and one for Elijah: not knowing what he said" (Luke 9:33). He was proposing that they build three tabernacles, booths, like those used at the Feast of Tabernacles in the fall. While Peter was speaking, a cloud, symbol of the presence of God in the Old Testament, appeared and overshadowed them. A voice out of the cloud said, "This is my beloved Son, in whom I am well pleased; hear ye him." The voice, confirming the heavenly message Jesus heard previously at his baptism, brought fear and consternation to the three disciples, who immediately fell to the ground. When they finally looked up, only Jesus was there with them (Matt. 17:4–8).

No doubt such an experience strengthened the disciples in their conviction that Jesus was truly the Son of God, thus preparing them for the trying days of the trial and crucifixion. The striking feature of the whole event is conveyed by the words of Luke: "they saw his glory" (9:32). They could not forget Jesus' splendor. Second Peter records the words of the apostle: "For he received from God the Father honor and glory, when there was borne such a voice to him by the Majestic Glory, This is my beloved Son, in whom I am well pleased: and this voice we ourselves heard borne out of heaven, when we were with him in the holy mount" (1:17–18). Jesus had informed them only a few days previously that he must suffer and die; how were they to reconcile this grim fact with the glory and majesty they had witnessed on the mount? Only after the cross and resurrection would they discern that out of death comes life; out of suffering comes glory; and out of apparent defeat comes triumph. This is the paradox of the gospel.

(6) A Question About Elijah   As they descended from the mountain Jesus commanded them, "Tell the vision to no man, until the Son of man be risen from the dead" (Matt. 17:9). This remark constitutes the second time that Jesus spoke of his coming resurrection.

Having seen Moses and Elijah on the mount, the disciples asked Jesus a question concerning the latter. "Why then say the scribes that Elijah must first come?" (v. 10). Their question was sparked by a passage in Malachi: "Behold, I will send you Elijah the prophet before the great and terrible day of Jehovah come. And he shall turn the heart of the fathers to the children, and the heart of the children to their fathers; lest I come and smite the earth with a curse" (4:5–6).

Jesus' answer was clear: Elijah had already come. "Then understood the disciples that he spake unto them of John the Baptist" (Matt. 17:13). The fearless preacher of the Jordan valley was the fulfillment of Malachi's prediction made several centuries previously. It is true that John the Baptist disclaimed being Elijah; when priests and Levites asked him if he were Elijah, he replied, "I am not" (John 1: 19–21). By this he meant he was not Elijah in person come back to earth, as many of the Jews expected would occur. John the Baptist fulfilled Malachi's Elijah passage spiritually, not physically.

8. The Demoniac Boy

Jesus, Peter, James, and John returned and met the remaining disciples, who were engaged in controversy with some of the scribes at that very moment. A man complained to Jesus that he had brought his demon-possessed son to the disciples, and they had been unable to cast out the demon. Jesus said, "O faithless and perverse generation, how long shall I be with you? how long shall I bear with you? bring him hither to me" (Matt. 17:14–17). Then he proceeded to heal the boy. When the disciples asked their Master why they failed, Jesus informed them that the reason was their lack of faith. "If ye have faith as a grain of mustard seed, ye shall say unto this mountain, Remove hence to yonder place; and it shall remove; and nothing shall be impossible unto you" (Matt. 17:20). "Faith as a grain of mustard seed" would be faith of a small amount, while "removing a mountain" would apply to that which at first glance would seem impossible.

9. Further Teaching in Galilee

Returning to the territory of his youth, Jesus again spoke of his coming death and resurrection. "The Son of man shall be delivered up into the hands of men; and they shall kill him, and the third day he shall be raised up." This brought great sorrow to the disciples (Matt. 17:22–23). Mark added that they failed to understand what he meant, but were afraid to question him concerning it (9:32). They were just not ready to accept the role of a suffering Messiah for their Master.

Every male Hebrew was required by the Mosaic law to pay an annual tax of a half shekel to the Temple (Ex. 30:13–16). When Jesus and his group of followers returned to Capernaum, the collectors of this tax approached him, seeking payment. Jesus instructed Peter to pay the tax for both of them and to secure the money in a very strange way. "Go thou to the sea, and cast a hook, and take up the fish that first cometh up; and when thou hast opened his mouth, thou shalt find a shekel: that take, and give unto them for me and thee" (Matt. 17:27).

On the same visit to Capernaum the disciples contended with one another about who was the greatest. Jesus used an object lesson to teach the twelve about greatness in his kingdom. He set a little child in their midst and said: "Except ye turn, and become as little children, ye shall in no wise enter into the kingdom of heaven. Whosoever therefore shall humble himself as this little child, the same is the greatest in the kingdom of heaven" (Matt. 18:3–4).

Humility is the criterion of greatness in Jesus' kingdom. Our Lord never discouraged one's having ambition to be great; greatness, however, must be achieved according to the principles of the kingdom of God, not according to worldly standards. Entrance into the kingdom comes through becoming like a child; therefore, greatness would consist in becoming even more like a child.

While still in Capernaum John was guilty of an incident of mistaken zeal. "Teacher, we saw one casting out demons in thy name; and we forbade him, because he followed not us" (Mark 9:38). The man was successfully operating in Jesus' name, but John thought he should have been stopped because he was not in their immediate following. Probably expecting Jesus' commendation, he heard Jesus say, "Forbid him not: for he that is not against you is for you" (Luke 9:50). Then Jesus continued with what is known as his great stumbling-block passage. "Whoso shall cause one of these little ones that believe on me to stumble, it is profitable for him that a great millstone should be hanged about his neck, and that he should be sunk in the depth of the sea. Woe unto the world because of occasions of stumbling! for it must needs be that the occasions come; but woe to that man through whom the occasion cometh!" (Matt. 18:6–7).

Jesus was referring to man-made obstacles in the lives of little ones, causing them to be hurt or led astray. "Little ones" would refer not merely to those young in age, but to all people in all realms of life, any of the followers of Jesus.

Peter asked Jesus how often he should forgive his brother. Would seven times be enough? Seven was considered in Jewish thinking a complete number; anything less than that was incomplete. Jesus replied that seven times was not sufficient, that one should forgive "seventy times seven." By this statement he did not mean a legalistic 490 times—he meant that one should go on forgiving endlessly. Jesus then told the parable of the unmerciful servant in order to illustrate the kingdom demands of forgiveness (Matt. 18:21–35). People who do not forgive their fellowmen cannot expect God to forgive their own sins.

About this time three would-be followers of Jesus were warned to count the cost of discipleship and to reckon with the conflicts of loyalties that following him would involve. Jesus then added, "No man, having put his hand to the plow, and looking back, is fit for the kingdom of God" (Luke 9:62).

10. The Feast of Tabernacles

The Feast of Tabernacles, one of the three major festivals of the Jews, begins on the fifteenth of the Jewish month Tishri (late September or early October) and lasts seven days. It is not only a feast for the summer crop; it is a memorial of the forty years of wilderness wandering. It is also the most joyous of all the feasts. When the time of the feast arrived, Jesus' brothers, who at that time did not believe him about who he was, urged him to go to Jerusalem ''that thy disciples also may behold thy works that thou doest.'' Jesus replied that his time was not yet come. After the brothers left for the feast Jesus also went up (John 7:2–10).

Luke added a significant comment: ''And it came to pass, when the days were well-nigh come that he should be received up, he stedfastly set his face to go to Jerusalem'' (9:51). When the time for the cross drew near he purposely started toward the headquarters of both Pharisees and Sadducees, knowing that they would seize him and crucify him. Several times he had escaped their grasp as they plotted to capture and kill him, but the time had arrived for the sacrifice consummating all sacrifices. This would take place in Jerusalem.

13.

The Late Judean Ministry

The later Judean ministry probably lasted from the Feast of Tabernacles to the Feast of Dedication—approximately three months. It is presented only by the Gospels of John and Luke, with John giving mainly that in Jerusalem and Luke that in Judea.

1. Jesus at the Feast of Tabernacles

We have already seen that Jesus visited and ministered in Jerusalem and Judea almost two years prior to this time. Again he was received with contention and bitterness in Jerusalem and with favor and popularity in Judea.

The Jews sought Jesus at the feast, and the multitudes were murmuring and disputing concerning him. Their opinions of him varied greatly, but they were afraid to state their opinions openly for fear of what the Jewish authorities might do. "Some said, He is a good man; others said, Not so, but he leadeth the multitude astray" (John 7:12). About the fourth day Jesus appeared in the Temple and began expounding such striking truths that the Jews marveled at his wisdom. "How knoweth this man letters, having never learned?" By this they meant that he had not attended the rabbinical school in Jerusalem.

Jesus proclaimed that his teaching came from God and that this truth would be recognized by anyone doing the will of God. Many looked upon him favorably and believed. But his enemies, the Pharisees and the chief priests, sent officers to arrest him. When Jesus said to his hearers that they would seek him but would not find him and that where he was going they could not come, the Jews again misunderstood his real meaning. They even asked if he would go outside the country and teach the Greeks (John 7:14–36).

On the last day of the feast two very dramatic and symbolical rituals took place. One was the lighting of the candelabra in the court of the women. The candelabra were placed high above the people's heads so that light went out to the other courts and even extended over the city. This light was representative of the glory of God symbolized by the pillar of cloud during the wilderness wanderings. There was also the procession of priests carrying water to be poured out at the pool of Siloam. As the water was poured from the golden vessels, the trumpets were blown and the priests quoted from the book of Isaiah: "Therefore with joy shall ye draw water out of the wells of salvation" (12:3).

As a contrast to this water, Jesus stood and proclaimed the saving power of another water. "If any man thirst, let him come unto me and drink. He that believeth on me, as the scripture hath said, from within him shall flow rivers of living water" (John 7:37–38). Such a startling claim stirred up a division among his hearers. Some declared him to be the prophet; some thought he was the Christ; some were filled with doubt because of his Galilean connection. "What, doth the Christ come out of Galilee?" (John 7:37–44).

When the officers sent by the Sanhedrin (chief priests and Pharisees) to take Jesus returned without him, they said, "Never man so spoke." Nicodemus, the influential Pharisee with whom Jesus held a conversation at night (John 3:1–21), spoke in behalf of Jesus, saying that he could not be arrested without a charge. Nicodemus was then sarcastically accused, "Art thou also of Galilee?" (John 7:45–52).

It may have been that the radiant light furnished by the candelabra was the basis for another startling claim made by Jesus: "I am the light of the world: he that followeth me shall not walk in the darkness, but shall have the light of life." This brought an immediate accusation from the Pharisees that Jesus' seemingly self-made witness was not true. Jesus proceeded to defend himself and his claim, stating that the Father, who sent him, also stood by him. (Here are two of the many witnesses set forth in John's Gospel to the divinity of Christ.) Jesus said to his accusers, "Ye know neither me, nor my Father: if ye knew me, ye would know my Father also." Then, according to John, "no man took him; because his hour was not yet come." The hour was the hour of the cross, and the appropriate moment for that signal event had not arrived (John 8:12–20).

2. Adulteress Brought to Jesus

More than once Jesus' enemies endeavored to snare him and to catch him off guard with some remark or act that they could twist into an accusation leading to condemnation. At one point they placed before Jesus a woman guilty of breaking one of the Ten Commandments (Ex. 20:14) and asked him what should be done to her. There was no doubt as to her guilt, for she was caught in the very act of adultery. They addressed him,

"Now in the law Moses commanded us to stone such: what then sayest thou of her?" John said overtly that they were "trying him, that they might have whereof to accuse him" (John 8:5–6).

Jesus, stooping, wrote with his finger on the ground, the only case in the four Gospels where his writing something is mentioned; we are not informed of what he wrote. His accusers continued to question him. Looking up, he said, "He that is without sin among you, let him first cast a stone at her" (v. 7). Again stooping, he continued his writing. They had not anticipated words that would direct their thinking from the woman's sin to their own shortcomings. One by one they all began to slink away; finally none remained. Jesus questioned her about her condemners and then forgave her, adding that she should "sin no more" (v. 11). Compassion, forgiveness, and mercy were much higher on Jesus' priority list than the legalistic exaction of punishment for wrongdoing. His enemies' attempt to discredit him had failed.

3. Denunciation of the Pharisees

Somewhere in Jerusalem, probably in the Temple, Jesus had a clash with the Jews. He said that he would go away, that they would seek him and would die in their sins, and that where he was going they could not come. Again they misunderstood and asked, "Will he kill himself?" (John 8:22). Then Jesus entered into a long dialogue with the people, some of whom believed him and some of whom did not. He told them that if they became his disciples they would know the truth and that the truth would make them free. Again they misunderstood, stating they were not in bondage to anyone. Physically they had been in bondage to Egypt, Assyria, Babylonia, Persia, Greece, and Rome; spiritually they were in bondage to sin at the time of their statement.

When they claimed to be sons of Abraham, he told them they were sons of the devil. He stated his preexistence when he said, "Before Abraham was born, I am" (v. 58). Due to this and many other claims made in his address, the Jews tried to stone him; but he escaped from them (vv. 21–59).

4. Healing of a Blind Man

It was the custom for beggars to sit at the Temple gates. As Jesus left the Temple one day, his eyes fell on a man who had been blind from birth. The disciples said to their Master, "Rabbi, who sinned, this man, or his parents, that he should be born blind?" (John 9:2). This question revealed the false concept regarding suffering that prevailed among the people of Jesus' day, that every bit of observable suffering could be traced back to

A GUIDE FOR NEW TESTAMENT STUDY

sin on the part of the sufferer or someone closely connected with him. If one's life were filled with suffering, God was punishing; if it were seemingly void of suffering, God was blessing. If one were destitute and poor, God was punishing; if one were prosperous, God was blessing. Not to have children made a woman disgraced.

Jesus pushed aside this false concept by saying, "Neither did this man sin, nor his parents: but that the works of God should be made manifest in him" (v. 3). They were not to speculate about the cause of the man's blindness, for this was an opportunity for the glory of God to shine forth. Had Jesus not just declared himself to be the light of the world? Jesus made clay of saliva and anointed the eyes of the man with the clay, commanding him to go wash in the pool of Siloam. He did so and came away seeing. Even the neighbors disputed about whether or not he was the same man who had been blind, questioning him about the healing. He explained to them what Jesus had done.

The Pharisees, calling the man before them, demanded an explanation of his restoration of sight. When the man explained, there was even a division of opinion among the Pharisees. They condemned Jesus for healing the man on the sabbath, an act they considered work and thus a breaking of their sabbath rules. Persisting in their unbelief concerning the healing, they called the parents of the restored man and questioned them. The parents, fearing they might be put out of the synagogue, toned down their answers and suggested that the Pharisees question their son. This they did a second time. The man replied, "I told you even now, and ye did not hear; wherefore would ye hear it again? would ye also become his disciples?" (v. 27). Finally they took the man's synagogue privilege away from him. When Jesus found him, he questioned him about his faith. The man said, "Lord, I believe," and then worshiped Jesus (v. 38).

5. The Good Shepherd

One of the most famous of the parables of Jesus is that of the good shepherd, a picture of the hostile Pharisees in contrast to the good shepherd who lays down his life for the sheep. Jesus is the good shepherd, while the hireling, who flees when the wolf comes, is representative of the Pharisees. "He fleeth because he is a hireling, and careth not for the sheep." But the good shepherd knows his sheep and is known by them.

Jesus further extended his parable: "Therefore doth the Father love me, because I lay down my life, that I may take it again. No one taketh it away from me, but I lay it down of myself. I have power to lay it down, and I have power to take it again. This commandment received I from my

Father'' (John 10:17–18). It was hard for his listeners to comprehend the real meaning of such a parable, especially since they heard the story prior to Calvary and the resurrection. A division arose among his hearers, some declaring he had a demon and some accepting him (John 10:1–21).

6. Mission of the Seventy

Jesus probably left Jerusalem soon after the Feast of Tabernacles. During the Galilean ministry he sent out the twelve apostles, two by two, on a preaching mission (see Chapter 11). That experiment was quite successful (Luke 9:6). At this time, late in his ministry, he sent out seventy disciples on a similar charge. The previous mission had been in Galilee; this one was in Judea. He "sent them two and two before his face into every city and place, whither he himself was about to come." Theirs was to be a healing and preaching ministry. His final word to them was: "He that heareth you heareth me; and he that rejecteth you rejecteth me; and he that rejecteth me rejecteth him that sent me" (Luke 10:1–16).

The seventy returned with joy, declaring that they had control even over the demons, that the demons were subject to them in the name of Jesus. He replied, "I beheld Satan fallen as lightning from heaven." Jesus could see in the spiritual accomplishments of his followers a foreshadowing of Satan's doom. He advised his followers not to concentrate on the fact that the demons were subject to them but to "rejoice that your names are written in heaven." Jesus said a prayer of thanksgiving to the Father, a prayer that revealed the intimate relationship between the Father and the Son. Then Jesus informed the seventy "that many prophets and kings desired to see the things which ye see, and saw them not; and to hear the things which ye hear, and heard them not" (Luke 10:17–24).

7. The Good Samaritan

A cunning lawyer asked Jesus, "Teacher, what shall I do to inherit eternal life?" (Luke 10:25). Jesus referred the man to the Mosaic law, questioning him about what was written there. He replied by quoting what is termed the *Shema* (so named from the opening word in the Hebrew language), found in Deuteronomy and Leviticus. "Thou shalt love the Lord thy God with all thy heart, and with all thy soul, and with all thy strength, and with all thy mind; and thy neighbor as thyself" (Deut. 6:5; Lev. 19:18). Jesus commended him on his answer, adding that if he so did he would live.

The lawyer then asked Jesus, "And who is my neighbor?" (v. 29). Evidently he wanted to release himself from any embarrassment by making

Well at traditional site of the parable of Good Samaritan

the identity of one's neighbor the significant issue in the case. Jesus answered him with the parable of the good Samaritan. This parable, found only in Luke, is one of the most famous of our Lord. The priest and the Levite passed by the robbed and beaten man on the Jericho road, but a Samaritan stopped and befriended him. When Jesus finally questioned the lawyer about who was neighbor to the destitute and suffering man, he answered, "He that showed mercy on him." Jesus said, "Go, and do thou likewise" (v. 37). Jesus gave the word *neighbor* a new connotation, for the word to him meant one who renders help to any in need. To the Jew of Jesus' day, a neighbor would have been another Jew. Jesus made a Jew admit that a despised Samaritan could be a neighbor also (Luke 10:25–37).

8. A Favorite Home in Bethany

At this time Jesus was a guest in the house of Mary, Martha, and Lazarus in Bethany, two or three miles southeast of Jerusalem. (There was another Bethany that lay beyond the Jordan, mentioned in John 1:28.) He returned to this home later on, during Passion Week, and made it his own during those trying days. Mary and Martha, devout followers of Jesus, were entertaining their Master with a meal. Mary was listening to Jesus speak more than she was helping with the food. "Martha was cumbered about much serving" (Luke 10:40). When she asked Jesus to insist that Mary help her with the preparation, Jesus remarked to Martha that she was "anxious and troubled about many things" and that "but one thing" was needful. Only one dish was necessary. Mary was placing her priorities in the right sequence; the teaching of her Lord came first. She was responsive to spiritual matters (Luke 10:38–42).

9. The Model Prayer

What we have termed the Lord's Prayer should probably have been called the Model Prayer. Jesus gave it to his disciples as a guide. One of the disciples requested, "Lord, teach us to pray, even as John also taught his disciples" (Luke 11:1). Jesus responded by giving the model prayer (Luke 11:1–4). Matthew also gave the model prayer in the Sermon on the Mount, Matthew 6:9–13. It is very doubtful that Jesus expected his followers to memorize the prayer and to recite it by rote in a ritualistic manner, thinking little of the meaning of the words involved. It was meant to be a guide in the preparation of the individual, personal prayers of the disciples.

Jesus then said a word about the need for persistence in praying. He told the parable of the importunate friend, which is the story of a man who arose at midnight to give a friend bread so he could feed a visitor. The man did so because of the great need, despite the unusual hour. To this Jesus added, "Ask, and it shall be given you; seek, and ye shall find; knock, and it shall be opened you." If a human being can be persuaded to befriend someone in an hour of desperate need, how much more will the heavenly Father grant the requests made by his children. If parental love can safely guide children, how much more can heavenly love bestow the right gifts (Luke 11:1–13).

10. False Accusation Concerning Beelzebub

"And he was casting out a demon that was dumb. And it came to pass, when the demon was gone out, the dumb man spake; and the multitudes marvelled." But the multitudes were not unanimous, for some accused him of casting out demons by the power of Beelzebub, the prince of demons. Jesus tried to show them the absurdity of their thinking by saying that Satan is not divided against himself; else his kingdom would not stand. Beelzebub would not cast out his own. "But if I by the finger of God cast out demons, then is the kingdom of God come upon you" (Luke 11:20). He refuted the accusation that the exorcism was performed by the aid of Beelzebub; instead, it was accomplished by a power derived from God. One cannot remain neutral in his relationship to Jesus. "He that is not with me is against me; and he that gathereth not with me scattereth" (Luke 11:14–26).

Jesus continued his discourse by calling that generation an evil generation, one that sought after a sign; and no sign would be given it but the sign of Jonah. As Jonah was a sign to the people of Nineveh, the son of man would be a sign to that generation. The irony lay in the fact that the queen of Sheba was amazed at the wisdom of Solomon, and there was someone wiser than Solomon; the men of Nineveh repented at the preaching of Jonah, and there was someone there greater than Jonah. At the day of judgment, Jesus said, the queen of Sheba and the men of Nineveh would condemn the generation that turned a deaf ear to his preaching (Luke 11:27–36).

11. Clash With the Pharisees

A Pharisee asked Jesus to dine with him, and Jesus willingly accepted the invitation. When Jesus began to eat without bothering to wash his hands, as was the custom of the Pharisees, his host was amazed. Sensing the feeling of the man, Jesus remarked that a Pharisee meticulously cleaned the outside of a cup and a platter before using them, while his inward life was "full of extortion and wickedness" (Luke 11:39). To Jesus such was hypocrisy, so he vividly pronounced three woes on the Pharisees for their insincerity. When one of the lawyers remarked that Jesus' pronouncements of woes hit them as well as the Pharisees, our Lord immediately pronounced three woes on the lawyers also. Jesus' remarks must have burned both groups deeply; as he left that place, they "began to press upon him vehemently, and to provoke him to speak of many things; laying wait for him, to catch something out of his mouth" (Luke 11:37–54).

12. Further Discourses

Luke recorded several discourses that probably took place one after another. They were addressed to various parties and were disturbed by constant interruptions, as was typical of Jesus' teaching. As found in the twelfth chapter of Luke, they were addressed to the disciples (vv. 1–12), to one out of the crowd (vv 13–21), to the disciples again (vv. 22–40), to Peter (vv. 41–53), and to the crowds (vv. 54–59). His main subjects were hypocrisy, covetousness, worldly anxieties, watchfulness, and his own approaching trial and crucifixion.

During this ministry in Judea Jesus' popularity with the multitudes was tremendous. As he taught, "many thousands of the multitude were gathered together, insomuch that they trode one upon another" (Luke 12:1). He warned his disciples to beware the hypocrisy so well exemplified by the Pharisees. Saying and acting one thing and being another was very disgusting to Jesus. He told them that whatever they said in private would be revealed openly. His injunction to them was to have no fear of the ones on earth who could threaten their bodies, but to fear God, the one who controlled their eternal destiny. "Yea, I say unto you, Fear him" (v. 5). He told them that, when they were apprehended and brought before rulers and authorities, the Holy Spirit would guide them in what to say. He did not promise that they would not experience suffering; but he did assure them that God would sustain them in their suffering (1–12).

Jesus warned the crowd against covetousness. "Take heed, and keep yourselves from all covetousness: for a man's life consisteth not in the abundance of the things which he possesseth" (v. 15). To illustrate the power of covetousness he told the parable of the rich fool, the story of the man whose fields produced an abundance. This man claimed and used it all in a miserly fashion, only to be called suddenly to give an account to God. "So is he that layeth up treasure for himself, and is not rich toward God" (vv. 13–21). Jesus' admonition against covetousness went back to the Tenth Commandment found in the Decalogue (Ex. 20:17).

He also cautioned the disciples about being overly anxious concerning the things of this world, even the necessities such as food and clothing. "For the life is more than the food, and the body than the raiment" (v. 23). The raven and the lilies are good examples of how God cares for things in his created order. Jesus' followers were urged to place God's kingdom first in their priorities; then God would see that they had the necessities of life. He warned them to always be ready for the coming of the Son of man, for they did not know in what hour he would return. To illustrate the need for watchfulness, Jesus told the parable of the waiting servants (vv. 22–40).

When Peter asked if this parable was meant for the disciples or for the crowd, Jesus answered by giving a further parable, the parable of the wise steward. It is the story of the steward who was ready and prepared for his master's return, no matter at what hour it occurred. This shrewd steward stood in contrast with the unwise one, who acted wickedly and was not ready. Jesus announced that his coming to earth to set up his kingdom would bring divisions upon earth, even dividing households. Some would accept him; some would not. In this sense his coming would not bring peace but conflicts (vv. 41–53).

Jesus warned the people of Jerusalem of their need of repentance, for the whole city would be destroyed if they did not repent. He mentioned two tragedies of the past in order to illustrate his urgent demand: Pilate's killing of some Galileans as they offered sacrifices and the collapse of the tower of Siloam, which fell on and killed eighteen people in Jerusalem. Jesus asserted that these people were no more deeply involved in sin than all the others present in Jerusalem at the same time. To his hearers he urgently said, "Nay: but, except ye repent, ye shall all in like manner perish" (13:1–5).

Jesus gave the parable of the barren fig tree to illustrate that God expected of his people righteous and productive living. The unproductive tree was to be given one more chance to produce; results of no fruit that year would mean that the tree would be cut down and discarded. Jesus was implying that the Jewish nation was even then in a probationary period. If fruits of righteousness were not produced, the people could expect God's condemnation and rejection (13:6–9).

13. Healing of a Crippled Woman

The sabbath healing of a crippled woman in one of the synagogues brought a clash with the ruler of that synagogue. Jesus addressed the woman, unable to stand straight for eighteen years, with the welcome news, "Woman, thou art loosed from thine infirmity." Laying his hand upon her, Jesus healed her of the crippling condition; and she glorified God. Immediately the ruler of the synagogue responded that the people should use the other six days of the week, not the sabbath, to come and be healed. Jesus immediately defended his action with a comparison. Men perform work on the sabbath in leading an ox or an ass from the stall for watering. Should not a daughter of Abraham, of more value than a dumb brute, be loosed from the power of Satan on a sabbath? The multitude rejoiced with Jesus' verbal victory over all his adversaries (Luke 13:10–17).

Our Lord illustrated the kingdom of God with two parables: the parable of the mustard seed and the parable of the leaven. The frequency with which Jesus referred to the kingdom vividly shows that it was the key concept in the new order he was bringing.

14. At the Feast of Dedication

The Feast of Dedication was initiated after the cleansing and rededication of the Temple following the purge of the Syrians during the Maccabean revolt. It occurs during December (during the Jewish month Kislev) and is also called Hanukkah (meaning "rededication") as well as the Feast of Lights. Since it was started in 165 B.C., the Old Testament does not mention it. Though not one of the three major feasts, it is both a patriotic and a religious festival.

John's Gospel says, "And it was the feast of the dedication at Jerusalem: it was winter; and Jesus was walking in the temple in Solomon's porch" (10:22–23). The Jews, surrounding him, asked for a clear and open statement about his identity. "If thou art the Christ, tell us plainly." This question was probably posed with the intent of ensnaring him so he could be accused before Roman authority. He responded, "I told you, and ye believe not: the works that I do in my Father's name, these bear witness of me" (v. 25).

He then spoke of the deep relationship existing between him and his Father: "I and the Father are one" (v. 30). This short remark became the cause of more controversy about the person of Christ in the early church than any other one biblical statement. The Jews took up stones to stone Jesus, saying he blasphemed by making himself God. He told them that if they did not believe him, to "believe the works: that ye may know and understand that the Father is in me, and I in the Father" (v. 38). When they tried to take him, he went away (John 10:22–39).

14.

The Perean Ministry

This ministry lasted from the Feast of Dedication until the last journey to Jerusalem, just prior to the trial and crucifixion—a period of about three and a half months. Most of the written account comes from Luke and John. The territory of Perea lay east of the Jordan, extending from the southern border of the Decapolis down to the land east of the Dead Sea. It was the southern part of the two disconnected regions ruled by Herod Antipas, mainly Hebrew in population but highly influenced by the Gentiles. Therefore, the people presented quite a contrast with those in and around Jerusalem. The chronology in the life of Christ pertaining to this period is somewhat hard to establish; it is unwise to speak definitely concerning the order of events during these weeks.

1. Withdrawal Beyond the Jordan

After Jesus was rejected by the Jews in Jerusalem he went to Perea. "And he went away again beyond the Jordan into the place where John was at the first baptizing; and there he abode." The people who were present at the preaching of John believed that Jesus fit the description of the one of whom John spoke. "And many believed on him there" (John 10:4–42). Evidently the people in Perea received Jesus and benefited from his ministry while in that territory.

2. Teaching in Perea on a Journey to Jerusalem

"And he went on his way through cities and villages, teaching, and journeying on unto Jerusalem" (Luke 13:22). A man asked him if there are few who are saved. Again Jesus did not answer categorically but said, "Strive to enter in by the narrow door: for many, I say unto you, shall seek to enter in, and shall not be able" (v. 24). There is a subtle suggestion to the man to cease speculating about the total number saved and to dwell more on the surety of his own salvation. Jesus then emphasized the short time element through the parable of the unwelcome latecomers. It is the story of the householder who shut the door and latecomers, knocking in vain, who sought entrance (vv. 23–27). According to our Lord, many Jews will be greatly troubled when they see Gentiles sitting down and eating at the messianic banquet with Abraham, Isaac, and Jacob, while they themselves are excluded. "There are last who shall be first, and there are first who shall be last" (vv. 28–30). There will be many surprising reversals in the last days.

It was at this time that some of the Pharisees warned Jesus concerning Herod Antipas. "Get thee out, and go hence: for Herod would fain kill thee" (v. 31). It is hard to determine whether they genuinely had his safety at heart or whether they were trying to drive him out of the territory and back into the hands of Jewish rulers, as has been suggested. At any rate, the men were not successful in frightening Jesus. Jesus' answer was a classic one. "Go and say to that fox, Behold, I cast out demons and perform cures to-day and to-morrow, and the third day I am perfected" (v. 32). ("Am perfected" means "end my course," or "am made complete.") Then he added that he must continue on his journey, "for it cannot be that a prophet perish out of Jerusalem" (vv. 31–33).

The compassion of Jesus for those who persisted in rejecting his salvation is clearly seen in his lament over the capital city. "O Jerusalem, Jerusalem, that killeth the prophets, and stoneth them that are sent unto her! how often would I have gathered thy children together, even as a hen gathered her own brood under her wings, and ye would not!" (v. 34). God's divine protection would soon run out for the beloved city, and desolation would set in (vv. 34–35).

3. Dining with a Chief Pharisee

After the meal in the house of the Pharisee previously mentioned, Jesus told three parables. He gave the parable of the seats at feasts to show humility. This parable, addressed to all present, advised them not to go into a marriage feast and seek out the most important places but to wait until they were told to occupy such. He addressed to his host the parable of the feast for the poor; the lesson was one of hospitality. When one gives a dinner or a supper (more exactly, according to the Greek, a breakfast or a dinner), he should not invite merely friends, relatives, or the rich. He should also invite the underprivileged who cannot return the invitation. To a certain individual at the meal Jesus addressed the parable of the great supper, but the parable was really meant for all present. It told that all who failed to accept the gospel invitation would not be included in the messianic meal—the places intended for them would be occupied by those from the "highways and hedges." Those "bidden" at first were the Jews, and those "constrained to come in" were the Gentiles (Luke 14:7–24).

4. Cost of Discipleship

Jesus' popularity continued with the crowds; Luke said "there went with him great multitudes" (Luke 14:25). To these he taught the cost of what it means to follow him in kingdom service. "If any man cometh unto me, and hateth not his own father, and mother, and wife, and children, and brethren, and sisters, yea, and his own life also, he cannot be my disciple" (v. 26). The term *hate,* as used in this passage, does not connote what it does in the language of today: to have an extreme dislike for a person or thing. It is used in this passage as the relative preference of one person over another; it really means "love less." This passage should be compared with a similar one in Matthew 10:37, where the word *love* is used rather than the word *hate.* There we are told to love our Savior more than those dear to us on earth. Jesus would never have declared that we are to manifest an utter dislike for our parents, relatives, and dear ones. What he is asking is that our loyalty to him be stronger and superior than the loyalty we have for those very close to us.

To this statement Jesus added, "Whosoever doth not bear his own cross, and come after me, cannot be my disciple" (v. 27). According to the prevailing custom of that time, anyone being crucified was compelled to bear his cross to the place of crucifixion. Jesus was implying that his followers also should expect suffering and should be willing to accept it. Never did Jesus picture the conditions of following him as easy or inviting. He always displayed the terms of discipleship as hard and exacting, involving suffering and self-denial of some kind or another. He did not want his followers to be deceived in any way.

To urge his followers to count the cost of discipleship, Jesus gave two parables. The parable of the man building a tower states that one who wishes to build a tower first sits down and figures the cost. The parable of the king going to war states that any ruler about to encounter an enemy in warfare ascertains whether his forces are strong enough to attain a victory before he fights (Luke 14:28–32). "So therefore whosoever he be of you that renounceth not all that he hath, he cannot be my disciple" (v. 33).

5. Associating with Sinners

While Jesus' relationship with the multitudes continued in a marvelous vein, the scribes and Pharisees were drawing their net around him tighter and tighter. When Jesus associated with publicans and sinners, his enemies were also there with their barbs of criticism. "And both the Pharisees and the scribes murmured, saying, This man receiveth sinners and eateth with them" (Luke 15:2). The publicans were those of Israelite blood who collected taxes from their fellow countrymen for the Romans. Sinners were Israelite descendants who were not trying to keep the Mosaic law. To associate with publicans and sinners was extremely below the plain upon which a good Pharisee lived. One might as well associate with Samaritans and harlots. These people were strongly attracted to Jesus, who in turn received them gladly and gave them his message of hope. Jesus was even more than they had longed for!

To show his attitude toward fallen and sinning humanity, Jesus told three parables. They are the parables of the lost sheep, lost coin, and lost son. When the sheep, and the coin, and the son were finally found, there was great rejoicing. Likewise, there is great rejoicing in heaven when a spiritually lost person is found and comes to God. "There is joy in the presence of the angels of God over one sinner that repenteth" (v. 10).

If any of the sinners with whom Jesus was associating were to experience salvation through the good news he was presenting, the Pharisees should have rejoiced, as the angels would in heaven. Instead, they felt only contempt. Their attitude is found in the person of the elder brother of the last parable, who, in his jealousy and self-complacency, was furious because his father rejoiced when his son returned (Luke 15:1–32). All three parables hinge on one great truth: the high value of the human soul in the sight of God.

6. Teaching on Stewardship

Stewardship is the use of all that we possess—mind, heart, will, talent, time, and possessions—to the glory of God. Jesus had much to say about stewardship, and many of his thoughts on the matter are recorded in Luke 16:1 to 17:10.

To the disciples Jesus related the parable of the unjust steward. As the earthly steward dealt wisely in the use of the possessions of his rich master, so the "sons of light" would do well to imitate the "sons of this world" and use their possessions to lay up eternal treasures. They should use the "mammon of unrighteousness" in such a way that, when it is no more, "they may receive you into the eternal tabernacles." He impressed upon his hearers the impossibility of serving two masters. "Ye cannot serve God and mammon" (16:1–13). "And the Pharisees, who were lovers of money, heard all these things; and they scoffed at him." Jesus remonstrated with them by telling them that they tried to justify themselves with men, but God knew their hearts. What appears good in the sight of men can be an abomination in the sight of God (16:14–15).

The story of the rich man and Lazarus is one of the most famous in the

New Testament. It depicts men who are eventually held responsible for what they do with their possessions upon earth. The scene of the first part of the story is upon earth, while the scene of the latter part is in hades. On earth the rich man lived in wealth and luxury, and the poor man sat at his gate in destitution. Both died and were buried, after which there was a complete reversal of conditions. Lazarus was accepted by Abraham, the acme of bliss for a true Hebrew. The rich man was in torment and anguish—not because he possessed wealth while upon earth, but simply because of his ill use of that wealth. No other sin is mentioned in connection with his earthly life; the point of the whole narrative is his defective view of stewardship. The consequences of his earthly course were final. There was no relief for him, even though he pleaded for such (Luke 16:19–31).

The parable of the unprofitable servant, addressed to the disciples, says that men are not to be thanked or rewarded for doing their duty. To the parable Jesus added the injunction, "Even so ye also, when ye shall have done all the things that are commanded you, say, We are unprofitable servants; we have done that which it was our duty to do" (17:10). The servants of Christ are to follow him humbly and to obey him explicitly. Even then, what they do for Christ will be small compared to what Christ does for them (Luke 17:5–10).

7. Raising of Lazarus From the Dead

Mary, Martha, and Lazarus lived in Bethany, just a short distance from Jerusalem. Lazarus became ill, so the sisters sent for Jesus: "Lord, behold, he whom thou lovest is sick" (John 11:3). It was Jesus' love for Lazarus that the sisters remembered, not that of Lazarus for Jesus. Jesus stated, "This sickness is not unto death, but for the glory of God, that the Son of God may be glorified thereby." After receiving the message Jesus purposely delayed two days and then stated, "Let us go into Judea again." Because of the Jewish hatred for Jesus in Judea, the disciples were afraid for him to go there. He informed them that Lazarus was dead and that he was going to awaken him.

When they arrived in Bethany Lazarus had been dead four days, and many of the Jews had come to console the sisters. Martha went to meet Jesus, saying, "Lord, if thou hadst been here, my brother had not died. And even now I know that, whatsoever thou shalt ask of God, God will give thee" (vv. 21–22). Jesus reminded her that her brother would rise again, to which she responded, "I know that he shall rise again in the resurrection at the last day" (v. 24). Then Jesus expressed to Martha one of the most meaningful and significant statements of his earthly career. "I am the resurrection, and the life: he that believeth on me, though he die, yet shall he live; and whosoever liveth and believeth on me shall never die" (vv. 25–26). This statement, the climax of the story, is one of many "I am" sayings found in the Fourth Gospel. Jesus was informing Martha and all his followers that he is the source of all resurrection—that from his being, as the Son of God, all resurrection stems. The power of the resurrection in the final age was already present in the person and work of the incarnate Christ.

When he asked if she believed this, she answered, "Yea, Lord: I have believed that thou art the Christ, the Son of God, even he that cometh into the world" (v. 27). Martha returned to Mary; and Mary in turn went out to meet Jesus, making the same initial statement that Martha had made to him. When Jesus observed the weeping of Mary and her friends, "he groaned in the spirit, and was troubled" (v. 33). We are told that Jesus wept. Why? Those around him misunderstood, thinking the reason was love of Lazarus. Nor, in all probability, does the reason lie in the fact that he was calling back to this suffering and mundane world one who had briefly seen the glories of the next. The reason evidently resides in the fact that they had faith that he could have healed Lazarus, but their faith did not extend to the point of Jesus' raising his friend from the dead. Again, "groaning in himself," Jesus came to the tomb.

It was a cave, with a stone against the opening. When he commanded the stone to be removed, Martha reminded him that the body of her brother, dead already four days, had begun to decay. First lifting his eyes and thanking the Father above for hearing him, Jesus cried in a loud voice, "Lazarus, come forth." And Lazarus did so, "bound hand and foot with grave-clothes; and his face was bound about with a napkin." Jesus ordered that they loose him and permit him to depart. The four days magnified the miracle, making it even more astounding. Decomposition had set in. Besides, there was a rabbinical teaching at that time that the soul lingered near the body for three days with the hope of being reunited with it. After this, with the beginning of decay, it took its flight to another realm.

John's story of the resurrection of Lazarus marks the third such in the earthly ministry of Jesus (John 11:1–44). It must be placed alongside of the raising of the widow's son at Nain (Luke 7:11–17) and the raising of Jairus' daughter (Luke 8:41–42, 49–56). The difference lies in the fact that the restorations recorded in Luke occurred soon after death, while that of Lazarus was four days after death.

We have seen that the miracles in John's Gospel are termed *signs* and that from each radiated the glory of God. The glory of God was disclosed in Lazarus' resurrection. As Jesus could give physical life, he could also give spiritual life, eternal life. This ability would be completely revealed in the cross-resurrection experience soon to come.

What were the effects of the raising of Lazarus? Many of the Jews believed Jesus and became his followers. Others of the Jews reported to the Pharisees all that Jesus had done, probably with a desire to spur the Pharisees to take action against Jesus. These enemies of Jesus gathered a council together to decide what should be done to curtail the activities of the popular wonderworker and teacher from Galilee. "If we let him alone, all men will believe on him: and the Romans will come and take away our place and our nation." They had defied Jesus many times, and each time Jesus' manner had caused them embarrassment. The miracle of Lazarus' resurrection was the climax. Jesus must go! "So from that day forth they took counsel that they might put him to death" (John 11:47–53).

There was also an effect upon Jesus himself. "Jesus therefore walked no more openly among the Jews, but departed thence into the country near to the wilderness, into a city called Ephraim; and there he tarried with the disciples" (v. 54). He was no longer safe in Jerusalem, and the time of the cross had not yet come.

8. Journey Through Samaria and Galilee

Evidently Jesus remained in Ephraim till the Passover was approaching, at which time he proceeded north through Samaria and into Galilee. Luke said, "And it came to pass, as they were on the way to Jerusalem, that he was passing along the borders of Samaria and Galilee" (17:11). In a certain village of the Samaritans he was met by ten lepers, all standing far off and saying, "Jesus, Master, have mercy on us." Mosaic law decreed that one suffering from this dread disease, so prevalent in that era in the Near East, be considered ceremonially unclean. He was to dwell apart from the rest of humanity and yell, "Unclean, unclean" so others would know not to approach him. This quarantine condition was imposed not for medicinal purposes but for a religious one (Lev. 13:45–46). When the lepers called on Jesus for help he cleansed them. He first told them to prove to the priest that they were whole (Lev. 13:49); as they were going, the healing took place.

The striking thing involved in the whole incident is the fact that only one out of the ten turned back to thank Jesus, who said, "Were not the ten cleansed? but where are the nine?" Jesus informed the man that his faith had made him whole (Luke 17:12–19). Jesus probably healed many lepers during the course of his ministry. Why, it might be asked, was this incident selected and recorded by Luke? Could the reason have been due to the sequel, the return of the lone man to express his gratitude to Jesus?

The ever-present Pharisees, archopponents of Jesus, again approached him with a question about when the kingdom would come. He replied that the kingdom of God is an inner, spiritual thing. "The kingdom of God is within you." They seemed to desire a better understanding of what his concept of the term might mean. He informed them that his kingdom comes "not with observation." It is subjective, spiritual, and invisible. He did not come for an earthly, physical restoration of the golden age of David, with all its pomp and outward glamour. Turning to the disciples, he continued to draw his verbal picture of future events, especially of "the days of the Son of man." As they were not prepared in the days of Noah, nor also in the days of Lot, so shall it be in "the day that the Son of man is revealed" (Luke 17:20–37).

Apparently at this same time Jesus gave two parables concerning prayer. One was the parable of the importunate widow, given "to the end that they ought always to pray, and not to faint." This, of course, means not to give up faith. As the earthly, human judge fulfilled the request of the widow, so shall God fulfill the request of these who "cry to him night and day" (Luke 18: 1–8). In the parable of the Pharisee and the publican, Jesus lashed out against those who were smugly complacent in their self-righteousness and "set all others at nought." As the Pharisee prayed, he reminded God of all his virtues and merits. As the publican prayed, he looked toward the ground, beat upon his breast in self-subjugation, and said, "God, be thou merciful to me a sinner" (v. 13). Jesus praised the publican, calling him justified. He said, "Every one that exalteth himself shall be humbled; but he that humbleth himself shall be exalted" (v. 14). The righteousness of a child of God is not derived through self-attainment, but through grace following a repentant and believing expression on the part of the sinner. This type of righteousness would never warrant looking on others with disdain (Luke 18:9–14).

9. Teaching About Divorce

Jesus also spoke on the subject of divorce. The Gospel of Matthew says that Jesus "departed from Galilee, and came into the borders of Judea beyond Jordan," which would be into Perea again. There, as usual, he healed and taught great multitudes (Matt. 19:1–2). Again tempting him, the Pharisees asked, "Is it lawful for a man to put away his wife for every cause?" (v. 3). They probably expected an answer based on the Mosaic law, but Jesus lifted the case out of the age of Moses and went back to the beginning of the human race, when God made male and female and instituted the home. God expected a man to "leave his father and mother" and to "cleave to his wife," after which the two would become "one flesh." After that they are not two, but one flesh. "What therefore God hath joined together, let not man put asunder."

When the Pharisees asked Jesus why Moses allowed divorce, he said that this was a concession Moses had made due to their "hardness of heart." But God from the very beginning had not planned it so. Jesus cited the revelation of God as found in Genesis, for there marriage is placed as the bedrock of the purpose of creation itself. The union of man and wife was not to be dissolved.

At that time there were two schools of thought among Jews regarding divorce. There was the school that followed a prominent rabbi named Hillel, who took a liberal view toward divorce, with the dissolving of a marriage being permitted for the most trivial reasons. This view had popular support, with the result that there was a high degree of laxness in granting divorce. The other school was that which followed another prominant rabbi, Shammai. This school of thought took a conservative view toward divorce; a dissolution of a marriage was granted for unchastity only. If the Pharisees had in mind embarrassing Jesus by making him choose one side, thus discrediting him with the side not chosen, he sidestepped their plot (Matt. 19:3–12).

10. Jesus and Little Children

We have already seen that Jesus used a little child to teach humility to the disciples and that humility is the criterion of greatness in his kingdom. At this time some people brought little ones to Jesus that he might place his hands upon them and pray. The disciples seemed to have had the prevailing attitude of that day toward children, for they rebuked the ones who wanted their little ones blessed. Jesus said, "Suffer the little children, and forbid them not, to come unto me: for to such belongeth the kingdom of heaven" (19:14). With this statement he laid his hands upon them and then departed (Matt. 19:13–15). What Jesus was actually saying was that the childhood traits of simplicity, faith, teachability, and love are the characteristics of one who is in the kingdom.

Jesus' attitude toward children in regard to his kingdom stands in contrast to Herod the Great's attitude toward children in regard to his kingdom. Jesus made childlikeness the basis of all who would enter his realm; Herod the Great slaughtered all the male infants around Bethlehem in a jealous fear that one of them would one day replace him as King of the

Jews. Wherever Christianity has spread, childhood and womanhood have been raised to a loftier plane.

11. The Rich Young Ruler

A rich and influential young man came to Jesus with a very piercing question: "Teacher, what good thing shall I do, that I may have eternal life?" Evidently this young man, unlike the lawyer who came with a similar question about eternal life (Luke 10:25–37), was very sincere in his desire for any answer the amazing teacher might give him. His question was no trick question, for he was humble and honest in his interview with Jesus. When Jesus told him to keep the commandments, he replied that he had done so. When the young man added "What lack I yet?" he revealed the void in his life that a meticulous observance of Judaism could not fill. Then Jesus imposed a severe test upon the rich young man. "If thou wouldest be perfect, go, sell that which thou hast, and give to the poor, and thou shalt have treasure in heaven: and come, follow me" (v. 21). The demand for a complete self-surrender seems to have been too exacting, for the young man turned away in sorrow. His possessions proved too dominant a force in his life (Matt. 19:16–22).

Jesus declared, "It is hard for a rich man to enter into the kingdom of heaven" (v. 23). He added that it is easier for a camel to go through the eye of a needle than for a rich man to enter into the kingdom of God. The popular notion toward wealth was that extensive material possessions indicated God's blessing upon the owner; so wealth could not be considered as unholy or ungodly. Jesus' request of the young man, as well as his decree that riches made it difficult for the owner to enter into heaven, was a complete reversal of what his listeners had been taught concerning abundance and prosperity.

To the disciples Jesus made salvation appear an almost impossible feat. "Who then can be saved?" they asked. Jesus replied that salvation can be accomplished only by divine power—that it is impossible for a man to be saved without God's grace (Matt. 19:23–26). Peter asked what they would receive, since they had left all to follow Jesus. Jesus promised that the spiritual rewards would far outweigh any earthly sacrifices they had made (vv. 27–30). He then gave a parable, the parable of the laborers in the vineyard, to reveal to his disciples that the rewards of those in the kingdom would be of grace, not of debt. God will reward as he sees fit, not necessarily as the child of God preconceives his worth in God's sight to be. Perhaps the rewards will be quite reversed over what is anticipated. "So the last shall be first, and the first last" (Matt. 20:1–16).

12. Traveling Toward Jerusalem

At this time Jesus and his disciples proceeded toward Jerusalem. Some who followed him were amazed; others were afraid. They were filled with anxiety, probably because "Jesus was going before them" (Mark 10:32). They evidently sensed that something was soon to happen, but certainly they could not have realized the momentous events that would soon transpire in the holy city. Jesus took his disciples aside and informed them of exactly what would occur.

"Behold, we go up to Jerusalem; and the Son of man shall be delivered unto the chief priests and the scribes; and they shall condemn him to death, and shall deliver him unto the Gentiles: and they shall mock him, and shall spit upon him, and shall scourge him, and shall kill him; and after three days he shall rise again" (Mark 10:33–34). Again Jesus revealed his approaching suffering and death in plainly understood terms. The time for phrases such as "the sign of Jonah" were past. The disciples must know exactly what to expect.

James and John, the sons of Zebedee, came to Jesus with a self-centered request, a petition that revealed they still possessed the old view of the Messiah's kingdom. They said, "Grant unto us that we may sit, one on thy right hand, and one on thy left hand, in thy glory." The two were thinking of sitting beside Jesus in Jerusalem, as he sat on the restored throne of David, not as he sat on his transcendent, heavenly throne in celestial glory. The "glory" of their request had an earthly connotation, not a heavenly one. It is probable that all the disciples conceived of Jesus' kingdom as one in which there were many places of honor. That thought would in turn lead to the question, What spot will I occupy?

Jesus told the two followers that they did not realize what they were asking. "Are ye able to drink the cup that I drink? or to be baptized with the baptism that I am baptized with?" (Mark 10:38). They had asked for an imposing part in his triumph; he asked if they were able to share in his suffering. They responded, "We are able." Jesus promised them that they would certainly suffer with him, but that their places in eternal glory was not his to give (Mark 10:35–40).

The presumptuous request had an adverse effect upon the other ten disciples; it filled them with disgust and indignation. As a result, Jesus turned again to a discussion of true greatness, kingdom greatness. At this time he made service the requirement of greatness. He said that true greatness does not consist in the privilege of exercising authority over others; true greatness lies in serving others. "Whosoever would become great among you, shall be your minister: and whosoever would be first

Jerusalem, Beautiful Gate, from the Garden of Gethsemane

among you, shall be servant of all'' (v. 44).

He added that he himself came to minister, not to be ministered unto. Again we see the paradox of the gospel, that greatness springs from service. The world had never heard of service and humility as the seeds of greatness (Mark 10:41–45).

Jesus also added that he came "to give his life a ransom for many." By the use of this graphic metaphor, ransom, Jesus spoke of his coming death, the fourth time that he had done so since Peter's great declaration at Caesarea Philippi. His life of self-sacrifice, ultimately to end in death, would be the acme of service for others (v. 45).

13. Blind Bartimaeus

Jesus and his group finally crossed the Jordan and entered Judea. Near Jericho two blind men appealed to Jesus to heal them. Mark and Matthew said that Jesus was going out from Jericho; Luke said he was drawing near Jericho. What probably happened is that the healing took place as he left old Jericho and was approaching new Jericho, which Herod the Great had built some distance away. Therefore, two writers had reference to old Jericho and one to new Jericho.

As Jesus was passing by, the blind men cried out, "Lord, have mercy on us, thou Son of David." When the crowd rebuked them and demanded them to cease their clamoring, they cried out the more, repeating their urgent request. Moved with compassion, Jesus touched their eyes; and they received their sight. Then they followed Jesus. One was named Bartimaeus, which means "son of Timaeus" (Matt. 20:29–34; Mark 10:46–52; Luke 18:35–43).

14. Zacchaeus, Chief Publican

Luke alone recorded that Jesus, passing through Jericho, encountered a man in a very unusual circumstance. His name was Zacchaeus, and he was the chief collector of taxes for Rome in that area, a position that had made him very rich. Being small of stature, he climbed a sycamore tree so that he could get a better view of the famous teacher as he passed through town. Coming near the tree, Jesus called to him, "Zacchaeus, make haste, and come down; for to-day I must abide at thy house" (Luke 19:5). He obeyed and joyfully received Jesus into his home. The people remarked of Jesus, "He is gone in to lodge with a man that is a sinner." Zacchaeus' occupation would make the other inhabitants of Jericho dislike him.

However, the hated publican gave proof of a radical change within his life by promising to restore all that he had gained by wrong exaction. Jesus declared, "To-day is salvation come to this house, forasmuch as he also is a son of Abraham'' (v. 9). Then he made a clear statement of the purpose of his incarnate life. ''For the Son of man came to seek and to save that which was lost'' (Luke 19:1–10).

Jesus also told the parable of the pounds. Luke informed us that Jesus gave the parable ''because he was nigh to Jerusalem, and because they supposed that the kingdom of God was immediately to appear'' (19:11). The cross was close at hand; yet the disciples still retained a false concept of the kingdom and what Jesus was about to do. Jesus himself is the nobleman in the parable, the one who went into a far country to receive a kingdom. What he was endeavoring to do was to check their wild enthusiasm to make him king in Jerusalem. The disciples were to go on working and not to be sitting and waiting (Luke 19:11–27).

''And when he had thus spoken, he went on before, going up to Jerusalem'' (v. 28).

15.

The Last Week

The last week of Jesus' life has been termed *Passion Week,* for the word *passion* in this case refers to the sufferings of Christ. It was a week of intense suffering for our Lord. In the famous "servant songs" found in the book of Isaiah (42:1–9; 49:1–13; 50:4–11; 52:13 to 53:12), it had been foretold that the coming Servant would endure great persecution and suffer a shameful death. Jesus knew himself to be the fulfillment of these vivid declarations by the prophet of old.

That he would be a suffering and dying Messiah was a notion hard to grasp. Too long had his followers been used to hearing of the popular concept of their anticipated Messiah, that of a militant and glorious king restoring the pomp of their glamorous David. From the time of his baptism Jesus had known that his atoning act would involve intense suffering, even to the point of a shameful death. All temptations to stray from this costly giving of himself in behalf of mankind had been thrust aside. The hour of the cross so often mentioned in John's Gospel was at hand. It was time for the "grain of wheat" to fall in the earth and die (John 12:23–24).

1. Jesus Arrives at Bethany

This Bethany was the village just two miles south of Jerusalem, where Jesus had visited several times previously. One of those visits became renowned due to the raising of Lazarus from the grave (John 12:1). Since the Passover, the most popular of the Jewish festivals, was at hand, many people were winding their way to Jerusalem to arrive early enough to make themselves ceremonially pure for the religious activities. Many people looked for Jesus in Jerusalem; and the common people of Bethany sought him in that neighboring village. The spectacular raising of Lazarus from the dead, not to mention the myriad of other miraculous deeds of Jesus, made him an object of search.

They wanted to see not only Jesus but Lazarus, also. Since the raising of Lazarus caused many Jews to believe in Jesus, the chief priests began to plot Lazarus' death also (John 11:55–57; 12:9–11). As Jesus approached Jerusalem the aura of expectation among his followers increased. Luke presented a clue to their anticipation: "They supposed that the kingdom of God was immediately to appear" (19:11). However, in opposition to the joy and the loyalty of his followers was the intense hatred of the Pharisees; they had commanded that anyone knowing Jesus' whereabouts should reveal his location (John 11:57).

This visit to Bethany seems to have taken place on a Friday, since it was six days before the Passover (John 12:1). If the appearance in Bethany took place on Friday, Saturday was spent in privately visiting his friends in the small Judean town. This would be the Jewish sabbath, a day the chief priests and Pharisees in Jerusalem may have devoted to their plotting and scheming against Jesus. The sabbath started at sundown on Friday and extended to the same time on Saturday. We may well imagine that Jesus went to the synagogue for worship, as was his custom. Then the remainder of the day was spent in the home of Lazarus.

2. Sunday

Sunday was the day of Jesus' dramatic entrance into Jerusalem, the Holy City. The spectacular ride has been erroneously termed *the triumphal entry*. A triumphal entry into the home city or capital was customarily made by a king as he returned home, having conquered his enemies and rounded up his captives. The crowd would watch him as he stalked through the city, followed by his cohorts and his chained prisoners of war. Jesus indeed effected a mighty conquest, a defeat of the forces of evil and the powers of this world. But his victory was on Calvary! On the cross he turned apparent defeat into triumph. On the cross he reigned and overcame the world (John 16:33).

(1)   Entrance into the City   The entrance into the Holy City was Jesus' offering of himself publicly as the Messiah. Though he refrained from using the terms *Messiah* and *Christ* for himself, when the term was used by others to describe him, he acknowledged and accepted it. At last the hour ·had arrived for him to vividly manifest himself as their Messiah. He deliberately brought forth the occasion whereby his followers could acclaim him as King. He knew that such a striking demonstration on the part of the people would hasten the cross. And the cross must be!

The prophet Zechariah had announced years before the Jerusalem-entry event, "Rejoice greatly, O daughter of Zion; shout, O daughter of Jerusalem: behold, thy king cometh unto thee; he is just, and having salvation; lowly, and riding upon an ass, even upon a colt the foal of an

Gethsemane (left) with traditional road of the royal entry

ass'' (9:9). He was not to ride upon a horse, the symbol of war; he was to ride upon an ass, the lowly beast of burden, a goodly animal associated with missions of peace. (Solomon rode his father's mule when he went to be anointed king in place of David, we read in 1 Kings 1:38). Jesus said to two of his disciples, ''Go your way into the village that is over against you: and straightway as ye enter into it, ye shall find a colt tied, whereon no man ever yet sat; loose him, and bring him'' (Mark 11:2).

Evidently the owner of the animal had been previously prepared and needed only the confirming word to deliver the colt to the two disciples. Coming to Jesus with the animal, they spread their garments on its back; and Jesus sat on their garments. The road from Bethany to Jerusalem passed by the Mount of Olives. As he approached Jerusalem, the crowd increased and the tumult became greater. There was intense rejoicing. The crowd ''spread their garments in the way; and others cut branches from the trees, and spread them in the way'' (Matt. 21:8). (This is the reason that day has been known through the years as Palm Sunday.) They cried, ''Hosanna to the son of David: Blessed is he that cometh in the name of the Lord; Hosanna in the highest'' (v. 9). Truly they hailed him as the one initiating the messianic kingdom. The word *hosanna* is very significant, for it is derived from the Hebrew and means ''save, pray.'' It was customarily used as an exclamation to God for deliverance.

John said that the Pharisees remarked, ''Behold how ye prevail nothing: lo, the world is gone after him'' (12:19). Such a commanding influence on Jesus' part demanded a drastic action on the Pharisees' part. Luke added that the Pharisees demanded that Jesus rebuke his disciples, which he vehemently refused to do, saying the stones would cry out if the disciples did not shout their praise (19:39–40). As Jesus came nearer Jerusalem he wept over it and voiced a lament over it. He predicted the approaching destruction of the city (Luke 19: 41–44), an event that took place in A.D. 70.

When Jesus entered the Holy City, the multitudes exclaimed, ''This is the prophet, Jesus, from Nazareth of Galilee'' (Matt. 21:11). Prior to this event Jesus had discouraged such a demonstration of messianic recognition; at this time he welcomed it. He healed many who were blind and lame, and after a time left the city and returned to Bethany (Matt. 21:17).

(2) The Self-Composure of Jesus The composure and self-possession that characterized our Lord stood him in good stead. He was completely at ease, completely in command. Standing face to face with death, confronting its somber eventuality, and realizing only too well the intense suffering that lay ahead—all this did not alter the dignity of his

person and the grandeur of his character. His whole bearing was sublime and continued to be throughout the degrading trial and the excruciating death! He knew that the inevitable hour had arrived. This is not to say that deep down inside there were not conflicting emotions surging back and forth within his breast; anguish and peace were strangely mixed. Both disappointment and joy were present, much like the ebb and flow of mighty ocean currents. Yet the serenity of his being ironically caused Pilate to stand in judgment before Jesus.

3. Monday

(1) Cursing of the Fig Tree Matthew stated, "Now in the morning as he returned to the city, he hungered" (21:18). When Jesus saw a fig tree with leaves and no fruit, he did the unusual. He pronounced a curse on it and said, "Let there be no fruit from thee henceforward for ever" (v. 19). Mark added that "it was not the season of figs" (11:13). In Palestine the fruit and the leaves of a fig tree appear at the same time, so there should have been fruit. Therefore Jesus pronounced a doom of eternal barrenness on the tree.

The explanation set forth by most scholars for Jesus' strange action is that he saw in the barrenness of the tree a symbol of the barrenness of Israel. Israel, like the tree, had been carefully cultivated; but Israel had produced no fruit for God. Therefore, in pronouncing judgment upon the tree, Jesus was pronouncing judgment upon the covenant nation as well. This miracle might well be termed an "acted parable," a parable fraught with distress and woe.

(2) Cleansing of the Temple Jesus proceeded to Jerusalem and entered the Temple, a spot extremely dear to him. It should have been a very sacred place, one surrounded by an aura of reverence; but conniving Sadducees and hypocritical Pharisees had profaned it by putting it to an unworthy use. They had defeated the original intent of God. The sacrificial emphasis had been transformed from an aid to worship to a shameful system of graft. Prayer had been blotted out by the clanging shekel, and the lucrative business of money-changing had superseded meditation on the glory of God.

Jesus' actions as he entered the Temple were so dramatic that all three of the Synoptic Gospels present the event. Matthew's version reads: "And Jesus entered into the temple of God, and cast out all them that sold and bought in the temple, and overthrew the tables of the money-changers, and the seats of them that sold the doves; and he saith unto them, It is written, My house shall be called a house of prayer; but ye make it a den of robbers'' (Matt. 21:12–13).

What the Master found in the Temple angered him just as it had years earlier, at the beginning of his public ministry. At that time he cleansed the Temple of those who had degraded and thwarted its purpose (John 2:13–17). Again, late in his ministry, he had to repeat his act of purging that sacred spot; those who had desecrated it must again be cast forth. Since the Sadducees had most of the priests within their ranks, Jesus' bold action that day was more a thrust at them than at the Pharisees. As was usual in many of the deeds he performed and in the truths he taught, Jesus quoted Scripture. Isaiah 56:7 states that the Temple was to be a house of prayer for all people, and Jeremiah 7:11 states that it had been converted into a den of robbers. Evidently Jesus combined these two passages in his denunciatory remark to the Temple authorities.

It has been said that Jesus' startling actions had a symbolic aspect relating to his work as the Messiah. He wanted to free the Jews from all commercial and materialistic expressions in their religion, elements that tended to downgrade the spiritual nature of true worship.

For years scholars have debated the one-cleansing and the two-cleansing theories. John presents an early cleansing, one in the second chapter of his Gospel; the Synoptics present a late cleansing, one just prior to the trial and crucifixion. Those who adhere to one-cleansing theory say that all four writers are talking of the same event and that John was not interested in a chronological order of events. He was concerned more with a topical arrangement. Those who adhere to the two-cleansing theory say that the depraved conditions surrounding the Temple and the sacrificial cult necessitated that Jesus repeat the purging ordeal. One was not sufficient to impress upon the minds of the priests the fact that they had desecrated and profaned that holy place; the house of prayer had been turned into a den of robbers. It is very possible, and quite probable, that Jesus had to repeat his denunciatory act aimed at demolishing the profitable racket of the chief priests.

(3) Some Greeks to See Jesus   Only the Gospel of John reveals the visit of some Greeks to Jesus (John 12:20–50). ''Now there were certain Greeks among those that went up to worship at the feast.'' This would make them ''God-fearers,'' Gentiles who read the Septuagint, offered prayers to the God of the Hebrews, and even worshiped in the court of the Gentiles, but who had not completely embraced Judaism. Those becoming Jews would be termed *proselytes*. God-fearers were just one step away from being proselytes. These Greeks said to Philip, ''Sir, we would see Jesus.'' Then Philip and Andrew brought them into the presence of their

Master.

Prior to this event, Jesus had repeatedly referred to his "hour," an hour that always had "not come." Finally, when some Greeks desired to hear what Jesus had to say, Jesus declared, "The hour is come that the Son of man should be glorified" (12:23). This glorification would come through the cross; the object of shame would be transformed into the object of glory. In that moment of extreme suffering, ridicule, and degradation, men would see God's radiant glory shine forth. Jesus had come to be the Savior of all men; when Gentiles finally came to question him, he knew unquestionably that the climactic hour was imminent.

Jesus said, "Verily, verily, I say unto you, Except a grain of wheat fall into the earth and die, it abideth by itself alone; but if it die, it beareth much fruit" (John 12:24). By his death he would bring life to many, for he himself was the grain of wheat soon to "fall into the earth and die." Even to the incarnate Son of God, the extreme agony of his approaching death brought grim reflections (vv. 27–28).

Jesus, perfect Son of God, prayed that God's name would be glorified. Immediately there was a responsive voice from heaven, saying, "I have both glorified it, and will glorify it again" (v. 28). The Father's name had already been glorified in the life and ministry of the Son and would soon be glorified anew at Calvary. This is the third recorded time that a voice from heaven, the *bath-kol,* came with divine approval and reassurance of Jesus' activities. The other two times were at his baptism and at the moment of transfiguration. Some of the multitude thought they heard thunder, while others thought an angel had spoken to Jesus. Jesus assured them that the voice had not come for his benefit, but for their benefit (29–30).

He stated that he would be "lifted up from the earth" and thereby draw all men unto him. They evidently knew that by "lifted up" he meant the cross, but again they were unable to understand why he had to die. In fact, they were puzzled about why he used for himself the phrase "Son of man." They asked, "Who is this son of man?" (12:32–34). He continued to counsel with them, a counseling that had the overtones of a warning concerning their acceptance or rejection of him.

4. Tuesday

(1) Wonder Concerning the Fig Tree   The next morning, when Jesus and his disciples were returning to Jerusalem, the disciples observed that the cursed fig tree had withered away from the roots. Peter called attention to the tree, and Jesus emphasized the importance of the combination of faith and prayer. "All things whatsoever ye pray and ask for, believe that

ye receive them, and ye shall have them.'' To faith and prayer Jesus added a third ingredient in his spiritual formula, forgiveness. ''And whensoever ye stand praying, forgive, if ye have aught against any one; that your Father also who is in heaven may forgive you your trespasses'' (Mark 11:20–25).

(2) Questions to Ensnare Due probably to Jesus' public proclamation of his messiahship when he rode into Jerusalem on the donkey, coupled with the people's favorable response to his action, the Jewish leaders endeavored to discredit him by a series of questions, all set forth with the intent of ensnaring and embarrassing him.

a. Question of the Sanhedrin The first group to ask Jesus a question was made up of the Sanhedrin. Their question challenged his authority; it demanded that he show his credentials for being a recognized teacher, a rabbi. Little did they realize that he had an authority higher than any they possessed. ''By what authority doest thou these things? or who gave thee this authority to do these things?'' (v. 28). Jesus responded by thrusting at them a return question: ''The baptism of John, was it from heaven, or from men? answer me'' (v. 30). They reasoned among themselves that if they said it was from heaven, he would ask why they did not believe him; and if they said it was from men, they would be in danger due to John's large following. They found themselves in a dilemma; they would be condemned by either response. They answered, ''We know not'' (v. 33). Jesus told them he chose not to answer their question (Mark 11:27–33).

At this time our Lord reinforced his argument by giving three parables, all three of which exposed and discredited the Jewish leaders. First is the parable of the two sons, one of whom refused to work in the vineyard of his father, but afterward repented and did so. The second son promised to work, but did not. The former son represents the harlots and publicans who repented and came to Jesus; the latter son represents the Jewish religious leaders who pretended to be righteous but were not. The point of the parable is that one shows his respect for authority by being obedient to that authority (Matt. 21:28–32).

The second parable is that of the wicked husbandmen. Again the theme of rebellion against authority and the dire consequences of that rebellion come to the fore. It is a parable set in the form of an allegory, much like the parable found in Isaiah 5:1–7. God is the owner of the vineyard, while the tenants are the Jewish leaders. The servants are the prophets, and the son is Jesus. The ones to whom the vineyard is finally entrusted are the ones who have accepted Jesus. The Jewish leaders are like vinedressers who hold back from their master what is rightfully his of the fruit of the vine. Their place will be given to a people who will give faithful service to this master (Matt. 21:33–46).

The third parable is that of the marriage feast of the king's son, in which the kingdom of God is likened to a marriage feast given by a king for his son. The king is God and the son is Jesus; the invited guests are the Jewish people. The guests who are finally gathered in, not included in the first invitation, are the Gentiles (Matt. 22:1–14). In both the second and third parables Jesus was declaring that the kingdom of God will be taken away from the Jews and be given to the believing Gentiles.

b. Question of the Pharisees and the Herodians The Pharisees and the Herodians combined in their verbal attack on Jesus. The Herodians were those who were faithful to the line of Herod the Great. They wished to see one from this dynasty back on the throne. The envoys of these two groups first complimented Jesus by declaring that he taught "the way of God in truth" (Matt. 22:16), caring not what men might say. Then they asked, "What thinkest thou? Is it lawful to give tribute unto Caesar, or not?" Jesus discerned their spurious air of innocence and called them hypocrites, saying they were tempting him. They expected Jesus to take one side or the other and therefore to defy those of the remaining view. If he said yes, the common people would disapprove, for they longed to throw off the Roman yoke. If he said no, he could easily be accused of sedition against Rome.

Jesus asked for a piece of the tribute money. When a small coin was brought to him he said, "Whose is this image and superscription?" They answered, "Caesar's." Then he said, "Render therefore unto Caesar the things that are Caesar's; and unto God the things that are God's." They were, in effect, under an obligation both to Caesar and to God; but they were tending to forget their obligation to God. They marveled at Jesus' wisdom and then departed (Matt. 22:15–22).

c. Question of the Sadducees "On that day there came to him Sadducees, they that say there is no resurrection" (Matt. 22:23). This Jewish group rejected the oral tradition built upon the Mosaic law as found in the Pentateuch; the oral law was the man-made section that had accumulated through the years. Here they were unlike the Pharisees. The Sadducees accepted only the Pentateuch, the first five books of the Hebrew Scriptures, as their holy writings. There is virtually nothing in the Pentateuch about life after death. The resurrection passages are in the later sections (as in Dan. 12:2). So when the Sadducees stepped forth to pose their question to Jesus, it was natural that they would ask about the resurrection; they wanted to make the idea appear absurd.

They said to Jesus, "Teacher, Moses said, If a man die, having no children, his brother shall marry his wife, and raise up seed unto his brother. Now there were with us seven brethren: and the first married and deceased, and having no seed left his wife unto his brother; in like manner the second also, and the third, unto the seventh. And after them all, the woman died. In the resurrection therefore whose wife shall she be of the seven? for they all had her" (Matt. 22:24–28).

The first part of their question involved what was known as Levirate marriage, a custom explained in Deuteronomy 25:5–10. If a man died and his widow had no son remaining with her, the brother of the deceased man was to marry the widow. The first son born from this union was to be considered the son of the deceased man, so that his name would not be "blotted out in Israel."

Jesus' answer declared them ignorant on two scores. "Ye do err, not knowing the scriptures, nor the power of God. For in the resurrection they neither marry, nor are given in marriage, but are as angels in heaven" (v. 30). God is powerful enough to accomplish a resurrection; Jesus had already proved that with the resurrection of Lazarus and others. "God is not the God of the dead, but of the living" (v. 32). Besides, in the future life there will be no marriages. The multitudes were astonished at the wisdom that Jesus displayed (Matt. 22:23–33).

d. Question of the Lawyer Concerning this episode Matthew used the term *lawyer,* while Mark used *scribe.* (The scribe was the lawyer of his day, for to the Jews religious and civil law were so intertwined that they were considered as one.) The scribe of this incident put forth a question that had been debated by the rabbis for years. "Teacher, which is the great commandment in the law?" (v. 36). Jesus' answer was without hesitation. "Thou shalt love the Lord thy God with all thy heart, and with all thy soul, and with all thy mind. This is the great and first commandment" (vv. 37–38). But Jesus did not stop here. He continued, "And a second like unto it is this, Thou shalt love thy neighbor as thyself. On these two commandments the whole law hangeth, and the prophets"(Matt. 22:34–40). The first commandment Jesus stated is found in Deuteronomy 6:4–5; the second is found in Leviticus 19:18.

Mark added that the scribe agreed with Jesus, that loving God with one's whole being and loving one's neighbor with a feeling equal to the love for self "is much more than all whole burnt-offerings and sacrifices." Jesus commended him by saying, "Thou art not far from the kingdom of God" (Mark 12:32–34). His skillful reasoning put to flight any others who might wish to ensnare him.

e. Jesus' Question for the Pharisees Jesus asked the Pharisees a counterquestion concerning his messiahship. He asked them from whom the Christ or the Messiah would be descended. They said, "David." He replied that David called him "Lord" in one of the Psalms (110:1). How then could he be David's son? How could David call one of his own descendants by the term Lord? Though a Jewish son might call his father lord, the opposite would never be true. Jesus was not, however, denying his Davidic descent when he posed this question; his purpose in setting forth his inquiry was to get the people to think about true messiahship. Not only were the Pharisees unable to answer Jesus; no one asked him any more questions (Matt. 22:41–46).

(3) Denouncing the Scribes and Pharisees In what was probably his last public discourse, Jesus denounced the scribes and the Pharisees in a very harsh sermon. To all the people Jesus advised, "The scribes and the Pharisees sit on Moses' seat: all things therefore whatsoever they bid you, these do and observe: but do not ye after their works; for they say and do not" (Matt. 23:2–3). Jesus abhorred the hypocrisy of these people, saying that "all their works they do to be seen of men" (v. 5). He said they loved the chief places at the feasts and in the synagogues and greetings in the marketplaces. They also loved to be called by the term Rabbi.

Jesus heaped upon the hypocritical scribes and Pharisees seven woes in which he condemned their sins of legalism, pride, and self-righteousness. He called them "sons of hell," "serpents," and "off-spring of vipers" (vv. 15,33). He concluded his discourse with a lament over Jerusalem, repeating the name of the city to show his great love for it (Matt. 23:13–39).

(4) The Poor Widow's Mite After Jesus delivered his convicting sermon he went over to the treasury of the Temple and sat down, where he observed the poor widow casting two mites into the treasury. Jesus commended her, saying that she, by casting in all she possessed, had given more than those who had cast in far greater amounts from their abundance (Mark 12:41–44).

This is not only the last time Jesus appeared in the Temple; it is the last occasion that he taught publicly. He later taught the disciples and made comments at the trial and from the cross; but this was his last public teaching. It had grown too late to plead with the opposition to try to understand and accept him. What little time remained needed to be spent in preparing the disciples for the death-resurrection experience. As yet they had failed to understand, much less accept, the mystery of that tragic yet splendid event.

(5) Discourse on Last Things   As Jesus left the Temple one of his disciples made a comment that set off an intimate talk with the disciples. "Teacher, behold, what manner of stones and what manner of buildings!" (Mark 13:1). Jesus replied that there would not be left one stone upon another, that all would be thrown down. Later, as Jesus and his disciples sat on the Mount of Olives looking across the Kedron valley at the Temple, he gave a discourse that concerned two things: the destruction of the Temple and his second coming. All three of the Synoptic Gospels present the teaching Jesus gave at this time (Mark 13:1–37; Matt. 24:1–42; Luke 21–5:36).

To the disciples the Temple seemed built for eternity; therefore, they could not conceive of its destruction. It was God's holy place, where he met his people; he would not allow it to be overthrown. Besides, if the Temple were to go, what would happen to the city, the nation, and the covenant people? Peter, James, John, and Andrew asked Jesus privately, as he sat on the Mount of Olives, when the destruction would take place and what would be the sign of the approaching doom (Mark 13:3–4). Jesus' answer involved the destruction of the Temple and the Holy City and a warning against misinterpreting these events, as well as his second coming and the consummation of the age. The destruction took place in A.D. 70, when Titus, as a result of the Jewish rebellion, descended on the city with Roman fury. The second coming is still to take place. This discourse has been termed the *Little Apocalypse,* while the book of Revelation is called the *Apocalypse.*

Matthew recorded several parables given at the end of this discussion, not contained in the other two Synoptics. These are the parable of the master of the house, the parable of the faithful servant and the evil servant, the parable of the ten virgins, the parable of the talents, and the parable of the sheep and the goats (24:43 to 25:46). Much of the teaching of these parables centers around the theme of being prepared for the second coming of our Lord. (There are two other parables set within the context of the discourse itself, the parable of the fig tree and the parable of the porter, as found in Mark 13:28–37.)

Watchfulness is demanded of every believer, for no one knows when the end of this age will come. Jesus' final picture of the last judgment, when the sheep will be separated from the goats, is a very dramatic one (Matt. 25:31–46). It has been termed the "inasmuch" passage. Jesus said, "Inasmuch as ye did it unto one of these my brethren, even these least, ye did it unto me" (v. 40). Horizontal service to our fellowman is equivalent to vertical service to Christ.

(6) Prediction of the Crucifixion Immediately after the last public discourse, Jesus announced his death as imminent. "And it came to pass, when Jesus had finished all these words, he said unto his disciples, Ye know that after two days the passover cometh, and the Son of man is delivered up to be crucified" (Matt. 26:1–2).

At this same time things were coming to a head with the Sanhedrin. Jesus had done many things contrary to their pattern of thinking. The raising of Lazarus, the royal welcome into Jerusalem, the cleansing of the Temple, and the scathing denunciation of the religious rulers—all of these unusual activities necessitated his being put out of the way. As a result, the Sanhedrin met at the palace of Joseph Caiaphas, the high priest, where "they took counsel together that they might take Jesus by subtlety, and kill him" (Matt. 26:4). Since Jerusalem would be filled with many people (it was the Passover season), the Sanhedrin decided to wait till after the feast to make the fatal blow. They wanted to prevent a riot protesting the execution of Jesus. They said, "Not during the feast, lest haply there shall be a tumult of the people" (Mark 14:2).

(7) Anointing of Jesus at Bethany There had already been an anointing of Jesus more than a year earlier by a sinful woman in the house of Simon the Pharisee. (See chapter 11, section 25.) It was probably on Tuesday evening that Jesus was visiting in the home of Simon in Bethany. Here a second anointing took place, done by Mary, devout sister of Martha and Lazarus. She took an alabaster vase containing a precious ointment and anointed Jesus. When certain of the disciples criticized her act, with the excuse that the expensive ointment might have been sold and the money given to the poor, Jesus defended her lavish giving.

"For ye have the poor always with you; but me ye have not always. For in that she poured this ointment upon my body, she did it to prepare me for burial. Verily I say unto you, Wheresoever this gospel shall be preached in the whole world, that also which this woman hath done shall be spoken of for a memorial of her" (Matt. 26:11–13). Jesus would be the last person to discredit acts of charity, for he taught that such are integral parts of the gospel itself; but here he maintained that charitable deeds can never be a substitute for the worship and homage due Christ himself.

At the first anointing Jesus promised the woman forgiveness; here he promised Mary perpetual and worldwide honor. Here also Jesus connected the action with his death, something he had not even mentioned when the previous incident took place. (It is necessary to read Mark 13:3–9; Matt. 26:6–13; and John 12:2–8 to secure the full picture of the anointing at Bethany in the final week of Jesus' ministry.)

(8)   Judas Bargains with the Rulers   Judas Iscariot, one of the twelve, went to the chief priests and captains to negotiate a deal with them for delivering Jesus to them. This was probably late on Tuesday evening. Luke said that Satan entered into Judas, thus motivating him to his base treachery (22:3). Judas said to the priests, "What are ye willing to give me, and I will deliver him unto you?" (v. 15). They immediately weighed out to him thirty pieces of silver, after which he sought any opportunity to perform his infamous deed (Matt. 26:14–16).

It has been maintained, and rightly so, that in a sense Judas sold himself for thirty pieces of silver, not Jesus. It is striking that this was the price of a slave in that era. At any rate, it was the price he accepted in place of his honor. There is hardly any sin held in more contempt by mankind than that of betrayal.

While there may have been several motives at work in Judas to make him betray his Lord, the Gospels seem to imply that the love of money was the paramount one. John informed us that Judas, when suggesting that Mary's expensive ointment used to anoint Jesus should have been sold and the money used for the poor, did not have a real love for the destitute ones. Instead, "he was a thief, and having the bag took away what was put therein" (12:6). Evidently his greed grew until it overcame all that was noble in him, even to the point of betraying the Son of God into the hands of his enemies. He seemed to have been truly Satan possessed.

5. Wednesday

As far as we can ascertain, the Gospels tell of no activities on Wednesday. It is to be imagined that Jesus spent Tuesday night, Wednesday, and a part of Thursday in seclusion with his friends in Bethany. To maintain that he did this or did that would be to speak from supposition alone.

6. Thursday

(1)   Preparation for the Passover   Thursday was the day of preparation for the Passover. The disciples said to Jesus, "Where wilt thou that we go and make ready that thou mayest eat the passover?" Jesus sent Peter and John into Jerusalem, where he said they would meet a man bearing a pitcher of water, a very unusual sight in any Oriental city. Women, not men, carried water pitchers. The two were instructed to follow him and to say to the owner of the house where they were led, "Where is my guest-chamber, where I shall eat the passover with my disciples?" They would then be shown a large and furnished upper room.

The disciples obeyed, finding everything as Jesus had said. They made ready for the celebration of the famous feast with their Master (Mark

14:12–16). This was on the fourteenth day of Nisan. After sunset would be the fifteenth of Nisan, the day of the Passover itself and of the eating of the paschal meal. (*Paschal* is an adjective derived from the Greek word translated *Passover* and means "pertaining to the Passover.")

(2) Observance of the Passover The Passover was the most solemn and meaningful of all the Jewish feasts, for it commemorated the deliverance of the Israelites out of Egyptian bondage into the freedom of the land of promise. The leader at the feast recalled to the participants of the meal all the dramatic incidents connected with God's great deliverance of his people. The mighty acts of God connected with their early history as a nation were orally passed in review. "And this day shall be unto you for a memorial, and ye shall keep it a feast to Jehovah: throughout your generations ye shall keep it a feast by an ordinance for ever" (Ex. 12:14). At sunset the trumpets would announce the arrival of the fifteenth of Nisan with a blast, after which the paschal meal could be eaten. This day was also the first of the seven days of unleavened bread, during which only unleavened bread could be eaten by the Israelites. "Seven days shall ye eat unleavened bread" (Ex. 12:15). Therefore the Feast of Unleavened Bread and the Feast of Passover were practically synonymous in Jewish thinking.

"And when the hour was come, he sat down, and the apostles with him. And he said unto them, With desire I have desired to eat this passover with you before I suffer" (Luke 22:14–15). As the leader Jesus must have been the one who presented the explanation of the feast and reviewed the great events connected with the exodus. The elements of the supper were roast lamb, unleavened bread, bitter herbs, a paste of crushed fruit with vinegar, and wine. This was all eaten in a prescribed manner, along with the singing of the *Hallel* (Pss. 113 to 115; 118). (*Hallel* is a word related to the more familiar term *hallelujah,* a Hebrew word of praise.)

It must have been very disappointing to Jesus to realize that a contention had broken out among them as to who was the greatest (see p. 194). He advised them that their greatness would not be akin to that of the kings of the earth, a worldly authority. Rather, it would be that derived through serving. "I am in the midst of you as he that serveth" (v. 27). Their greatness would be very apparent when they ate and drank at his table in his kingdom (Luke 22:24–30). Service, set forth here as a criterion of greatness, is added to that of humility, seen earlier as a criterion (Matt. 18:4).

(3) Washing the Disciples' Feet John said that Jesus arose from the supper, laid aside his garments, took a towel and girded himself, poured water in a basin, and then began to wash the feet of his disciples. As he came to Peter, this impetuous one said, "Thou shalt never wash my feet"

(v. 8). Jesus informed him that if he could not wash his feet, he would have no part of him. When he had finished the procedure, he replaced his garments, sat down with the disciples, and explained his actions. He reminded them that they called him Lord and Teacher. "If I then, the Lord and the Teacher, have washed your feet, ye also ought to wash one another's feet. For I have given you an example, that ye also should do as I have done to you" (v. 15). Jesus wanted to show that the spirit of his kingdom stood in vivid contrast to the spirit of this world.

(4) The Betrayer Revealed Jesus began to express to the disciples the intense sorrow that was engulfing him, for one of the twelve was soon to betray him. "And as they sat and were eating, Jesus said, Verily I say unto you, One of you shall betray me, even he that eateth with me" (Mark 14:18). At this point they, too, felt his sorrow and began to say, "Is it I?" Jesus' reply was that the person was the one who dipped with him in the dish and that it would be better for that one if he had not been born (vv. 19–21). He identified the betrayer with a sign, not an overt declaration of speech. According to John, Jesus remarked, "He it is, for whom I shall dip the sop, and give it him" (v. 26). With this statement he dipped the sop and presented it to Judas Iscariot, son of Simon Iscariot. Immediately Satan entered into Judas, and Jesus ordered him to do quickly whatever he had to do. With that Judas departed into the night (John 13:21–30). How symbolic was the blackness of the night for the blackness of the deed soon to be enacted!

(5) Inception of the Lord's Supper In the context of the Passover meal, Jesus instigated the Lord's Supper as a rite for Christians. This was all very appropriate; as the Passover was a memorial feast for the Hebrew people of their deliverance from human bondage in Egypt, so the Lord's Supper is a memorial feast for Christians of their deliverance from the spiritual bondage of sin and death. (See Luke 22:17–20.)

God had enacted a covenant with Israel at Sinai and made them his special people; he enacted a covenant with believers in Christ at Calvary to replace the old covenant and to make Christians his special people. Therefore, what the Passover symbolizes to the Jew, the Lord's Supper symbolizes to the Christian—and much more! As the first covenant was sealed with the blood of animal sacrifices, the new covenant was sealed with the blood of the Lamb of God himself. The bread symbolizes his body and the cup his blood—blood that was "poured out," not "shed," as it is translated in the King James Version. "Shed" is too mild a term with which to translate the Greek term, which means "poured out." "The life is in the blood" is a recurrent Old Testament theme, and the animal gave its life by the pouring out of its blood. We are "saved by his life" (Rom. 5:10) because Jesus gave his life in the pouring out of his blood.

Baptism and the Lord's Supper symbolize the life we have in Christ. Baptism stands at the beginning of the Christian life and symbolizes the life obtained through faith in the atoning death of God's Son. The Lord's Supper appears repeatedly in the Christian life and symbolizes the continuation of that life through the Bread of life, Christ Jesus himself. Paul said that Jesus is our Passover (1 Cor. 5:7).

(6) Warning Against Desertion Jesus informed the disciples that that very night they would be embarrassed because of him. He quoted Zechariah 13:7 to substantiate his statement. "I will smite the shepherd, and the sheep of the flock shall be scattered abroad" (Matt. 26:31). He added that after he was raised up, he would go before them into Galilee. Peter spoke forth and declared that even if all the others were offended, he would never be offended (v. 33). "Lord, with thee I am ready to go both to prison and to death," he said to his Master. To this Jesus responded, "Peter, the cock shall not crow this day, until thou shalt thrice deny that thou knowest me" (Luke 22:33–34). Peter vowed that he would never deny him, that he would die with him first. All the others said the same (Matt. 26:35).

(7) Farewell Discourse to Disciples Jesus and his disciples may have spent two or three hours in the upper room; here they ate the paschal meal and the Lord's Supper and reviewed the miracles of the past connected with the Exodus. Jesus also previewed the expectations of the future that would involve his followers. He gave to his disciples what has been termed "the farewell discourse," beginning in the upper room and continuing as they walked toward the Mount of Olives. This discourse is found in John 14—16. Chapter fourteen seems to have been presented in the upper room. It ends with the words "Arise, let us go hence" (v. 31). This would relegate chapters fifteen and sixteen to the procession out of the eastern gate of Jerusalem, down across the Kedron valley, and up the slopes of the Mount of Olives to the garden of Gethsemane. (Some books have "Kedron," while others have "Kidron.")

This discourse should be studied verse by verse, since it presents the deep thoughts of our Savior at this very crucial stage of his ministry. The disciples were troubled and fearful whenever he mentioned leaving them, which explains the opening statements of the discourse. "Let not your heart be troubled: believe in God, believe also in me. In my Father's house are many mansions; if it were not so, I would have told you; for I go to prepare a place for you. And if I go and prepare a place for you, I come again, and will receive you unto myself; that where I am, there ye may be also. And whither I go, ye know the way'' (John 14:1–4).

To Thomas' inquiry about knowing the way, Jesus gave the famous statement, ''I am the way, and the truth, and the life: no one cometh unto the Father, but by me'' (v. 6). He promised not to leave them orphans, but to come again (v. 18).

Jesus spoke of the Holy Spirit several times in this discourse, for whom he used the term *Paraclete* or *Comforter*. The Father would send the Comforter to them, not only to be their teacher and guide, but also to convict them of sin. The Holy Spirit would bear witness to Jesus the Son and would glorify him.

In the fifteenth and sixteenth chapters of John's Gospel is a continuation of our Lord's words on this occasion. He called them his friends and said, ''Greater love hath no man than this, that a man lay down his life for his friends. Ye are my friends, if ye do the things which I command you'' (15:13–14). He promised them the hatred and the persecution of the world. He also predicted that very soon they would be scattered, ''every man to his own,'' thus leaving him alone. But the Father would be with him (16:32). He endeavored to cheer them with the statement ''I have overcome the world'' (v. 33).

(8) High-priestly Prayer John 17 contains Jesus' prayer to the Father, which has been termed Christ's high-priestly prayer as well as Christ's intercessory prayer. It possibly occurred near Gethsemane; completing the discourse, he lifted his eyes to heaven and addressed the Father in a very intimate way. He declared that the hour for the Father to glorify the Son and for the Son to glorify the Father had arrived. This, of course, was the hour of the cross. As Jesus continued his prayer, it became not only one of self-consecration but one of intercession for all those believing on him, both in that day and in the years to come.

(9) Garden of Gethsemane ''When Jesus had spoken these words, he went forth with his disciples over the brook Kidron, where was a garden, into which he entered, himself and his disciples'' (John 18:1). Matthew and Mark stated that he went to the Mount of Olives, to a place called Gethsemane. This was an olive orchard, the name meaning ''oil press,'' from the fact that an oil press probably existed or had existed there. Jesus was in the habit of resorting to this spot with his disciples, so Judas and the other disciples knew it well (John 18:2). It was located about half a mile east of the Golden Gate that opened in the east wall of Jerusalem.

When they arrived at the garden, he requested the disciples to be seated.

Gethsemane, ancient tree

However, he took Peter, James, and John, the same three who had been with him when he was transfigured on the mount, with him into the garden (Matt. 17:1–8). It was at this point that he "began to be sorrowful and sore troubled," even admitting to them, "My soul is exceeding sorrowful unto death" (vv. 37–38). Telling them to wait there and to watch, he walked further into the garden and prayed (Matt. 26:36–39). The time of crisis had arrived. His redeeming activity had moved to the point of intense suffering and extreme cost, shown by the striking language with which he expressed the deep gloom that had engulfed him.

Throughout his ministry there had been the subtle temptation lurking at every turn to take the easy way out. Even though the matter was virtually settled in his heart and soul during the wilderness temptations (Matt. 4:1–11), the enticement to redeem man in a spectacular and more comforting manner was constantly raising its head. It was vividly discerned at Caesarea Philippi, when Peter told him it was not necessary for him to be killed. Jesus' prayer in Gethsemane, as he faced the cross in overwhelming grief, is reminiscent of the inducement to escape the foreboding ordeal of a Roman cross. "My Father, if it be possible, let this cup pass away from me: nevertheless, not as I will, but as thou wilt" (Matt. 26:39). The writer of Hebrews expressed the moment beautifully when he said, "Who in the days of his flesh, having offered up prayers and supplications with strong crying and tears unto him that was able to save him from death, and having been heard for his godly fear, though he was a Son, yet learned obedience by the things which he suffered" (5:7–8).

Three times Jesus prayed, and three times he returned to Peter and the two sons of Zebedee to find them sleeping. No event in all of history has been sung about, written about, and preached about more than has the final passion of our Lord. The irony of the situation lies in the fact that these three had an intimate part in that crushing ordeal, and they were asleep! This is a clear example of insensitivity to a moment of extreme gravity. The third time Jesus returned to find them slumbering, he said, "Sleep on now, and take your rest: behold, the hour is at hand, and the Son of man is betrayed into the hands of sinners. Arise, let us be going: behold, he is at hand that betrayeth me" (Matt. 26:45–46).

16.

The Trial and Crucifixion

It has been said that earth's blackest day and earth's brightest day were just three days apart. The arrest, trial, and crucifixion of Jesus constitute the tragedy of the ages; the crucifixion was truly the moment of abysmal darkness. On the day the Son of God was forced to submit to the most shameful of deaths, the depravity of man sank to its lowest ebb. Yet God changed shame into glory, apparent defeat into triumph, and a seeming tragedy into victory. This is the paradox of the cross, something that goes beyond human comprehension and plummets to the very depths of life's deepest meaning.

Thursday and Friday merged into one long, extended day for Jesus. After eating the farewell meal with his disciples he made his way to Gethsemane, conversing as he went. Then he endured the agony in the garden as he prayed, the arrest, the various trials, and finally the rude crucifixion on Friday morning. By the middle of the afternoon he was pronounced dead and removed from the cross for burial. At sundown the sabbath began, as well as the bleak and forlorn interval between Calvary and the open tomb.

The arrest, trial, crucifixion, and burial are all part of the last week of Jesus' life, commonly known as Passion Week. Therefore, technically, they should be included in the previous chapter entitled "The Last Week." However, it seems fit to discuss them as preliminary to the resurrection, the event that is complementary to the cross and brings it to fruition.

1. The Betrayal and Arrest

As Jesus was speaking to the disciples and asking them to arise, Judas and the mob from the chief priests and elders, along with a band of soldiers and officers, came with swords, staves, lanterns, and torches to arrest him. Jesus stepped forward and asked them who they sought, to which they answered, "Jesus of Nazareth." He replied, "I am he." At this answer they fell backward to the ground. Again he said, "Whom seek ye?" Again they replied, "Jesus of Nazareth," to which Jesus a second time responded, "I told you that I am he" (John 18:2–9).

Judas had previously agreed with the search party that he would identify Jesus with a kiss. A kiss on the hand was the usual greeting that a disciple gave to his rabbi. Judas walked up to Jesus and said, "Hail, Rabbi," and kissed him. Jesus' response to Judas was a very simple command: "Friend, do that for which thou art come." Then the mob seized Jesus (Matt. 26:48–50). Luke added that when Judas kissed him, Jesus asked, "Judas, betrayest thou the Son of man with a kiss?" (22:48). The height of reversals would be to use the symbol of affection for the symbol of betrayal, and this is exactly what Judas did.

The disciples must have been very bewildered by all that was going on. Simon Peter, the impulsive one, drew a sword and struck Malchus, servant of the high priest, cutting off his right ear. Jesus said to Peter, "Put up the sword into the sheath: the cup which the Father hath given me, shall I not drink it?" Again Jesus employed the term *cup* as the symbol of suffering. He was affirming the truth that the way of redemption was not to be through the sword but through the cross (John 18:10–11). Luke added that Jesus touched the ear of the servant and healed him (22:51).

They seized Jesus and bound him in order to escort him away, much as they would have a common criminal. Jesus asked them why they came with swords and staves. He had taught daily in the Temple, and they had not arrested him there. He declared that his arrest was a fulfillment of the Old Testament prophecies. The picture was made even more desolate by the desertion of his most intimate followers. "Then all the disciples left him and fled." Those who had vowed, along with Peter, to die with him rather than leave him disappeared into the darkness of the night (Matt. 26:55–56). To those arresting him Jesus made a very dramatic statement: "This is your hour, and the power of darkness" (Luke 22:53). The forces of evil seemed to be gathered up in this moment in all their devastating power.

Mark added one incident occurring at the arrest that is not recorded by any other Gospel writer. "And a certain young man followed with him, having a linen cloth cast about him, over his naked body: and they lay hold on him; but he left the linen cloth and fled naked" (14:51–52). Tradition says that this young man was Mark himself, the author of the Gospel.

2. Nature of the Trials

The trials of Jesus constitute one of the greatest legal disgraces of all history. There was nothing legitimate about them, for there was no honest process to determine the guilt or innocence of Jesus. They were partial from beginning to end. His enemies conspired to destroy him and to rid him from their presence. They determined to kill him, so they merely used the trials as a cloak of justification thrown around their proceedings to give some aspect of legality.

There were two trials: a Jewish or ecclesiastical trial and a Roman or civil trial. The death sentence could be imposed only by a Roman court. Jesus' trials were before three Jewish authorities: Annas, Caiaphas, and the Sanhedrin prior to daylight, and the Sanhedrin during daylight. The trials before Roman authorities were also three in number: Pilate, Herod Antipas, and Pilate the second time.

3. The Jewish Trials

(1) Before Annas Jesus' appearance before Annas, the ex-high priest and father-in-law of Caiaphas, was a preliminary hearing that can hardly be called a trial. (See John 18:12–13.) Annas had the preëminence; even though Caiaphas was legally the high priest at this time, Annas still retained much of his previous power. His judgment was highly respected by the people. It is also probable that the appearance of Jesus before Annas gave them something to do with him while the seventy-one members of the Sanhedrin were being convened. Rounding up the whole council would be quite a task, especially in the middle of the night.

Annas questioned Jesus concerning both his disciples and his teaching, to which Jesus avowed that he had always taught openly, in both the synagogues and in the Temple. Therefore, all Annas had to do was to question those who had heard him teach. One of the officers struck Jesus with his hand and accused him of lack of respect, saying, "Answerest thou the high priest so?" Failing to get the reaction from Jesus that he desired, Annas sent him bound to Caiaphas, the high priest (John 18:19–24).

(2) Before Caiaphas and the Sanhedrin By this time the various members of the Sanhedrin had assembled at the house of Caiaphas. The seventy-one members were composed of the chief priests, elders, and scribes. Many times when the New Testament mentions these three terms together, it is referring to the Sanhedrin. The palace of the high priest was not the usual place for the council to meet; it customarily assembled in the Temple in a room called the *Gapith*. Also, this particular assembly of the council was occurring during the night; and no important case could be tried during a night session. The meeting was probably around three or four o'clock in the moring, definitely before dawn.

"Now the chief priests and the whole council sought false witness against Jesus, that they might put him to death; and they found it not, though many false witnesses came. But afterward came two, and said, This man said, I am able to destroy the temple of God, and to build it in three days" (Matt. 26:59–61). The law of the Jews required two witnesses to condemn a person. The Jews secured false witnesses against Jesus but were unable to get two to agree; finally they secured two who stated that Jesus claimed he could rebuild the Jerusalem Temple in three days. In reality Jesus' prior statement was to rebuild the temple of his body (John 2:19); this they did not comprehend, however, for they had no idea about the death-resurrection event soon to be enacted. The inconsistency of the whole matter lay in the fact that the same law that required two witnesses against a person (Deut. 19:15) also spoke out adamantly against false witnesses (Deut. 5:20; Ex. 20:16). The Sanhedrin obeyed one requirement and flagrantly violated the other.

The high priest remonstrated with Jesus for his silence. "Answerest thou nothing?" Jesus held his peace and uttered not a word (Matt. 26:62–63). One of the four great servant passages in Isaiah predicted this very incident. "He was oppressed, yet when he was afflicted he opened not his mouth; as a lamb that is led to the slaughter, and as a sheep that before its shearers is dumb, so he opened not his mouth" (53:7).

Caiaphas demanded that Jesus openly confess whether or not he was the Christ, the Son of God. Jesus answered that he was. Then he added a statement about his second coming, something that threw the high priest into a fit of frenzy. "Henceforth ye shall see the Son of man sitting at the right hand of Power, and coming on the clouds of heaven" (Matt. 26:64). Such a remark harks back to Psalm 110:1, where "Jehovah saith unto my Lord, Sit thou at my right hand, Until I make thine enemies thy footstool" and to Daniel 7:13–14, where "there came with the clouds of heaven one like unto a son of man" to whom was given "dominion, and glory, and a kingdom."

Caiaphas then rent his garments, accused Jesus of blasphemy, and declared that there was no need of further witnesses. The council declared, "He is worthy of death," and then began to spit in Jesus' face and to abuse him (Matt. 26:65–68). Their pent-up hatred broke loose with uncontrolled abandon. The religious leaders of the nation, who should have acted with dignity and decorum at all times, behaved like hoodlums: they spit upon Jesus, struck him, and mocked him. It was a pitiful scene of vulgar brutality enacted by the leaders of the nation. We can only imagine how Jesus felt during the ordeal!

The charge finally brought against our Lord was blasphemy, a religious charge. To blaspheme means to speak evil against. Therefore, their charge against Jesus was that, by claiming to be the Christ and to have supernatural and divine power, he had spoken evil against God. Leviticus 24:16 says, "And he that blasphemeth the name of Jehovah, he shall surely be put to death; all the congregation shall surely stone him." Caiaphas thought Jesus was worthy of the death required in a violation of this binding law found in the book of Leviticus. Of course, the high priest mentioned death but not the manner of death. Jesus was finally crucified, but not stoned.

It is also very evident that Caiaphas pronounced Jesus guilty of blasphemy before the Sanhedrin had even voted. When they did so, the vote was unanimous; and our Lord was sentenced to death, thus making him equivalent to a common criminal in the eyes of those who did not know him.

(3) Peter's Denial A house in Jerusalem such as Caiaphas would have occupied was usually built around a quadrangular court; the front entrance opened into the street and was protected by a heavy gate. The house of Caiaphas had such a court, for here it was that Peter three times denied his Lord.

Peter followed Jesus, as did another unnamed disciple—probably John, the son of Zebedee. Because he knew the high priest, this unnamed disciple gained entrance into Caiaphas' courtyard. He was also able to secure an entrance for Peter by speaking to the maid at the door. When the girl asked Peter if he were a disciple of Jesus, Peter answered, "I am not" (John 18:15–17).

All those not permitted to enter the house where the questioning of Jesus was taking place had to remain outside in the courtyard. Here a fire was built, and Peter was warming himself. The one who had made his boast about dying with Jesus was consorting with those who were condemning Jesus; and he was warming himself at their fire (John 18:18). Twice more he was charged with being a follower of Jesus, and twice more he denied it.

The second time he "denied with an oath," saying he did not know him. At the third denial he "began to curse and to swear." Immediately the cock crowed (Matt. 26:71–74). Luke added, "And the Lord turned, and looked upon Peter." It would be hard to imagine the depth of embarrassment overwhelming the apostle at that moment, for he remembered vividly that Jesus had foretold that before the cock crowed, Peter would deny him three times. "And he went out, and wept bitterly" (Luke 22:61–62).

(4) Before the Sanhedrin Again The third Jewish trial was held after daybreak, when a formal session of the council was held in its usual

meeting place in the Temple (Luke 22:66–67). Meeting after daybreak would give the proceedings of the assembly a semblance of legality. At this session Jesus was questioned, but no witnesses were brought forward to present evidence against him. When they asked him to make a definite statement about whether or not he was the Christ, he told them that they would not believe him. He made a lucid remark about his second coming, however, just as he had at the previous night session. "But from henceforth shall the Son of Man be seated on the right hand of the power of God" (v. 69). When they asked him if he were the Son of God, he responded, "Ye say that I am" (v. 70). At this they declared that they had no need of witnesses, that Jesus' own words condemned him (vv. 70–71).

(5) *Illegal Aspects of the Jewish Trials*   There were certain aspects of the Jewish trials that made them flagrantly illegal. Besides the Jewish leaders' paying false witnesses to testify against Jesus, Jesus was given no opportunity to defend himself. At the same time he was placed under oath to condemn himself. No legal requirement was met by bringing Jesus before Annas initially. A meeting of the Sanhedrin in the dark hours of the night was definitely illegal. The formal condemnation of the Sanhedrin after morning had arrived was merely an effort to give the proceedings an aura of legality. Here was another effort to obey a law that did not interfere with their purpose, but they threw out others that did interfere.

Jesus was subjected to all sorts of indignities, mockings, and abuse, which should never happen in a smoothly run court proceeding. They pronounced Jesus "worthy of death," but Rome had taken away from the Jews the privilege of pronouncing sentence of death. Jesus was also accused of blasphemy, but no reasons for such a charge were given. Also, no one was invited to present testimony that would have aided Jesus.

(6) *Death of Judas*   Matthew and Acts are the two books that tell of Judas' death. Matthew places this event before the trial of Jesus. "Then Judas, who betrayed him, when he saw that he was condemned, repented himself, and brought back the thirty pieces of silver to the chief priests and elders, saying, I have sinned in that I betrayed innocent blood" (Matt. 27:3–4). Receiving little comfort from the Jewish authorities, he threw down the pieces of silver in the sanctuary, went out, and hanged himself (vv. 4–5).

The chief priests decreed that the money was unholy and could not be placed in the sacred treasury. It was the "price of blood." Therefore, they decided to purchase a field to be used as a place for burying strangers (vv. 6–7). The term strangers is used here for foreigners and therefore designates people from foreign lands dying in Jewish territory with no family to bury them. The place received the name Akeldama, meaning "field of blood" (Acts 1:19).

4. The Roman Trials

(1) Before Pilate Pontius Pilate, notorious for his condemnation of Christ, was the Roman procurator (governor) of Judea and Samaria from A.D. 26–36. He received his authority from Emperor Tiberius. Writings at that time picture him as harsh and cruel, though at times unstable and indecisive. The trial of Christ would be an example of these traits. Early in his Palestinian rule he introduced the imperial insignia into Jerusalem, which made the Jews so angry that he had to remove them. One of the worst things he did was to use funds from the Temple treasury to build a needed aqueduct. When the Jews protested, he had his troops attack and disperse the crowd. Eventually his cruel acts resulted in his recall to Rome in A.D. 36.

Mark said that they "bound Jesus, and carried him away, and delivered him up to Pilate" (15:1). John told us more about this first appearance before the Roman procurator than the other Gospel writers. He stated that, when they took Jesus to the palace of Pilate, they themselves did not enter the building; it belonged to a Gentile, and entering such an edifice would make them unholy and unable to partake of the Passover festivities. Therefore, Pilate walked out to meet them and to inquire of the accusation against Jesus. Pilate must have had some knowledge of the situation—not only concerning Jesus and his claims, but also how the Jews felt about the famous teacher. The Jews answered to the effect that their bringing Jesus before him implied that Jesus was an evildoer (John 18:28–30). The Jewish crowd accused Jesus of three things: perverting the nation, refusing to give tribute to Caesar, and claiming to be a king (Luke 23:2).

Pilate's response to the Jews constituted his first attempt to evade the responsibility of dealing with the touchy matter. "Take him yourselves, and judge him according to your law." They quickly reminded Pilate that they couldn't put a man to death (John 18:31–32).

The Jews' statement about Jesus' claim to be a king must have intrigued Pilate, for he returned inside to Jesus and asked, "Art thou the king of the Jews?" Jesus clearly stated the nature of his kingdom. "My kingdom is not of this world: if my kingdom were of this world, then would my servants fight, that I should not be delivered to the Jews: but now is my kingdom not from hence" (v. 36).

From this the interview proceeded to a discussion of the nature of truth. Finally Pilate moved outside to the Jews and stated, "I find no crime in him'' (John 18:33–38). If this were true in Pilate's thinking, and if he really believed such, he should have released Jesus. This was Pilate's second attempt to evade his responsibility. When Jesus made no reply to the accusations, Pilate said to him, ''Answerest thou nothing? Behold how many things they accuse thee of.'' Jesus continued to maintain his silence, at which Pilate marveled (Mark 15:3–5). The procurator had mixed emotions; he was amazed at the unswerving composure of Jesus, but at the same time he feared the Jewish reaction if he should free Jesus. He had dealt with the Jews' riotous moods on previous occasions. Little did he realize that in reality he was on trial before Jesus.

The Jewish mob made one remark that gave Pilate a ray of hope in his judging ordeal. They stated that Jesus had stirred up the people with his teaching ''throughout all Judea, and beginning from Galilee even unto this place'' (Luke 23:5). As soon as he heard the word Galilee, Pilate asked whether Jesus was a Galilean. Of course, the crowd answered in the affirmative. This gave the trial a new twist, for it set forth Jesus as coming from the territory of Herod Antipas, not Pilate. Therefore, Pilate sent Jesus to stand before Herod Antipas, tetrarch of Galilee and Perea, who was in Jerusalem for the feast (vv. 6–7). This was Pilate's third attempt to rid himself of the responsibility of pronouncing a verdict of condemnation on Jesus.

(2) **Before Herod Antipas** ''Now when Herod saw Jesus, he was exceeding glad: for he was of a long time desirous to see him, because he had heard concerning him; and he hoped to see some miracle done by him'' (Luke 23:8). This ruler over Galilee and Perea was the one who had had John the Baptist beheaded. Evidently his only concern was to see Jesus perform some miracle such as a magician might perform to entertain a crowd. To his questioning, Jesus answered nothing. When Herod saw that he was going to elicit neither answer nor miracle from Jesus, he, with his soldiers, began to mock him. Arraying him in gorgeous apparel, he sent him back to Pilate. The striking thing about this whole incident was that the two rulers ''became friends with each other that very day: for before they were at enmity between themselves'' (Luke 23:8–12). How ironical that the treating of our Lord as a common criminal should have been the means of reconciliation between these two tyrannical rulers!

(3) **Before Pilate the Second Time** When Jesus was returned to Pilate, the morning was still early. The governor immediately conversed with the chief priests and rulers, telling them, ''Ye brought unto me this man, as one that perverteth the people: and behold, I, having examined him

before you, found no fault in this man touching those things whereof ye accuse him: no, nor yet Herod: for he sent him back unto us; and behold, nothing worthy of death hath been done by him" (Luke 23:13–15).

It is striking that the charge against Jesus in the Jewish trials was blasphemy, for which they said he was worthy of death. That charge was never brought to either Herod or Pilate. Several completely different accusations were brought to the Romans.

There was a custom at that time for the governor to release to the Jews at the Feast of Passover any prisoner they designated. The most infamous prisoner in Jerusalem at the time was a man named Barabbas—an insurrectionist, a murderer, and a robber (Luke 23:19; John 18:40). The crowd had picked him for release, for they asked Pilate "to do as he was wont to do unto them" (Mark 15:6–8). However, Pilate clung to the faint hope that they might permit him to release Jesus as the fulfillment of the annual custom.

Pilate seemed to have a certain degree of insight into the motive of the Jewish rulers concerning their desire to rid themselves of Jesus. This was Pilate's fourth attempt to shelve the responsibility of condemning Jesus; and it, too, failed. The Jewish rulers persuaded the multitudes to ask that Barabbas be released and that Jesus be destroyed. The governor said to the crowd, "Which of the two will ye that I release unto you?" The answer, of course, was Barabbas (Matt. 27:20–21). Tradition based on strong evidence maintains that Barabbas' name was also Jesus. If so, Pilate was asking the Jews if he should deliver to them Jesus the Christ or Jesus Barabbas.

Matthew recorded one incident not given by the other Gospel writers, one that occurred while Pilate was sitting on the judgment seat. His wife sent to him, saying, "Have thou nothing to do with that righteous man; for I have suffered many things this day in a dream because of him" (27:19). Tradition says that her name was Claudia Procla and that she was a proselyte from paganism to Judaism.

Pilate ignored his wife and had Jesus scourged, at which time the soldiers put on Jesus' head a crown of thorns and on his body a purple robe—all mock symbols of royalty. They yelled, "Hail, King of the Jews!" and struck him with their hands. Pilate then went to the Jews and announced that he found no crime in Jesus. When Jesus came out, decked in his regal apparel of mockery, Pilate said, "Behold the man." By this time the hatred of the Jews toward Jesus had reached a climax. They cried, "Crucify him, crucify him." At this interval the governor tried again to bypass the responsibility of pronouncing a verdict, his fifth attempt. He said to the Jews, "Take him yourselves, and crucify him: for I find no crime in him." Again Pilate's effort was to no avail; the Jews answered, "We have a law, and by that law he ought to die, because he made himself the Son of God" (John 19:1–7).

This statement perturbed the procurator greatly, so he entered the palace (or "praetorium," as it is termed in John's Gospel) to question Jesus again. He said, "Whence art thou?"; Jesus made no reply. When the governor reminded Jesus that he had power either to crucify him or to release him, Jesus reminded him that any power he had was God-given (John 19:8–11).

Pilate then made a sixth attempt to free Jesus and thus absolve himself from responsibility in the case, but again his effort was thwarted. John said "Upon this Pilate sought to release him: but the Jews cried out, saying, If thou release this man, thou art not Caesar's friend: every one that maketh himself a king speaketh against Caesar" (19:12).

With these caustic words from the Jews, Pilate realized that the case was settled as far as his Jewish subjects were concerned. They would settle for nothing less than crucifixion! Bringing Jesus out to them, he sat on the judgment seat to make a formal verdict. He said to the clamoring mob, "Behold, your King!" When they reminded him that they had no king but Caesar, he gave Jesus to them for the purpose of crucifixion. This occurred at six o'clock in the morning (19:13–16).

Matthew alone related Pilate's dramatic action at this decisive moment. When he saw that all his efforts to dismiss Jesus were to no avail but that the whole scene was bordering on a tumult, "he took water, and washed his hands before the multitude, saying, I am innocent of the blood of this righteous man; see ye to it. And all the people answered and said, His blood be on us, and on our children" (27:24–25).

This might be considered the seventh attempt of Pilate to absolve himself of responsibility in regard to the settlement of Jesus' case. He symbolically transferred all responsibility from himself to the Jews. However, this also failed. Shakespeare's Lady Macbeth said that all the perfume of Arabia could not wash the guilt from her murderous hands; the same applied to Pilate. He could not escape the full responsibility for cowardly surrendering Jesus to the Sanhedrin in order to insure stability to his Roman appointment as procurator.

(4) *Illegal Aspects of the Roman Trials* Just as was true in the Jewish trials, the Roman hearings contained glaring violations of justice. The charge of blasphemy, brought against Jesus when he stood before the Jewish rulers, was never pressed when he was assailed before the Roman authorities. The Sanhedrin had condemned him on this charge, but they

knew that such a religious accusation would not warrant the death penalty in a Roman court. So they conceived of other charges. Pilate had stated he found no crime in him, but he nevertheless "delivered him unto them to be crucified" (John 19:16). Again, as in the Jewish trials, no witnesses were brought to testify in behalf of Jesus. Also, Jesus suffered all kinds of indignities—being scourged, beat upon, spit upon, mocked, and embarrassed. He was taken out immediately after the final hearing under Pilate and crucified; there was no waiting period whatsoever.

5. Mocking by the Roman Soldiers

Jesus was led away by the Roman soldiers into the palace, where the whole cohort began to harass him. (A cohort was a tenth of a Roman legion. It consisted of several hundred men.) The soldiers could do as they pleased with a condemned criminal, and Jesus fit in this category after Pilate released him for crucifixion. After stripping Jesus, they put a scarlet robe and a crown of thorns on him; then they put a reed in his right hand. They mocked him, kneeling and saying, "Hail, King of the Jews!" They not only spit upon him; they beat him on the head with the reed (Matt. 27:27–30).

6. On the Way to Golgotha

After the mocking they changed Jesus' apparel to his own clothes and led him out to crucify him (Mark 15:20). This occurred sometime prior to nine o'clock that Friday morning. Jesus went out, "bearing the cross for himself" (John 19:17). The way by which Jesus proceeded from the palace to Golgotha became known as the *Via Dolorosa,* meaning "way of sorrow." However, the exact path he took is not definitely known. Today pilgrims to Jerusalem along the *Via Dolorosa* are pointed out what are known as "stations of the cross," but these stations did not become known as such until about the middle of the fourteenth century.

The Synoptic Gospels present an event that must have taken place soon after the march had started. The soldiers compelled one named Simon, who was passing by, to carry the cross for Jesus. Simon was from the city of Cyrene on the northern coast of Africa. He was a Jew, probably back in Jerusalem for the Passover.

Luke alone added a second incident that happened on the way to the execution, the lament of the women and Jesus' remark to them. He told them not to weep over him, but to weep for themselves because of the terrible days that lay ahead. There was to be a divine retribution upon Jerusalem that would bring great devastation and suffering (23:26–31).

Jerusalem, Via Dolorosa

Finally they arrived at a place called Golgotha or Calvary. (*Golgotha* is the Aramaic word for skull; *Calvary* is the Latin translation for the same. The Greek term is *kranion*.) The actual place of the crucifixion has been debated for years. For a long time it was considered to be the site on which the Church of the Holy Sepulcher, a Greek Orthodox church, now stands.

Today, however, another spot is considered likely by New Testament scholars. It is a hill outside the walls of Jerusalem about a quarter of a mile north of the Damascus Gate. This is called Gordon's Calvary, named for a British army officer, General Charles Gordon. There is the profile of a skull, with holes for the eyes, nose, and mouth in the hillside. Very near it is the Garden Tomb, a sepulcher hewed out of rock with a trench for a rock cylinder to be rolled across the entrance. This place is located north of Herod's Gate and was definitely outside the wall of Jerusalem at that time. John said that the place where Jesus was crucified was "nigh to the city" (19:20).

7. The Crucifixion of Jesus

The Romans had been practicing crucifixion since the third century B.C. However, it had been employed as a means of execution by the Egyptians, Babylonians, Phoenicians, and other people for centuries. Being a Roman citizen exempted one from this form of death; crucifixion was reserved for runaway slaves, common criminals, and rebels against Rome. The cross carried with it a stigma of dishonor.

One destined for crucifixion was first scourged, a gruesome Roman custom in which a man was tied to a post and beaten with leather whips having pieces of metal and bone tied in. Sometimes the victim was lashed with this instrument of torture almost to the point of death, each stroke cutting into the quivering flesh. Almost always it ended with the fainting of the one being scourged. We have seen that Jesus suffered this act of cruelty. The one destined for crucifixion was also forced to carry his cross, as Jesus was compelled to carry his. Such suffering prior to the actual crucifixion was severe in itself.

When they arrived at the place for Jesus' death, "they offered him wine mingled with myrrh," but he refused it (Mark 15:23). This was a drugged drink used to soften the extreme pain. Jesus did not wish to die in a mental stupor; he felt the necessity to experience the entire act in all its excruciating pain. He was suffering for man's sin; that act of expiation for man's sin must not be altered by decreasing the suffering.

About nine o'clock Jesus was placed on the cross (Mark 15:25). None of the Gospel writers described the actual crucifixion in detail, for it was a well-known sight to the readers of that day. Mark said simply, "And they

260 A GUIDE FOR NEW TESTAMENT STUDY

crucify him'' (15:24). What usually happened was that the condemned one carried to his place of execution only the crossbeam, which weighed between eighty and ninety pounds. At the place of execution he was stripped of his clothing and made to lie down so he could be lashed to the beam. Jesus' hands were also nailed to the wood with spikes. The beam was then raised, with the body, to be securely fastened to the upright beam previously fixed in a hole in the ground. The feet were also tied or spiked to the upright beam. Suspended in such a manner, Jesus was left to hang in physical and mental anguish—exposed, racked with pain, tormented by insects, railed on by the passing, jeering multitude, subjected to the agony of hunger and thirst. Death followed sometimes in ten to twelve hours, sometimes not for two or three days. Jesus' living hours on the cross were relatively short, about six hours.

Matthew said, ''And when they had crucified him, they parted his garments among them, casting lots; and they sat and watched him there'' (27:35–36). Psalm 22 has many details that are strikingly similar to the details of Jesus' crucifixion. Verse 18 reads, ''They part my garments among them,/And upon my vesture do they cast lots.'' Verse 16 says, ''A company of evil-doers have enclosed me;/They have pierced my hands and my feet.'' Verses 14 and 15 read, ''I am poured out like water,/And all my bones are out of joint:/My heart is like wax;/It is melted within me./My strength is dried up like a potsherd;/And my tongue cleaveth to my jaws;/And thou hast brought me into the dust of death.''

Above Jesus' head Pilate had placed an inscription: ''Jesus of Nazareth, the King of the Jews,'' written in three languages: Hebrew, Latin, and Greek. The title reflected many attitudes: a note of revenge on Pilate's part toward the Jews for the distressing position into which they had thrust him; a note of official contempt toward Jesus for his claim to be a king; a declaration that, with the crucifixion of Jesus, Jewish nationalism had come to an end. Whatever Pilate's motive might have been, the Jewish leaders were very disconcerted because of the inscription and asked Pilate to alter it. They said to him, ''Write not, The King of the Jews; but, that he said, I am King of the Jews.'' Pilate's answer has almost become a proverb: ''What I have written I have written'' (John 19:19–22).

Along with Jesus were crucified two robbers, one on his right and one on his left. It was a custom at that time to crucify in groups, so the crucifixion of three at this time was not unusual. According to Mark and Matthew, both of the robbers reproached Jesus (Mark 15:27,32; Matt. 27:38,44); according to Luke, one of them repented and asked Jesus to remember him when he came into his kingdom (Luke 23:39–43).

Jerusalem, Gordon's Calvary

Those who passed by the crucifixion scene railed on Jesus and challenged him to save himself by coming down from the cross. The Sanhedrin also mocked him: "He saved others; himself he cannot save. He is the King of Israel; let him now come down from the cross, and we will believe on him. He trusteth on God; let him deliver him now, if he desireth him: for he said, I am the Son of God" (Matt. 27:42–43). How much this sounds like Psalm 22:8: "Commit thyself unto Jehovah;/let him deliver him:/Let him rescue him, seeing he/delighteth in him." Even the soldiers joined in the mockery of Jesus, offering him vinegar, a drink indulged in by Roman soldiers (Luke 23:36–37).

8. The Seven Sayings of Jesus

The seven utterances of Jesus upon the cross, sometimes known as the seven last words, are familiar to Christians throughout the world. They have been set to music and sung as oratorios during the Easter season for many years. Luke recorded three utterances; John recorded three; and Matthew and Mark recorded one, the only one found in more than one Gospel. We cannot speak authoritatively on their proper sequence. However, it is very probable that three occurred from nine till twelve o'clock, the hours of light, and four from twelve till three, the hours of darkness. The first three sayings of Jesus were made in reference to others; the last four were made in reference to himself. The traditional order of the sayings is presented here.

(1) "Father, forgive them; for they know not what they do" (Luke 23:34). This was a prayer of intercession for his executioners. In his ministry he had taught his disciples to pray for the ones persecuting them (Matt. 5:44); in his death he exemplified his teaching by this prayer for the ones treating him so cruelly. Even in the agony of extreme suffering, his heart yearned for a depraved humanity.

(2) "Verily I say unto thee, To-day shalt thou be with me in Paradise" (Luke 23:43). This was a promise to the repentant thief being crucified at his side. This robber, after remonstrating with the other one for rebuking Jesus, turned to our Lord and said, "Jesus, remember me when thou comest in thy kingdom." Immediately Jesus gave his glorious promise. The first and second sayings are recorded in the Gospel of Luke.

(3) "Woman, behold, thy son! . . . Behold, thy mother!" (John 19:26–27). This was a charge to his mother and to "the disciple whom he loved," taken by most scholars to be John, the son of Zebedee. John is never mentioned by name in the Gospel that bears his name, but "the disciple whom Jesus loved" is referred to many times. Most scholars

believe that these two are synonymous. The disciple referred to accepted the challenge and took Mary into his own home. Evidently Joseph was dead; he was not mentioned in the life of Jesus after the incident in the Temple when Jesus was twelve (Luke 2:41–51).

(4) "My God, my God, why hast thou forsaken me?" (Mark 15:34; Matt. 27:46). This cry of desolation, given in both Mark and Matthew, is the only one found in more than one Gospel, and it is the only saying that either of these Gospels presents. On the surface it might seem that Jesus felt neglected by the Father, but there is more to the saying than that.

Jesus was probably quoting the opening line of Psalm 22. This is the psalm already referred to, the psalm that fits the crucifixion in so many details. This psalm, so familiar to our Lord, would be in his mind while he hung on the cross. Pious Jews were in the habit of quoting Psalm 22 in times of adversity. It begins with a forlorn note, but it ends in triumph. In this case it would be Jesus' shout of victory, not his shout of abandonment. Also, never has there existed the moment when the motive, thought, will, or desire of one person of the Trinity ran counter to that of another person of the Trinity—not even during the throes and extreme agony of the cross. This would be an inconsistency within the Godhead. The old thought, so often voiced, that the Father turned his back on Jesus during Calvary, is without foundation. The attitude of one was the attitude of the other at all times and in all places.

Jesus had already been rejected by his own people (John 1:11). He had been convicted by false witnesses and illegal Roman justice. His disciples had fled (Mark 14:50). Peter had denied him, and Judas had betrayed him. There was darkness over the whole land from noon till three o'clock, and it was at about three that Jesus uttered this forlorn saying (Matt. 27:45–46). It may have even seemed that all nature had deserted him. Death itself was very near, so his agony was extremely great—even to the point that, apparently, the Father had forsaken him. It was necessary that Jesus suffer alone in his salvation of a depraved humanity. He must have experienced a more complete isolation than ever befalls the common man as he passes through the gates of death. The salvation of a lost humanity was coming into being through the agonizing death that, from all appearances, marred the beauty and winsomeness that he so richly possessed. Truly he tasted death for every man (Heb. 2:9).

In his death he conquered Satan and all his forces. "Now shall the prince of this world be cast out" (John 12:31). There was never a moment during his incarnate life that the Father was more pleased with the Son nor nearer the Son than at this moment, the climax of all his suffering. When Jesus asked the Father to glorify his name, the Father responded from heaven, "I have both glorified it, and will glorify it again" (John 12:28). Jesus had glorified it in his ministry and would glorify it in his death.

Mark said Jesus cried with a loud voice, "Eloi, Eloi, lama sabachthani? which is, being interpreted, My God, my God, why hast thou forsaken me?" Matthew used "Eli, Eli" instead of "Eloi, Eloi." It is easy to see why some of those standing around misunderstood him and thought he called for Elijah (Mark 15:35; Matt. 27:47).

(5) "I thirst" (John 19:28). This, the cry of physical anguish, is found only in John. The thirst that accompanied the agony of crucifixion must have been horrible. John stated that "they put a sponge full of the vinegar upon hyssop, and brought it to his mouth" (v. 29).

(6) "It is finished" (John 19:30). This, the cry of victory, is also found only in John. Evidently this saying immediately followed the preceding one, for John said, "When Jesus therefore had received the vinegar, he said, It is finished." It was a word of accomplishment as well as of victory. The English is a translation of a Greek word meaning to complete, to accomplish, to finish, to fulfill. Jesus was crying out in a sense of relief that the great transaction was done. The ransom had been paid (Matt. 20:28)!

(7) "Father, into thy hands I commend my spirit" (Luke 23:46). This is presented only by the Gospel of Luke. Immediately after the cry of resignation, Luke added, "He gave up the ghost" (v. 46). John added, "And he bowed his head, and gave up his spirit" (19:30).

It is estimated that Jesus died around 3 P.M. on a Friday in April, probably in A.D. 30. (Other books say anywhere from A.D. 27 to A.D. 33.)

9. Miracles of Nature

Besides the darkness from noon till three in the afternoon, there were several other miracles that occurred during the last phases of the crucifixion. The elaborate and significant veil that separated the holy place from the holy of holies in the Temple was torn from the top to the bottom (Mark 15:38). What was the significance of this mysterious tearing? The high priest was the only person to enter through the veil from the holy place to the holy of holies, and he only did so on the Day of Atonement. With the atonement of Jesus, effected through Calvary, the earthly holy of holies was no longer needed. Jesus is our high priest, who lives to make intercession for us in heaven above, our holy of holies (Heb. 9:24). Calvary was the beginning of a high priesthood, that of Christ, which goes on forever (Heb. 4:14). Therefore, the tearing of the veil was a symbol that every believer has bold access to the throne of grace itself, made possible by the death of Jesus.

Besides these two miracles there was also an earthquake, accompanied by the splitting of rocks. Matthew stated, "The earth did quake; and the rocks were rent" (27:51).

The fourth miracle consisted of the opening of the tombs and the bodily emerging of many of the saints who had died (Matt. 27:52). Matthew added in his Gospel that after the resurrection of our Lord, these saints entered Jerusalem and appeared to many (v. 53). This is another indication that the resurrection of Jesus is the source of our resurrection also.

These miraculous happenings seemed to have a tremendous effect on those standing by, especially for the centurion in charge of the Roman soldiers crucifying Jesus. This Gentile man of war, hardened to the cruel Roman expectations for one of his military position, "feared exceedingly, saying, Truly this was the Son of God" (Matt. 27:54).

The ones most faithful to Jesus were the women, who stayed on, "beholding from afar." Among them were Mary Magdalene, Mary the mother of James and Joses, and the mother of James and John, sons of Zebedee (Matt. 27:55–56). Mark said there were many other women besides these three (15:41).

10. The Burial of Jesus' Body

The sabbath began at sunset. According to Jewish law, no body could be left on the cross on a sabbath day (John 19:31); therefore, the bodies of Jesus and the two thieves had to be removed before sunset. The Jews requested of Pilate that their legs be broken, an act by which death would be hastened and the bodies could be removed in time to observe the law. This was probably done with a heavy mallet. After they broke the legs of the two thieves they came to Jesus, only to find that he was dead already. They did not break his legs, which John considered a fulfillment of Scripture. Psalm 34:20 reads, "He keepeth all his bones:/Not one of them is broken." Also, a requirement of the Mosaic law was that not a bone of the Passover lamb was to be broken (Ex. 12:46; Num. 9:12). Nevertheless, one of the soldiers pierced Jesus' side with a spear, and blood and water gushed out. Evidently he wanted to make sure Jesus was dead (John 19:31–37).

Most victims of crucifixion were outcasts, with no friends or loved ones to bury them, so their bodies were placed in a special plot. A man named Joseph, of the nearby village of Arimathea, went to Pilate and requested the body of Jesus. Mark and Luke said he was a "councillor of honorable estate,'' one who "was looking for the kingdom of God" (Mark 15:43; Luke 23:50–51). Matthew and John stated that he was a disciple of Jesus (Matt. 27:57; John 19:38). Pilate marveled that Jesus had died in so short a time and called the centurion for verification of the matter. Learning that Jesus was dead, he granted Joseph his request (Mark 15:44–45). John said that Nicodemus, mentioned twice previously in the Fourth Gospel, brought "a mixture of myrrh and aloes" and helped Joseph with the preparation of the body and with the burial (19:39–40). They wrapped the body in a clean linen cloth, folding in the spices as they did so.

The tomb was near the place of crucifixion. "Now in the place where he was crucified there was a garden; and in the garden a new tomb wherein was never man yet laid. There then because of the Jews' preparation (for the tomb was nigh at hand) they laid Jesus" (John 19:41–42). This tomb, Joseph's own possession, was hewn directly from the rock and had never been used. They rolled a great stone against the opening to secure the tomb, then departed (Matt. 27:60).

The Galilean women, so faithful at the cross, were also faithful at the tomb. These women followed the men carrying the body of Jesus to the tomb and watched the burial procedure. Then they went home and prepared more spices; but they rested on the sabbath, as all pious Jews did (Luke 23:55–56).

There was still fear and anxiety on the part of the Jewish leaders. Jesus' following had been so great, his personality and his ministry so distinct, and his crucifixion so characterized by supernatural events that the chief priests and Pharisees made a special request of Pilate: "that the sepulchre be made sure until the third day" (v. 64). Their reason was that Jesus' disciples would come and steal him away, then claim he had arisen. Pilate advised them to use their guard and make the seal as sure as possible. This was all done on the day after the crucifixion (Matt. 27:62–66), which would be on the morning of the sabbath. This was a special day, for it was the sabbath of the Passover.

This sabbath day ended at sunset, at which time the first day of the week for the Jews began. After sunset, therefore, and at the beginning of the new day, Mary Magdalene and the other Mary came to the tomb bringing spices (Matt. 28:1).

17.

The Resurrection and Ascension

The four Gospels present little evidence concerning the feelings and thoughts of Jesus' followers during the time he was in the tomb. However, they must have felt desolate and forlorn, with their hopes and expectations faded. Their mood must have been one of defeat and disillusionment as they saw their Master taken down from the cross and laid away in a dark tomb. The words of two travelers on the way to Emmaus convey to us something of the despair of their state of mind. "But we hoped that it was he who should redeem Israel" (Luke 24:21). This statement was made by men who had already heard of the empty tomb; so the dejection of the disciples during the hour of the actual entombment was probably much more acute.

They were bewildered and perplexed by the startling turn of events. Jesus had informed them on several occasions that he must suffer at the hands of men, be killed, and the third day be raised up. On the first occasion Peter had remonstrated with him. Matthew stated that one time "they were exceeding sorry." Generally, they made no comments and asked no questions. They did not want to accept the deplorable concept of a dying Messiah, so they evidently dismissed it from their minds.

If they had really believed Jesus when he said that on the third day he would be raised up, would they not all have been at the tomb in eager anticipation, waiting for the exact moment? It appears that not one of them expected him to step forth alive. The great cause he had taught seemed to be eclipsed. Their great love for him and the constant awareness of his absence heightened their grief. It appeared that he had been conquered by death, that his kingdom had come to an end, and that his enemies had triumphed.

1. The Empty Tomb

Suddenly amazing things took place! Early on the first day of the week, even before sunrise, the tomb was miraculously opened. "And behold, there was a great earthquake; for an angel of the Lord descended from heaven, and came and rolled away the stone, and sat upon it. His appearance was as lightning, and his raiment white as snow: and for fear of him the watchers did quake, and became as dead men'' (Matt. 28:2–4). Just as startling things occurred during the final moments of the crucifixion of Jesus, startling things transpired at his resurrection. It was a very dramatic moment, a moment that was destined to revitalize the dejected band of devotees.

It seems that Mary Magdalene was the first to witness the empty tomb, arriving there even before dawn. She came ''early, while it was yet dark, unto the tomb.'' When she saw that the stone had been rolled away from the entrance, she ran to tell Peter and John what she had witnessed (John 20:1–2).

Next were the Galilean women, who came at dawn bringing prepared spices. When they, too, saw that the stone was rolled away, they entered the tomb and found that his body was gone. While they were standing there in a perplexed state of mind, ''Two men stood by them in dazzling apparel: and as they were affrighted and bowed down their faces to the earth, they said unto them, Why seek ye the living among the dead? He is not here, but is risen: remember how he spake unto you when he was yet in Galilee, saying that the Son of man must be delivered up into the hands of sinful men, and be crucified, and the third day rise again'' (Luke 24:4–7). Then they recalled Jesus' words and went immediately to inform the eleven apostles and the others of the wonderful news (Luke 24:1–10).

Matthew said that the angel who rolled away the stone spoke reassuring words to the women and commanded them to go relate the good news to the disciples—that Jesus was going before them into Galilee and that they would see him there. The women, filled with mixed emotions of fear and joy, ran to the disciples with the marvelous news (Matt. 28:5–8).

The third party to witness the tomb void of Jesus' body consisted of Peter and John. (The Gospel of John designates, for the second and unnamed man, the ''disciple whom Jesus loved.'' It will be assumed here that this was John, the son of Zebedee.) Mary Magdalene hurried to them with the news that Jesus' body was no longer there. Both of them ran to the tomb; John outran Peter and arrived first. With reverence he stood outside, stooped down, and looked in, where he viewed the linen cloths. Peter came up and, true to his impulsive nature, entered immediately into the tomb. There he found the linen cloths and the napkin that had been on Jesus' head. Then John entered, ''and he saw, and believed.'' Then the writer of the Gospel added a word of explanation. ''For as yet they knew not the

Jerusalem, traditional tomb of Jesus

scripture, that he must rise again from the dead." They departed for their homes (John 20:2-10). The overwhelming evidence is that the disciples, even the faithful Galilean women, did not anticipate Jesus' resurrection. They were surprised when it occurred.

2. The Appearances of the Resurrected Lord

The empty tomb, along with the angelic verification that Jesus had arisen, presented substantial evidence of the resurrection. Weightier yet as evidence were the many appearances of Jesus in bodily form to his disciples throughout the next forty days. These came at various times and in various places, sometimes in Galilee and sometimes in Jerusalem. Jesus' main objective in the appearances was to convince his disciples that he was alive and that he had conquered death. The first five appearances took place on the day of the resurrection itself, and the subsequent six appearances occurred during the remaining forty days.

(1) To Mary Magdalene Mark said that Mary Magdalene was the first person to whom Jesus appeared after he was risen on that first day of the week (16:9). John informed us that when she stooped to look into the tomb, she saw two angels, one sitting at the head and one at the foot, where the body had been. When they asked her why she wept, she replied that they had taken away her Lord and she did not know where they had laid him. When she turned around, she saw Jesus but failed to recognize him. Jesus asked her the same question. Thinking the man was the gardener, she said to him, "Sir, if thou hast borne him hence, tell me where thou hast laid him, and I will take him away." Jesus said, "Mary," to which Mary replied with the term "Rabboni." (This is the Aramaic form of Rabbi.) Jesus said to her, "Touch me not; for I am not yet ascended unto the Father: but go unto my brethren, and say to them, I ascend unto my Father and your Father, and my God and your God" (v. 17).

The words "Touch me not" would best be translated from the Greek as "Do not continue to hold on to me." Jesus was not requesting that she not touch him physically, for he was not thinking of the nature of the resurrected body. He was advising her to discontinue clinging to him for security, for his ascension was soon to take place and he would not be bodily present. Mary left the scene and went to bring word of the startling event to the other disciples (John 20:11-18). Mark added that they disbelieved (16:11).

(2) To the Other Women Jesus met the other women and said to them, "All hail" (v. 9). They immediately grasped him by the feet and worshiped him. He said, "Fear not: go tell my brethren that they depart

into Galilee, and there shall they see me'' (Matt. 28:9–10).

Matthew here related an incident involving the guard who had been stationed around the tomb. When these men reported all the events connected with the tomb and the resurrection, a council was held to determine how to meet the crisis. It was decided to bribe the soldiers to say, ''His disciples came by night, and stole him away while we slept.'' The soldiers took the money and did as directed (Matt. 28:11–15).

(3) *To the Two Disciples on the Road to Emmaus*   On the evening of the day of the resurrection, two disciples were traveling on the road to the village of Emmaus, which was about seven miles northwest of Jerusalem. One was named Cleopas, but the name of the other is not mentioned. As they walked and conversed of the recent events that had taken place in Jerusalem, Jesus appeared and accompanied them. ''But their eyes were holden that they should not know him'' (Luke 24:13).

When Jesus quizzed them concerning their conversation, they seemed surprised that he should have been in Jerusalem and did not know the strange events that had transpired there. They spoke of Jesus and the crucifixion and of the hopes they had placed in him for the future of Israel. They also mentioned the reports of the angels and the women. Jesus replied, ''O foolish men, and slow of heart to believe in all that the prophets have spoken! Behooved it not the Christ to suffer these things, and to enter into his glory? And beginning from Moses and from all the prophets, he interpreted to them in all the scriptures the things concerning himself'' (vv. 25–27).

When they arrived at the village they invited him to come in with them. They recognized him at the blessing and breaking of the bread, after which he vanished from their sight, probably even quicker than he had appeared. That very hour the two returned to Jerusalem to bring to the others the joyous news (Luke 24:13–35).

(4) *To Simon Peter*   This appearance is one mentioned briefly in two places, Luke and 1 Corinthians. When the two from Emmaus returned to the disciples in the capital city bearing news of Jesus' visit and of his conversation with them, their friends also had glorious words. ''The Lord is risen indeed, and hath appeared to Simon'' (Luke 24:34). Evidently this is the identical incident of which the apostle Paul spoke, ''he appeared to Cephas'' (1 Cor. 15:5).

(5) *To the Disciples; Thomas Absent*   Even while the group of disciples was eagerly listening as the two from Emmaus related their recent experience, Jesus suddenly stood in their midst, saying, ''Peace be unto you.'' Their joy was mixed with fear, for ''they were terrified and affrigh-

ted, and supposed that they beheld a spirit." Jesus reassured them, challenging them to view his hands and feet. "Handle me, and see; for a spirit hath not flesh and bones, as ye behold me having." Even when he pointed out his hands and his feet, "they still disbelieved for joy, and wondered." To add further proof of his identity and of the reality of his presence, he ate a piece of broiled fish before their eyes (Luke 24:36–43).

John recounted the same appearance, adding that the doors were shut "for fear of the Jews." Suddenly Jesus was standing in their midst, challenging them: "Peace be unto you: as the Father hath sent me, even so send I you." After saying this he breathed on them and said, "Receive ye the Holy Spirit." Thomas, also called Didymus (Twin), was not with them. As they related to him later their glorious encounter with the risen Lord, he stated that unless he could see and feel the print of the nails in Jesus' hands and could put his hand into the hole in his side, he would not believe (John 20:19–25).

(6) To the Disciples; Thomas Present   This appearance took place on Sunday night a week later. Again Jesus suddenly appeared, even though the doors were shut. He said, "Peace be unto you," after which he seemed to direct his conversation directly to Thomas. He said to him, "Reach hither thy finger, and see my hands; and reach hither thy hand, and put it into my side: and be not faithless, but believing" (v. 27). It must have been very embarrassing for Thomas, for he replied, "My Lord and my God." Jesus then added, "Because thou hast seen me, thou hast believed: blessed are they that have not seen, and yet have believed" (v. 29).

Thomas did not carry out what he had declared necessary before he would believe; the stark reality of the presence of his Lord brought forth his frank statement of faith (John 20:26–29).

(7) To Seven Disciples Beside Galilee   John vividly described Jesus' appearing to seven on the shore of the lake. Evidently the disciples had returned from Jerusalem to Galilee, and seven were assembled by the water: Simon Peter, Thomas, Nathanael, James, John, and two unnamed ones. Simon Peter said, "I go a fishing," to which they responded, "We also come with thee." They fished that night but caught nothing.

At daybreak Jesus stood on the shore, but the disciples did not know he was their Master. When he directed them to cast their net on the other side of the boat, they accepted his suggestion. The catch was miraculous—153 fish in all, a catch so large that the net was almost torn. It seems that John was the first to recognize Jesus, for he said to Peter, "It is the Lord." After they finally reached the shore with their enormous catch, they had breakfast there with Jesus. None of the disciples inquired of Jesus concerning his identity. John said, "And none of the disciples durst inquire of him, Who art thou? knowing that it was the Lord" (John 21:1–14).

John added the famous questioning to which Jesus subjected Peter immediately after the meal. Three times he asked Peter if he loved him, and Peter responded three times in the affirmative, being grieved the third time when Jesus put forth the question. One wonders if Jesus purposely made Peter contradict every denial with a declaration of love.

"Jesus saith to Simon Peter, Simon, son of John, lovest thou me more than these? He saith unto him, Yea, Lord; thou knowest that I love thee. He saith unto him, Feed my lambs. He saith to him again a second time, Simon, son of John, lovest thou me? He saith unto him, Yea, Lord; thou knowest that I love thee. He saith unto him, Tend my sheep. He saith unto him a third time, Simon, son of John, lovest thou me? Peter was grieved because he said unto him the third time, Lovest thou me? And he said unto him, Lord, thou knowest all things; thou knowest that I love thee. Jesus saith unto him, Feed my sheep" (John 21:15–17).

Immediately after the conversation Jesus predicted, in somewhat cryptic words, that Peter would die through crucifixion and that his death would glorify God (John 21:18–19). With that he issued to Peter a very succinct injunction: "Follow me" (v. 19). The call that had challenged Peter at the beginning of Jesus' ministry was once again cast at the feet of this impetuous but lovable disciple.

(8) To More Than Five Hundred in Galilee The apostle Paul wrote of an appearance of Jesus to more than five hundred people: "then he appeared to above five hundred brethren at once, of whom the greater part remains until now, but some are fallen asleep" (1 Cor. 15:6). It is probable that this meeting mentioned by Paul is the same as that recorded by Matthew as the appointed meeting on a mountain in Galilee (28:16). This may have been the meeting in Galilee referred to by the angel to the women at the tomb: "and lo, he goeth before you into Galilee; there shall ye see him" (Matt. 28:7). We are told that some worshiped him, while others doubted. On this occasion Jesus gave what is known as the Great Commission. (See Matt. 28:19–20.) Jesus was appointing the disciples as his witnesses throughout the whole world and was promising them his presence unto "the consummation of the age" (a better translation of the Greek than "the end of the world"). Jesus may have wanted to commission his "flock" while in Galilee, the place of his greatest reception (Matt. 28:16–20).

(9) To James, the Brother of Jesus None of the Gospels speaks of this appearing; an account is found only in 1 Corinthians. "Then he

appeared to James'' (15:7). The appearances of Jesus that Paul lists before
and after this one make it appear that this is the best place for it in the
chronological order. This brother of our Lord became a Christian of great
influence in the Jerusalem church. It is possible that this appearance led to
James' conversion.

(10) To the Disciples   Jesus reminded his disciples that the things
written in the law, the prophets, and the Psalms were fulfilled in him, after
which ''opened he their mind, that they might understand the scriptures.''
He claimed that his death and resurrection on the third day were written in
the Hebrew Scriptures and that the disciples were to preach repentance and
forgiveness of sins in his name unto all nations, starting in the capital city.
They were to remain in Jerusalem until such time as they would be
''clothed with power from on high'' (Luke 24:44–49). Acts also describes
what, from all semblance, is this same appearing. (See Acts 1:3–5). Being
''clothed with power from on high'' and being ''baptized in the Holy
Spirit'' are phrases referring to the same event, an event fulfilled a few
days later. From Acts we learn that the appearances of Jesus covered a span
of forty days.

The disciples asked Jesus an urgent question: ''Lord, dost thou at this
time restore the kingdom to Israel?'' Even on the day of the ascension, a
distorted concept of Jesus' motive in coming to earth was voiced.

Then Jesus informed them that with the coming of the Holy Spirit they
would receive power and be his witnesses ''in Jerusalem, and in all Judea
and Samaria, and unto the uttermost parts of the earth'' (Acts 1:6–8).

(11) To the Disciples on Olivet   The last appearance of the resurrected Lord took place on the Mount of Olives and near Bethany. Luke said
that Jesus led the disciples out ''until they were over against Bethany.''
There he lifted up his hands and blessed them and, while doing so, was
''carried up into heaven'' (Luke 24:50–51). In Acts Luke added that a
cloud received him out of their sight. As they gazed into heaven, two men
dressed in white clothing stood by them and said, ''Ye men of Galilee, why
stand ye looking into heaven? this Jesus, who was received up from you
into heaven, shall so come in like manner as ye beheld him going into
heaven'' (v. 11).

With this joyous news they made their way back to Jerusalem from
Olivet. This return was ''with great joy,'' followed by a continual blessing
of God (Luke 24:52–53). Their doubts had vanished and had been replaced
by certainty. Their fears had changed to joy. Their hopes, almost crushed
into extinction, had been resurrected along with their Lord. They knew he
was risen, alive, and glorified and that he had ''sat down at the right hand

of God" (Mark 16:19)! He who on Calvary had been the world's burden-bearer had on Olivet become eternity's scepter-bearer.

3. The Nature of Jesus' Resurrected Body

Various views have been set forth concerning the nature of the resurrected body of Jesus, the body of the Jesus of the appearances. Some New Testament scholars believe that it was a spiritual body, that the physical body he had prior to his death was in some way changed into one of spiritual nature only. His body was no longer subject to natural law because it was no longer a natural body. This would be tantamount to saying that he was no longer mortal, that the incarnation had ceased to exist, that his humanity had disappeared and had left only the divine nature. Hence his resurrection ministry was conducted in this seemingly natural body. Those who hold such a view point to certain recorded incidents in the resurrection story. His grave clothes were undisturbed (John 20:6-9), as though he had emerged from them as only a spiritual being could have done. Closed doors did not constitute a hindrance to his sudden appearances (John 20:19,26). His disappearances were sometimes instantaneous, as occurred at Emmaus (Luke 24:31). He seemed to have no specific place of residence during the appearance days; they occurred through the entire field of his previous ministry.

Other New Testament scholars believe that Jesus had the same body after the resurrection that he had had during his ministry and during his passion. They cite the incidents in which the Gospel writers stress his human nature. He ate, he walked, he talked, he pointed to his wounded hands and side. At one of his appearances the disciples were afraid, thinking they had seen a spirit. He reassured them that he was not a spirit and charged them, "See my hands, and my feet, that it is I myself: handle me, and see; for a spirit hath not flesh and bones, as ye behold me having." He then "showed them his hands and his feet," after which he ate before them a piece of broiled fish (Luke 24:36-43).

Since some scriptural passages seem to point one way, while some seem to point the other way, divergent theories concerning the nature of Jesus' resurrected body have emerged. It is impossible to speak categorically and decisively. But the fact of Jesus' resurrection is the all-important consideration!

4. False Theories Concerning the Fact of the Resurrection

Through the years certain false and unbiblical explanations about Jesus' resurrection have been discussed. They explain away rather than explain the resurrection.

(1) The Swoon Theory   This view maintains that Jesus did not actually die but that the coldness of the tomb, plus the spices, revived him. In answering such a view, one points to the issuing of blood and water from his side while on the cross (John 19:34) and to the fact that the centurion told Pilate that he was dead (Mark 15:44–45). A hardened Roman soldier would have been able to recognize genuine death. Also, in such a theory as this, who would have rolled away the stone? What about the presence of the angel bearing good news?

(2) The Spirit Theory   According to this view, Jesus really died; but only his spirit returned from the grave. His spirit gave the disciples proof of his continued life. But his body did arise from the tomb, for the tomb was empty and the linen clothes were lying in an orderly fashion (John 20:6–7). Jesus himself denied being merely a spirit but was one composed of flesh and bones (Luke 24:39). Peter preached that his flesh did not see corruption (Acts 2:31).

(3) The Vision Theory   This theory states that there were no objective appearances at all, just subjective appearances. The followers of Jesus experienced hallucinations that led them to believe that Jesus had arisen. Mary Magdalene had such a subjective experience, a vision that spread from her in a contagious manner to the others. Since the followers expected Jesus to work miracles, the subjective visions followed the lines they expected. We reply by saying that his disciples did not expect his resurrection; they had to be convinced of such by the actual appearances of our Lord. Again, there was the empty tomb; where does it fit in such a theory? The women went to the tomb to embalm a dead body, not to see a risen Savior. Besides, hallucinations do not transform human lives and change people without hope into flaming evangelists of the gospel story.

(4) The Mistake Theory   Those who hold to this view believe that the women made a mistake and went to an old deserted tomb, not the one in which Jesus had been placed. Thinking that this tomb was the burial place of their Lord, they departed to circulate the report that he had risen from the dead. In reply we state that people do not easily forget such a place and the happenings surrounding it, written indelibly on their minds. Matthew revealed that the women were there when he was placed in the tomb (27:61), and the time between the burial and resurrection was a relatively short one. There is no parallel case in history of such a preposterous blunder as this charge made against the faithful Galilean women. Even if such a highly improbable failure at recognizing a recently observed burial place did take place, would not the disciples have soon corrected such an

error?

(5) The Fraud Theory   Here it is maintained that Jesus' disciples stole into the tomb by night, took the body of Jesus and hid it, and then circulated the report that he had risen. This is perhaps the oldest erroneous theory concerning the resurrection of Jesus, for it is discussed in Matthew's Gospel (28:11–15). When the soldiers stationed around the tomb went to the chief priests to recount the happenings there, the chief priests bribed them to say that Jesus' disciples had come and had stolen the body while the guards slept. They accepted the bribe and did as they were commanded, "and this saying was spread abroad among the Jews, and continueth until this day" (v. 15). We respond by asking how the guards would know what took place if they were asleep. Also, this act on the part of the disciples would be a fraud; and to accuse the disciples of such an unethical deed would be to blaspheme their character. There was only one Judas. Besides, a movement as ethical and upright as Christianity would not have been thrust forward in the world in such a dynamic way had it been motivated by deception. Men do not march forth as martyrs, having been impelled by a lie they have told themselves.

5. The Significance of Jesus' Resurrection

The resurrection is the most wonderful of all the miracles related to the ministry and great atonement of our Lord. So much is undergirded by it.

(1) The Witness of His Deity   Paul said Jesus "was declared to be the Son of God with power, according to the spirit of holiness, by the resurrection from the dead" (Rom. 1:4). The resurrection gave meaning to Jesus' own statement, "I am the resurrection" (John 11:25), for it filled his claim with divine verification. The whole book of Acts rings with the theme that it was the resurrection of Jesus, substantiated by his appearances, that convinced the disciples that he was the divine Son of God who had come to redeem sinful humanity. He had brought life out of death. None of the great sermons found in Acts mentions the virgin birth of Jesus as a basis of the faith of the disciples. It is the resurrection that is set forth time and again as the cornerstone of their belief in the divinity of Jesus and of their faith in his power to save them from sin to eternal life. Peter preached, "This Jesus did God raise up, whereof we all are witnesses" (Acts 2:32).

(2) The Consummation of Calvary   The resurrection of Jesus was complementary to the death of Jesus. It completed, fulfilled, his atoning sacrifice on the cross. The resurrection did not rectify a mistake made on Calvary, for on the cross Jesus reigned. There the ransom was discharged and the debt paid. "It is finished" was the cry of victory. The resurrection

triumphantly brought to fruition that which was accomplished on Calvary. This is what Paul meant when he declared that Jesus "was delivered up for our trespasses, and was raised for our justification" (Rom. 4:25). Paul very vividly reminded us that "if Christ hath not been raised, your faith is vain; ye are yet in your sins" (1 Cor. 15:17). Many writers speak of the cross-resurrection event, thus depicting the vital connection of the two.

(3) The Guarantee of Our Resurrection   Because Jesus arose, we believe that we will arise also. His resurrection is the basis of our hope, for it guarantees to us life beyond the grave. Paul stated, "For if we have become united with him in the likeness of his death, we shall be also in the likeness of his resurrection" (Rom. 6:5). He also said, "But if the Spirit of him that raised up Jesus from the dead dwelleth in you, he that raised up Christ Jesus from the dead shall give life also to your mortal bodies through his Spirit that dwelleth in you" (Rom. 8:11). The same truth is taught in 1 Corinthians 15.

(4) The Assurance of the Triumph of the Kingdom   The resurrection of Christ is the Christian's guarantee of the triumph of the kingdom of God. As the glorified Christ, Jesus is extending his kingdom through the church and will bring it to a glorious fulfillment someday. The final triumph of the kingdom is lucidly depicted in the book of Revelation, a victory that will occur because Jesus Christ is King of kings and Lord of lords (19:16). He declared, "Fear not; I am the first and the last, and the Living one; and I was dead, and behold, I am alive for evermore" (1:17–18). He is the Lamb in the midst of thousands of angels and of created beings who sing that he is worthy of all power, riches, wisdom, blessings, honor, and glory (5:8–14).

PART FOUR

The Acts of the Apostles: Holy Spirit Extending the Church

18.

The Church in Jerusalem

Luke, in his Gospel, which he addressed to Theophilus, presented the story of Jesus from birth through the ascension. In his sequel, the book of Acts, also addressed to Theophilus, Luke continued the story, repeating the ascension event and depicting the expansion of the church through the work of the Holy Spirit. In the preface of Acts (1:1-5) Luke reminded Theophilus of his "former treatise" and that it concerned "all that Jesus began both to do and to teach." In Acts there is a continuation of that which Jesus began—a flowering, so to speak, of a mighty spiritual movement destined to produce a momentous impact on the world.

1. The Significance of the Book of Acts

Outside the New Testament there is very little literary reference to the Christian movement from about 30 to about 100. Roman writers of that era made only casual statements about the new religion that had its source in Palestine. Josephus, the Jewish historian, in his *Antiquities* (XVIII, iii, 3) concluded his remark about Jesus with the statement: "And even to this day the race of Christians, who are named from him, has not died out."

To these few sporadic literary references to the early Christian movement, archaeology contributes nothing. There is an inscription at Delphi which helps to fix the time of Gallio's rule in Corinth, which in turn helps to ascertain the time of Paul's stay in that city. Excavations that have uncovered church ruins reveal that these churches date from the middle of the third century and later.

This striking scarcity of information from sources outside the New Testament makes the New Testament documents immensely important. It is to the Acts of the Apostles and to the following New Testament books that we owe what knowledge we have of the period of the growth of the early church. Each author makes his contribution from his own viewpoint and with his own purpose in mind.

The chief source of knowledge about the early church is Acts. Since it is so important to us today, it is striking that we can find no trace or mention of it in the writings of the early Christians. The first definite references to it appear in works dated about 180. It is mentioned by Irenaeus of Lyon, by Clement of Alexandria, by Tertullian of North Africa, and by an unknown author of a Latin writing.

2. The Author of the Book of Acts

The work known as the Acts of the Apostle is, in a certain sense, anonymous, since it does not have the name of the author embedded in the text. Early tradition says that Luke, a physician and companion of Paul on his third journey, was the author. Colossians 4:14 mentions "Luke, the beloved physician," while Philemon 24 mentions Luke among Paul's "fellow-workers." 2 Timothy 4:11 states, "Only Luke is with me." It appears that Luke was a Gentile; and if this is so, he is the only Gentile writer of any of the New Testament documents. A study of Colossians 4:10–14 makes it apparent that Luke was of Gentile birth, since Paul placed Luke's name in the Gentile list and not in the list of those of Hebrew birth and Jewish background. Also, the prologue of a manuscript of the Gospel of Luke, dated in the second century, states that Luke was a Syrian hailing from Antioch, one who became a convert to Christianity in his middle age due to the church in that city.

It has been well established that whoever wrote the third Gospel wrote Acts also. There are three lines of evidence to this effect. *One,* both works are dedicated to a man named Theophilus, a name meaning "friend of God." He is called "most excellent" in Luke 1:3, which would denote a man of high social standing, great political prestige, or aristocratic status. *Two,* the writer of the sequel, Acts, referred to his "former treatise," the Gospel (1:1). *Three,* the style of writing and the vocabulary are found to be strikingly similar in the two works. Obviously, when the terms style and vocabulary are used, the Greek is the language concerned.

The author of Luke-Acts was a very important contributor to our New Testament canon for two reasons. One has to do with quantity, for his writings constitute over one fourth of the pages of the New Testament. They almost equal the total number of pages that Paul contributed in his thirteen epistles. The other reason has to do with quality, for both Luke and Acts are quite distinctive in many ways. The third Gospel has more independent material in its composition than any of the other three, and the material having to do with Jesus' postresurrection days is very enlightening. Also, Acts is our only account of the beginning years of the early church, for the Pauline epistles give very little material in this regard.

3. The Purpose of the Book of Acts

Although probably not attached to the original work, the full title, The Acts of the Apostles, was accepted and used by the end of the second century. Both Tertullian and Clement employed the full name around 200. In a sense this title is not fully appropriate since it deals with so few of the apostles. Acts is mainly the story of the activities of Peter and Paul. After a list of the eleven, John is mentioned several times in the third and fourth chapters and James once in the twelfth chapter (12:2). Evidently the author did not intend to set forth in vivid detail the work of all the apostles. The full title was probably added as the canon was being formed, for the early church had a deep respect for the two main apostles, Peter and Paul.

Nor did the writer intend to record pure history *per se*. Objective history is concerned with presenting all the details in a precise chronological order, with full descriptions of all the events. Luke did not tell about all the twelve apostles. He did not tell about all the seven assistants (6:5–6), but concentrated on Philip and Stephen. Barnabas and Saul (Paul) are the only ones mentioned of the special five at Antioch (13:1). The brothers of Jesus became Christians after the resurrection. How? James rose to a position of leadership in the Jerusalem church. How? How did Christianity spread to Alexandria?

Luke wrote with a purpose, that of showing how the gospel story was spread after Jesus' death and how the early churches were formed and successfully fought the rising heresies that would have thwarted the true story of God's redeeming love. Luke selected his episodes with his literary aim in mind; he displayed the events and arranged them with that same purpose constantly before him. He painted his own picture of the young church, with all of its heartaches and struggles, as well as its joys and victories. When one writes with a passion, he cannot record a dispassionate narrative, overlaid with minute details that do not contribute directly to the overall aim.

We might say that Luke was a historian, but a historian with a controlling purpose. In fact, Luke might be classified as the first church historian. He had predecessors in writing a Gospel (Luke 1:1), but he had no predecessor in writing church history. In this area he plowed new ground; therefore, he might be considered the father of church history.

4. The Holy Spirit in the Book of Acts

We have already seen how the Gospel of Luke places great stress on the activity of the Holy Spirit. (See "Luke" under Chapter 7, "A View of the Four Gospels.") Time and again, especially in the first part of his Gospel,

Luke mentioned what the Holy Spirit accomplished through key individuals. In the book of Acts there is even more emphasis upon the directive work of the Holy Spirit. It has been suggested that an appropriate title for the book would be "The Acts of the Holy Spirit"; for Luke's theme, pulsating throughout the book, is the accomplishment of the Holy Spirit through the consecrated leaders of the early church. Where the Gospel concerns the work of the Son, Acts concerns the continuing work of the Holy Spirit.

The outpouring of the power of the Spirit at Pentecost (2:1–13) was a supernatural occurrence of paramount importance, for it thrust the apostles into a very effective evangelistic mission. They entered not just into the streets of Jerusalem but into far-distant lands of the empire.

People are said to be "filled with the Spirit." Some are said to be prompted by the Spirit, while others are said to be guided by the Spirit. Sometimes the Spirit predicted future happenings. Since the Spirit was in control in the early church, the whole movement was characterized from time to time by supernatural events. Luke depicted these events in vivid portrayal.

5. The Organization of the Book of Acts

A reading of this remarkable book reveals that it has a geographical structure. The expansion of Christianity moves from Jerusalem to Judea to Samaria to the coastal area of Palestine to Antioch to the province of Galatia to the region of the Aegean and finally to Rome. The overall movement is west through the Mediterranean world with the capital of the empire as the goal. However, it must be kept in mind that Rome is not merely a geographical goal; it is a spiritual goal, a gospel-fulfilling goal. Luke did not exhaust this subject; he did not relate the spread into Egypt, Galilee, Armenia, Parthia, and other regions where the church had an early growth. He does not speak of the founding of the Roman church or of the Ephesian church or of the Colossian church. When Paul finally wrote his letter to the church in the capital city, it was a strong church; and he had never been there. Someone else carried the gospel there for the first time.

Even though Acts follows a geographical pattern of expansion, it is hard to discern a precise outline that Luke followed. Some scholars divide the book into as few as two parts and some into as many as six parts. This book will employ an outline of the book of Acts involving three major divisions, each division evolving from one of the three divisions in Jesus' Great Commission as recorded in the first chapter of Acts. "Ye shall be my witnesses both in Jerusalem, and in all Judea and Samaria, and unto the uttermost part of the earth'' (1:8). The Jerusalem section is 1:1 to 8:3. The Judea and Samaria section is 8:4 to 12:25. The ''uttermost-part-of-the-earth'' section is 13:1 to 28:31; it concerns Paul's missionary travels in the Mediterranean world. This chapter deals with the proclamation of the gospel in the Jerusalem church, as found in the first seven chapters of Acts.

6. The Jerusalem Church

The first local church arose in Jerusalem. Here a small band of the followers of Jesus were aroused by the resurrection and formed the nucleus of the church in the Holy City. The basis of their close fellowship was a commitment to their resurrected Lord in fulfilling his commission to them.

The organization of this first church was extremely simple; it had little rigid structure, no fast-bound church organization, no hymnbooks, no church buildings, no specifically Christian scriptural writings. The followers of Jesus were not even called Christians at this early stage, but were referred to as those of ''the Way'' (Acts 9:2; 19:9,23; 24:22). They were disciples committed to their Master, those who were walking in ''the way of the Lord'' (18:25). They numbered about 120 (1:15).

A word in the people's daily vocabulary meaning an assembly of citizens was the Greek term *ekklesia,* the called-out ones. The early Christians used this term and applied it to themselves as the ones called out in a common commitment to the Lord Jesus. This is the term that is translated with the English word *church.* The little band of faithful followers at Jerusalem constituted a church or *ekklesia* in the full sense of the word.

This small group was not a powerful one, as the world judges power. They were from a race universally despised. Most of them were Galilean peasants. They had no wealth, no political prestige, no social status, very little educational accomplishments. They possessed the weaknesses characterizing the common man. However, they were a people committed to their Lord, people who were willing to die for their faith. These facts made the difference!

7. A Promise of Power

Matthew and John did not tell of Jesus' ascension into heaven from Olivet. Mark's Gospel has one brief statement concerning it. ''So then the Lord Jesus, after he had spoken unto them, was received up into heaven, and sat down at the right hand of God'' (16:19). Luke spoke of the ascension twice, once at the end of his Gospel (24:51) and again at the beginning of his sequel, the book of Acts (1:9–11).

Just prior to his ascension Jesus gave to his band of faithful followers a promise, his word of a future event that was destined to produce in them an extraordinary spiritual impetus. He said, "I send forth the promise of my Father upon you: but tarry ye in the city until ye be clothed with power from on high" (Luke 24:49). In Acts Luke also presented Jesus' promise to his followers, his word to them that they would "be baptized in the Holy Spirit not many days hence" (Acts 1:5). Jesus' further statement is as follows: "But ye shall receive power, when the Holy Spirit is come upon you: and ye shall be my witnesses both in Jerusalem, and in all Judea and Samaria, and unto the uttermost part of the earth" (Acts 1:8).

Subsequent to this double-edged statement, containing both a promise and a commission, "he was taken up: and a cloud received him out of their sight" (v. 9). Then the band of disciples returned to the Holy City and "went up into the upper chamber, where they were abiding" (1:12–13).

8. Selection of Judas' Replacement

Evidently the apostles thought they might as well dispense with one important task while they were waiting for the fulfillment of the promise, the replacement of Judas Iscariot among the twelve. For some reason or other, the eleven felt that the original number of apostles should remain intact. Peter made a short speech, telling of the defection of Judas and of his tragic end, to all the 120 faithful followers of Jesus. Already assuming the leadership of the Jerusalem church, Peter clearly stated the qualifications for the one to be selected. "Of the men therefore that have companied with us all the time that the Lord Jesus went in and went out among us, beginning from the baptism of John, unto the day that he was received up from us, of these must one become a witness with us of his resurrection" (vv. 21–22).

Two men were put forward, "Joseph called Barsabbas, who was surnamed Justus, and Matthias." They then prayed, asking God to select the one he wanted to replace Judas. With the casting of lots the lot fell upon Matthias, who was then included among the twelve (1:15–26).

Matthias is never mentioned again after his appointment to the ranks of the twelve. Only Peter, James, and John are mentioned after the first chapter of Acts. There is no indication that the twelve, other than Peter, possessed any kind of official leadership in the Jerusalem church; they were merely participating members along with the others.

9. Outpouring at Pentecost

The Jewish Feast of Pentecost occurred fifty days after the Feast of Passover. *Pentecost* is from the Greek word for fifty and is the Hellenistic name for the Jewish Feast of Weeks, Feast of Harvests, or Feast of First

Fruits. Since Jesus' death occurred at Passover and since Jesus' appearances took place during a space of forty days, there were about ten days between the ascension and the supernatural events that happened to the believers of Pentecost.

To the Jew, Pentecost represented a centuries-old feast of historical origin. It was a thankgiving feast for the winter grain crop, even though it was not observed until our month of June. Joy and gladness permeated the air during the days of the feast. To the devout follower of Christ, Pentecost represented the outpouring of spiritual strength in great abundance upon the beginning, struggling church. It has been called "the birthday of the church," though such a phrase poses a difficulty. Many beginning points have been suggested for the church: the birth of Christ, the start of his ministry, the calling of the twelve apostles, the cross, the resurrection, the giving of the Great Commission, the ascension, and Pentecost. One thing is certain: somcting happened at Pentecost that gave to the small, faithful nucleus a great impetus that thrust them forward in a mighty missionary endeavor.

The group was "all together in one place" at the time of the strange happenings on the day of Pentecost (2:1). They had been eagerly awaiting the fulfillment of the promise of their Lord. "And suddenly there came from heaven a sound as of the rushing of a mighty wind, and it filled all the house where they were sitting. And there appeared unto them tongues parting asunder, like as of fire; and it sat upon each one of them. And they were all filled with the Holy Spirit, and began to speak with other tongues, as the Spirit gave them utterance" (2:2–4). Here we see the elements of wind and of fire, both symbolic of the Spirit of God. Luke was telling us that the Holy Spirit came with an energizing force that gave the disciples an enthusiasm that became contagious to all who heard their testimony.

It must be remembered that what was new at Pentecost was not the presence of the Spirit, for the Holy Spirit had been with Jesus and the disciples all along. (See "Luke" in chapter 7, "A View of the Four Gospels," for a discussion of the Holy Spirit in relation to Jesus in his earthly life.) God's Spirit is omnipresent (a word meaning "present everywhere"). He always has been and always will be present everywhere. What was new in the happening at Pentecost was the power brought by the Spirit, for it enabled those present to march forth as Jesus' witnesses "in Jerusalem, and in all Judea and Samaria, and unto the uttermost part of the earth" (1:8).

Since Pentecost was one of the three major feasts (Ex. 23:14), there were great multitudes of Jews in Jerusalem for the occasion. These came from distant places, many of them speaking their own languages and not the Aramaic of Palestine. Luke said that these devout men were "from every nation under heaven." Hearing the tumult caused by the strange happenings, they came together and were very amazed "because that every man heard them speaking in his own language." Since the ones doing the speaking were Galileans, the Jerusalem visitors were at a loss to understand how each man heard and understood in the language of home. Luke listed fourteen different nations or localities from which the visiting Jews and proselytes came. They remarked, "We hear them speaking in our tongues the mighty works of God." They were amazed and perplexed, stating, "What meaneth this?" However, there are generally some who always take the negative side and scoff in any situation, and Pentecost was no exception! Some said, "They are filled with new wine" (2:5–13).

This experience of speaking in tongues was quite different from the tongues mentioned in 1 Corinthians 14. In Acts the visitors heard in their native tongues and understood; in 1 Corinthians the tongues were not understood and required an interpreter. The Acts variety of speaking in tongues edified the church; the Corinthian variety was tearing the church apart. (*Glossolalia* is the term used for speaking in tongues, being derived from two Greek words, "tongue" and "speech.")

10. Peter's Sermon at Pentecost

Peter, standing up with the eleven other apostles, began his memorable sermon on the day of Pentecost. The first thing he did was to correct the erroneous idea that the men were drunk with wine; instead, the strange happenings, he maintained, were the fulfillment of the prophecy of Joel, through whom God predicted that he would pour forth his Spirit upon all flesh and that wonders would be seen in the heavens and signs upon the earth (Joel 2:28–32).

Peter went on to assert that Jesus had fulfilled this prophecy, for mighty works, wonders, and signs had been done by him. He accused the Jews of crucifying and slaying Jesus "by the hand of lawless men," but told how God raised him from the dead. They were all witnesses of that resurrection. Jesus, raised up and exalted, "hath poured forth this, which ye see and hear." The final statement of the sermon bore down with convicting power: "Let all the house of Israel therefore know assuredly that God hath made him both Lord and Christ, this Jesus whom ye crucified" (2:14–36).

The effect of this first sermon after Jesus' ascension was amazing. Convicted of their sin and of their need for Christ, they cried out, "Brethren, what shall we do?" Peter's quick answer was for them to repent and be baptized; then they would receive the gift of the Holy Spirit. "For to you is the promise, and to your children, and to all that are afar off, even as many as the Lord our God shall call unto him" (Acts 2:39). Due to Peter's sermon about 3,000 people repented, believed, and were baptized on that day (2:37–41).

The results of the empowering miracle had a lasting effect, for these new converts "continued stedfastly in the apostles' teaching and fellowship, in the breaking of bread and the prayers." But the consequences of that day were not confined to the new members of the church; "fear came upon every soul; and many wonders and signs were done through the apostles." There was a common fund used to serve the needy. Day by day the devout followers worshiped in the Temple, praised God, had joy in their hearts, and possessed the favor of all the people. The Lord added more saved ones to their Christian community day by day (2:42–47).

Luke said that "the Lord added," meaning to emphasize that the marvelous things that happened in the early church were of God's doings, not man. They were results of the work of the Spirit. Truly, it was necessary that the disciples witness, for the signs and wonders of God did not come about without men used as God's instruments. God was the agent; man was the instrument.

11. The Addresses in Acts

In Acts there are at least sixteen addresses or sermons as given at one time or another by four prominent men: Peter, Stephen, James (the brother of Jesus), and Paul. These addresses make up more than one fifth of the book, Stephen's being the longest one of all (7:2–53). Paul's are not only the most numerous; they vary more in the content than those of any other man. Stephen and James only have one each. The addresses are as follows:

Peter	At Pentecost	2:14–40
	At Solomon's Porch	3:12–26
	Before the Sanhedrin	4:8–12
	Again before the Sanhedrin	5:29–32
	At house of Cornelius	10:34–43, 47
	Before Jewish Christians in Jerusalem	11:5–18
	Before the Christian Council in Jerusalem	15:7–11
Stephen	Before his accusers	7:2–53
James	Before the Christian Council in Jerusalem	15:13–21

Paul	In synagogue in Antioch of Pisidia	13:15–41
	On the Aeropagus in Athens	17:22–31
	Before the elders from Ephesus	20:18–35
	On the stairs in the temple	22:3–21
	Before Felix	24:10–21
	Before Agrippa	26:2–29
	Before chief Jews in Rome	28:17–20

In writing the book of Acts, Luke used those speeches to great advantage. They show us several things. *One,* they are lucid examples of the preaching of the apostles, the type of message expounded by those who had known Jesus in the flesh and had been in a close relationship with him. Preachers of today can learn much from these apostolic, scriptural sermons. *Two,* they manifest the boldness with which the messages were proclaimed. There was no fear or trembling as the story of Jesus' redeeming love, the *kerygma,* was recounted. This shows the extent of the spiritual power released by the Holy Spirit at Pentecost. Peter was at last the rock that Jesus had predicted he would become. Stephen did not tone down his sermon one bit, although near the end of his message he probably saw his accusers gathering the rocks used to bring on his death. *Three,* there is great unanimity of thought in the sermons; they all heartily agree in the aspects of the gospel story that are presented. If the name of the man presenting a certain speech were not identified, it would be hard to identify the messenger. Peter's sermons and Paul's sermons could be interchanged with no violation of thought or doctrine whatsoever.

What theme or themes do the sermons of Acts show us? Each one consists of a brief narrative of the life and ministry of Jesus, a brief mention of the cross, a witness to the resurrection, and a call to repentance and to faith in Jesus' name. Though many sermons from the modern pulpit never mention the resurrection of our Lord, the apostolic sermons make it a central issue.

The sermons are highly biblical in nature. Since the New Testament had not been written and placed in the hands of both proclaimer and audience, the sermons abound in either allusions to or quotations from the Old Testament, especially prophecies. In the first sermon, Peter quoted from both the book of the prophet Joel and from the book of Psalms. Stephen, in his lengthy address, gave a review of Hebrew history, showing an unbelief concerning the death of Jesus.

Some of the sermons are examples of the earliest Christian apologetic—that is, the earliest speeches intended to answer accusations and challenges thrown out by hostile groups. Stephen's address fits well into this category.

But the overall theme of the sermons is the necessity of belief in the resurrected Messiah, which, along with repentance, will issue in the reception of the Holy Spirit.

12. Record of Growth in Acts

We have seen that the faithful group of Jesus' followers, waiting for the power that had been promised, was composed of 120 people (1:15). After Peter's sermon on Pentecost, the number was increased by about 3,000 (2:41). Then the Lord added "day by day those that were saved" (2:47). Later "the number of the men came to be about five thousand" (4:4). Later yet "believers were the more added to the Lord, multitudes both of men and women" (5.14). Luke indicated even further growth: "And the word of God increased; and the number of the disciples multiplied in Jerusalem exceedingly; and a great company of the priests were obedient to the faith" (6:7). A still further statement notes that the church in Judea, Galilee, and Samaria "was multiplied" (9:31). Later we read, "But the word of God grew and multiplied" (12:24). Later still we read that "the churches were strengthened in the faith, and increased in number daily" (16:5). Concerning Paul's work in Ephesus Luke said, "So mightily grew the word of the Lord and prevailed" (19:20).

What is Luke endeavoring to manifest in these numerous allusions to increases in the church? One is an *outward* growth in numerical strength. Many members were being added constantly. Jesus' "little flock" (Luke 12:32) was fast becoming a big flock. A second thing is an *inner* growth in depth, a spiritual growth in faith and commitment. Luke says the churches were "strengthened in the faith" (16:5). Acts is concerned with the development of the church in both these phases.

13. Miracle at the Gate Beautiful

What happened to Peter and John on a certain day as they entered the Temple was the first instance of persecution of the Jews who had become Christians by the Jewish authorities in Jerusalem, mainly the Sadducees. The Sadducees consisted mostly of the priests and the aristocracy of Judea. The new group, the devout and committed Christian community, posed a threat to the power held by the Sadducees. It was mainly the chief priests, Sadducees, who had sought Christ's death. The proclamation of Christ as the Messiah by the disciples, the miracles they performed in his name, the enthusiasm of the group, the rapid growth in their numbers—all led to fear and alarm on the part of the Sadducees.

As Peter and John went up into the Temple at the ninth hour (in the Hebrew reckoning of time, 3 P.M.), the hour of prayer, they encountered at the Beautiful Gate a beggar who had been born lame forty years before. Daily this one was carried and placed at the Temple gate to beg alms. Seeing Peter and John, he expected a coin or two. As Peter and John gazed upon him, Peter commanded him, "Look on us." Naturally the unfortunate man expected an expression of charity from the two worshipers. Peter said, "Silver and gold have I none; but what I have, that give I thee. In the name of Jesus Christ of Nazareth, walk" (3:6).

Peter grasped his right hand and helped him to his feet; the man stood up and went walking and leaping into the temple, praising God as he did so. The beggar had asked for so little and had received so much; he asked for the materialistic and received something money cannot buy. Recognizing the man as the pitiful sight they had witnessed so often at the Beautiful Gate, the people "were filled with wonder and amazement at that which had happened unto him" (3:1–10).

14. Peter's Sermon on Solomon's Porch

The effect of the miracle was the gathering of a crowd of people congregated at Solomon's Porch to see the two disciples who had effected the amazing cure. They came "greatly wondering." With this Peter immediately launched out on one of his frequent sermons, one that contained many of the same elements that he had used in his sermon on the day of Pentecost. He first disclaimed any power at having performed the miracle, for he said it was the work of the God who "hath glorified his Servant Jesus." He accused the Jews of having "killed the Prince of life; whom God raised from the dead." It was this Jesus who had effected the healing of the beggar. Peter then called on the people to repent, saying, "Repent ye therefore, and turn again, that your sins may be blotted out, that so there may come seasons of refreshing from the presence of the Lord." He continued his sermon, basing his appeal on the Old Testament prophets and their foretelling of the coming One who would bless them. "Unto you first God, having raised up his Servant, sent him to bless you, in turning away every one of you from your iniquities" (3:11–26).

Twice in the sermon Peter brought a verbal witness to the resurrection of Jesus, a central theme in all the addresses in the book of Acts. In the thinking of the early church at Jerusalem, the resurrection was a very significant event, for it was an indication that Jesus was the Christ, the Son of God. It brought a whole new concept to the term kingdom of God, for the early Christian had begun to understand what Jesus meant when he used the phrase "my kingdom." God's great act of redemptive love was completed at the cross-resurrection event, and the messianic reign had begun. The resurrection instituted a new age, the age of the church. Some Jews had left

Judaism for the *ekklesia,* "the called-out ones"; and Christ had begun to reign in their hearts eternally. Such a situation produced a cleavage between Christianity and Judaism. No longer were they compatible. The start of the conflict between the chief adherents to Judaism and the followers of Christ is discerned in the incident of the healing of the lame man. But it was not the healing that brought the divergence; it probably was not even the proclamation of Jesus as the long-awaited Messiah. It was the preaching of the resurrection, the fact that God raised Jesus from the dead, that brought conflict with the Sadducees and other Jewish authorities.

15. Peter's Sermon Before the Sanhedrin

The miraculous cure and Peter's sermon on Solomon's Porch are found in Acts 3; the ensuing conflict with the Sanhedrin and Peter's address before the members are contained in Acts 4. "And as they spake unto the people, the priests and the captain of the temple and the Sadducees came upon them, being sore troubled because they taught the people, and proclaimed in Jesus the resurrection from the dead" (4:1–2). Arresting Peter and John, they locked them up until morning; for it was near evening. Luke announced that many believed, bringing the number of men believers to about five thousand (vv. 3–4).

The following morning the Sanhedrin assembled, including Annas, Caiaphas and others. The trial of the men began with a question by the council: "By what power, or in what name, have ye done this?" With this Peter, "being filled with the Holy Spirit," launched out into another sermon, his third in the book of Acts. In a sense his address was an apologetic for Christianity. The question that spurred on the sermon had a barb in it, for it was not the query of those seeking light but of those seeking a springboard for accusation. It came from enemies, not friends. It was a challenge to their qualifications as religious teachers, for the Jewish authorities knew the two had not been in attendance at the rabbinical college in Jerusalem.

The Holy Spirit gave Peter boldness of speech. His sermon had much the same content as the two previous ones. He accused the Jews of having killed Jesus Christ of Nazareth, "whom God raised from the dead." It was through Jesus that the lame man was made whole, and it is through Jesus alone that salvation is made possible; "for neither is there any name under heaven, that is given among men, wherein we must be saved" (4:5–12). "Now when they beheld the boldness of Peter and John, and had perceived that they were unlearned and ignorant men, they marvelled; and they took knowledge of them, that they had been with Jesus" (4:13). The Sadducees could not discount the boldness with which the two apostles affirmed their faith in Jesus; nor could they deny that the man had been miraculously healed. To these two factors there was probably added a third to increase the difficulty of the situation in which they found themselves: the esteem of the people toward Peter and John. Therefore, they resolved not to take any further action against the two, but to command them to silence in their preaching and teaching, charging them "not to speak at all nor teach in the name of Jesus."

The answer of Peter and John, recorded by Luke, is classic as an affirmation of fearlessness. "Whether it is right in the sight of God to hearken unto you rather than unto God, judge ye: for we cannot but speak the things which we saw and heard" (vv. 19–20). Again it is easily discerned that Peter is the rock Jesus predicted he would become, not the weak and unfaithful one who thrice denied his Lord. Such a bold response brought forth a further warning aimed at intimidating Peter and John. Again they were commanded not to speak in the name of Jesus, after which they were released (4:13–22).

After being set free, Peter and John returned to the place where their fellow believers were meeting and gave a full report of the recent happenings—arrest, trial, threats, and all. Everyone present lifted up his voice to God in a prayer asking for his help in disregarding the warnings of the Sanhedrin, for boldness in further speaking the gospel message, and for signs and wonders to be done in the name of Jesus. This is one of the few places the Scriptures record a prayer spoken in unison, a spontaneous response to the disconcerting news brought by the two apostles. There was an immediate answer from God, an answer manifested in a physical sense. "And when they had prayed, the place was shaken wherein they were gathered together; and they were all filled with the Holy Spirit, and they spake the word of God with boldness" (4:23–31).

The word that recurs time and again in these chapters is the term boldness. Luke was trying to show the complete lack of fear and trepidation on the part of the ones preaching and teaching the kerygma, the story of Jesus and the hope lying within that story. There was absolutely no dread, no trembling, even when the accused were brought before the august body of chief priests, elders, and scribes. Their conviction lay in the truth of their message, and their power resided in the indwelling presence of the Holy Spirit. "They were all filled with the Holy Spirit"—this was the secret of their boldness.

16. The Common Fund

The Jerusalem church was unique among the early churches in that it had a common fund used to relieve any suffering on the part of any of the members in need of the physical necessities of life. This might be compared to the benevolence fund in the budget of a modern church. "And all that believed were together, and had all things common; and they sold their possessions and goods, and parted them to all, according as any man had need" (2:44–45).

Luke resumed the topic two chapters laters, stating that the ones who believed "were of one heart and soul" and did not consider that the things they possessed were their own. Instead "they had all things common." No one lacked a necessity of life. Those possessing lands or houses sold them, bringing the money to the apostles. From the common fund, distribution was made to the needy. Even though the membership of this early Christian community numbered in the thousands, there was as much concern for each person as there was when there were just 120. It was a case of practical stewardship put into effect in the Jerusalem church.

Evidently the situation of many destitute people in the Jerusalem company of Christians was desperate. The church had grown rapidly. Many poor people were probably won; the gospel story would have made a great appeal to these destitute ones. Probably many visitors in Jerusalem had joined; there were many Galileans in the small, original group; and there were probably people from distant lands who also decided to stay on. Their funds would have soon been exhausted. It is also very probable that, as the opposition to Christianity increased, a boycott was put into effect against any disciples who had businesses. A famine could cause extreme suffering. We know there was one in the days of Claudius that brought forth hardships in Judea (11:28–29). Also, it could be that the early believers expected a speedy return of Jesus, in which case material possessions would have been of little value.

Whatever the cause or causes, there was an acute need on the part of many members; and the church arose to the occasion. The plan was so successful that Luke could observe that "neither was there among them any that lacked" (4:34). Even distant churches, churches built in Gentile areas from Gentile membership, sent offerings to "the brethren that dwelt in Judea" (11:29–30) and to "the poor among the saints that are at Jerusalem" (Rom. 15:26).

17. The Sin of Deception

However, the success of the charitable plan was not destined to be a permanent feature of it. Effective for a time in relieving physical distress, it eventually slipped into a chaotic condition. The element of human weakness intervened to cause a disruption in the seemingly smooth operation of the plan.

Barnabas, a Hellenist Jew of the Dispersion whose homeland was the island of Cyprus, was a Levite. (His name was really Joseph; Barnabas, meaning son of exhortation, was a nickname or surname.) Back in Hebrew history the Levites could not own property; instead, they were allotted cities to dwell in (Num. 35:1–8). That regulation had been altered by the time of the New Testament era. Although not a Judean Jew, Barnabas was highly regarded in the Jerusalem church. Luke described him as "a good man, and full of the Holy Spirit and of faith" (11:24). He, "having a field, sold it, and brought the money and laid it at the apostles' feet" (4:36–37). His deep concern for the poor at Jerusalem was expressed in this tangible and concrete manner.

In contrast to Barnabas, Ananias and his wife Sapphira also sold a possession with the intent of giving to the common fund of the Jerusalem church. However, they gave part of the proceeds of the sale and kept back part of it for themselves. It appears that the withholding of their personal share was a private arrangement known only to them; evidently they wanted the praise accorded to men who did what Barnabas did, but they wanted the "cost" of the praise not to be too exorbitant. Peter remonstrated with Ananias for the fact that Satan had manipulated him to lie to the Holy Spirit and to keep back part of the price. Ananias immediately fell dead, and "great fear came upon all that heard it." Young men took him out and buried him. When Sapphira returned three hours later, Peter quizzed her about their mutually planned deception just as he had her husband. He accused them of agreeing "to try the Spirit of the Lord." Then he made the jarring announcement that those who had buried her husband were on hand to do the same for her. She immediately died, and they buried her by Ananias. The effect upon the entire Christian community was overwhelming, for "great fear came upon the whole church, and upon all that heard these things" (5:1–11). This is the first time Luke used the term church.

Their sin was deception. They were not punished because they did not bring the entire proceeds of the sale, but because they pretended to have brought the whole amount. Thus they were guilty, according to Peter, of lying to the Holy Spirit. Certain questions rise to the surface that are difficult to answer. Why was Ananias buried before his wife had returned home? Why was the punishment so harsh? Why was their sin any more an affront against the Holy Spirit than it was against the Father or the Son? These questions pose difficulties in interpretation to the very best of scholars. Lack of full details in the narrative causes difficulty in answering these questions.

18. Growth in Miracles and in Numbers

At this point in his lively account of the early church in Jerusalem, Luke interjected a note about the abundant miracles performed by the apostles, as well as the spiraling growth in the number of members. The apostles performed "many signs and wonders" among the people; and in spite of the fear and trembling at the might of God discerned in the Ananias and Sapphira event, "believers were the more added to the Lord, multitudes both of men and women." Throngs were still expressing faith in Jesus as Lord and Christ in spite of the unsavory actions of people like Ananias and Sapphira. God's work still continued to blossom in the beginning church even though there was underlying sin on the part of some. The sick were carried out into the streets and placed upon pallets in the hopes that Peter's shadow might fall upon them. The sick were even brought into Jerusalem from the neighboring cities for the purpose of being healed (5:12–16).

19. The Persecution Renewed

An accelerating church was too much for the Sadducees, so they instigated another attempt to curtail its growth. Their motive seemed to have been jealousy. They arrested the apostles "and put them in public ward"; but an angel opened the doors of the prison and released them. The angel then commanded, "Go ye, and stand and speak in the temple to the people all the words of this Life." The apostles obeyed, and at daybreak entered the Temple and began teaching (5:17–21).

Calling an assembly of the Sanhedrin, the high priest sent to the prison for Peter and the apostles, only to have the officers return with the perplexing news that the men were not in the prison. At about this time a man arrived with further news: the men were "in the temple standing and teaching the people." The apostles were then rearrested and brought before the council, where the high priest reminded them of the charge previously made that they were not to teach in Jesus' name. His further statement betrayed a tinge of an uneasy conscience, for he remarked, "Behold, ye have filled Jerusalem with your teaching, and intend to bring this man's blood upon us" (5:22–28).

Peter's reply was the paragon of boldness and spiritual confidence: "We must obey God rather than men." This was the apostle's opening statement of a short but powerful sermon addressed to the Sanhedrin, Peter's second to the Sanhedrin and fourth in the book. He accused that stern body of killing Jesus, of "hanging him on a tree." God raised him from the dead and exalted him to be "a Prince and a Saviour" to give remission of sins. Peter stated that both they and the Holy Spirit were witnesses of the things he proclaimed (5:29–32).

20. Gamaliel's Advice

The reaction of the Sanhedrin to Peter's sermon was a very violent one, for they were "cut to the heart, and were minded to slay them." Their rage was so great that they were at the point of murdering the apostles, but a man named Gamaliel stepped forward to wield a leveling influence on the incensed council. This very learned and wise man, one of great reputation among all the Jewish people, was a grandson of the famous Rabbi Hillel. Since he was the outstanding rabbi of his time, many young men came to the rabbinical school in Jerusalem to study for the rabbinate under his teaching. Paul, the apostle from Tarsus, was one of his pupils (22:3). Luke added that Gamaliel was a Pharisee. Opposition to the followers of Christ up to this point had been mainly Sadducees; now we see the Pharisees beginning to oppose them also.

Gamaliel's advice was good. At his request the accused men were asked to leave the room, after which he made an address requesting that nothing drastic be done to the men. He first cited two cases in which men had endeavored to lead out in movements of national liberation, one movement spurred by a man named Theudas and one by a man named Judas of Galilee. These men failed, and their followers were either killed or scattered. Then the famous Pharisee advised, "Refrain from these men, and let them alone: for if this counsel or this work be of men, it will be overthrown: but if it is of God, ye will not be able to overthrow them; lest haply ye be found even to be fighting against God" (vv. 38–39).

The influence of Gamaliel was so great that the Sanhedrin agreed on a policy of moderation. Calling the apostles before them, the council beat them, charged them not to speak in Jesus' name, and then released them. The surprising thing is that the Sadducees, having the majority of seats on the Sanhedrin (the Pharisees constituted the minority) consented to vote on the advice of a Pharisee. It could be that they were afraid not to do so, for they knew that most of the common people were lined up with the Pharisees.

The apostles went away, "rejoicing that they were counted worthy to suffer dishonor for the Name." This shows the exalted brand of Christianity that these early heralds of the gospel possessed—rejoicing in the privilege of suffering for Christ's sake! Not only did they rejoice in their being flogged and in their being threatened to remain silent; they continued daily, in the Temple and in the homes, the proclamation of the good news, for "they ceased not to teach and to preach Jesus as the Christ" (5:33–42).

21. Choosing of the Seven

At the time of the beginning of the early church in Jerusalem there were many Jews of the Dispersion in the Holy City. These were known as Grecian Jews as well as Hellenists. Many of these had accepted the gospel and had become part of the church. One, Barnabas, who has already been mentioned, had an early place of leadership. Soon others arose to prominent positions in the church.

There was a certain degree of questioning between the Grecian Jews and the Judean Jews. Each looked upon the other suspiciously, a feeling that was not entirely erased when they were brought together in the bonds of Christian fellowship in the church. This feeling broke into overt expression when the Grecian Jews expressed the opinion that their widows were being neglected in the daily distribution from the common fund. They felt that there was a discrimination against their widows in favor of the widows of the Palestinian Jewish group. It seems that the problem was somewhat related to the rapid growth of the church, for Luke mentioned that the dispute arose "when the number of disciples was multiplying." Calling for an assembly of the church, the apostles very appropriately suggested, "It is not fit that we should forsake the word of God, and serve tables. Look ye out therefore, brethren, from among you seven men of good report, full of the Spirit and wisdom, whom we may appoint over this business. But we will continue stedfastly in prayer, and in the ministry of the word" (vv. 2–4).

The business of the distribution had become so immense that a special delegation was needed to care for it; this would allow the apostles to spend more time in praying and preaching. Since the suggestion seemed a wise one, the church agreed to the proposal. Seven men were chosen: Stephen, Philip, Prochorus, Nicanor, Timon, Parmenas, and Nicolaus. After Stephen's name is a remark: "a man full of faith and of the Holy Spirit"; and after Nicolaus' is another remark: "a proselyte of Antioch." Following the choosing of the seven they were placed before the apostles, who then prayed and laid their hands on them (Acts 6:1–6).

All the names are Greek names, not Hebrew names; but this does not necessarily indicate that all the seven were Grecian Jews or Hellenists. There is a good probability they were, however. One was a Gentile who had become a Jew (a proselyte) and then had become a Christian. Two became famous, Stephen as the first Christian martyr and Philip as the first evangelist outside Jerusalem. After the mentioning of their names nothing is again related of the other five. The significant thing is that this whole incident shows that Grecian Jews, Hellenists, were emerging as leaders in the church.

Although the word *deacon* is not used in this passage, it is assumed by many scholars that this incident constitutes the origin of the office of deacon and that these seven men were the first ones elected to that responsibility in the church. It is to be noted that they were elected to serve tables, not to rule or exercise authority. The word deacon means servant and is derived from the Greek verb "to serve tables."

22. Continued Growth

After his word about the election of the seven special servants, Luke added another comment about the rapid expansion of the Jerusalem church. "And the word of God increased; and the number of the disciples multiplied in Jerusalem exceedingly; and a great company of the priests were obedient to the faith" (6:7). Even many of the archenemies of Christianity, the Sadducees, were entering the fold of the devotees of Christ. Luke was emphasizing not only the number of new Christians, but also the diverse ranks from which they came. For Sadducees to see some of their own group becoming Christians would increase their hatred and opposition to the church.

23. Stephen's Arrest

Stephen, whose name means "crown," was a man full of faith and the Holy Spirit (6:3); he was also "full of grace and power" and performed "great wonders and signs among the people" (6:8). Such ability placed him somewhat on the level of the apostles themselves. Many of the Grecian Jews who persisted in stubbornly opposing the acceptance of Jesus as the Messiah set themselves against Stephen. It may have been that Paul was among the agitators, since he was a Grecian Jew and since he was present later at the stoning of Stephen. The Jews were no match for Stephen, who was fortified two ways: with wisdom and with the Holy Spirit. They concluded that this winsome and forceful preacher had to be stopped right away! They hired witnesses against Stephen, who said, "We have heard him speak blasphemous words against Moses and against God." This led to his arrest and to his being brought before the council, where false witnesses were again employed against him. The accusations were strongly worded. "This man ceaseth not to speak words against this holy place, and the law: for we have heard him say, that this Jesus of Nazareth shall destroy this place, and shall change the customs which Moses delivered unto us"

(vv. 13–14).

These words and charges were not completely false; rather, the Jews took Stephen's words and twisted them around to give a false slant, a distorted implication. At any rate, a very startling thing happened; at the moment that charges were made, all who sat in the council chamber looked on Stephen and "saw his face as it had been the face of an angel." There surely was no vestige of fear written on that face. Was Paul present in the room during this dramatic moment? If so, we can surmise that it was from him Luke received an account of the proceedings (6:8–15).

24. Stephen's Sermon and Death

The high priest at this time was Caiaphas, the same one who presided at Jesus' trial. The double charge against Stephen was that he preached that Jesus of Nazareth (1) would destroy the Temple, and (2) would alter the Mosaic law. Caiaphas questioned Stephen, "Are these things so?" The response Stephen gave to the query was a sermon, the longest in Acts. It takes up almost all of the seventh chapter of the book, for Stephen started out by recounting the history of Abraham and wound up with an accusation of the murder of Jesus directed to the Jews. Stephen made no attempt to defend himself, but he used forceful words to defend his faith in Jesus as the Christ, the Righteous One, who had come to redeem mankind.

He maintained that God's revelation was made to the great characters in the history of Israel in many lands and in many places. God did not restrict himself to one locale or one country. He conversed with Abraham beyond the Euphrates, with Joseph in Egypt, and with Moses at Sinai. Solomon built the Temple, but "the Most High dwelleth not in houses made with hands." And Moses received from God "living oracles" to give to their forefathers, but those forefathers were not obedient. They asked Aaron to help them return to the calf worship they had known in Egypt. So Israel had been guilty of rejecting Moses from years back. Moses and the prophets told of the coming of the Christ; but when he came, they murdered him. They had resisted the Holy Spirit both in their history and at that present time. They had "received the law as it was ordained by angels, and kept it not." Stephen endeavored to refute both issues in the double charge made against him (7:2–53).

The sermon infuriated the Jewish opposition. Not only were they "cut to the heart"; they "gnashed on him with their teeth." The narrative further says, "But he, being full of the Holy Spirit, looked up stedfastly into heaven, and saw the glory of God, and Jesus standing on the right hand of God, and said, Behold, I see the heavens opened, and the Son of man

A GUIDE FOR NEW TESTAMENT STUDY

standing on the right hand of God'' (vv. 55–56).

Crying out in rage, the mob stopped their ears as a protest of what they heard. They rushed upon Stephen, cast him out of the city, and stoned him. The spirit with which Stephen accepted his martyrdom is significant. As they stoned him he said, "Lord Jesus, receive my spirit." Kneeling down, he cried out, "Lord, lay not this sin to their charge." Then "he fell asleep." Both of Stephen's remarks are reminiscent of two sayings of Jesus while on the cross. By his death Stephen obtained the crown, symbolized for so many years by his name itself (7:54–60).

One wonders how the Jews were able to stone Stephen without first receiving permission from the Roman authorities. The martyrdom probably took place in 33, while Pilate was still the procurator. (He was not recalled to Rome till 36.) Pilate's home was in Caesarea, so he may not have heard about the stoning until days later. Even then, if a large group of the Jews in Jerusalem approved of the death, Pilate may not have wanted to muddy the waters by expressing disapproval.

25. Persecution by Saul the Pharisee

While stoning Stephen, "the witnesses laid down their garments at the feet of a young man named Saul" (7:58). "And Saul was consenting unto his death" (8:1). This is the first time the name of this dynamic young man is mentioned in the New Testament. He is known better by his Roman name, Paul, which Luke switched to later in his book.

The persecution was renewed with vigor that very day "against the church which was in Jerusalem." Saul became a leader in this persecution. As a result of the opposition "they were all scattered abroad throughout the regions of Judea and Samaria, except the apostles" (8:1). This persecution was conducted mainly by Pharisees, whereas up to this time it was mainly the work of the Sadducees.

Luke presented a great contrast, that between "devout men" and Saul. He revealed that devout men buried Stephen and lamented his death. In contrast to these, Saul "laid waste the church, entering into every house, and dragging men and women committed them to prison" (8:2–3). The term "laid waste" is too mild a translation for the Greek; a better term is *ravaged*. Saul acted like a savage animal blinded by destructive passion. Luke's further word (9:1) verifies the extreme hatred Saul manifested toward the followers of Christ.

19.

The Church in Judea and Samaria

Chapters 1—7 in Acts deal with the establishment of the church in Jerusalem; chapters 8—12 deal with its beginning in Judea and Samaria. (The second section really begins in Acts 8:4.) With the death of Stephen there began an intense persecution of the followers of Jesus in the Jerusalem area. It was a Jewish persecution, not a Roman persecution. Rome had no part in it. As a result of the disruption, there was a scattering of the believers into new territory with the word of redeeming love. Really the persecution was a blessing in disguise. Instead of causing the destruction of the church, it gave new challenge and life to the church. Tertullian has said, "The blood of martyrs is the seed of the church." This was certainly true in the Jerusalem persecution.

1. Philip in Samaria

Philip (not the Philip of the twelve original disciples), listed second in the special seven selected to dispense the common fund in Jerusalem (6:5), was the first to appear as an evangelist marching out of the Holy City to present the good news. "And Philip went down to the city of Samaria, and proclaimed unto them the Christ. And the multitudes gave heed with one accord unto the things that were spoken by Philip, when they heard, and saw the signs which he did" (vv. 5–6).

Philip was appointed to look after the material needs of the poorer members of the church at Jerusalem; but he seems equally to have been captivated by the spiritual needs of men, especially those outside the Judean locale. Evidently he did not want to be confined merely to waiting tables. He has been known through the centuries as "Philip the evangelist." The Samaritans not only gave ear to his preaching; they were amazed at the signs he did. Christianity always brings joy, wherever it is proclaimed, accepted, and applied; and Philip's work in Samaria was no exception (8:4–8).

Luke did not state that Philip received any special call from the Holy

Spirit to go to Samaria; the Holy Spirit, mentioned so often in Acts in connection with the spread of the church, is not mentioned here. Jesus listed Samaria in the three areas pointed out in the Great Commission. Maybe Jesus' famous injunction was passed on to Philip, making an impression he could never forget. If so, that was all the prompting Philip needed to travel north to Samaria.

He went to the country of the people the Jews avoided as much as possible. "For Jews have no dealings with Samaritans" (John 4:9). The Samaritan people and the reasons they were held in such low esteem by the Jews have already been discussed. As a Christian of Grecian Jewish origin, not Judean Jewish origin, it was easier for Philip to launch out in a Christian ministry to these people than it would have been for one of the apostles.

Luke said Philip went to "the city of Samaria." The article *the* shows it was a place quite important and not a mere village or town. It may have been Sebaste, a city that was rebuilt by Herod the Great from the site of the old city of Samaria (the capital of the Israelite kingdom in the Old Testament period). Another guess is that Philip preached in Sychar, where Jesus spoke to the Samaritan woman. Other possibilities are Nablus, which was the same as old Shechem, the center of Samaritan worship, and Gitta, the birthplace of Simon Magus, of whom we read a few verses later in Acts. In spite of all these theories, Sebaste is the most likely spot for Philip's preaching. It was the chief city in the territory of Samaria at the time of the early church.

2. Simon Magus

Luke introduced into the narrative at this time a man named Simon, known as Simon Magus or Simon the Magician, one who had a great following among the Samaritans because of his feats of magic and sorcery. This one "amazed the people of Samaria, giving out that himself was some great one: to whom they all gave heed, from the least to the greatest." The people of Samaria even believed that his powers came from God, for they said, "This man is that power of God which is called Great." For quite some time the people had been amazed at his ability to perform sorceries (8:9–11) and had been taken in by his quackery. Simon had built a thriving business as a magician; sorcerers of Simon's type were quite common in the world of that era. The people were very superstitious, conceiving of the world as infested with demons and evil spirits. Protection from them necessitated acts and incantations performed by a magician, a sorcerer, or someone versed in spiritualism, such as Simon.

Due to Philip's preaching many of the people who formerly had pinned their hopes and fears on Simon heard the good news of the kingdom of God made accessible through faith in the name of Jesus Christ. As a result, they believed and "were baptized, both men and women." Simon also was impressed and became one of their number.

3. Peter and John in Samaria

News of the great ingathering of Samaritans into the community of the believers reached the ears of the church in Jerusalem, and "they sent unto them Peter and John." It is to be noted that the Jerusalem church *sent* the two apostles; so they went under the authority of the whole church, not under a self-conceived notion. The Jerusalem church was at last functioning in obedience of Jesus' command in the Great Commission (8:14). It is also to be noted that this is the same John who, with his brother James, wanted to call down fire from heaven to consume the Samaritans when they would not receive Jesus during his ministry in that country. Jesus rebuked James and John at that time for their vindictive attitude (Luke 9:54–55). The "son of thunder" (Mark 3:17) had changed considerably since those earlier days.

When Peter and John arrived in Samaritan territory, great things took place. The major incident has been called the "Samaritan Pentecost," since what happened is so similar to the startling occurrence at the Jewish Pentecost in Jerusalem (2:1–4). When Peter and John arrived they "prayed for them, that they might receive the Holy Spirit: for as yet it was fallen upon none of them: only they had been baptized into the name of Jesus" (vv. 15–16).

When the two apostles laid their hands upon the Samaritans, the new believers received the Holy Spirit (8:15–17). This event is quite an advance in Christian thinking; Jews touching Samaritans would have been unheard of up to this time. The gospel was certainly growing, and the barrier between Jew and Samaritan was falling. This is the last appearance of John in the book of Acts, although his name is mentioned in 12:2.

The coming of the Holy Spirit upon the Samaritans gave vindication from heaven that the Samaritan enterprise was the work of God. There was an overt divine approval. That the Holy Spirit, previous to the coming of Peter and John, had "fallen upon none of them" does not mean that their conversion experience was not genuine, that the Holy Spirit had not produced in them true regeneration. Luke spoke in a manner assuming that their baptism was genuine and valid. Just as there were external signs that followed the miraculous outpouring of the Spirit at Pentecost (2:4–12), there were probably external signs that followed the coming of the Spirit upon those in Samaria. The experience gave assurance to the born-again Samaritans that they had full status in the family of God.

4. Simon Magus' Request

No sooner had the Holy Spirit been bestowed on the Samaritans through the laying on of the hands of the apostles than Simon Magus offered money to the apostles to give him power to do the same thing. Peter's answer was to the point and somewhat tinged with contempt: ''Thy silver perish with thee, because thou hast thought to obtain the gift of God with money. Thou hast neither part nor lot in this matter: for thy heart is not right before God. Repent therefore of this thy wickedness, and pray the Lord, if perhaps the thought of thy heart shall be forgiven thee. For I see that thou art in the gall of bitterness and in the bond of iniquity'' (vv. 20–23).

Such a sharp rebuke left no doubt where Peter stood in the matter and how he felt toward Simon. Simon evidently accepted Peter's advice; he said to him, ''Pray ye for me to the Lord, that none of the things which ye have spoken come upon me'' (8:18–24). After his plea for mercy Simon Magus is not again mentioned in the book of Acts. Various legends sprang up in the second and third century about Simon, but they are not supported by definite evidence. One of these is that he was the founder of a Gnostic sect. The validity of Simon's Christian experience has been debated. Some say he was never converted, for his underlying motive was selfish. He sought to further selfish interests. Others say he was a believer but had a shallow experience. He was not yet truly mastered by Jesus Christ. However, we really have no right to pass judgment on Simon's status with God.

We have already seen that very early in the Jerusalem church, sin raised its head to mar the fellowship in the dispute about the distribution of the common fund and the deception of Ananias and Sapphira. Very early in the Samaritan church, sin raised its head also in Simon's attempt to purchase spiritual power. From his unusual request came the term *simony,* the selling and buying of church offices, a custom quite prevalent in the church in the Middle Ages.

6. Philip and the Ethiopian

God used an angel to send Philip in another direction, this time southwest instead of north. He was to travel into the desert country on the road to Gaza. There were two roads he could have taken out of Jerusalem, one going east and one going south by way of Bethlehem and Hebron. Gaza had figured prominently in the Old Testament, especially in the Sampson narratives. It was one of the five cities of a Philistine confederation.

"And he arose and went"; this tells us that Philip obeyed God immediately. On the way he met "a man of Ethiopia, a eunuch of great authority under Candace, queen of the Ethiopians, who was over all her treasure, who had come to Jerusalem to worship; and he was returning and sitting in his chariot, and was reading the prophet Isaiah" (8:26–28).

Candace was a hereditary title for all the Ethiopian queens. This one reigned at the city of Meroe and was probably the queen mother. At that time in the East, eunuchs were commonly placed in the offices of the court; this one was the treasurer. He had been to Jerusalem to worship and was returning home. Early in Israel's history eunuchs were excluded from the Temple services (Deut. 23:1); later this rule was changed to a more lenient attitude. Isaiah 56:3–8 states that all eunuchs and foreigners were welcome to the Temple services. However, it appears that the Judaism of the first century A.D. had ignored Isaiah's words. This or any other eunuch could not have become a Jew. That is, he could not have become a proselyte; he was therefore probably a God-fearer, a Gentile who worshiped the God of Israel, offered his gift at the Temple, observed the sabbath, and read the Scriptures, but who had not become a Jew in the full sense of the term.

The eunuch was returning to his home. Sitting in his chariot, he was reading from the Bible of the Jews—very probably a Septuagint. It was usual among the people of that era to read aloud. The ancient manuscripts required it; there were no punctuation marks, no divisions of words, and no divisions of sentences. All the letters ran together. It was easier to spell out the words by reading aloud than by reading silently. The passage he was reading is found in Isaiah 53:7–8, a part of the fourth Servant Song, telling of the suffering servant of the Lord. Jesus knew that he himself fulfilled the prophecy in Isaiah 53.

The Holy Spirit (not an angel, as previously) told Philip to go to the chariot of the eunuch. When he did so, Philip asked the eunuch if he understood what he read. The man answered, "How can I, except some one shall guide me?" He immediately invited Philip to join him.

Philip began his witnessing by explaining the Scriptures and "preached unto him Jesus." Going on their way, they came to some water, where Philip baptized the treasurer. With that "the Spirit of the Lord caught away Philip; and the eunuch saw him no more." The new convert proceeded on his way in spiritual joy. Irenaeus, writing much later (second century), informed us that the eunuch became a missionary to the people of Ethiopia. This may very well have happened. Philip, beginning at Azotus, went through city after city preaching the gospel all the way. Finally he came to

Caesarea (8:29–40). The villages to which Philip preached were mostly of Gentile population.

Luke was showing us that there is no hindrance to the gospel in bringing the grace of God to all people. Just prior to his baptism the Ethiopian asked Philip a question with apprehension: "Behold, here is water; what doth hinder me to be baptized?" He had probably been denied a full place in Judaism, as a proselyte. He wondered if anything would prevent his becoming a follower of Jesus. All that Philip required was an assurance of his faith in Jesus the Lord. An inner spiritual experience was the determining factor. Neither race nor physical mutilation could keep him out of the kingdom of God.

Within Jerusalem, the gospel brought God's saving power to Jews; north of Judea, it did the same to the despised Samaritans; southwest of Jerusalem, it reached out to a Gentile eunuch; and west of Jerusalem, it brought peace and hope to forlorn Gentiles. Philip, a Grecian Jew who became a Christian, understood the universal nature of Christianity at a time when the apostles were still holding on to their narrow horizons and Judaistic prejudices. Luke ended Acts with a Greek adverb meaning "without hindrance." He wanted very much to show that God meant the gospel for all people, that it was to be freed from narrow provincialism and from the confinement of an exclusive Judaism.

Luke also revealed in the Philip-eunuch incident how the Septuagint was used to win new converts, especially those out of the range of the Aramaic and Hebrew languages. The New Testament documents had not been written at this time; the sayings and teachings of Jesus, as well as the miraculous acts and signs which he did, were still in the oral stage of transmission. The Septuagint became the Bible of the early Christians and was used in winning new believers, as is seen in the case of Philip and the treasurer of Ethiopia. (See also Acts 18:28.)

7. A New Apostle

Luke at this point told of the conversion, call, and commission of a new apostle named Saul. He had already mentioned him as one witnessing the stoning of Stephen and being the mainstay in the Jewish persecution of the church in Jerusalem (7:58; 8:1–3). It has been maintained that the conversion of Saul is the most important happening in the history of Christianity after Pentecost. Luke gave three accounts of Saul's experience, one in the third person (9:1–19) and two in addresses by the apostle himself (22:3–21; 26:12–18).

Saul, meaning "asked for," was his Hebrew name, while Paul was his

Tarsus, Cleopatra's Gate

Roman name; he had Roman citizenship. (In the Latin the name is *Paulus*, and *Paul* is an English form of the Latin.) A Jew could legally hold citizenship in the empire, a factor that the apostle used to his advantage more than once (16:37–40; 22:25–30; 23:26–30; 25:10–12). In Acts 13:9 Luke switched from Saul to Paul and used the Roman name from that time to the end of the book.

Saul, who was born about A.D. 1, had a Jewish background combined with a Greek influence; he was a Jew hailing from a city in Cilicia named Tarsus. It was just south of the Famous Cilician Gates, the pass through the Taurus range, and therefore a main gateway between the eastern and western sections of the empire. When the apostle called it "no mean city" he was not stretching the point, for only Athens and Alexandria excelled it in culture. There was a Greek university there. This great cosmopolitan center, situated on the major trade routes of that area, had a population of about half a million people. Here the culture of the East met the culture of the West, and here great commercial enterprises held sway.

Being a Hellenistic Jew from such a center made Saul one versed in both Greek and Hebrew (21:37–40), as well as Aramaic. When he said an Old Testament quotation, he took the passage directly from the Septuagint. Since he was a Pharisee (Phil. 3:5), he probably did not study at any of the Greek universities. He studied under Gamaliel, the most prominent rabbi in Jerusalem, a privilege that made him well versed in Judaism. He was born into his Roman citizenship (22:28), but we do not know how his father obtained his. He was of the tribe of Benjamin, as was also Saul, first king of the Hebrew nation. He had a sister living in Jerusalem, who had a son (23:16). Saul's trade was tentmaking (18:3). Such a varied background equipped this young man for the arduous task of being God's special apostle to the Gentiles.

8. Saul's Conversion

Damascus, about 140 miles north and a little to the east of Jerusalem, was the capital of Syria during the Old Testament period; but since the days of the Seleucid kings, Antioch, far to the north on the Orontes, had been the Syrian capital. Damascus had the distinction of being the city with the longest continuous habitation in the world. It lay on the main trade route between Egypt and Mesopotamia. There were many Jews in Damascus; therefore, the city provided a place of security for Jerusalem church members fleeing the persecution in their home cities. But what authority would the high priest in Jerusalem have in a remote city like Damascus? Technically, none, but his influence there among the Jewish populace would be considerable; they would be willing to cooperate with him in any way. Therefore he gave to Saul official approval to proceed to Damascus, to arrest the followers of Jesus, and to bring them back to Jerusalem for judgment.

The believers were called those "of the Way." Later, in Antioch, the name *Christian* was used for the first time. It seems that at this time in Damascus the Christians worshiped in the synagogues, for the complete separation of Jews and Christians had not been effected. Ananias, the Christian who was sent by the Lord to Saul after his arrival in the city, was "a devout man according to the law, well reported of by all the Jews that dwelt there" (22:12). There was no antipathy between the Jews and the Christians.

The hatred for the followers of Jesus that boiled in the heart of Saul was vividly portrayed by Luke, who pictured him much as he would a legendary dragon. He said that Saul was "breathing threatening and slaughter against the disciples of the Lord." (9:1). From Luke's description of the stoning of Stephen, it appears that Paul displayed a passive attitude at that infamous event (7:58). By the time of the journey to Damascus, his zeal was white hot, however. At about midday, as Saul came near the city, the miraculous event happened. He was surrounded by a heavenly light and fell to earth. He heard a voice in the Hebrew language calling him by name and asking why he was persecuting him. The men who were accompanying him heard the voice but saw no man. Saul must have known it was Jesus, for he said, "Who art thou, Lord?" Jesus identified himself and then commanded Saul to enter the city and wait for further directions. Because Saul was blind when he arose from the ground, he had to be led into Damascus. For three days he had no sight, no food, and no water (9:3–9).

The two accounts of the conversion experience from Saul's own testimony are found in 22:5–11 and 26:12–20. In the former he asked Jesus, "What shall I do, Lord?" In the latter Jesus stated to Saul, "It is hard for thee to kick against the goad." The term kicking *against the goad* (*pricks* in the King James) reveals that Saul had certain misgivings, certain questions about the followers of Jesus that were pressing on his mind and preying on his conscience. Goads were used by herdsmen to urge the animals to hasten on. To kick back at the goad, thus showing displeasure, was painful. Saul had been kicking at certain concepts pertaining to Jesus, all with a vain attempt at reconciling them in his thinking.

Why did not the tormented men and women strike back? How could they possibly pray for their persecutors? What about Stephen's face that resembled that of an angel? How could the high moral standards of the believers be explained? What was the secret of their inner spiritual strength? Why had his Judaism not satisfied his deep spiritual yearnings? Why had it failed so completely (Rom. 7)?

Yet if Jesus had really been the Messiah—and Saul yearned for the Messiah's coming as much as any other Jew—why had he come to fishermen, such as Peter and John; to publicans, such as Matthew; to Zealots, such as Simon the Canaanean; and to Samaritans, such as the Samaritan woman at Jacob's well? Why had he not presented himself to self-respecting Pharisees, or even to the ruling Sadducees? Also, if Jesus had really been the Messiah, why had he not set up the kingdom the Jewish people had expected him to inaugurate? Why had his Judean throne turned out to be a Roman cross? Was the preposterous story of the resurrection of Jesus true after all?

Saul's transformation was complete. The whole experience revolutionized his thinking and altered his entire purpose in living. In three days of meditation and retrospection, his thoughts struck out in many directions, searching for the overall meaning of his recent experience. His Judaism, with all its legalistic exactions, came tumbling down; in its place was the resurrected Jesus, his Lord and Master. The things that were "gain" to him he found to be "loss for Christ." Years of Pharisaical study suddenly became "refuse" after once knowing "him, and the power of his resurrection, and the fellowship of his sufferings" (Phil. 3:1–11).

9. Ananias, Reluctant Servant

The next step in Saul's momentous experience took place through a relatively unknown disciple of Jesus at Damascus named Ananias. Luke termed him "a certain disciple." In one of his own descriptions of his conversion experience, Saul described Ananias as a "devout man according to the law, well reported of by all the Jews that dwelt there" (22:12). Both the believers in Jesus and the Jews thought highly of him. The Lord appeared to Ananias in a vision, saying, "Arise, and go to the street which is called Straight, and inquire in the house of Judas for one named Saul, a man of Tarsus: for behold, he prayeth; and he hath seen a man named Ananias coming in, and laying his hands on him, that he might receive his sight" (9:11–12).

Even though his commission came directly from God, Ananias had misgivings and expressed a reluctance in obeying God's request. This is understandable, in view of the fact that knowledge of the dreaded activities of this ardent tormentor of the ones faithful to Jesus had spread as far as Damascus. Ananias knew why Saul had come to their city, and he reminded God of this fact; but God answered him, "Go thy way: for he is a chosen vessel unto me, to bear my name before the Gentiles and kings, and the children of Israel: for I will show him how many things he must suffer for my name's sake'' (9:15–16).

God would not accept a negative answer; Ananias must go directly to the one he feared most. God had even prepared Saul with a vision of Ananias' coming to him. Saul's commission was plain: he was to carry the gospel to ''Gentiles and kings, and the children of Israel.'' His ministry was to be to his own people and to those outside his own people. Also, God promised him suffering, a suffering that would occur for God's name's sake. He would suffer as a consequence of his obedience to God's orders.

Ananias obeyed God's directive, going to Judas' house on the street called Straight. He addressed the new convert ''Brother Saul'' and informed him that he had been sent of the Lord Jesus that he might receive his sight ''and be filled with the Holy Spirit.'' Immediately Saul saw, arose, was baptized, and accepted food. The Holy Spirit, who would lead and guide him throughout his preaching and writing ministry, was with him in full measure from the beginning.

Saul received his physical sight at that very moment, seeing Ananias and also Judas' house, where he had been staying for three days, for the first time.

10. Saul in Damascus and Arabia

Luke continued to call the apostle ''Saul,'' and did so until a certain stage on the first missionary journey. The new ''preacher of the gospel'' remained ''certain days'' in Damascus, an indefinite term that leaves us in doubt as to the length of his stay in the old Syrian city. In the synagogues he proclaimed Jesus as the Son of God, the place of his preaching denoting that as yet there was no open breach between the believers in Christ and the Jews. All those who heard Saul were amazed to see and hear him as a follower of the Lord. But Saul continued his message of salvation in Christ Jesus, with the Jews being confused and mixed up about the issue. Saul was ''proving that this is the Christ.'' A better translation for ''proving'' would be ''putting together.'' What he was actually doing was comparing the prophetic Hebrew Scriptures with their fulfillment in Jesus of Nazareth, the crucified-resurrected Messiah (9:19–22).

However, peace did not reign long; for when ''many days'' were drawing to an end the Jews plotted to kill Saul. This became known to the apostle. Since the Jews watched the gates of the city day and night, his friends let him down over the wall in a basket so he could escape (9:23–25).

The next verse (v. 26) states that Saul went to Jerusalem. The problem that presents itself at this juncture of the story is where to place Saul's "Arabian visit," as well as the location of "Arabia," as he used the term. This visit is mentioned in the book of Galatians but not in Acts. In Galatians he stated that, when God saved him and called him to preach, he did not go to Jerusalem to confer with the apostles, but to Arabia, after which he returned to Damascus. "Then after three years I went up to Jerusalem to visit Cephas, and tarried with him fifteen days" (Gal. 1:15–18). Since Galatians mentions the visit and Acts does not, where does it fit in Luke's narrative in Acts? Did it occur immediately after his conversion and before he preached in Damascus, or did it occur after the escape from Damascus and before he went to Jerusalem (as is stated in v. 26)? In either case, he spent three years in Damascus *after* the brief period in Arabia. It appears as though he preached for a while, then went to Arabia, and then returned to Damascus for three years, at which time he must have preached also. Then he went to Jerusalem to visit Peter.

Also, where was the Arabia visited by Saul? Arabia was a very large area. On the north was the Euphrates River, on the east the Persian Gulf, on the south the Indian Ocean, and on the west the Red Sea. About the time of Saul's conversion Emperor Tiberius placed Damascus under the protecting arm of Aretas IV (9 B.C. to A.D. 40), king of Arabia. Petra was his capital. At one time Damascus had been in the Arabian kingdom, but since 64 B.C. it had been part of Syria. It could be part of Syria and still be protected by Aretas. Therefore, to go to Arabia all Saul had to do was to leave Damascus through one of its gates. He probably did not travel far from Damascus itself; and when he did so, he probably went east of the city.

11. Saul in Jerusalem and Tarsus

When Saul arrived in Jerusalem, he went to the followers of Jesus and tried to join them. However, because of disbelief that this archpersecutor could really be a follower of Jesus, they were all afraid of him. What Barnabas did leads us to believe he was previously acquainted with Saul, for he informed the church "how he had seen the Lord in the way, and that he had spoken to him, and how at Damascus he had preached boldly in the name of Jesus" (9:27).

Due to the recommendation of Barnabas, Saul was accepted into the Jerusalem church; and while he was in the city, he continued to preach "boldly in the name of the Lord." This preaching took on a different aspect and developed into a disputing with the Grecian Jews, creating an opposition that grew to such a degree that they wanted to kill him. These

Grecian Jews were Hellenists, as was Saul. So Saul knew their thinking well, plus the fact that he had been called and commissioned by Jesus and had the Holy Spirit as his ally. Therefore, in debate the Grecian Jews could not cope with Saul. They had already killed Stephen; now they desired to mete out the same fate to Saul. Knowing this, the church feared for his life; so they sent Saul to Caesarea, and then on to his home in Tarsus (9:26–30).

Galatians 1:18 informs us that this visit to Jerusalem lasted only fifteen days, but they were profitable days to Saul. He saw and had fellowship with both Peter and James, the half brother of Jesus. It is very possible and quite probable that Saul got much of his information about Jesus' ministry from Peter. It is also quite possible that he secured many of the details of Jesus' family life from James.

We know very little of Saul's activities while he was in Tarsus. Acts 9:30 says he went there; Acts 11:25–26 says that Barnabas sent to Tarsus seeking Saul to get him to come to Antioch. Luke did not write a complete and unabridged life of the great apostle; he had a purpose in writing and therefore added and omitted incidents according to his purpose. Saul gave a brief statement about this period of his life, that he "came into the regions of Syria and Celicia" (Gal. 1:21); he stated that it lasted fourteen years, after which he went up to Jerusalem (Gal. 2:1). We surmise that he spent the time in Syria and Celicia preaching.

12. Peace and Growth

Luke at this point summarized the condition of the church: "So the church throughout all Judea and Galilee and Samaria had peace, being edified; and, walking in the fear of the Lord and in the comfort of the Holy Spirit, was multiplied" (9:31).

To what cause or causes can this peace be assigned? Since the statement immediately follows the remark that Saul left Jerusalem for his home territory, the era of tranquillity may have been largely due to the absence of zealous and fervent preachers such as Saul, Stephen, and Philip. It must be remembered that these men had been Grecian Jews, not Judean Jews, prior to their becoming disciples of the Lord Jesus. Men of this caliber kept things stirred up. However, other factors may have also contributed to the peace. Emperor Caligula, who ruled the empire from 37 to 41 (the date of his assassination), let it be known that he intended to set up his statue in the Temple at Jerusalem. This would have been so disconcerting to the Jews that they would have had little time to think of persecuting the Christians.

Again Luke used the term *church*. It is very likely that he was signifying all the local churches in the entire territory west of the Jordan. And again

Jerusalem, Jaffa Gate

Luke did not tell us about the activities of these churches, except that there was peace and a building up.

13. Peter in Lydda and Joppa

Luke turned next in his narrative to Peter and to those closely associated with him. Peter began traveling toward the coastal area known in Old Testament times as the plain of Sharon. In the city of Lydda he healed a man who had been confined to his bed with palsy for eight years. When "all that dwelt at Lydda and in Sharon" saw the man made whole, they believed in Jesus (9:32–35). Then Peter went from the inland city of Lydda to the coastal city of Joppa, famous in the Old Testament as the city where Jonah caught a ship in his endeavor to run away from God.

At Joppa there was a believer named Tabitha, an Aramaic name which in Greek was Dorcas. This woman, who filled her life with deeds of kindness, was especially noted for the garments she made. When she became ill and died, her friends prepared her body, placed it in an upper room, and sent two men for Peter, still at Lydda, requesting him to hurry to them. Putting the attending widows from the room, Peter knelt, prayed, and then addressed the body with the words "Tabitha, arise." The woman opened her eyes and sat up. Then Peter presented her to the widows and to the other believers at Joppa. "And it became known throughout all Joppa: and many believed on the Lord." Peter stayed for several days in Joppa, living in the home of a tanner named Simon (9:36–43).

Here we see not only a deep Christian concern for the needs of others—those of a palsied man and of mourners in the presence of death—but we also see a further advance of the gospel into another area of Judea. We discern a liberal attitude on the part of Peter, for he stayed in the home of a tanner. Since tanners had to deal with the hides of dead animals, they were considered ceremonially unclean (explanation in Lev. 11:39–40).

14. Caesarea, a Roman City

Caesarea was not merely a Gentile city; it was a Roman city, one symbolic of Roman power. It was a seaport site also. The Phoenicians built the Tower of Straton in the fourth century B.C., and Pompey freed it in 63 B.C. Augustus, the emperor, gave it to Herod the Great, who in turn rebuilt it over a period of twelve years into an elegant city, renaming it Caesarea in honor of Augustus Caesar. The city rivaled Jerusalem in prestige and surpassed it in magnificence and artistic splendor. It was founded in 22 B.C. and dedicated in 12 B.C., becoming the Roman seat of government. The procurators lived there, making visits to Jerusalem during the great Jewish feasts and other prominent activities. It was considered a Jewish city until the procurators began their rule in A.D. 6; then it came under direct Roman rule and was considered a Roman city. There were many public buildings, such as an amphitheater, theater, hippodrome, and a temple visible for miles out at sea. The hippodrome seated 20,000 people. Two aqueducts carried fresh water from the Carmel Range six miles to the north down into Caesarea. There was a huge breakwater encircling the harbor going down into the water to a depth of 120 feet. There were elaborate buildings and statues at the entrance to the harbor. Titus marched forth from Caesarea when he sacked Jerusalem in 70.

15. Peter in Joppa and Caesarea

At this point Luke introduced another character into his story, a centurion named Cornelius, who lived at Caesarea and was "a devout man, and one that feared God with all his house, who gave much alms to the people, and prayed to God always" (10:1–2). Cornelius was a God-fearer, a Gentile who worshiped the God of the Jews and accepted a great portion of Judaism. He had not, however, become a proselyte, one with a complete acceptance of Judaism in all its ritualistic requirements. There were many of these God-fearers throughout the empire, attending the synagogue services and reading from the Septuagint translation of the Hebrew Scriptures. The Ethiopian eunuch had been a God-fearer; but God did not have to prepare Philip for his witness to the eunuch in the way he had to prepare Peter for his witness and acceptance of Cornelius.

Cornelius and Peter were prepared for meeting each other by two concurrent visions. Cornelius' vision occurred in Caesarea at the ninth hour, or about three o'clock in the afternoon. This was the hour of prayer. The centurion saw and heard an angel of God addressing him and calling him by name. Very afraid, he said, "What is it, Lord?" The angel informed him that his prayers and his alms had "gone up for a memorial before God" and that he was to send to Joppa for one named Simon Peter, who was at that time staying with a tanner also called Simon. Cornelius immediately sent a soldier and two of his servants to Peter at Joppa (10:3–8).

The next day, as the three men neared Joppa, Peter ascended to the housetop to pray. This was at about the sixth hour, or at noon. While Peter was waiting for his meal to be prepared, he too had a vision—that of the opening of heaven and the descent of a vessel like a great sheet down upon the earth. In it were "all manner of fourfooted beasts and creeping things of the earth and birds of the heaven." When Peter was told to kill and eat, he remonstrated, declaring that he had never eaten anything "common and unclean." He then heard a voice saying, "What God hath cleansed, make not thou common." The vision was repeated two times, after which the vessel was received back into heaven (10:9–16).

Peter was perplexed over the meaning of what he had seen and heard, little realizing that God was preparing him to consider Gentiles as fit candidates for the church and for Christian fellowship. The command to eat animals that the Jews had for centuries considered ceremonially unclean was puzzling to the apostle. God's new revelation to Peter seemed to run counter to an old revelation. God's will for Peter's life at this moment seemed to be contrary to God's will for Peter's forefathers. This concept always produces perplexities. It happened several times when Jesus said, "Ye have heard it said of old," each time followed by a "but I say unto you." Jesus' new revelations were so disconcerting to the Pharisees and Sadducees that they nailed him to a cross. So the protest Peter made to God at this time was only natural.

While Peter was pondering the vision, the three men appeared at the gate of the tanner's house and asked about Simon Peter. The Holy Spirit informed the apostle that the men were present and that he should go with them, for he himself had sent them. Going down to see the men, Peter inquired of their visit; they told him of what had happened at Cornelius' house and of how Cornelius was commanded by God to send for Simon Peter. Peter invited them in to lodge that night (10:17–23).

Peter's disturbance of mind was somewhat steadied by the fact that the men appeared with news of Cornelius' vision and that it was related to his own vision. God's overall preparation of the matter was conforting to the apostle. Joppa had been the scene of Jonah's disobedience centuries prior to this; it would not now be the scene of Peter's disobedience. Jonah's love for the Ninevites was not as strong as God's love; Peter's love for Gentiles was strong enough to send him to Caesarea without hesitation. God got Jonah to Nineveh by a painful and circuitous route; he got Peter to Caesarea directly and immediately. The ultimate result of two men at prayer, Peter and Cornelius, would be a Gentile Pentecost.

The next day Peter arose and went to Caesarea, accompanied by the three visitors and "certain of the brethren at Joppa." Taking six of the believers at Joppa with him was a wise move; they could verify to the church at Jerusalem any unusual happenings in Caesarea. When Peter arrived in the city and entered the house of Cornelius, he found that the centurion had invited his relatives and close friends. All had been anticipating Peter's arrival. Cornelius greeted him with an attitude almost to the point of reverence. The significant thing is that Peter had crossed what to the Jews was a formidable barrier: he had entered the house of a Gentile. He said to the whole company, "Ye yourselves know how it is an unlawful thing for a man that is a Jew to join himself or come unto one of another nation; and yet unto me hath God showed that I should not call any man common or unclean; wherefore also I came without gainsaying, when I was sent for" (10:28–29).

Peter revealed that he understood the unusual vision at Joppa. As Calvary had removed the "clean and unclean" distinction for foods in the Mosaic system, it had also removed the "clean and unclean" status among God's highest creatures, man. All men, both Jews and Gentiles, are lost; all men are candidates to receive God's redeeming love poured forth at Calvary.

16. Peter's Sermon

When Peter asked the reason for the invitation to come to Cornelius' home, the Roman officer vividly recounted his vision. He made it plain that God's will was back of the summons (10:30–33). Immediately after Cornelius' explanation, Peter began to preach. He started his message with a momentous statement for one of Peter's background: "Of a truth I perceive that God is no respecter of persons: but in every nation he that feareth him, and worketh righteousness, is acceptable to him" (vv. 34–35).

The concept Peter expressed harks back to the Old Testament; Deuteronomy 10:17 states that God "regardeth not persons," and 2 Chronicles 19:7 states that with God there is "no respect of persons." The literal translation of the Greek phrase is "God is no face-receiver," meaning that God does not look on the outward man but upon the inner man. What Peter stated in his sermon had been expressed by many of the Old Testament prophets, but such a theme was minimized in the Judaism of Peter's day. Exclusive Judaism found no place for the missionary outlook of the prophets.

Peter continued his sermon, with Jesus and his great atoning act as the core of his message. He proclaimed that Jesus is Lord and that the Holy Spirit gave him God's power. His ministry was one of teaching and of merciful acts of healing. He accused the Jews of rejecting and crucifying him; but despite their efforts God raised him up on the third day and ordained him "to be the Judge of the living and the dead." Then Peter announced that everyone believing in Jesus would have forgiveness of sins. The ministry, the cross, the resurrection, the judgment—Peter included it all in his dynamic message, ending with an invitation that included every member of the human race (10:34–43).

God immediately stamped the whole event with his divine approval. "While Peter yet spake these words, the Holy Spirit fell on all them that heard the word. And they of the circumcision that believed were amazed, as many as came with Peter, because that on the Gentiles also was poured out the gift of the Holy Spirit. For they heard them speak with tongues, and magnify God" (10:44–46).

Just as there had been a Jewish Pentecost (2:1–4) and a Samaritan Pentecost (8:14–17), there was a Gentile Pentecost (10:44–46). Peter was involved in all three. Again there was speaking in tongues. To Jews, then to Samaritans, then to Gentiles—this was the everwidening circle for God's redemptive love and the pouring out of his Spirit.

Peter challenged all present to show reasons why the new converts should not be baptized: "Can any man forbid the water, that these should not be baptized, who have received the Holy Spirit as well as we?" It may have required more mental anguish for Peter to do what he did at Caesarea than for what he did at Jerusalem. Evidently there was no voiced disapproval, for he commanded baptism for all the new believers. After such a day, a stupendous one in the history of Christianity, the people requested Peter to stay with them for awhile. Luke, through silence, implied that he did so (10:46–48).

17. Peter Back in Jerusalem

When Peter returned to Jerusalem, what he had anticipated happened. There was an element in the Jerusalem church that believed in an adherence to many of the requirements of Judaism, even though the members had come to know the richness of the spiritual blessings in Christ. The whole Jerusalem church heard "that the Gentiles also had received the word of God." So the "strict group" was waiting to contend with Peter concerning his entering a Gentile house and his table fellowship with Gentiles. Their charge was direct: "Thou wentest in to men uncircumcised, and didst eat with them" (11:1–3).

Peter recounted the whole story, starting with the vision he had while praying on a housetop in Joppa and going through the falling of the Holy Spirit on Gentiles in the house of Cornelius in Caesarea. On the day of the first Pentecost, he had interpreted the pouring out of the Spirit as a fulfillment of Joel's prophecy (2:16–21); here he interpreted the pouring forth of the Spirit as a fulfillment of Jesus' ascension promise (1:5). He concluded his sermon with words that silenced his challengers: "If then God gave unto them the like gift as he did also unto us, when we believed on the Lord Jesus Christ, who was I, that I could withstand God?" (v. 17).

Not only were his objectors speechless; they glorified God and said, "Then to the Gentiles also hath God granted repentance unto life" (11:4–18).

Here we see a mild foreboding of the activities of a group that would cause Paul consternation later on: the Judaizers. This strict group might be the nucleus of those who were to insist that anyone entering the church must enter through the door of Judaism. Paul's answer to those of such persuasion is found in Galatians.

18. The Gospel in Antioch

It has already been pointed out that there was a scattering of the disciples in Jerusalem because of the persecution and that these went out preaching the gospel. Some went to Phoenicia, some to the island of Cyprus, some to Antioch, speaking to Jews only (11:19). Some men of Cyprus and Cyrene (North Africa) also came to Antioch, preaching the Lord Jesus to Greeks only (11:20). The phrase "of Cyprus and Cyrene" leaves us in doubt as to whether they came directly from these two locales or whether Luke was inferring that these two places were their homes. There was a synagogue in Jerusalem especially for people from Cyrene. People from this synagogue, as well as from others, disputed with Stephen (6:9). Stephen's preaching may have been instrumental in bringing these Cyrenians to a faith in Jesus. The Greeks to whom the men of Cyprus and Cyrene preached may have been God-fearers.

Significantly, a church grew up in Antioch. The city had received many favors from Rome, even being freed. It was adorned with beautiful statues and edifices; it was called "the Queen of the East" as well as "Antioch the Beautiful." However, it was not all beauty; it was the home of pagan and sensual religion. The famous Groves of Daphne, known for the immoral rites practiced there, were located in Antioch.

Was it a providential act of God that this great metropolis became the new center of the missionary enterprise? Did God desire a new church in a new location, free from the legalistic restrictions of Judaism, so that the gospel could be spread in an unhindered manner and with a universal outlook? If so, God found that location in Antioch, a city of cosmopolitan character, where people of all races mingled and settled. Here the first great church outside of Jerusalem was located. It was a church composed of Jews and Gentiles, but the latter highly dominated the scene. In fact, the main difference between the Jerusalem church and the Antioch church was the Gentile character of the latter. The church at Antioch was destined to surpass the church at Jerusalem in its role of expansion of Christianity.

The unnamed disciples who went as evangelists to Antioch had great results in their preaching. "And the hand of the Lord was with them: and a great number that believed turned unto the Lord" (11:21). In fact, the growth of the Antioch church was so great that the news filtered down to the church in Jerusalem. The Jerusalem church members sent Barnabas to Antioch to observe the situation.

When Barnabas arrived in Antioch he saw the results of "the grace of God." His message to the church was one of exhortation, "that with purpose of heart they would cleave unto the Lord." The effect of Barnabas' presence must have had no small influence; for Luke, after telling of his visit, stated that "much people was added to the Lord." Apparently Barnabas fulfilled the same role in Antioch that Peter and John played in Samaria (8:14).

Evidently Barnabas sensed a need for additional help in the work of the Lord. Conversions were multiplying at Antioch, and there was no end to the possibilities for future growth. He remembered Saul of Tarsus, the young man he had befriended years before in effecting his acceptance by the Jerusalem church (9:27). "And he went forth to Tarsus to seek for Saul: and when he had found him, he brought him unto Antioch." In the church at Antioch the two labored side by side for a year. Luke did not go into details about the results of that ministry, but it must have been a very profitable one. Luke mentioned "that the disciples were called Christians first in Antioch" (11:26). Other names found in Acts for the Christians are "those of the Way," "the ones being saved," "the disciples," "the saints," "the brethren," "the faithful ones," "the sect of the Nazarenes," and "the ones believing." The believers would not have initiated the name Christian for themselves; they would have had too much respect for their Lord. The Jews would not have used it of the believers, for the term Christ is the Greek form for the term Messiah. It is probable that the Gentiles of the city heard the believers frequently use the name Christ and added a suffix to the name. Hence the name Christian came into being.

19. Famine in Judea

At this juncture Luke told of a group of prophets who went from Jerusalem to Antioch predicting "by the Spirit that there should be a great famine over all the world: which came to pass in the days of Claudius." A prophet named Agabus was their spokesman for the prediction (11:27–28). Claudius reigned as emperor in Rome from 41 to 54, so the famine had to have been sometime in this span of years. "All the world" probably means the Roman world.

Prophets are frequently mentioned in Acts (11:27; 13:1; 15:32; 21:9–

10). Although a prophet did, on many occasions, predict future events, this was not his primary function. His main concern was to speak from God to man, to bring to man God's revelation of himself and his will for man. His message generally concerned the events of his own day more than those of a future day.

The main concern of Luke in recording this occasion was to show the feeling of compassion on the part of the Antioch church for the Jerusalem church. The Christians in Antioch sent relief to those dwelling in Judea (11:29–30). Although differences of opinion existed between the two Christian communities, an urgent need brought forth a helping hand, with no questions asked.

20. Deliverance of Peter

Since the death by sword of James, Jesus' brother, "pleased the Jews," Herod Agrippa I courted their favor during the Feast of Passover by putting Peter in prison under a strong guard, "intending after the Passover to bring him forth to the people" (12:3–4). Did this mean that he would have given Peter over to the people in the same manner that Pilate gave Jesus over to the people? This is hard to determine. However, one thing is certain: the church was earnestly praying for Peter (v. 5).

Peter had been in prison in Jerusalem one other time for his proclamation of the gospel. At that time God used an angel to unlock the prison doors and release him and the other apostles that had been arrested with him. (5:17–21). Then Peter had been between two guards, chained to each one, with other guards placed at the prison door. "And behold, an angel of the Lord stood by him, and a light shined in the cell: and he smote Peter on the side, and awoke him, saying, Rise up quickly. And his chains fell off from his hands" (v. 7).

When the angel led him forth from the cell, Peter was so startled that he thought he saw a vision. They went past the first guard, then the second guard, then through the iron gate—which miraculously opened for them—and on out into the street. Then the angel disappeared; and Peter, coming to himself, realized it was not a dream, that God had sent an angel to effect his deliverance (12:6–11).

Peter went to the house of Mary, mother of John Mark, "where many were gathered together and were praying." There he knocked at the outer gate, and a servant girl named Rhoda answered. She recognized the voice of the famous apostle; but, due to the mixed emotions of joy and unbelief, she did not open the gate but ran back and informed the others that Peter was there. They said to her, "Thou art mad." Not believing, they also said, "It is his angel." We are amused by Luke's declaration that "Peter continued knocking." When they finally opened the door to him, he revealed to them all the wondrous happenings during the night. Requesting that they inform James also, as well as the brethren, he departed from them (12:12–17). James, half brother of Jesus, was to become the recognized leader of the Jerusalem church. Luke evidently wanted us to observe this Jerusalem leadership as it began to emerge.

The next morning, due to Peter's absence from the prison, there was great confusion among the soldiers of the guard. After Herod Agrippa I had investigated the matter, he ordered the guards executed. With that, he returned to his home in Caesarea (12:18–19).

21. Death of Herod Agrippa I

One day this pompous ruler, arrayed in regal splendor, made an oration to the people. They shouted, "The voice of a god, and not of a man." Immediately a miracle occurred, for "an angel of the Lord smote him." Luke's interpretation for God's action was that "he gave not God the glory." Luke also said, "He was eaten of worms, and gave up the ghost" (12:21–23). Josephus has left a vivid description of the death of Herod Agrippa I, one in which he says the king was suddenly struck with violent internal pains, was taken home, and died five days later.

"But the word of God grew and multiplied" (v. 24). With these terse words Luke added another of his frequent comments about the growth of the church, a comment that sets the ongoing of the church in vivid contrast to the miserable, final moment of a despotic king. The church was destined to advance in spite of religious and civil opposition.

At this phase of his narrative, Luke told of the return of Barnabas and Saul to Antioch from Jerusalem, having fulfilled their "famine visit" (11:29–30). They took with them John Mark (12:25), whose mother had a home in Jerusalem (12:12). He was a cousin of Barnabas (Col. 4:10) and later served on missionary ventures with Barnabas.

22. A Difficult Question

Galatians 2:1–10 speaks of a visit to Jerusalem made by Saul, Barnabas, and Titus that presents quite a problem. Where does this "Galatian visit" fit in Luke's Acts account? "Then after the space of fourteen years I went up again to Jerusalem with Barnabas, taking Titus also with me. And I went up by revelation; and I laid before them the gospel which I preach among the Gentiles" (Gal. 2:1–2).

Is this visit the same as the "famine visit" of Acts 11:29–30 and 12:25? Or is it the same as the one to come later, that recorded in Acts 15:1–35,

A GUIDE FOR NEW TESTAMENT STUDY

which tells of the Jerusalem controversy occurring between the first and second missionary journeys? The opinion of scholars is divided. It would require too much space to present both sides of the matter in a book of this nature; there are commentaries that fulfill this need.

The Galatian account does present an agreement worked out by the personalities of both Antioch and Jerusalem. It reads, "when they perceived the grace that was given unto me, James and Cephas and John, they who were reputed to be pillars, gave to me and Barnabas the right hands of fellowship, that we should go unto the Gentiles, and they unto the circumcision" (Gal. 2:9).

20.

The Church in Asia Minor

Chapters 1—7 of Acts deal with the growth of the gospel in Jerusalem and the development of the Jerusalem church. This was a Christian community composed mostly of those who had previously been Jews. Chapters 8—12 deal with the spread of the gospel into Judea and Samaria. Here Samaritans and God-fearers, such as the Ethiopian treasurer and Cornelius the centurion, were won to the Lord Jesus. Chapters 13—15:33 deal with the proclamation of the gospel and the founding of churches in Asia Minor. We will concern ourselves with this third phase in the present chapter of this book.

1. Separation of Saul and Barnabas

Luke mentioned five names at the beginning of chapter 13, men who were part of a group of "prophets and teachers" in the church at Antioch. These men were "Barnabas, and Symeon that was called Niger, and Lucius of Cyrene, and Manean the foster-brother of Herod the tetrarch, and Saul" (13:1). Barnabas and Saul, then, continued to serve in the Antioch church after their return from the "famine visit" to Jerusalem (12:25); this ministry continued until they left on their first extensive missionary endeavor.

Galatians 2:11-14 tells of a visit of Peter to Antioch, which seems to fit into the Acts account better at this juncture than at any other. Peter ate at the same table with the Gentiles until some of the Jerusalem Christians, those who had formerly been Jews, came to the city. At their arrival, however, Peter drew back and would not have table fellowship with the Gentile Christians, an example that drew others away also. Even Barnabas was affected by Peter's action. Saul contended with Peter, openly and before the whole church; he believed that Peter and the others "walked not uprightly according to the truth of the gospel" (v. 14).

In the first of the three phases of Acts, the names of the remaining apostles after Judas' death, plus Matthias who replaced him, are listed

(1:13,26). However, the activities of only two of these, Peter and John, are featured by Luke. In the second phase of Acts the names of seven men are listed, probably the original seven deacons (6:5). Again the activities of only two, Stephen and Philip, were discussed by Luke. In the third phase of Acts the names of five men are listed (13:1); and only two, Barnabas and Saul, are brought into the picture. The remaining ones are never mentioned again.

In Acts, Luke placed great emphasis upon the leadership of the Holy Spirit, a fact very apparent in the call of Barnabas and Saul into a much wider circle of missionary endeavor. (See Acts 13:2–3.) Antioch became the center of the broader evangelistic thrust; the church in that community took the initiative in the work. The endeavor was directly inspired by the Holy Spirit.

2. Beginning of First Missionary Journey

Barnabas and Saul, accompanied by young John Mark, who had returned with them to Antioch from their "famine visit" in Jerusalem (12:25), started on an extensive missionary campaign that took them first to Seleucia, the port of Antioch, and then to the island of Cyprus (13:4). We wonder what the duty of John Mark might have been. Was it to care for the material needs of the party; to do the baptizing; to act as a teacher of the basic truths set forth by Jesus, as well as the significance of his person and of his advent into the world? The term used for John Mark is "attendant" (13:5), which means more than *valet* and even more than *assistant*.

Due to Greek influence Cyprus became highly Hellenized. During New Testament times it was extensively populated, with about two hundred thousand of its population Jews. Barnabas, Saul, and Mark were not the first Christian evangelists to reach the island; Christians from the island were among those first bringing the gospel to Antioch (11:20).

The three emissaries for Christ went first to the port of Salamis, where "they proclaimed the word of God in the synagogues of the Jews" (13:5). At this stage of the Christian movemet the synagogues were open to preachers of the gospel, so the men made a habit of going to the synagogues first in their evangelistic efforts, as was done on the island and throughout the province of Galatia (13:14,44; 14:1).

3. Winning of a Proconsul

The men next went "through the whole island," finally coming to Paphos on the southwestern shore, the capital of Cyprus (13:6). Luke said that at Paphos "they found a certain sorcerer, a false prophet, a Jew, whose name was Bar-Jesus; who was with the proconsul, Sergius Paulus, a man

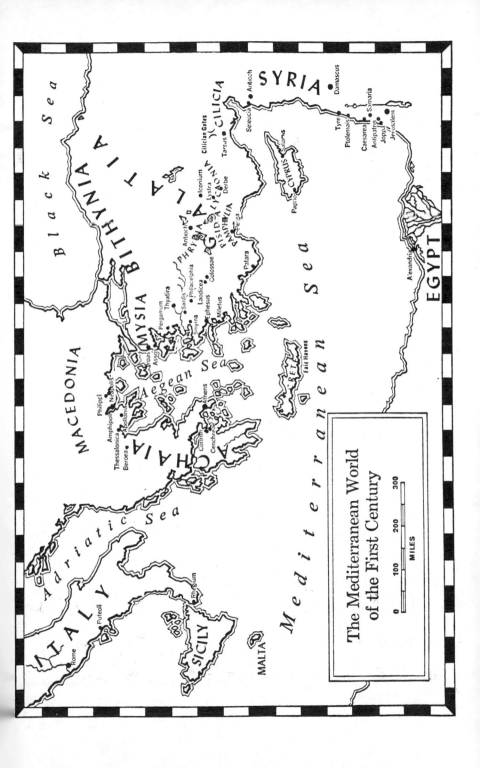

The Mediterranean World
of the First Century

0   100   200   300
MILES

of understanding'' (13:6–7).

The province of Cyprus was a senatorial one, one ruled by the senate rather than the emperor; a province ruled by the emperor was termed an imperial province. A senatorial province had a proconsul, while an imperial province had a procurator. Sergius Paulus, described in Acts as a man of understanding, "called unto him Barnabas and Saul, and sought to hear the word of God'' (v. 7). This was a significant event, since it constitutes the first recorded case of Christian preachers before a Roman ruler. A false prophet named Bar-Jesus, also called Elymas, opposed the preachers in their efforts to win Sergius Paulus, "seeking to turn aside the proconsul from the faith'' (13:7–8).

In Acts 13:9 Luke introduced two changes in terminology; the first was a change of name for "Saul, who is also called Paul.'' Also, up to this point the order of the two names is that of "Barnabas and Saul.'' It is so used in Acts 11:30; 12:25; 13:2; and 13:7. This would indicate that Barnabas was in some degree the leader, a fact that corresponds with Barnabas' having taken the initiative in seeking out Saul as his aide in the Lord's work (11:25). From this point on Luke replaced Saul, the Hebrew name, with Paul, the Roman name; and he also reversed the order of the two names Barnabas and Saul. Paul is placed in the leadership spot, as is discerned in the order of names and in such phrases as "Paul and his company'' (13:13).

Paul's conflict with Bar-Jesus, the sorcerer at Paphos, reminds us of Peter's conflict with Simon Magus in Samaria. (The Greek work translated *sorcerer* is *magus*.) Paul used strong words on this occasion, as had Peter previously. Paul, filled with the Holy Spirit, and looking directly at Bar-Jesus, said: "O full of all guile and all villany, thou son of the devil, thou enemy of all righteousness, wilt thou not cease to pervert the right ways of the Lord? And now, behold, the hand of the Lord is upon thee, and thou shalt be blind, not seeing the sun for a season'' (vv. 10–11). Bar-Jesus means son of Jesus, but Paul called him "son of the devil.'' The proconsul, witnessing the sudden blindness of Elymas, "believed, being astonished at the teaching of the Lord'' (13:9–12).

4. In Antioch of Pisidia

Paul and his two companions set sail from Paphos and went to the mainland of Asia Minor, the territory that today comprises Turkey. We do not know how long they were on the island of Cyprus, but probably two or three months at the most. Paul had set his sights on winning the entire Roman Empire.

They landed at Perga in Pamphylia, where John Mark left the company of the other two men and returned to Jerusalem (13:13). Many guesses have been set forth as to why he left. One is that he became homesick. Another is that he foresaw a broadening mission to the Gentiles, which did not appeal to him. Since he was a cousin of Barnabas (Col. 4:10), he may have resented Paul's new leadership role. Or he may have feared the hazards of the prospective missionary journey through the rough terrain of Asia Minor. Whatever the cause, Paul resented his forsaking them, a fact that prevented the apostle from accepting John Mark as a travel companion later (15:36–41). At the end of his career, however, Paul forgave John Mark; he later told Timothy to bring Mark with him when he came, for he would be useful to him (2 Tim. 4:11).

Luke left no record that Paul and Barnabas preached in the coastal province of Pamphylia. Instead, they continued over the Taurus range of mountains and moved into the province of Galatia, a very large province comprising the central area of Asia Minor. They came to Antioch of Pisidia, where, on the sabbath day, they attended the synagogue services. (The southern part of Galatia was known as Pisidia; and Antioch, its chief city, was called "Antioch of Pisidia" to differentiate it from "Antioch of Syria.") After the reading of the law and the prophets, the rulers of the synagogue invited the two visitors to speak. Paul accepted the invitation (13:14–16).

Paul's sermon (13:16–47), his first one recorded, is similar to others found in Acts. Just as Stephen, in the long sermon prior to his death (7:2–53), reviewed much of Israel's history and God's dealings with the nation, Paul reviewed much of the same history. Since Paul heard Stephen's sermon and witnessed his tragic death, maybe he was not able to erase from his memory that eventful scene. He then pictured Jesus' rejection and condemnation by the Jews, as well as his death and resurrection. He also used passages from the Old Testament to show that Jesus' resurrection was foretold there. Then he climaxed his message with a very dramatic statement: "Be it known unto you therefore, brethren, that through this man is proclaimed unto you remission of sins: and by him every one that believeth is justified from all things, from which ye could not be justified by the law of Moses" (vv. 38–39). This was followed by a quotation from the prophet Habakkuk (1:5) intended to serve as a warning to his hearers (13:16–41).

Evidently Paul's sermon impressed his hearers in a very significant manner; they invited him to return the following sabbath. Also, as they left the building, "many of the Jews and of the devout proselytes followed Paul

and Barnabas,'' whom Paul urged "to continue in the grace of God''
(13:42–43).

The six-day interval between the two sabbaths allowed ample time for
the news of Paul's sermon to spread; and there was a huge crowd to hear
him, "almost the whole city.'' Such a sight must have produced apprehension on the part of the Jewish leaders, for they became extremely jealous
"and contradicted the things which were spoken by Paul.'' However, Paul
and Barnabas answered them boldly, saying that since the Jews had
rejected the word of God, the two of them would "turn to the Gentiles.''
The missionaries even quoted the prophet Isaiah to support such a move,
all of which pleased the Gentiles tremendously. As a result, many believed. "And the word of the Lord was spread abroad throughout all the
region'' (13:44–49). From the nucleus of converts in Antioch the gospel
spread to outlying regions, much as Paul had planned it.

However, the Jews continued to oppose the work of Paul and Barnabas
by persecuting them and casting them out of that territory. The two
preachers "shook off the dust of their feet against them, and came unto
Iconium,'' a city eighty miles east of Antioch (13:50–51). "And the
disciples were filled with joy and with the Holy Spirit'' (v. 52).

5. In Iconium, Lystra, and Derbe

Again Paul and Barnabas entered the synagogue, preaching so persua-
sively "that a great multitude both of Jews and of Greeks believed.'' And
again the Jews who opposed the gospel brought on discontent; they
"stirred up the souls of the Gentiles, and made them evil affected against the
brethren.'' Yet Paul and Barnabas were able to preach for quite a while,
"speaking boldly in the Lord'' and doing "signs and wonders.'' Evidently
they were able to form a strong church. Again Luke used the word *boldly* to
characterize the manner of the preaching and of the ministry of the early
apostles and evangelists. Thus we see the continuing effect of Pentecost year
after year (14:1–3).

Yet the division of the people of the city, produced by the conniving of
the Jews, increased till there was a concerted effort to treat the two
evangelists shamefully—even to the point of stoning them. Hence they
departed from the city and went to Lystra, twenty miles distant, to preach
there (14:4–7). This was in the region called Lycaonia.

In Lystra there must have been no synagogue, since no mention is made
of one; the atmosphere in which Paul worked seems to have been predominantly pagan. Here he healed a man who had been lame from birth.
Perceiving the man's faith, Paul shouted, "Stand upright on thy feet.'' The

man leaped up and walked. Observing the miracle, the crowd said, "The gods are come down to us in the likeness of men." They mistook Barnabas for Zeus (Jupiter in the Roman pantheon) and Paul for Hermes (Mercury in the Roman pantheon). Luke said they called Paul Hermes "because he was the chief speaker." (The King James translators, relying heavily on the Latin Vulgate in their work, used "Jupiter" and "Mercury" rather than "Zeus" and "Hermes.") The priest of Jupiter brought oxen to sacrifice in order to recognize Paul and Barnabas as deities; but the two missionaries proclaimed with forceful words and actions that they were "men of like passions" as those around them. They informed the people that they were bringing them good tidings and that they "should turn from these vain things unto a living God." They were scarcely able to restrain the people "from doing sacrifice unto them" (14:8–18).

Troublemaking Jews came from Antioch and Iconium to Lystra to cause distress for the emissaries of the gospel. They were successful in stirring up the people to the point that they stoned Paul, dragged him out of the city, and left him for dead. However, he must not have been seriously hurt; when disciples came to him, he arose and again entered the city. The next day he and Barnabas left Lystra and went to the neighboring city of Derbe (14:19–20).

Luke did not describe the activities of the two evangelists at Derbe except to say that they preached the gospel there and "made many disciples" (14:20–21). There is no mention of adverse activities on the part of Jewish unbelievers at Derbe; things seem to have been quiet as far as persecution was concerned. It would not have been far to Paul's home from Derbe; the distance was approximately 160 miles. Though the idea might have appealed to Paul, he was committed to the spread of the gospel. He needed to retrace his steps and confirm the work already started, even to the extent of going back to a city where he had recently been stoned.

6. The Journey Home

The newly formed churches needed to be strengthened in the faith right away. Paul and Barnabas returned to Lystra, to Iconium, and then to Antioch of Pisidia, "confirming the souls of the disciples, exhorting them to continue in the faith." They appointed elders in every church and prayed and fasted with the congregations. Then they proceeded through Pisidia to Pamphylia and, arriving at Perga, preached the word there. Then they came to the port of Attalia and set sail for Antioch of Syria, their point of original departure. Arriving in Antioch and gathering the church together, "they rehearsed all things that God had done with them, and that he had opened a door of faith unto the Gentiles." They stayed in Antioch for some time (14:21–28). This first campaign lasted approximately two years. It probably went from 46–48, although it is impossible to speak authoritatively concerning dates. It was of the shortest duration of any of the three journeys and covered less territory.

7. Dissension in the Church

The two evangelists found that all was not well at Antioch; troublemakers had come from Jerusalem to sow seeds of discontent in the city. "And certain men came down from Judea and taught the brethren, saying, Except ye be circumcised after the custom of Moses, ye cannot be saved" (v. 1). This led to argumentation and debate between the two missionaries and the visitors from Jerusalem who held opposing views. The crisis was so acute that the church at Antioch sent Paul and Barnabas and certain others to the apostles and elders in Jerusalem to investigate the matter (15:1–2).

The problem boiled down to the question of what is necessary to be saved. Is faith alone, accepting the grace of God offered in the atoning sacrifice of Jesus Christ, all that is necessary? Or does one have to become a Jew first, submitting to circumcision and various other legalistic exactions of the Mosaic system, before his faith in Christ will redeem him? The problem arose due to the acceptance of many Gentiles into the Christian fold. What should be the attitude of the church, each and every local church, toward these new converts?

There had always been a "strict group" in the Jerusalem church, those who had formerly been such strong Pharisees that they were not able completely to shelve their pre-Christian Judaism when they came into a saving knowledge of Jesus Christ. They wanted to interpret the Christian faith in terms of Judaism, for they felt that one could be a Christian and still observe many of the old requirements of Judaism. Luke called this group "the sect of the Pharisees who believed" (15:5). We must remember that most of the members of the Jerusalem church were formerly Jewish, and therefore devotees of Judaism; but some of these people, now Christian, were more strict than others about keeping the Jewish ceremonial law. This group became known as Judaizers. They were willing to welcome Gentiles into the church, but these converts must enter through the door of Judaism; according to the Judaizers, Christianity consisted of "Christ plus the law."

Paul and Barnabas had ample proof of the spiritual freedom of the Gentiles and were willing to fight to prevent their coming under the shackles of Judaism. Therefore, they immediately proceeded to Jerusalem, "passing through Phoenicia and Samaria, declaring the conversion of the

Gentiles.'' This caused "great joy unto all the brethren.'' When they arrived in Jerusalem and were received by the church there, they related all that God had done through them. However, the story of God's gracious dealings with the Gentiles as told by the two evanglists did not satisfy the Judaizers. Instead of expressing joy over the salvation of the Gentile pagans, they voiced their discontent (vv. 3–5).

8. The Jerusalem Controversy

"And the apostles and elders were gathered together to consider this matter.'' Thus began what has been termed the most significant council ever to sit in the history of Christianity, for what was discussed was the basic requirement in being saved. Was it faith in Christ, or faith in Christ *and* observance of the law? The details of the controversy are found in Acts 15:1–29.

"Much questioning'' arose, after which Peter, a man well respected by both groups, made an important contribution to the matter under dispute. He reminded all present that God had decreed that by his preaching "the Gentiles should hear the word of the gospel, and believe'' and that God had given the Holy Spirit to believing Gentiles as well as to believing Jews. God made no distinction between Gentile and Jew. Peter accused the Judaizing element of endeavoring to put a yoke on the neck of the Gentiles that they, the Jews, had been unable to bear. Salvation is effected through the grace of the Lord Jesus, and this was true for both Gentile and Jew (15:7–11).

Peter's address was so effective that "all the multitude kept silence.'' The fact that Peter had been with Jesus constantly during his remarkable ministry gave him credibility in the eyes of the members of the Jerusalem church, coupled with the fact that God had placed his divine approval on everything that Peter had experienced in Caesarea at the house of Cornelius. After Peter's address Paul and Barnabas were permitted to tell of all "the signs and wonders'' God had effected among the Gentiles through them (15:12). Their speech substantiated all that Peter had just stated. Their experiences were very similar to Peter's experience with Cornelius.

The third address for the occasion was made by James, the half brother of Jesus, who was recognized for his Jewish allegiance even though an ardent follower of Jesus. At this time he seemed to have assumed the leadership of the Jerusalem church, a position probably favored by his physical relationshp to Jesus. Though still an observer of the law, he, like Peter, realized that salvation comes by grace alone and not through fulfilling legalistic requirements. He was just the one to smooth the waters and bring a decision from the church concerning the matter.

Quoting Amos 9:11–12, James endeavored to show the Hebrew Christians that God had planned all along that Gentiles should enter the kingdom. He strongly suggested that they "trouble not them that from among the Gentiles turn to God," meaning that Gentiles should not be required to submit to circumcision. This recommendation was followed by another, in the form of a compromise, that the Gentile Christians be admonished to "abstain from the pollution of idols, and from fornication, and from what is strangled, and from blood." The strange thing is that the first two requirements are moral and the last two are ritualistic, a peculiar mixture hard to comprehend. James' request for respect of certain Jewish customs grew out of a desire to conciliate the two groups, two factions quite diverse in backgrounds.

An acceptance of James' entire speech would require a bit of giving on the part of both sides, thus tending to maintain a very essential peaceful relationship. Even though the Gentile Christians were assured that they would not have to submit to circumcision, they should respect the feelings of their weaker Jewish brothers in Christ. After all, most of the Jewish Christians had not had experiences, as had Peter and Paul, that would free them from the old exactions of Judaism. Also, there was no compromise in regard to basic principles. It was a case of "peace at any cost" (15:13–21).

9. Report of the Council

The next step was to send a report of the decision made at the Jerusalem conference back to Antioch, as well as to other interested churches in Syria and Cilicia. Not only was the letter carried by Paul and Barnabas; two other men, "chief men among the brethren," accompanied them on their mission. These were Judas, called Barsabbas, and Silas, who could well verify the contents of the epistle carried by the two missionaries. The letter reported that the results of the conference were that the parties involved came "to one accord" and that Judas and Silas were being sent to substantiate the letter "by word of mouth." It did not have the tone of a command; it was more of a courteous suggestion, a request made to help solidify Christian harmony between the believers of Jewish learnings and those from Gentile ranks (15:22–29). If the Gentile Christians would courteously observe the requests of the letter, there would be no reason the Jewish Christians could not have table fellowship with them; and this would include observing the Lord's Supper in their company.

The epistle was delivered to the Antioch church and immediately read, producing great rejoicing at the exhortation that it contained. Judas and

Silas preached for a time to the Antioch church and then returned to their home in Jerusalem. However, it appears that Silas remained in Antioch with Paul and Barnabas for some time, while Judas made his way back to Jerusalem (15:30–35).

10. The Galatians Account

As was stated at the end of chapter 19 under "A Difficult Question," Galatians 2:1–10 speaks of a visit to Jerusalem made by Saul and Barnabas, who took Titus with them (2:1). Some scholars believe this visit is the same as the "famine visit" related in Acts 11:29–30 and 12:25. Others believe it is the same as the "Jerusalem Council visit" of Acts 15:1–35. Commentaries are filled with long discussions presenting each side of the question. There *are* shades of difference between the Galatians account by Paul and the Acts 15 account by Luke, such as the mentioning of Titus by Paul in his account and not by Luke in Acts. Also, the overall tone of the Acts account is harmony and peace, while that of Paul's account is bitter controversy and heated debate. But would not these apparent differences exist due to the variant purpose in writing by the two authors?

Both Acts 15 and Galatians 2 have as their theme the qualifications for the admittance of Gentiles into the church. Were circumcision and other Mosaic regulations to be imposed before Gentiles could be included in the Christian fold? Or was salvation by grace through faith alone, with no legalistic exactions required? Also, what was the relationship of Jews and Gentiles after having been admitted within the church? Paul in his Galatians account (2:1–10) emphasized freedom in Christ, a freedom that absolves one from the regulations of Jewish legalism. He implied in Galatians 2:1–10 that the debate was fierce. All, however, ended in harmony and victory for the great apostle; he stated that James, Peter, and John gave to him and Barnabas "the right hands of fellowship." He and Barnabas would relate the outcome to the Gentiles, and the Jerusalem "pillars" would do the same for the Jews (Gal. 2:9).

It appears to this author that the weight of evidence is for the acceptance of the Acts 15 account and the Galatians 2 account as both being reports of the highly significant Jerusalem controversy. There are difficulties of interpretation in going in either direction, but it seems there are less difficulties in this view of the matter.

21.
The Church in the Aegean World

During the days in Antioch following the Jerusalem Council, while Paul was preaching the word of God, his mind must have drifted constantly to the churches all along the route of his first extensive missionary endeavor. How were they progressing in their newfound faith? Had problems arisen to harass them in their Christian work? Had the Judaizers penetrated that far in their pernicious teachings? Within a few days he suggested to Barnabas that they return to every city where they had "proclaimed the word of the Lord" in order to determine the welfare of the brethren (15:36). Paul may have received word from some of the Galatian churches that stirred up a desire within him to be once again in their midst.

1. A Clash in Personalities

Differences arose, however, that were to disturb the tranquillity of the waters. Barnabas seemingly agreed immediately with Paul's suggestion; but when he "was minded to take with them John also, who was called Mark," Paul disagreed. He remembered too vividly that John Mark had left them on the previous journey. Luke said there arose a "sharp contention." Paul had already denounced Peter and Barnabas for not eating with the Gentile Christians when Jews from Jerusalem came to visit Antioch. At that time he accused them of not walking "uprightly according to the truth of the gospel" (Gal. 2:13–14). The disagreement over John Mark probably added fuel to the flame.

As a result of the dispute there was a parting of the ways, Barnabas taking Mark (Col. 4:10) and going back to Cyprus, and Paul taking Silas and departing through Syria and Cilicia (15:37–41). Silas was one of the two who accompanied Paul and Barnabas on their return trip from Jerusalem to verify the report of the Jerusalem Council. He must have stayed on in Antioch to aid in the work there and was, therefore, ready when Paul needed him most. In a certain sense the parting of Paul and Barnabas was a blessing in disguise, for two missionary expeditions

339

emerged from the turmoil. Would there not be just as much need to return to Cyprus and revisit those churches as there would be to revisit the ones in Asia Minor? And could not Barnabas be very effective in the work of the Lord in his home territory?

There is also a possibility that more was involved than merely a clash in personalities over John Mark. It could be that Barnabas, not quite so adamant and determined about the "freedom of the gospel" as his companion Paul, would favor a mission to the Jews more than one to the Gentiles. Luke spoke no more of Barnabas and Mark after mentioning that they sailed for Cyprus. We are left to wonder how they fared on their second evangelistic effort on this strategic island. Later on in his life, Paul was reconciled to John Mark, for he found him very useful in his work (2 Tim. 4:11) and considered him a fellow-worker (Col. 4:10–11). In 1 Corinthians 9:6 Paul spoke in a friendly manner concerning Barnabas; so the "sharp contention" caused no permanent rift between these two famous personalities.

4. A New Worker

Luke said that Paul and Silas came "to Derbe and to Lystra" and that a disciple named Timothy was there. Does the word "there" refer to Derbe or to Lystra? The determination of Timothy's hometown depends on the answer to this question, a very difficult one. Most scholars believe he came from Lystra, however. At any rate he is called a "disciple" (16:1), so Paul must have won him on his previous journey, although Luke did not mention Timothy's name in connection with that journey. His mother was a Jewess named Eunice, and his grandmother was named Lois; his father was a Greek. Timothy was respected, for he was "well reported of by the brethren that were at Lystra and Iconium" (16:2). Paul invited the young man to go with them (16:3), possibly thinking of a replacement for young John Mark.

Then Paul did something that puzzles the reader of Acts. After inviting Timothy to accompany him "he took and circumcised him because of the Jews that were in these parts: for they all knew that his father was a Greek" (16:3). Why did Paul, one who felt so strongly concerning the freedom of the gospel from Jewish restrictions, feel it was necessary to require this of Timothy? He evidently felt that he was not compromising the truth, for he did it to maintain harmony and peace.

5. Reading of the Letter

As the three men went from city to city, "they delivered them the decrees to keep which had been ordained of the apostles and elders that were at Jerusalem" (16:4). This means that Paul read them the letter that he and Barnabas had brought back from Jerusalem to Antioch after the controversy there. Growth must have occurred because of their visit; Luke wrote that "the churches were strengthened in the faith, and increased in number daily" (16:5).

6. Leadership of the Holy Spirit

The province of Asia, with its capital at Ephesus, lay directly west of Galatia. This "Asia" must certainly not be confused with the continent of Asia, for it was merely a Roman province. It seemed to be an inviting field to the three missionaries, but evidently God had other plans. "And they went through the region of Phrygia and Galatia, having been forbidden of the Holy Spirit to speak the word in Asia" (16:6). The three men turned north and came "over against Mysia," the name of the northwestern part of the province of Asia. When they wished to turn in a northeasterly direction "to go into Bithynia," still in Asia Minor, the Spirit of Jesus prevented them from doing so (16:7). We have already seen that the directive force of the Holy Spirit in the expansion of the church is a major theme in the book of Acts.

Evidently God wanted the men to spread the gospel westward, not eastward; they then bypassed Mysia and entered Troas, a city on the Aegean Sea (16:8). It was near the site of ancient Troy. Once the missionaries were located in Troas the only ways to proceed further were northwest into Macedonia or southeast into Achaia (Greece proper). Macedonia was a Roman province, having been conquered by the Romans in 168 B.C. and made a province in 146 B.C.

Again the three men received God's directive, this time by a vision. "And a vision appeared to Paul in the night: There was a man of Macedonia standing, beseeching him, and saying, Come over into Macedonia, and help us" (16:9). The men immediately made plans to obey the call. Later Paul again visited Troas (20:6–12); at this time, however, the city was only an embarking point for a fruitful stay in Macedonia.

7. Another New Worker in Troas

In Acts are several passages that have become known as the "we" sections. The first one is 16:10–17. Luke turned in his narrative from the third person to the first person plural, which is a good indication that Luke joined the party of Paul, Silas, and Timothy at Troas, accompanying them from there to Philippi. Many students of the Bible believe that Luke kept a travel diary, which he later used in writing the book of Acts. This may well have happened, in view of the accuracy with which he recounted the

Egnatian Way, between Neapolis and Philippi

episodes in his book. Also, some scholars have suggested that the beloved physician himself may have been "the man of Macedonia" in the apostle's vision, which would correspond with Luke's joining the group at Troas. Some scholars, however, think that Luke's home was Pisidian Antioch and that he joined the party there. In this case he just refrained from using the first person till he got to Troas. If he started his travel diary at Troas, this would account for the start of the "we" sections at this point. A lot of surmising is involved in such a theory, however.

8. A Convert in Philippi

The party of four did not cross the Hellespont, the narrow strait separating the provinces of Asia and Macedonia. (It is called the Dardanelles today.) Instead, they set sail from Troas and traversed the upper part of the Aegean Sea, going by way of Samothrace, an island rising five thousand feet above sea level, and on to Neapolis, a seaport town. Landing there, they proceeded by land nine miles to Philippi. Philippi, named for Philip of Macedon, father of Alexander the Great, was not the capital. However, it was located on the Egnatian Way, one of the important Roman roads of that day, and was noted for its gold mines. In fact, Philip of Macedon, seizing the gold mines, had fortified the city and named it for himself. Philippi also had the distinction of being a Roman colony, decreed so by Caesar Augustus. Not many cities had this honor, a privilege that furthered the protection of the empire.

After an important battle fought nearby in 42 B.C., a number of the veterans were settled there, and many of the legionnaires were granted land. After another battle in 31 B.C. more colonists were added. Being comfortably situated there would make the soldiers more concerned about the protection of that area; therefore, the purpose of the colony was really military. A Roman colony also had a certain degree of self-government, for it was like a part of Rome moved abroad. Being proud of their status as a colony, the inhabitants copied Rome in the titles of their officials: praetors, translated "magistrates" (16:20), and lictors, translated "sergeants" (16:35).

Luke said that the party stayed in Philippi several days and that on the sabbath they went out by the gate and down by the riverside, where they supposed "there was a place of prayer." Here they spoke to the women who had assembled, including one "named Lydia, a seller of purple, of the city of Thyatira." The river was the Gangites (or Angites), a tributary of the Strymon. Evidently the women were in the habit of meeting for prayer. Lydia, from Thyatira, a city in the province of Asia, may have come to know the Jewish religion when she was in her home city; there were Jews in Thyatira. (Thyatira is mentioned in Revelation 2:18–29 as one of "the seven churches" in the province of Asia.)

Lydia was a seller of purple cloth, probably made in her hometown, and was named for the region in Asia, Lydia, where Thyatira was located. She may have been rich; at least she was the head of her house. She is described as "one that worshipped God" and as one "whose heart God opened to give heed unto the things which were spoken by Paul." She was baptized, along with "her household." Her husband is not mentioned by Luke, which probably means she was either a widow or unmarried. "Her household" could have been composed of servants and other dependents. At any rate, she was Paul's first European convert and invited the party of evangelists to stay in her home. They accepted her offer (16:13–15).

The Philippian church that began with this event became a strong one, bringing much joy to the heart of "the great evangelist to the Gentiles." The people of the church aided him in his further labors, even sending gifts for his support (Phil. 4:15–17). He wrote to them one of his most joyous letters, Philippians.

9. A Demented Slave Girl Healed

There was a slave girl in Philippi, well known to the inhabitants, who had a "spirit of divination." This term literally means a "spirit, a python." In Greek mythology the god Apollo was thought of as embodied in a snake at Delphi, a town in ancient Greece where the oracle of Apollo was located. The snake in which the god was supposed to have been located was named Python. From this came the Grecian, pagan belief that a python was a spirit that possessed certain people, making that one inspired in speech. The python was considered as prophesying through the mouth of the one he possessed. Many of these people so possessed uttered words beyond their control. This poor girl, evidently suffering from a mild, chronic type of lunacy, was considered to be possessed by a pythonic spirit. She represented a profit to her masters because of her soothsaying, for they took advantage of those who consulted her as a fortune-teller.

Paul and his party met the girl one day as they were going to "the place of prayer." She followed them, crying out, "These men are servants of the Most High God, who proclaim unto you the way of salvation." The term "Most High God" was one used by both Jews and Greeks, but with a different connotation. It was employed here by the girl in its pagan sense, as one denoting the highest of many gods. The term salvation was also employed by both Jews and Greeks. The pagans thought of salvation as deliverance from the powers and principalities of the physical world that tend to dominate man and determine his fate. The girl continued day after day to follow the evangelists and to utter her cry. Finally Paul turned around and commanded the spirit possessing her, "I charge thee in the name of Jesus Christ to come out of her." The exorcism took place immediately, for the spirit "came out that very hour" (16:16–18).

10. Roman Opposition

Immediately there was concerted opposition to the attempt of the missionaries to bring peace of mind to a tormented girl. "But when her masters saw that the hope of their gain was gone, they laid hold on Paul and Silas, and dragged them into the marketplace before the rulers" (v. 19). For the first time in Acts we encounter the persecution of Christians by pagans rather than by Jewish leaders; and the reason was economic, not religious or doctrinal. The girl was now valueless to her masters; their source of unethical gain was gone.

When Paul and Silas were brought before the rulers of the city and the charges were made, the real reason for their arrest was not mentioned. The masters of the girl claimed, "These men, being Jews, do exceedingly trouble our city, and set forth customs which it is not lawful for us to receive, or to observe, being Romans" (16:20–21). The accusation against the two men was charged with race prejudice: "These men being Jews . . . [we] being Roman." On this foundation the two men were accused of endeavoring to change Roman customs, a thought that would especially draw wrath from the citizens of a Roman colony such as Philippi. The citizens of such a city considered themselves to be superior to the Greeks around them; this feeling was probably even greater toward Jews that had wandered into town. Paul and Silas were the ones who were arrested and accused; Luke, a Greek, and Timothy, a half-Greek, were not bothered. Men of another race were tampering with the customs of proud Roman citizens, and the citizens arose to help the girl's masters in their denunciation of the two evangelists.

When "the multitude rose up together against them," the magistrates, hastily and without investigation, had the men beaten with rods. The irony is that, since Paul and Silas were Roman citizens, the magistrates were defying Roman law; and the charge against the men was that they were altering Roman customs. After the men were beaten, they were cast into prison; and the jailer was commanded "to keep them safely." As a result, he not only put them in the inner prison; he put their feet in stocks (16:22–24).

11. Winning of a Philippian Jailer

The deep, spiritual nature of Paul and Silas is revealed in the fact that, even though bruised and bleeding from the rods of the lictors, and even though uncomfortably confined in Roman stocks, they "were praying and singing hymns unto God" at midnight. Probably amazed at the unusual happenings around them, the other prisoners were listening. Then the miraculous occurred! "Suddenly there was a great earthquake, so that the foundations of the prison house were shaken: and immediately all the doors were opened: and every one's bands were loosed" (v. 26). When the jailer was aroused and saw the opened doors, he supposed that the prisoners had escaped and drew his sword with the intent of killing himself.

Paul cried out, "Do thyself no harm: for we are all here." Calling for lights, the jailer fell trembling before Paul and Silas. Then he brought them out and asked a very poignant question: "Sirs, what must I do to be saved?" Starting with the statement, "Believe on the Lord Jesus, and thou shalt be saved, thou and thy house," they preached unto him, and to those of his house, the gospel. That very hour the jailer bathed their wounds, after which "he and all his" were immediately baptized. "And he brought them up into his house, and set food before them, and rejoiced greatly, with all his house, having believed in God" (16:34).

12. Release of Paul and Silas

For some reason Luke did not record, when the morning arrived, the magistrates ordered that Paul and Silas be released. They sent the lictors with the order to the jailer, who in turn encouraged the two prisoners to go. The jailer was seemingly happy over being able to convey this news to the two prisoners and was probably surprised over Paul's answer. "They have beaten us publicly, uncondemned, men that are Romans, and have cast us into prison; and do they now cast us out privily? nay verily; but let them come themselves and bring us out" (v. 37).

We wonder why Paul did not appeal to his Roman citizenship the day before, just prior to being beaten with the rods. Would the riotlike situation of that hour have made his appeal useless? Later on he will claim his right at Jerusalem, thus preventing a flogging with the cruel scourge. Roman citizens were exempt by Roman laws (passed between 509 and 195 B.C.) from any form of degrading punishment—beating with rods, scourging, crucifixion.

When the magistrates were informed of Paul's answer and realized what they had done, they were afraid. They responded personally and came to the prison to escort the men to their freedom. Whatever Paul's reason for

Philippi, ruins of forum

his strange action, it probably protected the new Christian converts in the city from any possible persecution inflicted because of their association with men who had broken the law. Leaving the prison after their victory over the magistrates, Paul and Silas went to the home of Lydia, comforted the brethren, and then departed (16:35–40). Evidently Luke stayed in Philippi for some time. His "we" passage ended when Paul and Silas were put in prison (vv. 16,19), and another "we" passage does not start till 20:5. We know that the church at Philippi grew into a splendid one, for it was one of the greatest established by Paul. It was his "joy in Christ." He thanked God upon every remembrance of the members there (Phil. 1:3).

13. In Thessalonica

Leaving Philippi, Paul, Silas, and Timothy traveled by the Egnatian Way west to Amphipolis, the capital of the first district of Macedonia, to Apollonia, and then on to Thessalonica, the capital of the second district of Macedonia. It was the most important city in the province and was later (146 B.C.) made the provincial capital. Even today, known as Salonika, it is a significant city.

There was a synagogue in Thessalonica; and here Paul preached for three sabbaths using the Old Testament Scriptures to verify Jesus as the Messiah of the Hebrew Scriptures. Some Jews and many devout Greeks believed, including some of the "chief women." It seems that the Jews, along with God-fearing Gentiles attached to the synagogue, formed a group around the evangelists in the synagogue. However, there were some Jews who were envious. These people rounded up rabble of the city and created a mob, setting the city in an uproar. They entered the house of one called Jason, seeking the evangelists. Not finding them, they dragged Jason and other Christians before the rulers of the city, charging, "These that have turned the world upside down are come hither also; whom Jason hath received: and these all act contrary to the decrees of Caesar, saying that there is another king, one Jesus" (vv. 6–7).

The phrase "have turned the world upside down" is an indication of the tremendous effect that Christianity was having throughout the Roman empire. The charge against the men was treason against Rome, and Jesus was depicted as the rival of Caesar. Thessalonica was made a free city in 42 B.C., and it is possible that the citizens wanted to avoid any appearance of sedition against Rome so that their status would not be revoked. Claudius not long before this time (A.D. 49) had expelled all the Jews from Rome. Luke said the rulers of the city were troubled when they heard the charge against the men, an accusation that was purely political and not religious.

They took "security" from Jason, a sort of peace bond, and let him go. However, Paul was evidently afraid that if he continued his work in the city, he might endanger Jason and others; so the brethren "sent away Paul and Silas by night unto Beroea," a city about sixty miles to the west of Thessalonica (17:1–10).

14. In Beroea

This city, just off the Egnatian Way, was located in a farming district. Again Paul and Silas went first to the synagogue. Timothy seems to have stayed in Thessalonica, for his name is not mentioned as being sent away from Thessalonica (v. 10). When the missionaries opened their ministry in Beroea, the people received the truth gladly. Their interest in the Old Testament Scriptures gave verification to Paul's gospel message as preached to them. Their spiritual hunger offered a fertile field for the sowing of the word. As a result many believed in Jesus, some of whom were influential Greek women.

However, troublemaking Jews from Thessalonica, on hearing that Paul was proclaiming the truth in Beroea, came there to stir up turmoil among the multitudes. As a result the brethren rushed Paul away. Luke said that Silas and Timothy remained in Beroea, so at some time or other Timothy must have come to Beroea from Thessalonica. Paul's friends conducted him safely to Athens, where Paul wrote a message back to Timothy and Silas to hurry to him. Thus Paul's ministry in Macedonia was brought to an end for the time being (17:10–15).

15. Athens, Center of Culture

For centuries prior to Paul's arrival in Athens, this great city had been the cultural and intellectual center of the Mediterranean world. It was the most important of the Greek city-states and the cradle of democracy. Students came from all areas of the world to study under its famous teachers. Painting, music, drama, sculpturing, philosophy, oratory, government, architecture—all played significant parts in the life of this famous citadel of learning. The golden era of Athens' history had passed, however, by the time of Paul's visit. Paul found a city of pagan idols and corrupt practices.

16. Paul Reasons in Athens

Luke said that Paul waited for Silas and Timothy to come to Athens (v. 16). While he waited, he spoke to the Jews and to the God-fearers in the synagogue. We do not know what success he had with the Jews in Athens, for Luke did not mention them again during Paul's stay at this time.

However, the Jews would agree with Paul in his disgust over the multiplicity of idols in that city of prestige. Why would the great city of cultural and philosophical learning stoop so low as to further the worship of things made by men's hands!

The great apostle did not confine himself to the synagogue, for he also taught every day in the marketplace or agora, as it was called. There was an agora in every Greek city, a wide place surrounded by porticoes and shops where brisk business and the selling of wares took place. Years before Paul's time Socrates had challenged the Athenians gathered around him in the agora. Even in the Christian era it was a place frequented by orators of every description. It was here that he encountered the Epicurean and Stoic philosophies (17:18).

The Epicurean school of thought (see chap. 2), conceived of the world as made of atoms that were eternal in nature. When one dies the atoms making up his body revert to impersonal atoms. Therefore, there is no such thing as immortality of the soul. At death the soul ceases to exist. The chief end of life is pleasure. However, this is not carnal pleasure but the pleasure of a tranquil life free from pain, passions, and other disturbing emotions. At the time of Paul, Epicureanism rivaled Stoicism. In modern times one who indulges in the ''eat-drink-and-be-merry'' manner of life is described as an Epicurean; this use of the term is wrong. A true Epicurean would forego this type of life in order to have a higher type of pleasure over a longer period of time.

The Stoic school of thought (see chap. 2) taught that man must live in harmony with nature. In nature there is a logos, which is reason or design. This is the way God pervades the universe. Therefore, the Stoics stressed reason and the rational aspect of life more than emotions. One of the key words in Stoicism is apathy—no feeling in regard to human need. One should strive for self-sufficiency, which would be tantamount to an egocentric life.

Paul received different reactions to his teaching in the agora. Some Athenians said, ''What would this babbler say?'' The term *babbler* literally means seedpicker, a slang term of Athens used to belittle Paul. It was used for one who, like a sparrow, lived on what he could pick up as scraps in the agora. When applied to Paul, it meant that his knowledge and wisdom consisted of odds and ends that he picked up at random. Other Athenians said, ''He seemeth to be a setter forth of strange gods,'' a remark made because he preached Jesus and the resurrection. The term strange gods really meant foreign deities. The Athenians were not familiar with the name Jesus and the term resurrection. In Greek, as used here by Paul, the term Jesus is a masculine word, and the term resurrection is a feminine one. Therefore, it has been suggested that they thought Paul was bringing them word of a new pair of gods, one masculine and the other feminine (17:18).

17. Sermon Before the Areopagus

As a result of his teaching Paul was brought before the Areopagus with the request, "May we know what this new teaching is, which is spoken by thee?" They wanted to know about his strange teachings. His sermon took place "in the midst of the Areopagus" (17:19–22). There was a Council of the Areopagus, which received its name from a place called the Areopagus west of the Acropolis and near the agora. A literal translation of Areopagus is Hill of Ares, or Ares Hill. Ares was the god of war in Greek mythology, who had the name Mars in Roman mythology. Therefore Ares Hill was the same as Mars Hill, or Areopagus. It is hard to determine whether Paul was brought *before* the Areopagus as a council or was brought *to* the Areopagus, or Mars Hill, for questioning. Luke could very well have meant that Paul was brought before the council to preach.

Paul's sermon in Athens is one of the most famous in the history of Christianity. The first thing he did was to compliment them on being very religious, a fact that was apparent due to the many objects of worship. He broached his subject by pointing out the many idols around him, calling attention to one altar with an inscription "To an Unknown God." This inscription Paul very artfully used as a springboard to preach Jesus, saying, "What therefore ye worship in ignorance, this I set forth unto you." He wished to introduce them to the God who was unknown to them.

As soon as he spoke of a resurrection of dead men, his sermon was forcefully concluded. The Greeks believed in an immortality of the soul but had never heard of the dead being raised. They considered the body to be inherently evil; their belief was that the soul is entombed in the body until its release at death. Therefore, some mocked, while others said they desired to hear more. There were a few believers, however, including one member of the council itself, whose name was Dionysius. Another believer was Damaris, a woman. Although Paul did not have striking success in Athens, a church was probably started due to his brief stay there.

18. Paul in Corinth

Corinth was more than fifty miles west of Athens, located on the Isthmus of Corinth connecting the mainland with the Peloponnesus, a peninsula constituting the southern part of Greece. It was a great commercial center,

Athens, ruins of the Parthenon

in contrast to Athens, the cultural center. It controlled the narrow isthmus and had access to the sea, for ships were hauled across the narrow isthmus between the Aegean and Adriatic Seas. Destroyed in 146 B.C., Corinth was rebuilt by Julius Caesar in 46 B.C. and was made the capital of the province of Achaia (Greece proper) in 27 B.C. It was not only the largest but also the most prosperous of the cities in Achaia. It was noted for immorality. "To Corinthinize" was tantamount to "to make immoral." The famous temple of Aphrodite (Venus in the Latin pantheon), goddess of love, was there; and in this temple were 1,000 sacred prostitutes or priestesses. In a sense, lust was a part of their pagan religion. How great was the need there for the gospel of the Lord Jesus!

19. Aquila and Priscilla

It is little wonder that Paul prolonged his stay in this center of both prosperity and vice to a year and a half, especially since he was in the company of a wonderful couple who held like interests. Aquila and Priscilla of Corinth were tentmakers, as was Paul; so Paul lived with them, and all three plied their trade (18:3). (The cloth that Paul used for his tent making was woven from goat hair from Cilicia, a tough fiber producing a strong cloth.) On the sabbath he preached in the synagogue.

20. News from Macedonia

At last Silas and Timothy arrived in Corinth from Macedonia, and Paul "was constrained by the word, testifying to the Jews that Jesus was the Christ" (18:5). This seems to imply that the two men brought Paul good news from the churches in Macedonia, thus encouraging him and giving him added power and zeal in proclaiming the gospel. The good news more than offset the discouragement that he had received at Athens. He preached "that Jesus was the Christ."

The Jews still looked for the Messiah, the Christ. Paul tried to show them that Jesus was their anticipated Christ. When Jewish opposition to his work grew, Paul renounced further work among the Jews, committed them to the dire result of rejecting Jesus, and announced his intention of turning to the Gentiles (18:6). Moving next door to the synagogue, to the house of one Titus Justus, a God-fearer, Paul seems to have continued his gospel ministry (v. 7). He would not be held back by unbelieving Jews; his ministry was destined to be greater than this. Even Crispus, the ruler of the synagogue, accepted Jesus, along with his household; and many Corinthians believed and were baptized (v. 8). The Jews were losing some of their most influential people to the Christian cause. Paul said in 1 Corinthians 1:14 that he baptized Crispus and Gaius; this must have been the same Crispus mentioned in Acts 18:8.

God encouraged Paul at this point by a vision in the night, saying, "Be not afraid, but speak and hold not thy peace: for I am with thee, and no man shall set on thee to harm thee: for I have much people in this place" (v. 9). This vision must have been just as vivid a message from God as Paul's vision in Troas of the man from Macedonia. God told him not to fear but to keep on in his ministry, for many people there needed to hear him. This may be part of the reason Paul stayed for a year and a half in cosmopolitan Corinth "teaching the word of God" among the people (18:9–11). The letters to the Christians at Corinth indicate that Paul established a strong church there, even though it was plagued with many evils and various heresies. It became the center for the work in the province of Achaia. Evidently persecution was not one of its problems.

21. The Thessalonian Epistles

The two letters to the church at Thessalonica were written while Paul was at Corinth, penned in response to the news that Silas and Timothy brought him from Macedonia. Paul endeavored to correct certain erroneous thoughts that were prevalent in the church. In the second letter he continued with many of the same subjects he had discussed in the first letter. The Thessalonians were concerned over the return of the Lord, especially since some of the members had died and were buried. Paul taught them concerning the second coming of Jesus, as well as giving them many suggestions and admonitions for holy living.

22. Paul and Gallio, the Proconsul

Gallio became proconsul about 51. About this time the Jews were able to bring Paul before him in judgment, charging that Paul persuaded "men to worship God contrary to the law." Their very indictment of Paul reveals the apostle's preaching success. Their charge was religious, not political, and was similar to the charge made against Paul at Philippi (16:21). However, at Philippi the charge was made by Gentiles; at Corinth it was made by Jews (18:12–13).

Gallio spoke before Paul could open his mouth to defend himself. He maintained that if the charge had been one of an immoral nature or had been a villainous crime, he would have been interested in the case. Since it was a matter of Jewish law, he had no interest whatsoever. He wanted nothing to do with a Jewish dispute over religion. Sosthenes, the ruler of the synagogue, bore the brunt of the frustration of the crowd; he was beaten before the judgment-seat. Presumably he was the new ruler of the synagogue, replacing Crispus, who had become a Christian. One wonders if this is the Sosthenes mentioned in 1 Corinthians 1:1 and termed "our brother."

23. Paul's Departure from Corinth

Paul sailed from Corinth, intending to go to Syria, and taking with him Priscilla and Aquila. It is very likely that Timothy accompanied Paul and his two tent-making friends to Ephesus. When they had crossed the Aegean Sea and had come to Ephesus, the capital of the province of Asia, Paul "entered into the synagogue, and reasoned with the Jews." Luke did not reveal the success of this "reasoning." When the Ephesians requested Paul to prolong his stay, he refused. However, he did promise to return, if it were God's will. Leaving Priscilla and Aquila in Ephesus, he sailed from there and landed at Caesarea on the Palestinian coast. Then "he went up and saluted the church, and went down to Antioch." After some time there he left and went through Galatia and Phrygia, "establishing all the disciples" (18:18–23).

24. Beginning the Third Journey

When Paul left Antioch, he started on what has traditionally been called the third missionary journey (Acts 18:22 to 21:15). It has been suggested by some scholars that, instead of three "missionary journeys," there were two "missionary campaigns," with the first journey constituting the first campaign and the second and third journeys constituting the second campaign. The first campaign was among the cities of Asia Minor, and the second campaign among the cities in and around the territory of the Aegean Sea. Thus Paul's trip to Jerusalem and to Antioch (18:22–23) would be merely a side trip during his Ephesian ministry and more or less during the second campaign.

25. Apollos, Eloquent Preacher

Leaving Antioch, Paul went through Galatia, revisiting the churches in that area (18:23), and then proceeded on to Ephesus, where he had stopped briefly some time before. All this gives the impression that his Ephesian work was interrupted and was now being resumed. There he had left Priscilla and Aquila, his two tent-making fellow workers. During his absence a very eloquent Jewish preacher named Apollos from Alexandria had come to Ephesus. Luke said "he was mighty in the scriptures." He also was fervent in spirit and "spake and taught accurately the things concerning Jesus." But he had one deficiency: he knew "only the baptism of John." Therefore, it seems that he knew of the life and the teachings of Jesus but did not know of Christian baptism. He did not understand that the death and resurrection of Jesus were symbolized in Christian baptism. At any rate, Priscilla and Aquila proceeded to instruct him more accurately in the way of God.

Apollos is a good example of the fact that others besides Paul and his associates were bearing the news of Christ throughout the Mediterranean world. In time, Apollos desired to cross the Aegean Sea into Achaia, which would evidently mean Corinth. When he did so, the Ephesian church wrote a letter to the disciples in Corinth to receive him. Evidently the letter fulfilled its purpose, for Apollos did go to Corinth and was able to be of great assistance to the ones there "that had believed through grace." He tried to prove to the Jews through their Scriptures that Jesus was their long-awaited Messiah (18:24–28).

Apollos may have created some problems at Corinth, judging from what Paul said in 1 Corinthians; if so, this may have been due either to his enthusiasm or to his immaturity. On the whole, however, his ministry there seems to have been very effective. Paul said in 1 Corinthians, "I planted, Apollos watered" (3:6); so Paul must have felt that Apollos continued the work that he himself had started. Paul almost gave Apollos the status of an apostle in 1 Corinthians 4:9. He even requested that Apollos make a second trip to Corinth (1 Cor. 16:12).

26. Paul and the Twelve Disciples

Apollos made his trip to Corinth before Paul came from Galatia to Ephesus, so Apollos was not there when Paul arrived. At Ephesus Paul began a very fruitful ministry. The first thing he discovered was a group of disciples, twelve in number, with an incomplete knowledge of the Christian faith (19:2–4). When he asked them if they had received the Holy Spirit when they believed, they replied in a manner showing no knowledge of the Holy Spirit. When he asked them into what they were baptized, they answered, "Into John's baptism." Paul explained to them the significance of John's baptism and the relation of John to the ministry of Jesus. They were immediately "baptized into the name of the Lord Jesus." When Paul laid his hands upon them, the Holy Spirit descended upon them. They spoke in tongues and prophesied (19:1–7). It was virtually an Ephesian Pentecost, much like the earlier ones at Jerusalem, at a city in Samaria, and at the house of Cornelius in Caesarea. This is according to the unfolding plan of Luke in Acts, the spread of an unhindered gospel, a gospel free of legalistic exactions.

27. Paul's Ministry in Ephesus

Ephesus, the leading city in all of Asia Minor, was one of the great ports of the Mediterranean. This great city, capital of the province of Asia, was located on the main road from Rome to the eastern countries. It was a free city, having its own senate and assembly. Because great privileges had been granted them, there were many Jews living in Ephesus. The famous temple of Artemis, one of the seven wonders of the ancient world, was located in this great coastal metropolis. Knowing of the significance of the city, Paul had desired to teach and preach there at a previous time; but he was "forbidden of the Holy Spirit to speak the word in Asia" (16:6).

When Paul arrived in Ephesus he first taught in the synagogue, "reasoning and persuading as to the things concerning the kingdom of God." This had been his custom in place after place, to go the the Jews first. He spoke boldly in the synagogue for three months. Some of the Jews accepted what Paul preached, and some rebelled against him, "speaking evil of the Way before the multitude." The preaching of the kingdom may have had something to do with the opposition that built up against him. At any rate, Paul voluntarily left the synagogue and began "reasoning daily in the school of Tyrannus." (The Greek says *school*; but the hall was probably used by lecturers and orators.) Paul was not evicted from the synagogue, as he evidently had been in other cities; he left of his own free will. His new ministry, which had great success, was to be to both Jews and Gentiles. It lasted for two years, and "all they that dwelt in Asia heard the word of the Lord, both Jews and Greeks" (19:8–10). Again Luke was emphasizing the spread of the word and the growth of the churches.

Luke did not go into detail about how the gospel was extended from Ephesus into the province. Many visitors came to the capital, Ephesus, thus hearing the word and returning home with it. Paul's fellow workers may have gone to other localities and preached, as well as Paul himself. The area was well populated, and the towns were many. A few decades later the book of Revelation was written, a book in which the seven churches of Asia, one of which was Ephesus, are set forth in dramatic view (Rev. 2:1 to 3:22). Early Christian writers have pictured Ephesus as a strong Christian center. Many believe that the Gospel of John was written in this metropolis.

28. The Power of the Gospel

Paul said that he "fought with beasts at Ephesus" (1 Cor. 15:32). Whatever Paul meant by such a remark, Luke did not mention it in Acts. He did tell of the "special miracles" Paul was able to perform, extraordinary acts of healing and of exorcism. God used "the hands of Paul" to do so. "Handkerchiefs and aprons" that had touched Paul's body were carried away to the sick, who were healed (19:11-12).

Exorcism of demons was practiced throughout the heathen world, many times by pronouncing a name sacred in heathen circles. When some wandering Jewish exorcists witnessed Paul's miracles of this nature, they endeavored to do the same by using the name of Jesus. They said, "I adjure you by Jesus whom Paul preacheth." They were borrowing the name of the Lord Jesus and using it in an unscrupulous manner. The specific example of this given by Luke concerns the effort of the "seven sons of one Sceva, a chief priest." The answer of the evil spirit to the seven has a ring of humor: "Jesus I know, and Paul I know; but who are ye?" With that, the man bearing the evil spirit leaped upon the men, overpowering them and sending them forth from the house "naked and wounded."

We see in such a story as this that spiritual power is void when disconnected from its source, the Holy Spirit. Speaking the name of Jesus without knowing Jesus is ineffective. The effect of the complete overthrow of the sons of Sceva upon both Jews and Greeks in Ephesus was tremendous; "fear fell upon them all, and the name of the Lord Jesus was magnified." Many who believed confessed and declared their sins (19:13-18).

The power of the gospel is not only seen in such miraculous healings and in exorcisms; it is also seen in the reformation of lives of the Ephesians who came to know Jesus as Lord. "And not a few of them that practised magical arts brought their books together and burned them in the sight of all; and they counted the price of them, and found it fifty thousand pieces of silver" (vv. 19-20). The presence of the indwelling Christ brought a radical change in regard to superstitious practices. The huge bonfire probably created quite a stir (19:18-19). Paul declared, "So mightily grew the word of the Lord and prevailed" (v. 20).

29. Riot in Ephesus

Luke said that at this time Paul intended to go to Macedonia and Achaia, then to Jerusalem, and then to Rome itself (19:21). The apostle stated twice in his epistle to the Christians at Rome his longing to visit them (Rom. 1:11; 15:23). According to the remainder of Acts, this is exactly what occurred; but it happened in a manner that he did not expect. He sent Timothy and Erastus into Macedonia and then tarried in Ephesus for a while, where trouble came to him (19:21-22).

The magnificent temple of Artemis has already been mentioned. One of the seven wonders of the ancient world, it was four times the size of the Parthenon in Athens. It burned during the fourth century B.C. but was soon built back. There was a silversmith guild in Ephesus that made small replicas of both Artemis and her temple. These replicas, purchased by the worshipers, were probably presented in the temple as part of the act of worship. They were made of gold, silver, terra-cotta, and stone—there was one to suit the pocketbook of any worshiper. The Artemis of Greek mythology was identical to Diana in Roman mythology. She was supposed to have been the daughter of Zeus. A virgin huntress, she became the goddess of the chase and of the moon. In her original character she was a fertility goddess and patroness of women in childbirth. This Artemis, however, was the Ephesian deity, the mother-goddess of Asia Minor. In early times she went under other names. The Ephesian Artemis is not to be confused with the virgin goddess of the chase and of the moon. The Ephesians believed that the image of their Artemis had fallen from the sky (19:35).

Since the people were turning from Artemis to Christ in large numbers, the lucrative trade of the guild of silversmiths was declining. Demetrius, one of the artisans, called his fellow workers together and made a very dramatic speech. He accused Paul of having turned away many people from the worship of Artemis and of speaking of the images as "no gods, that are made with hands." He reminded his audience that not only would their business come into disrepute but that the temple of Artemis, as well as Artemis herself, would decrease in the estimation of the people. Artemis would "be deposed from her magnificence." A near-riot ensued, and the people shouted, "Great is Diana of the Ephesians." (The King James and the American Standard Versions use *Diana* throughout this whole passage, probably an influence of the Latin Vulgate. *The Living Bible* uses Diana also. Today's English Version uses Artemis, which is the best—and literal—translation of the Greek term.)

In the confusion that ensued, the people seized Gaius and Aristarchus, the travel companions of Paul, and rushed with them into the theater. (This theater, which seated twenty-four thousand people, has been excavated in modern times.) Paul felt compelled to enter also, probably with the intention of helping his two friends; but the disciples constrained him from doing so. Some of the foremost men of the city also constrained Paul from entering the theater. These were officers who had charge of Roman festivals and ceremonies connected with emperor worship; their protection of Paul showed that Rome at this time felt no antipathy toward the Christian movement. Christianity was not yet an "illicit religion."

The confusion within the theater mounted. When Alexander, who had been set forth from the multitude, started to make his defense, the crowd noticed he was a Jew. For two hours they cried, "Great is Diana of the Ephesians." The town clerk, the highest non-Roman official in the city, was able to quiet the mob by reminding them that decisions such as this should be settled in the courts and that there was danger of their being accused of starting a riot. This would endanger the favorable status Ephesus enjoyed in the eyes of Rome. The speech must have been successful, for we are told "he dismissed the assembly" (19:23–41). At Philippi Paul had healed a demented girl and in doing so had touched the pocketbooks of her masters. At Ephesus he won so many people to Christ that the idol industry declined rapidly, and again the pocketbooks of those with vested interest were touched. In Philippi he was asked to leave the city; in Ephesus he himself deemed it best to depart. Entrenched wealth seemed to have won the battle.

30. The Corinthian Epistles

Ephesus and Corinth were on opposite sides of the Aegean Sea, about three days apart by sea journey. There would be many travelers going back and forth, since both cities were on the trade route between east and west. Paul had been God's agent in founding a great church in Corinth, so he had various friends there. During his stay in Ephesus many months later, he would have had several opportunities to learn of the welfare of the church in Achaia. In Acts Luke did not tell us of all the connections that Paul had with the Corinthian church while he was in Ephesus. We must turn to Paul's Corinthian correspondence to add to our knowledge in this respect.

Apollos preached in Ephesus, went to Corinth and ministered, and then returned to Ephesus (1 Cor. 16:12). Paul sent Timothy to Corinth (1 Cor. 4:17). Titus went to Corinth of his own accord (2 Cor. 8:16–17). The household of Chloe brought Paul word of divisions in the Corinthian church (1 Cor. 1:11). Three Corinthian members—Stephanas, Fortunatus, and Achaicus—brought Paul news from their church (1 Cor. 16:17–18). The Corinthian church wrote Paul a letter (1 Cor. 7:1). Paul spoke of a report that he had received concerning the church (1 Cor. 5:1). In 2 Corinthians 13:1–2 he mentioned a proposed third time to come to them. When did the *second* visit take place? Luke said nothing about it in Acts, yet it must have occurred. The proposed third visit would be that recorded in Acts 20:2–3, a three-month visit. This second visit would have given Paul news of the Corinthian church.

Through these sources and possibly through others, Paul received word from Achaia that necessitated his writing to them. We have two Corinthian letters in our Bible. In 1 Corinthians 5:9 Paul said, "I wrote unto you in my epistle." So there must have been a letter prior to what we now call 1 Corinthians, one that seemingly is lost. However, it may be included, in part at least, in the two letters in our Bible of today. So from Ephesus Paul wrote the lost letter; then he wrote what we now have as 1 Corinthians. These were probably written before the riot instigated by Demetrius.

Some scholars think that Paul sent a sharp letter to Corinth by Titus, who was very effective in straightening out the conditions there. This letter too is lost, or else incorporated, whole or in part, in our two existing letters. Then when Titus brought good news to Paul from Corinth after Paul had gone on to Macedonia, Paul wrote a fourth letter to Corinth. This letter is virtually our present 2 Corinthians. Much of this is theory; but it looks as though there were at least three letters, and possibly four, written by the apostle to the church at Corinth. Two or three of these were from Ephesus and one from somewhere in Macedonia.

31. On to Macedonia

After the riot at Ephesus had died down, Paul met with the disciples and then departed for Macedonia. Some of Paul's activities that Luke did not relate are found in the Corinthian correspondence. "Now when I came to Troas for the gospel of Christ, and when a door was opened unto me in the Lord, I had no relief for my spirit, because I found not Titus my brother: but taking my leave of them, I went forth into Macedonia" (2 Cor. 2:12–13). Paul was so upset over the fact that Titus was not at Troas with word from the Corinthian church that he could not take advantage of the evangelistic opportunity that presented itself to him. So he went on to Macedonia, probably to Philippi, to the church that was his "joy in Christ." Somewhere in Macedonia, probably in Philippi, Titus met him and brought news from the Corinthian church that caused him great rejoicing (2 Cor. 7:5–7). Then it seems that Paul sent another letter by Titus back to Corinth, which would consist mainly of what we now have in our Bible as 2 Corinthians.

32. The Illyricum Visit

Presumably Paul visited several of the churches in Macedonia. Luke's information on this score is brief, as well as Paul's in his epistles. In the book of Romans, however, Paul stated that he preached the gospel of Christ "from Jerusalem, and round about even unto Illyricum" (15:19). Illyricum was a Roman province, long and narrow, facing the Adriatic Sea and northwest of Macedonia. It paralleled Italy, just across the Adriatic. Part of Illyricum is today the coastal region of Yugoslavia. The problem for scholars is where, in Paul's travels, to place the Illyricum visit that he merely mentioned in Romans. Most scholars believe that it occurred between his Macedonian visit and his Grecian visit, both of which were depicted by Luke in two verses, Acts 20:1–2. Even then, we are not told what success—or disappointment—occurred on the visit. At any rate, Paul proceeded on south to Greece, probably to Corinth (20:2).

33. The Galatian Letter

Nothing has been debated more among New Testament scholars than the place and date of Paul's letter to the Galatians. This blazing and impassioned letter, Paul's attack on the Judaizers, has as its theme salvation by grace through faith. But where and when was it written? One theory is that it was penned at Antioch just prior to the great Jerusalem controversy between Paul's first and second journeys. If this is so, then what occurs in Galatians 2 has to be connected with Paul's "famine visit" to Jerusalem as depicted in Acts 1:29–30 and 12:25. Another theory is that it was composed at Antioch immediately after the Jerusalem controversy, which would allow Galatians 2 to be a record of the same event in Acts 15, the Jerusalem controversy. Both of these views would make Galatians the earliest of Paul's canonical epistles.

Another view is that Galatians was written during Paul's year-and-a-half stay in Corinth on his second journey. Still another view is that he wrote it at Antioch during his very brief visit between the second and third journeys. One theory is that it was written at Ephesus during his more than two-year stay on his third journey. Another opinion is that Paul penned it at Corinth during his three-month visit on the third journey. All of these varied and bewildering viewpoints are due to the lack of sufficient evidence in Acts and in the epistle itself that would warrant a definite answer. The comforting thought is that the contents of this mighty epistle are the relevant matter, after all.

34. The Roman Letter

It is generally agreed among scholars that Paul wrote his letter to the Romans during his last stay in Corinth. Therefore, the date of writing would be sometime between 56 and 58. This final stay lasted for three months (Acts 20:3). Paul seemed to have been reconciled with the Corinthian church. Probably most of their difficulties had been resolved. He had been collecting funds from among the churches in Galatia, Macedonia, and Greece to take to the poor Christians in Jerusalem (Rom. 15:25–27). He told the Romans that when he had completed his trip to Jerusalem to take the gift, he wanted to come to them for a visit. Then he would go on to the west to Spain. Though hindered many times from coming to them, he had wanted to do so for many years (Rom. 15:4–29).

The apostle was turning his eyes to the western section of the empire, with Rome as the center of his work. The fact that stands out clearly is that the Roman church was a strong one when Paul wrote to them. Therefore, someone else had been doing some missionary work besides Paul, a work that is not discussed by Luke in Acts. When we remember that Luke got most of his material from Paul, we surmise the reason for this silence.

Whereas most of Paul's writings were called forth due to some pressing need wanting an immediate solution, this letter was not. It was a systematic treatise of his view of the gospel, both for Jews and for Greeks. This, the most formal of all his letters, is considered by most people as Paul's greatest. It was taken to Rome by Phoebe, a member of the church of Cenchreae, an eastern port of Corinth (Rom. 16:1–2).

35. Paul Leaves Corinth

Paul seemed eager to return home to Jerusalem. Winter was over, and navigation was possible. He had been gone about four years since his last brief visit there; besides, he needed to get the offering safely to the Jerusalem church. Luke did not mention the offering in Acts; we are informed of it in Paul's epistles (Rom. 15:26; 1 Cor. 16:1–4; 2 Cor. 9:1–8). The offering is a good example of the concern of the Aegean churches for the "mother church" in Jerusalem.

Just as Paul was about to sail for Syria, a plot against his life on the part of the Jews was discovered. Luke did not present the motive for the planned murder, but we can imagine that the non-Christian Jews in Corinth disliked him, as they did in many other cities. His noted success at furthering the Christian movement made considerable inroads upon organized Judaism. Therefore Paul's departing group divided, some going the proposed way and Paul going by way of Macedonia. Luke mentioned the names of seven men who went the planned way, by ship. These men were from various churches where Paul had preached, probably going along as Paul's emissaries in carrying the offering to the Jerusalem church. They were Sopater, Aristarchus, Secundus, Gaius, Timothy, Tychicus, and Trophimus. They departed before Paul and waited for him and Luke at Troas. Paul and Luke, after observing the Passover in Philippi, sailed to Troas, arriving in five days (20:3–6). Luke started another "we" section in Acts 20:5; so it appears he joined Paul at Philippi. From this point on to the arrival in Jerusalem, Luke gave more details of the travel.

36. Paul in Troas

Paul stayed in Troas seven days. On the first day of the week (our Sunday), there was a large gathering of the church, along with the members of Paul's visiting group. Here Luke presented a glimpse into a first-century worship service. We also see a custom that grew in the early church, that of meeting on the first day of the week, the day of Christ's resurrection. This developed into our first-day, or Sunday, services. Paul himself added weight to the first-day-of-the-week services when he mentioned the custom in 1 Corinthians 16:2. The very early Christians were highly tied to the synagogue services; therefore, the Christian services were held on the Jewish sabbath. After the separation from the synagogue, the Gentile Christians had no reason for worshiping on the Jewish sabbath. So they turned to the first day of the week, which they called the Lord's day (Rev. 1:10).

Luke said that they "were gathered together to break bread." It is not known whether this refers to the observance of the Lord's Supper or to the *agape* feast—the love feast. It could have been a combination, one in which a common meal was shared in Christian love and fellowship (*agape*), which was in turn followed by the Lord's Supper (20:7).

Since Paul planned to leave Troas the next day, he prolonged his sermon till midnight. A young man named Eutychus, who was very sleepy, sat in a third-story window. As Paul continued to preach, Eutychus fell from the window "and was taken up dead." Then Paul went down, fell on him and embraced him, and said, "Make ye no ado; for his life is in him." One sentence says he was dead; the next implies he was not dead. It is hard to determine whether there was a restoration of life or not. At least the young man was completely recovered from the fall when Paul left the next day. After the interruptive incident of the fall, they broke bread, ate, and talked till the morning light. Then Paul departed (20:7–12).

37. Paul in Miletus

When they left Troas, Paul walked south to a place on the Aegean Sea named Assos; the others went by ship and took him aboard at Assos. Then they continued along the coast, stopping at various places on the way. Luke delighted in naming the stopping points. When they came to Ephesus they sailed on by, stopping at Miletus, south of Ephesus. Paul purposely went past Ephesus, for he did not want to stay there for an extended time. He was trying to get to Jerusalem to partake in the observance of the Feast of Pentecost. Paul loved his nation and its people. He had respect for the Jewish customs and wanted to share in Pentecost (20:13–16).

At Miletus (thirty miles from Ephesus) he called for the elders of the Ephesian church to meet him there, and they came. Paul then addressed them in a very moving manner, revealing the deep yearnings of his heart. His address at Miletus is different from all the other addresses in Acts, being more in both style and content what Paul expressed in his epistles. He talked of his labors among them and of the gospel he preached to them. He told them of his intent to go to Jerusalem and that the Holy Spirit had informed him of the bonds and afflictions awaiting him. He told them that they would see his face no more. He also warned them of those who would endeavor to bring in heresies. Then he reminded them that he had worked while among them so that he could support himself (20:17–35).

In one statement he called the elders *bishops,* a word meaning overseers (v. 28). Evidently in Paul's day the terms *elders* and *bishops* were synonymous. Later development in church organization caused the terms to designate two different capacities in the Christian ministry.

After the address to the elders, he knelt with them and prayed with them. Then they wept and fell on Paul's neck. What disturbed them most was the thought of never seeing him again. Then they brought him to the ship (20:36–38).

Paul quoted a statement of Jesus that we cannot find in any of the four canonical Gospels: "It is more blessed to give than to receive" (v. 35). He must have had some source for the statement, for it is commensurate with everything else our Lord taught.

38. On to Jerusalem

Paul and his party, including Luke, sailed from Miletus and went to Cos, then Rhodes, then Patara. Here they boarded another ship, sailed around Cyprus, and finally landed at Tyre in Phoenicia, where the ship unloaded its cargo. Paul stayed seven days with the Christians at Tyre. They informed Paul that the Spirit warned against his setting foot in Jerusalem, but Paul did not heed them. They went with him down to the beach, where they knelt and had prayer; then Paul and his group boarded ship and sailed away to the south. They stopped at Ptolemais and "saluted the brethren," staying one day. Then they sailed further south to Caesarea, where they stayed in the house of Philip the evangelist. Many years previously this same Philip, one of the seven of Acts 6:1–6, had brought the gospel to Samaria (8:5) and to Caesarea (8:40). Paul's fellowship with Philip must have been delightful. Luke mentioned that Philip had seven daughters who prophesied (21:1–9).

While Paul tarried at Caesarea a prophet named Agabus came down from Judea and prophesied in a vivid, pictorial manner, much as Ezekiel and Jeremiah would have done. He took Paul's sash, bound his own hands and feet with it, and said, "Thus saith the Holy Spirit, So shall the Jews at Jerusalem bind the man that owneth this girdle, and shall deliver him into the hands of the Gentiles" (v. 11). This may very well be the same Agabus who is mentioned in Acts 11:28. With this graphic demonstration of foreboding peril awaiting the famous missionary, both Paul's group of travelers and the Christians at Caesarea begged him not to go to the Holy City. He chided them for their weeping and for the grief it was causing him, adding, "I am ready not to be bound only, but also to die at Jerusalem for the name of the Lord Jesus." When they saw that all their pleading was to no avail, they said, "The will of the Lord be done" (21:10–14).

Paul was warned repeatedly not to go to Jerusalem, in every case by means of the agency of the Holy Spirit. He himself in his Miletus address said that the Holy Spirit testified unto him "in every city, saying that bonds and afflictions" were waiting for him (20:23). Then the Christians at Tyre warned Paul through the Spirit not to enter Jerusalem (21:4). Agabus at Caesarea very graphically relayed to Paul a message from the Spirit that he would be bound if he entered Jerusalem (21:11). In view of these messages from the Holy Spirit, it might be debated whether Paul did right in not heeding them. They were evidently messages from God conveyed by the Spirit, the third person of the Trinity. How could Paul disobey and be right? How could "the will of the Lord be done" (21:14) if Paul disobeyed the will of God revealed by the Spirit? Later, in his imprisoned state, he interpreted his bonds as furthering the gospel; so he says in one of his prison epistles (Phil. 1:12–13). He did write four of his greatest epistles while in prison. But, we might ask, could not these have been written just as well out of prison as within? Could Paul have done more out of prison than confined with chains and locked behind doors? Would he not have been free to preach in many needed areas, in much of the western area of the empire? Speculation about "what might have been" if another course of action had been pursued is futile. We will never know.

In a few days Paul, Luke (the "we" section still continues), and the others moved on to Jerusalem. Some of the disciples from Caesarea accompanied them. One Mnason of Cyprus also came, since the party was to stay in his home (21:15–16).

22.

The Later Years of Paul

Beginning with Acts 21:17 Luke told of the later years of the great apostle. Yet in a sense this is not entirely correct, for when the book of Acts ends with 28:31, Paul was still alive. How many more years did he have? There is convincing evidence from Paul's epistles that he had several more years. We shall sift the evidence for significant clues.

1. Report to the Jerusalem Church

Paul and his company experienced a joyous reception by the brethren in Jerusalem. On the very next day, the apostle met with James and the elders of the church of that city and related to them "one by one the things which God had wrought among the Gentiles through his ministry." Such a glowing report made those hearing it glorify God (21:17–20).

Yet all was not as it should be; there was tension in the air, as Paul soon learned. This tension arose due to the influx of many Gentiles into the fold of the church without their adherence to the laws and customs of Moses; and Paul was the chief agent for this large ingathering of non-Jews to the side of Christ. Alongside the large Gentile element, there were thousands of Jews in Jerusalem who believed in Christ and who were zealous in continuing to observe the laws and customs of Moses. These Jewish Christians in Jerusalem had heard that Paul was teaching the Jews out in the empire "to forsake Moses, telling them not to circumcise their children, neither to walk after the customs." The opinion was that as soon as these zealous-for-the-law Jewish Christians heard that Paul was again in Jerusalem, there would be trouble.

James seemed to fear the Christian Jews in Jerusalem, not the non-Christian Jews. Therefore, Paul's friends in the Holy City suggested to him a course of action to allay the slanderous report that was circulating concerning his intentions. They suggested that he align himself with four Jerusalem men who had made a vow, that he and the four men purify themselves according to the Jewish requirement, that the men shave their heads in completion of the vow, and that Paul pay the charges for all four of them (21:23–24). This would prove the error of the accusation brought against the apostle and that he still had great respect for the Mosaic law.

He was willing to comply with any Jewish regulation that was not posed as a requirement for salvation; to him this would not be to compromise. He himself said in one of his epistles, "And to the Jews I became as a Jew, that I might gain Jews" (1 Cor. 9:20). He maintained that all the things he did were for "the gospel's sake," that he might be "a joint partaker thereof." Paul was willing to submit personally to any requirement of Judaism in the interest of peace, as long as no requirements were imposed upon the Gentile Christians.

Had Paul not had Timothy circumcised because of the Jews (16:3)? And had he not made a vow and had his head shorn (18:18)? The very next day he took the men, purified himself with them, accompanied them to the Temple to declare the fulfillment of the purification, and paid the entire charges (21:20–26). According to Numbers 6:14–15, this required for each man two lambs, one ram, unleavened bread cakes, unleavened wafers, a meal offering, and a drink offering. All of this for four men would be expensive!

2. Paul's Arrest

Paul was only too willing to do what James and the others suggested if his actions would keep the Christian Jews in a peaceful state of mind. It was the non-Christian Jews who soon caused him great consternation— Jews from the province of Asia, probably from Ephesus. These Jews saw Paul out in Jerusalem with Trophimus, an Ephesian Gentile. Then later, on observing him in the Temple, they jumped to the conclusion that he had taken Trophimus into the holy portion of the Temple, the Court of Israel, where it was unlawful for a Gentile to be. This, according to Mosaic law, would be to defile the Temple. Paul would not have taken a Gentile, even though a Christian, into the holy section of the Temple; he had too much respect for the Jewish concept that surrounded the building. But the Jews made the charge that he did. In fact, their charge was twofold: that he taught everywhere "against the people, and the law, and the place," and that he brought Greeks into the temple, thus defiling it (21:27–29).

Paul's accusers set off a riot, for they "stirred up all the multitude" to the point that "all the city was moved, and the people ran together." They dragged Paul out of the Temple, and immediately the door was shut. Was it shut to prevent Paul from seeking security there? The mob became so enraged with Paul that the people sought to kill him and probably would have done so had he not been rescued. The Tower of Antonia, a Roman fortress in which was stationed a cohort (one thousand men), was very near the Court of the Gentiles. Two flights of stairs went down from the fortress to the outer court or Court of the Gentiles. The Roman soldiers, rushing in to disperse the crowd, rescued Paul. The soldiers were led by a military tribune, along with more than one centurion. During the festival seasons the number of soldiers was increased, and more sentries were used in the Temple area. When the city was crammed with visitors, or during feast days, riots were more easily instigated.

The tribune or captain commanded that Paul be bound with two chains, for he thought Paul had captured a notorious Egyptian who had recently stirred up trouble, leading four thousand men into the desert. He inquired who Paul was and what he had done, but he was unable to understand due to the tumult and uproar of the mob. Therefore he commanded that Paul be brought into the tower (or barracks or castle, as in some translations). They were able to get as far as the stairs, with the mob crying out, "Away with him" (21:30–36).

On the stairs leading up to the Tower of Antonia, Paul asked the tribune if he could say something. He spoke in Greek, surprising the tribune. When the officer inquired if he were the notorious Egyptian bandit, Paul responded by declaring that he was a Jew of Tarsus. When he asked to speak to the people, the tribune gave permission. Paul then spoke to the crowd in their native tongue (21:37–40).

3. Paul's Defense

Paul's addressing the Jews in the vernacular language had a needed quieting effect. (Even though Acts 21:40 in the Greek says "Hebrew," we should understand it to mean Aramaic, the language of the street, the market, and the home in Palestine.) The noted apostle, relating to the people his conversion experience, addressed them as "brethren and fathers." He identified himself as a Jew and said that, even though born in Tarsus of Cilicia, he had come to Jerusalem for his training "at the feet of Gamaliel," the most prominent rabbi of that day. Therefore his education was according to strict Mosaic principles. His zeal was shown in his persecution of the Christians and in his working under the authority of the high priest and the elders. Then he began to tell of his Damascus road experience, of his message from God delivered by Ananias in Damascus, of his Jerusalem ministry, and of his commission by God to preach to the Gentiles (22:1–21).

Paul very diplomatically threw all the credit back to God. He told the

Jews that the "God of our Fathers" appointed him to know "his will and to
see the Righteous One" (meaning Jesus) and to hear a directive from Jesus
(v. 14). He was "to witness for him" (Jesus), and this witness was to be
"unto all men" (v. 15). He, Paul, was merely obeying a divine directive
from heaven, for everything was God's idea, not Paul's. Even the trance
that he experienced while praying in the Temple shortly after his conversion and commission by God (vv. 17–21) was God's word to him that his
message had been rejected by the Jewish people and that he was to depart
from Jerusalem. He was told to go to the Gentiles (v. 21).

"And they gave him audience unto this word" (22:22). The Jewish mob
listened patiently to Paul's Aramaic words until he mentioned Gentiles. This
word threw them into a frenzied emotion! They declared Paul not fit to live,
cast off their garments, and threw dirt into the air. The tribune commanded
Paul to be brought into the fortress, to be bound, and then to be scourged.
Paul informed the centurion that he was a Roman citizen, which immediately brought consternation when relayed to the Roman tribune.
It was unlawful to scourge an uncondemned Roman. Roman scourgings
were more cruel than Jewish ones, sometimes crippling or killing. The
tribune informed Paul he had purchased his citizenship; Paul said he was
"a Roman born." The tribune was afraid of the fact that he had bound Paul
for scourging. Before the Jews on the stairs Paul's central theme had been
that he was a Jew; before the tribune and the Roman soldiers about to be
scourged it was that he was a Roman. The next day the tribune brought
Paul before the Sanhedrin, "desiring to know the certainty wherefore he
was accused of the Jews" (22:22–30).

4. Before the Sanhedrin

Paul stood again before the august Jewish council, the one with whom he
had at one time allied himself closely, but from whom now he expected no
mercy or understanding. He knew he would not receive a fair hearing from
so biased a group. After Paul made one sentence, addressing them as
"brethren" and declaring his clear conscience in God's sight, Ananias the
high priest ordered that he be struck in the mouth. (This man was cruel and
self-centered. He was finally deposed from authority in 58 or 59 and
assassinated in 66.) Paul called Ananias a "whited wall" and responded in
a flaming reply to the command that he be struck. When he was informed
of the identity of the high priest, Paul said, "I knew not, brethren, that he
was high priest." Some have said this remark shows poor eyesight. Others
have been of the opinion Paul really did not know who had spoken. Others
have maintained Paul was using sarcasm (23:1–5).

When Paul saw that there were both Sadducees and Pharisees on the council, he cried out, "Brethren, I am a Pharisee, a son of Pharisees: touching the hope and resurrection of the dead I am called in question" (v. 6). The Sadducees did not believe in the resurrection; the Pharisees did. Knowing of this diversity in belief, Paul attempted to drive a wedge in the doctrinal rift and cause confusion and bickering. He attempted to pit Sadducee against Pharisee. Maybe their prejudice for each other could make them forget, momentarily at least, their feelings about him.

It was a clever strategy; "there arose a great clamor," and the assembly was thrown into dissension. Some of the scribes of the Pharisees avowed they found no evil in Paul. Evidently the clamor grew worse, for the tribune feared that "Paul should be torn in pieces" by the dissenting council members. Again he rescued Paul and brought him into the tower. This was the second time a pagan Roman tribune had to rescue Paul from ferocious, "religious" Jews (23:6–10).

5. A Confirming Vision

During the night, following this day filled with exhaustive ordeals, the Lord Jesus must have thought Paul needed reassuring. He stood by the apostle and said, "Be of good cheer: for as thou hast testified concerning me at Jerusalem, so must thou bear witness also at Rome" (v. 11). Paul's purpose had been to teach and preach in Rome (19:21); this very event would eventually take place. (According to Acts, Paul received six visions: 9:4; 16:9; 18:9; 22:17; 23:11; and 27:23–24.)

6. A Plot Against Paul

The apostle knew what it meant to be plotted against. The day following the disorderly conduct of the Sanhedrin, a group of forty Jews vowed to "neither eat nor drink till they had killed Paul." They put themselves under a curse to this effect. These men may have been Zealots, those who wanted to overthrow the Romans by the sword. Naturally they would be against anyone desiring conciliatory peace with Rome. Informing the chief priests and the elders of their intent, the forty asked their help in the plot. They requested that a meeting of the council be called, supposedly with the intent of judging more of Paul's case; when Paul was being ushered to the meeting, they would fall upon him and kill him. Paul's nephew, his sister's son, heard of the plot and informed the tribune in a private conversation of the intended slaying of the apostle. Believing the young man, the tribune called two centurions and commanded that they prepare two hundred soldiers, seventy horsemen, two hundred spearmen—quite a guard for one man—at the "third hour of the night" (9:00 P.M.) and that they leave with

Paul for Caesarea. The tribune must have realized what forty fanatical men could accomplish, especially when spurred on by an oath. He had probably already seen acts of violence on the part of restless Jews (23:12–24).

7. Delivered to Felix the Governor

The name of the tribune was Claudius Lysias. (The Greek word for tribune is *chiliarch,* which means ruler of a thousand. A tribune was over a cohort, or a military unit of a thousand men.) Lysias wrote a letter to Felix, the procurator (provincial governor) at Caesarea, explaining his action in sending Paul to him—that Paul was about to be lynched by the Jews when he rescued him, that he was a Roman, that he had been before the Jewish council, and that he found nothing worthy of decreeing death or imprisonment. The immediate reason for his dispatching Paul to him was a plot to kill him. Lysias said nothing of the embarrassing intention to scourge Paul, a Roman (23:25–30).

The guard brought Paul by night to Antipatris, out of danger of the forty fanatical Jews. This town was about twenty-five miles south of Caesarea. Here they left Paul with the horsemen for the remaining trip to Caesarea, while they returned to Jerusalem to their barracks. The horsemen proceeded the remaining distance to Caesarea, delivering both Paul and the letter to Felix. From Jerusalem to Caesarea was approximately sixty miles.

Felix was made procurator of Judea and Samaria in 51 or 52. He had at one time been a slave of the mother of the Emperor Claudius. Maybe this accounts, in part at least, for his despotic and cruel tactics in ruling; Tacitus, the Roman historian, wrote to this effect. Felix asked for the name of Paul's province and was told that it was Cilicia. He then promised to hear about Paul when his accusers had arrived from Jerusalem. He assigned the prisoner "to be kept in Herod's palace" (23:31–35).

8. Paul Before Felix and His Defense

After five days Ananias, the unscrupulous high priest, came from Jerusalem, bringing with him "certain elders" and Tertullus, an attorney with great oratorical power. We do not know whether he was Roman, Greek, or Jewish. Their arrival was with the express purpose of informing Antonius Felix about Paul. Tertullus, after a very flattering appeal to Felix, brought the charge against the prisoner. He accused Paul of being "a mover of insurrections among all the Jews throughout all the world," of being a "ringleader of the sect of the Nazarenes," and of profaning the Temple. The Jews who had accompanied Tertullus affirmed his statements (24:1–9).

Paul presented his own defense, which he began with a sincere statement

Caesarea, ruins of theater

that Felix had had much experience in such matters. Paul denied being an insurrectionist, for he was not guilty of "disputing with any man or stirring up a crowd." As for profaning the Temple, it was just twelve days prior to this that he had gone to the Temple to worship. While in the Temple he disputed with no one. He even spoke of being "purified in the temple." He did confess to the second charge, however—that of being one of "the Way." Yet in the Way, which his accusers called a sect, he served the God of their fathers and believed the things written in the law and the prophets. He presented the Way as not being at variance with the true aspect of Old Testament revelation; in fact, it was the true form of Judaism. The hope that Israel had, he had also. The resurrection Israel expected, he expected. He added that the Jews from Asia, the ones bringing the original charge, should be there to bring their accusation against him (24:10–21).

Felix delayed making a decision, saying that he would await the arrival of the tribune Lysias. Luke said that Felix had knowledge concerning the Way, which he must have obtained from his wife Drusilla, a Jewess. He commanded the centurion to keep Paul "in charge" and to permit his friends to wait on him (24:22–23).

9. A Two-Year Wait

Felix's third marriage was to Drusilla, the daughter of Agrippa I and sister of Agrippa II and Bernice. Drusilla left her first husband to marry Felix, the Roman procurator. After a few days Paul was brought before Felix and Drusilla, for the procurator wanted to hear "concerning the faith in Christ Jesus." As Paul preached of "righteousness, and self-control, and the judgment to come," Felix became terribly afraid. It is little wonder that Felix felt condemned, for these were the very subjects that the procurator and his wife needed to hear. Felix then told Paul to depart, that when he had some spare time he would hear him again. This appearance before the procurator and his Jewish wife was in 53, or possibly a year or so later.

Luke maintained that Felix hoped to receive a bribe from Paul and that this was the reason for his arranging frequent interviews with the noted missionary. At any rate, Antonio Felix was replaced as procurator by Porcius Festus. Luke said that the change in office involving the two men was after the space of two years (24:24–27), which would make the change in office occur about 55 or later. What Paul did during the two years in Caesarea as Felix's prisoner we can only surmise, for Luke did not say. We may well guess that he wrote letters, mostly personal ones to his friends. He may have had many opportunities to preach. Some New Testament scholars believe Paul wrote Ephesians during this interval spent at Caesarea.

10. Paul Before Festus and His Appeal to Caesar

After Festus had been in Caesarea three days, he decided to make a visit to Jerusalem. While there he was approached by the Jewish leaders, who requested that he send for Paul and bring him to Jerusalem. Their plot was to kill Paul on the way to the Holy City. Festus replied that Paul was imprisoned at Caesarea, where he himself was going soon. If they had anything against Paul, they could return with him to Caesarea and make their accusation there (25:1–5). Again a plot to murder the great evangelist failed. Had not God promised Paul that he would bear his Christian witness at Rome (23:11)?

On the next day after returning to Caesarea, Festus had Paul arraigned before him, at which time the Jews who had come down from Jerusalem brought "many and grievous charges" against him. To these Paul replied, "Neither against the law of the Jews, nor against the temple, nor against Caesar, have I sinned at all" (v. 8).

Festus, wishing to appear in a good light to the Jews, suggested to Paul that he go to Jerusalem and stand trial before him there. Paul replied that he ought to be judged before Caesar's judgment-seat and that he had done nothing wrong in regard to the Jews. Evidently Paul knew he would stand no chance if the trial were held in that hotbed of Judaistic legalism and unscrupulous religious connivers. He said, "I appeal unto Caesar." Festus conferred with the council and then replied, "Thou hast appealed to Caesar: unto Caesar shalt thou go" (25:6–12). The emperor at this time was Nero (54–68).

11. Paul Before Agrippa II and Bernice

At this time Agrippa II ruled over certain areas in northern Palestine. He had been granted the power to appoint or to depose the high priest and to control the Temple. He had already deposed Ananias from the high priesthood and had appointed another man in his place.

Agrippa II and his sister Bernice came to Caesarea to make a visit of state with the procurator. Since the visit lasted several days, Festus had plenty of time to lay before Agrippa a complete description of Paul's case and what had happened so far. Agrippa and his sister seemed to have an interest in Jewish affairs. Evidently Festus thought Agrippa might be able to help decide about how to dispose of his prisoner. The charges that were brought against Paul by his Jewish accusers were not vicious evils or crimes, but were of a religious nature. They concerned "one Jesus, who was dead, whom Paul affirmed to be alive." He confessed to Agrippa that he was perplexed about such things. He also informed his visitor that Paul had appealed to Caesar. When Agrippa expressed a desire to hear Paul, Festus said that a hearing would be set the next day (25:13–22).

The public hearing turned out to be a scene of great pomp and display, with the chief dignitaries of the city being present. When Paul was brought in, Festus made a short presentation of him to Agrippa, stating that the Jews desired his death but that he himself found in him "nothing worthy of death." Since Paul had appealed to the emperor, he had determined to send him; but he had no certain accusations to send along with him. Therefore, he wanted Agrippa to examine the prisoner, so that he might "have somewhat to write" to the emperor (25:23–27). Luke presented Festus as being very fair in his statements concerning Paul.

Paul's defense of himself before the king and his sister was an excellent one. He informed Agrippa that he was happy to be able to make his defense before him; and this statement did not constitute flattery. Paul had the opportunity not only to defend himself, but to preach the gospel to the highest Jewish official in the land. He first told of his life and his loyalty to Judaism, which all the Jews knew. Then he told of his persecution of the Christians. Next came his conversion experience on the Damascus road; then the apostle told of his commission by the Lord Jesus to preach the gospel of redemption to both Jews and Gentiles.

He avowed his obedience to that commission: "Wherefore, O king Agrippa, I was not disobedient unto the heavenly vision." He continued his address by referring to the suffering and resurrected Christ, whereupon Festus interrupted him by declaring him to be mad. This Paul denied; his words were of truth and soberness. Surely Agrippa knew of the things he spoke of! His final appeal to the king was a personal one: "King Agrippa, believest thou the prophets? I know that thou believest." Paul implied to Agrippa that what he affirmed was anticipated by the prophets of old (26:2–27). The king said, "With but little persuasion thou wouldest fain make me a Christian" (v. 28).

Agrippa and Festus, in a private conference after the address, agreed that Paul had done nothing worthy of suffering death. If he had not appealed to Caesar he might have been set free. This event put Jewish authority and Roman authority in agreement as to Paul's innocence and lined up Agrippa and Festus with Lysias, the tribune, in their opinion (26:28–32).

12. Beginning of Journey to Rome

Paul and certain other prisoners were delivered to a centurion named

Julius, of the Augustan band, to be taken to Rome. Aristarchus of Thessalonica, one of those who had accompanied Paul to Jerusalem, was also in the party, as well as Luke. The remaining two chapters of Acts (27 and 28) constitute one of the "we" sections of the book, showing that Luke was present. Since it was autumn, and since the weather was unfit for sea travel in the winter, there would be little chance of getting a vessel going directly from Caesarea to Italy. They embarked on a ship that was a coasting vessel, a ship of Adramyttium in Mysia. In one day they reached Sidon in Phoenicia, where Julius permitted Paul to leave the ship and visit his friends. Sidon was about sixty-nine miles north of Caesarea. Julius was not only kind to Paul here, but all through the journey. Throughout all of Luke's writings, centurions are pictured in a good light.

Due to the nature of the winds at that time of the year, they sailed north of Cyprus, then westward along the coast of Asia Minor. They finally came to Myra of Lycia. Here they changed ships, embarking on a vessel from Alexandria sailing for Italy. Evidently it was a grain ship, for there was an extensive grain trade between Egypt and Rome. Due to the winds, the best route from Alexandria to Rome was by way of Myra. Leaving Myra, they sailed slowly for many days, passing north of Rhodes and arriving finally at Cnidus, at the southern tip of the province of Asia. Then, probably due to contrary winds, they sailed south to Crete and then westward along the southern coastline of the island. This was in the lee of the island, due to the high White Mountains bordering the southern shore. Finally they came to a place called Fair Havens, near the city of Lasea, about halfway down the island (27:1–8).

13. Shipwreck on Malta

Since good sailing weather was almost over, Paul cautioned the ones in charge not to proceed further—to do so would be to endanger both lives and cargo. Luke said that "the Fast" was over, which would be the Day of Atonement or Yom Kippur, the tenth day of Tishri. Paul may have observed Yom Kippur at Fair Havens. However, the centurion listened to the captain and to the owner of the ship more than to Paul. Most wanted to go to Phoenix, a city on the southern shore further to the west, since it would be a city with better facilities for spending the winter months. They started sailing westward along the coast, only to experience a sudden adverse wind that drove them south to a little island named Cauda. This tempetuous wind even had a name, the Euraquilo. This island was about fifty to sixty miles from Fair Havens.

Under the lee of the island they were able to hoist up the little lifeboat and to strengthen the ship by undergirding the hull, probably with cables.

The undergirding was to prevent the ship from falling apart due to wind and wave. What they feared most was being cast upon the quicksands off the coast of Africa, near Cyrene. Therefore "they lowered the gear, and so were driven," which probably means that they used very little sail. Luke said they "labored exceedingly with the storm." His use of "we" suggested that he, too, got in the act. During the next two days they threw cargo and even the tackle itself overboard. They had no way of knowing their location or direction, since they had neither sun nor stars. The storm kept on and on, like a small tempest. All hope of saving lives was very remote (27:9–20).

At this moment of no hope Paul arose to the occasion nobly and confidently. He assured them that no life would be lost; only the ship would be damaged. An angel of his God had appeared to him during the night, informing him he would stand before Caesar, that all lives would be saved, and that they would be cast upon an island (27:21–26).

For many days and nights they were driven on a westward path where the Mediterranean and Adriatic Seas meet, and during the fourteenth night the sailors surmised they were nearing land. The sailors attempted selfishly to lower the small boat and escape to the land; but Paul, easily the dominant man on the ship at this time, warned the centurion and the soldiers of their plan. The soldiers foolishly-cut the ropes on the lifeboat and let it fall into the sea, thus losing something they would need later. Paul suggested food for everyone. He took some, gave thanks to God, and ate it, with the others of the total 276 following his advice and counsel. Then they threw the remaining wheat overboard (27:27–38).

When day arrived they cut loose the anchors, hoisted the sail, and rammed the ship onto the shore. The rear of the vessel was about to break up by the force of the storm. The soldiers, the selfish ones at this time, wanted to kill all the prisoners lest they should have to give their own lives if any escaped. The centurion, Julius, refused to accept their suggestion, "desiring to save Paul." All escaped to the land, some by swimming and some on planks (27:39–44).

14. Three Months on Malta

The island upon which the wrecked men found themselves was Malta, or as it was termed in that day and in the New Testament, Melita. Luke called the natives of the island barbarians, which was not a term of disrespect but one which merely designated those who did not speak Greek. The Maltese were derived from the Phoenicians and therefore spoke a Phoenician dialect. Here the group stayed for three months—probably November,

December, and January. It was necessary to wait for spring sailing weather.

The natives, who treated them kindly, gave them immediate relief from the rain and cold. Paul was helping to gather sticks for the fire when a viper attached itself to his hand. When it dropped off, leaving him unharmed, the natives changed their opinion of him from that of a murderer, probably due to his chains, to that of a god. They had thought that Justice, one of their deities, was taking Paul's life by means of the snake. They very swiftly changed this concept of him because of his miraculous escape from the viper (28:1–6).

The chief man of the island, one named Publius, entertained the group for three days. During that time Paul healed the father of Publius, who was sick with fever and dysentery. Then many others also came and were cured of their diseases. The natives honored them "with many honors" (28:7–10).

15. Paul At Last in Rome

After three months on Malta the men sailed on another Alexandrian ship, probably another grain ship, which had weathered on the island. This was either in February or March, probably in the year 60. The figurehead on the ship was that of the twin brothers, Castor and Pollux, the patron gods of sailors. As Paul approached Rome he must have had mixed feelings. What could he expect from the Roman court? How would the Jews react to his presence? How would the Christians receive him? The ship went to Syracuse, chief city and port on the large island of Sicily just north of Malta, where they stayed three days. Then they went across the strait to Rhegium, a port on the toe of Italy. They proceeded north to Puteoli in the Bay of Naples, the usual port of entry for ships coming from the east, especially Alexandrian grain ships. This city was approximately 140 miles south of Rome.

Luke said that here they found "brethren," supposedly meaning Christians. These people entreated Paul and his party to remain there seven days, which they did. They also sent an advance notice to the Roman church that Paul was on his way to the capital city. As Paul and his group approached Rome, the brethren from there came out to meet them on the Appian Way, the road from Puteoli to Rome. They met them at the Market of Appius, about forty-three miles from Rome, and at the Three Taverns, about thirty-three miles from Rome. Evidently there were two groups, possibly even representing separate Roman congregations. When Paul saw the Christians from Rome "he thanked God, and took courage." He had

Rome, the Appian Way

reached the Eternal City at last, being somewhat encouraged by the fact that he was not friendless there. He had written the church an epistle approximately three years previously; now he was seeing them face to face. His wish had been granted (28:11–15).

16. Paul Preaches in Rome

Paul was permitted to live privately, even though a prisoner in his own dwelling. His constant companion was the Roman soldier who guarded him. This state of affairs lasted for two years in the Imperial City. For two years he was a prisoner in Caesarea; then there was the sea voyage of half a year at least; then there were two further years of imprisonment in Rome. Yet in all this time Paul was not idle, for he interpreted the things that happened to him to be "unto the progress of the gospel" (Phil. 1:12).

When Paul entered Rome he was apprehensive about the Jews of that city. After three days, just long enough to become settled in his new quarters, he invited the leading Jews to meet with him for dialogue. Luke gave the short defense Paul made for himself before his Jewish visitors, in which he claimed loyalty to his Jewish heritage. His ministry had not been in violation of the customs of their fathers in any way. When arrested, the Roman authorities found no cause demanding death and would have set him at liberty; but the Jews rebelled at such. Therefore he had appealed to Caesar. He brought his faith in Christ back to its foundation in the Jewish heritage when he declared that "because of the hope of Israel I am bound with this chain."

When they informed him that they wanted to hear more of his Christian beliefs, they used the word *sect* for Christianity. It seems that the synagogue and the church had no connection in Rome. The Jews in Rome had heard nothing about the charge of the Jerusalem Jews against Paul. Therefore, on an appointed day the Roman Jews came to Paul's place of lodging "in great number." Here he preached to them the kingdom of God and Jesus as the fulfillment of the law and the prophets. Luke did not give a verbal account of this sermon, but he did give the results: "And some believed the things which were spoken . . . and some disbelieved." Paul quoted a passage from Isaiah (6:9–10), one often quoted in the New Testament. He was evidently applying it to the rejection of his message by many of the Jews present. In other cities he had been rejected by the Jews and had turned to the Gentiles; here in Rome this scene was repeated. Paul's firm belief was that it was the Gentiles who would listen (28:16–28).

For two years Paul lived "in his own hired dwelling," receiving all who came to visit him. Where did Paul get the money necessary for such expenses? Some feel the various churches where he had ministered helped

Roman Forum with Arch of Septimus (left) and Temple of Saturn (right)

him, such as the Philippian church. Some feel that Paul, at some time or other, may have inherited his family property. During this time he preached the kingdom as fulfilled in Jesus—with all boldness and without hindrance (28:30–31).

Luke ended Acts on a triumphant note. The Jews rejected the blessings of the gospel, but that gospel could be proclaimed with no hindrance and no restriction! Did Luke reach his objective and then stop writing? He brought Paul to Rome, where the apostle proclaimed the gospel without hindrance. Did Luke plan to write a third volume, also to be dedicated to Theophilus? This is a subject for speculation. Some scholars think he did; some think otherwise. Yet we are puzzled by the fact that Luke did not continue his work in order to reveal the disposition of Paul's appeal to Caesar. Some New Testament scholars believe that Luke died before his work was finished. At any rate, when Acts ends, about 62, Paul is still alive and a prisoner in Rome in his own dwelling.

17. The Prison Epistles

Most students of the New Testament believe that Paul wrote four of his epistles during his two-year imprisonment in Rome. Therefore, these letters have become known as the prison epistles. However, even though most scholars believe that the epistles were written while Paul was in confinement, there is no unanimous opinion that the place of writing for all four was Rome. These epistles are Philippians, Philemon, Colossians, and Ephesians. So all of Paul's time was not consumed with preaching and winning new converts. The pen became one of his mightiest weapons. We do not know the exact order in which these four epistles were written; so one order for describing them will do as well as another. Each letter had its reason for being.

Philippians was written as a thank-you epistle, for the Christians of Philippi had sent Paul a generous offering by one of their ministers, Epaphroditus. While in Rome, Epaphroditus became ill. When he became better Paul sent an epistle to Philippi as their minister returned home. This is one of Paul's most informal and intimate letters.

Philemon was sent to one man. It concerned Onesimus, a runaway slave belonging to Philemon, a convert of Paul's. Paul was sending him back to his master, asking that he be received like a Christian brother. The letter was carried by Onesimus himself to Philemon at Colossae.

Colossians was written to the people of Colossae in the rich Lycus valley east of Ephesus. This epistle concerns the person of Christ, his true being. Heresies concerning his person were circulating; Paul wanted to correct these.

Ephesians is generally believed to be a circular or general letter, since the oldest manuscripts do not have "Ephesians" written in. It also contains no personal salutations. It concerns the nature of the Christian calling and certain admonitions.

18. Remainder of Paul's Life

The book of Acts furnishes us with a vivid and concrete account of Paul's ministry up through a two-year imprisonment at Rome, probably to the spring of 62. The chronology of his visits and his acts is not a matter of conjecture, for with Acts we are on firm ground. From here on out—or until his death—we are unable to speak categorically, for we must piece together the remaining portion from evidence found in various sources. Generally one man's piecing differs from another man's piecing, and different accounts ensue. Some scholars, mostly in the past, have surmised that Paul was found guilty and executed soon after the story in Acts ends. Today, however, the prevailing view is that Paul was acquitted and released in 62, that he had a five-year ministry, that he was imprisoned a second time, and that he was executed at Rome in 67. Yet a consistent picture of this phase of Paul's life is impossible to paint.

The evidence for the prevailing view today is based upon two sources: ancient tradition and the pastoral epistles. By ancient tradition is meant the letters of prominent Christians of the first few centuries of the Christian era. In the letter that Clement of Rome wrote to the Corinthian church about 97, it is maintained that Paul preached in both "the east and the west," reaching even to the "boundary of the west." Clement must have meant Spain. A writing called the Muratorian Fragment or Muratorian Canon, of about 170, agrees with the statement found in Clement's letter. It assumes that Paul's release from the Roman prison and his visit to Spain are both well known. Both Eusebius, the famous church historian, and Jerome, the translator of the Latin Vulgate, made statements in their works about Paul's release and his preaching in Spain.

The second source of material for Paul's latter years is found in his pastoral epistles, 1 Timothy, Titus, and 2 Timothy. There are some scholars of the New Testament who maintain that Paul did not write these three epistles, a decision based solely on a difference in style, in vocabulary, and in content from Paul's travel epistles and his prison epistles. Early tradition said that Paul wrote the three pastorals, and up to the nineteenth century the fact that Paul was the author of the pastorals was not questioned. Of course, if Paul did not write them, they are of little value in building a theory of the happenings in his latter years. It will be assumed in this book, however, that the great apostle to the Gentiles was the author, an opinion substantiated by many respected scholars of the modern era. Paul's style and vocabulary could have changed both with the years and with his purpose in writing.

In the pastoral epistles Paul talked of travels and journeys to many places that do not fit into the narrative Luke presented in Acts; therefore, they must have happened to Paul after his two-year imprisonment in Rome ending in 62. In two of the letters written during this time of confinement, Paul spoke of his hopes for future journeys. He told Philemon of Colossae that he hoped to visit him soon (Philem. 22). He told the Christians of Philippi that he hoped to be with them shortly (Phil. 1:25–26; 2:24) The pastoral epistles speak of the fruits of these travel expectations.

Paul asked Timothy to stay at Ephesus while he himself was going on to Macedonia (1 Tim. 1:3). This verse reveals Paul's visit to Ephesus and also various cities in Macedonia, probably Philippi and Thessalonica. He visited Crete and left Titus there (Titus 1:5). He told Titus to come to him at Nicopolis, a name meaning "city of victory" (Titus 3:12). Since there were nine cities by this name in the empire, it is hard to discern the one Paul had in mind when he made this remark. It was probably the one located in western Achaia, however. It seems he went to Corinth (2 Tim. 4:20), where he left Erastus. He definitely went to Miletus (2 Tim. 4:20), where he left Trophimus sick. He left his cloak and books with Carpus at Troas (2 Tim. 4:13). At the time of writing 2 Timothy, Paul was in a Roman prison, probably the Mamertine Dungeon near the Roman Forum (2 Tim. 1:16–17). He wanted Timothy to come to him (2 Tim. 4:9), even before winter (2 Tim. 4:21). This was probably the winter of 66–67. Luke alone was with Paul at that time (2 Tim. 4:11). Demas had forsaken him (2 Tim. 4:10), and he had sent Tychicus to Ephesus (2 Tim. 4:12). Crescens had gone to Galatia and Titus to Dalmatia (2 Tim. 4:10). He wanted Timothy to bring John Mark when he came (2 Tim. 4:11). His first hearing was over when he wrote; it had ended in his favor (2 Tim. 4:16–17). However, he felt that his end was soon to be (2 Tim. 4:6–8).

Some scholars take these varied references, set forth in three different epistles, and try to weave a definite pattern of travel for Paul during these five years. This is impossible to do, however, for they are too sporadic. They do show us that he traveled back and forth over the Aegean world and that he made a trip as far west as Spain. Nero burned Rome and blamed the act on the Christians in 64. It is believed that Paul suffered martyrdom in a Neroian persecution in 67 and that he was beheaded on the Appian Way outside of Rome. Nero's death occurred in 68.

QVESTA È LA COLONNA DOVE STANDO
LEGATI I SS·APOSTOLI PIETRO E PAOLO
CONVERTIRNO I SS·MARTIRI PROCESSO
E MARTINIANO CVSTODI DELLE CARCERI ET
ALTRI XLVII ALLA FEDE DI CRISTO QVALI
BATTEZZORNO COLL'ACQVA DI QVESTO
FONTE SCATVRITA MIRACOLOSAMENTE

Rome, Mamertine Prison

PART FIVE

The Epistles:
Conflicts Confronting the Church

23.
Pauline Correspondence

1. Paul the Writer

Paul of Tarsus was the major contributor to the spread of the gospel throughout the Aegean world. His extensive travels in that area, coupled with his forceful preaching and his warm teaching, resulted in the founding of many strong Christian communities. His ministry in Ephesus and Corinth, the two major cities of the territory, produced dual strongholds for Christianity from which the good news of Christ could spread to the more rural areas. Truly, the great apostle to the Gentiles did an amazing work in a territory predominantly Greek in culture and Roman in spirit.

However, all was not as bland as it sounds. Problems arose, both within and without the churches. Crisis after crisis called for Paul's return to locales where he had previously worked so that he could counsel the members and soothe over doctrinal differences. Heresies and false ideas that needed to be firmly refuted burst forth in place after place, and all had to be done diplomatically and with a spirit of compassion. This called for extensive travel, either by Paul personally or by one of his co-workers: Timothy, Titus, Gaius, Aristarchus, Luke, Mark, Silus, Epaphras, and even Demas, who finally forsook him. But this method did not suffice, and Paul had to resort to another device—the pen and parchment. As a result, the notable missionary emerged as one of the greatest writers of the age. Over a span of ten or twelve years he wrote many letters, some lost and some extant. The ones that we now possess as part of the inspired canon of the New Testament not only rectified many theological errors of that day, but have also constituted the basis of doctrinal beliefs through the centuries. These epistles, written both to individuals and to churches, are firm statements of faith for all those who believe in the Scriptures as the basis of spiritual authority. Paul the preacher and teacher became, through necessity, Paul the writer and correspondent.

2. General Form of Paul's Letters

The letters of the apostle Paul generally followed a definite pattern, a similar framework. This is as follows.

    (1)   An introductory paragraph, including his name, the name of those with him at the time, and a salutation bestowing grace and peace.

    (2)   An expression of thanksgiving for the recipients.

    (3)   The general body of the letter, including two parts:

        a.   Doctrinal section; beliefs and certainties.

        b.   Practical section; application of the doctrines.

    (4)   Messages to certain friends.

    (5)   A conclusion, containing a benediction.

All of the epistles do not contain every one of these features. For instance, a cyclical letter, such as the letter to the Ephesians is thought to be, would not contain personal messages to select friends. This would not permit its being sent to varied Christian communities. In most of Paul's letters, however, this outline can be detected.

3. An Amanuensis

In Paul's day there prevailed a custom of dictating letters to an amanuensis (secretary), and Paul many times seems to have followed this custom. In Romans 16:22 we read, "I Tertius, who write the epistle, salute you in the Lord." One can almost visualize Tertius sitting on the floor with a papyrus roll on his knees, while Paul walked to and fro dictating his letter. We can almost see and hear Paul as he gestures with his hands and as he displays in his voice the emotions of concern, of gratitude, of compassion, of disappointment, and of desire that his injunctions be obeyed. The sharp break between Philippians 2:30 and 3:1 seems to indicate that an interruption took place, after which Paul resumed his dictating. Sometimes Paul finished off the letter in his own handwriting, as he did in 1 Corinthians. "The salutation of me Paul with mine own hand" (16:21). He did the same in Colossians (4:18) and in 2 Thessalonians (3:17). The final message in his own hands gave a personal air to the epistle, as well as a stamp of genuineness.

4. Bearers of the Letters

There was no system of postal service in the vast Roman empire for private correspondence. Caesar Augustus instituted a system for dispatching official documents and imperial announcements, but all private letters had to be carried by friendly travelers. Paul named some of his bearers. Phoebe, of Cenchreae, bore Paul's letter to Rome (Rom. 16:1). Timothy bore 1 Corinthians to Corinth (1 Cor. 16:10). Epaphroditus took Paul's letter to Philippi (Phil. 2:25,28–29). Onesimus, the slave, took Paul's letter to Philemon, his master (Philem. 10–12).

5. Classification of Paul's Letters

Paul's letters may be classified in one of two ways, the order in which they appear in the New Testament or the order in which they were penned. The former arrangement is of little practical value, for in the New Testament they are placed in an order roughly according to their length Romans, the first, is the longest, while Philemon, the last, is the shortest. However, in this arrangement the nine letters to churches come first, while the four to individuals come last. In the canon of the New Testament there are thirteen letters attributed to Paul. (In the King James Version the epistle to the Hebrews has a superscription that attributes the letter to Paul; however, practically all scholars affirm today that Paul did not write this epistle. We do not know who wrote it, but Paul was probably not the author.)

The best way to arrange the epistles is in a chronological sequence, for then we are able to perceive a little of the historical development of Paul's theology and beliefs. Throughout these epistles Paul touched many topics and dealt with varied themes, all interspersed and blended to fulfill the purposes for which the writings were produced. It must be constantly kept in mind that each letter was composed with a purpose, and the purposes varied with the passing of time and from place to place. Examining the epistles according to their order of writing, we find them falling into three categories: travel epistles, prison epistles, and pastoral epistles. The travel epistles fall into two groups, those on the second journey and those on the third journey. First and 2 Thessalonians were written during his second missionary journey. First and 2 Corinthians, Galatians, and Romans were written during his third missionary journey. The prison epistles were written from a Roman confinement and are composed of Ephesians, Colossians, Philippians, and Philemon. The pastoral epistles were written during the five-year period of his release and second imprisonment in Rome. These are 1 and 2 Timothy and Titus. This makes four groups in all:

1 and 2 Thessalonians, A.D. 52–53
1 and 2 Corinthians, Galatians, and Romans, A.D. 55–58
Ephesians, Colossians, Philippians, and Philemon, A.D. 60–62
1 Timothy, Titus, 2 Timothy, A.D. 65–67

6. Second Journey Correspondence

(1) First Thessalonians   We have seen that on the second missionary journey Paul left Beroea and went south to Athens in Achaia, a distance of about three hundred miles. He left Timothy and Silas in Beroea to continue the work, but with the instructions that they were to join him very soon in Athens. He hoped that they would bring him a good word about the persecution in Beroea (Acts 17:10–15). Adding information contained in 1 Thessalonians to that of Acts, we find that Timothy and Silas did bring him word in Athens—news so disconcerting that Paul sent them back to Macedonia, Timothy to Thessalonica and Silas to somewhere else in the province (1 Thess. 3:1–5). Paul later left Athens and went on to Corinth (Acts 18:1), where Silas and Timothy soon met him, having just come from Macedonia (Acts 18:5). The news must have been good, for Paul began to preach the word more ardently (v. 5).

Paul stayed in Corinth about a year and a half and during this time wrote both of the letters to the Thessalonians. The letters were probably a few months apart. In the first letter the greeting includes the names of both Timothy and Silas. It is an epistle of gratitude to God for the steadfastness of the Christians at Thessalonica in spite of much affliction and persecution by the Jews. Paul was also endeavoring to correct some misunderstandings that had evolved among them, the main one being a mistaken concept concerning the return of Christ. Therefore, this epistle is the earliest discussion of Christ's second coming found in the New Testament. (Christ's second coming is referred to in Christian literature as the *parousia,* from the Greek word meaning presence.) Since no one knows when Christ will return, all believers should live lives of sobriety and watchfulness (5:1–6).

(2) Second Thessalonians   Paul's first letter about Christ's return did not succeed in calming the frustrated minds of many of the Thessalonians. The situation became more serious. They thought Christ's coming was imminent; many had ceased to work and were living off of the livelihood of other Christians. There seems even to have been a false letter, as though coming from the great apostle himself, which maintained "that the day of the Lord is just at hand" (2:2). Paul admonished them to work and eat their own bread (3:12).

7. Third Journey Correspondence

It seems that Paul wrote his letters to the Corinthian church, his letter to the Roman church, and his letter to the Galatian churches during his third missionary journey, although his letter to the Galatians is not surrounded by scholarly unanimity in this regard. Its writing has been placed from Antioch both before and after the great Jerusalem controversy, from Corinth during the extended visit there, from Ephesus during the long stay there, and from Corinth during the second and brief visit prior to his return to Jerusalem with the offering. It is maintained in this book that Galatians was written at either Ephesus or Corinth on the third missionary journey.

(1)   First Corinthians   During Paul's extended stay in Ephesus on his third missionary journey, he wrote to the Corinthian church what we now have as 1 Corinthians. In 5:9 of this letter he mentioned a previous letter he had written to them, one that is now obviously lost. In this lost letter he admonished them to separate themselves from all evil, a requisite due to the extreme immorality of the city. Some would make fragments of the lost letter appear in 1 Corinthians and 2 Corinthians, but this hypothesis is not without pitfalls.

Evidently Paul got little response from the lost letter, so he wrote again to the church at Corinth. He had received word from the members through the household of Chloe, through a visit from Stephanas, Fortunatus, and Achaicus, and through a letter (1 Cor. 1:11; 16:17; 7:1). The second letter that Paul wrote, now mainly our 1 Corinthians, is largely a pastoral letter, for it was written as a pastor to his flock. It was designed to clear up misunderstandings and to correct erroneous thinking. Problems needed to be straightened out.

This letter dealt with practical Christianity. Paul jumped from one item to another with no intention of adhering to continuity. Problems had to be solved one by one, so each is isolated and discussed in its turn. Here we see a church that was besieged by temptations and ungodly inclinations simply because it was embedded in a highly pagan society.

Some of the problems of which Paul spoke are divisions in the church, immorality, incest, lack of chastity, and Christians in court. Some of the questions put forward in their letter to Paul were concerning marriage, celibacy, meats offered to idols, the conduct of women in churches, Lord's Supper observance, spiritual gifts, and the resurrection. In Christian love and compassion Paul wrote this letter, one of his greatest, to help the church in whose midst he had spent a year and a half of his life in a very fruitful ministry. The letter is very informal in style, written just as Paul might have talked to the Corinthian church members had he been face to face with them. The thirteenth chapter of the book is the great hymn to love. The fifteenth chapter is one of our greatest sources for the nature of the resurrection of the believer. The problems faced in the Corinthian church are still present in churches today.

(2) Second Corinthians Evidently Paul made a personal trip to Corinth sometime after writing his other two letters, the lost letter and 1 Corinthians (2 Cor. 12:14; 13:1). He had sent 1 Corinthians by Timothy, and we can only surmise as to whether or not Timothy was able to help the situation. Paul said that his future coming would be his third visit to Corinth (2 Cor. 12:14); he must have made a visit sometime after Timothy's visit to Corinth carrying the letter. It seems that Paul's advice on this visit was rejected, that he may even have been insulted. Therefore he returned to Ephesus. In Acts Luke told nothing of this visit of Paul to Corinth.

In 2 Corinthians 2:4 Paul said he wrote to the Corinthians with "anguish of heart" and with "many tears." This is what has been called Paul's sharp letter or angry letter, which would be Paul's third letter to Corinth. First Corinthians is not of this nature, and what we have as 2 Corinthians was written later. Some scholars think that 2 Corinthians 11—13 may be, whole or in part, this sharp letter, but this theory can hardly be proven. Other scholars believe the letter has been lost. Titus took the epistle to Corinth (2 Cor. 7:8–13).

Paul went on to Troas and looked for Titus to arrive also, but he did not appear on the scene. Therefore Paul moved on to Macedonia (2 Cor. 2:12–13); and while he was laboring there, Titus came and brought him joyous news from Corinth. The church had changed; a repentant spirit had emerged. With great rejoicing Paul sent to the members what we now have virtually as 2 Corinthians, all in preparation for a third and happy visit with them. This makes four epistles in all that Paul sent to Corinth. It must be admitted, however, that the sharp-letter theory is not on so firm a ground as the theory there were at least three other epistles; its reality is not accepted by some scholars. All scholars agree, however, that there was a lost letter written first of all.

Second Corinthians deals more with personal matters than it does with doctrinal issues, as in Romans, or with ecclesiastical issues, as in the pastoral epistles. We see much of Paul's personality, his fears, his ambitions, his likes, his dislikes, his moral obligations. The letter moves more on the emotional side and is not quite so clear-cut in outline as 1 Corinthians. There seem to have existed a few criticisms leveled at the apostle on the part of the Corinthian church; Paul defended himself on these scores. His accusers even claimed he was not one of the original apostles, thus undermining the apostolic authority underlying his teaching. He claimed he was "not a whit behind the very chiefest apostles" (11:5). He showed the "signs of an apostle" among them (12:12). He also appealed to the

Corinthian church to give generously to the offering for the Jerusalem church and not to be outdone by the Macedonian churches (chapters 8 and 9). He presented a lengthy list of the persecutions and sufferings that he underwent for the gospel's sake (11:23–27); he announced to the Corinthians that he planned to come to them soon (12:14; 13:1) and pleaded for their repentance (12:21).

(3) Galatians One of the debatable issues concerning the book of Galatians is whether it is addressed to churches in North Galatia or in South Galatia. North Galatia was the territory inhabited by the Gauls in the third century B.C. South Galatia was the territory that Paul visited more than once, including Pisidian Antioch, Iconium, Lystra, and Derbe. Most scholars accept the South Galatian theory as the more plausible. The other debatable issue is the time of the writing of the epistle, something that has previously been discussed in this book. It is the view of this author that the writing took place either at Ephesus during Paul's extended stay there or at Corinth during his brief stay in that city prior to departing for his final trip to Jerusalem.

It was written by Paul to Gentile believers converted to Christianity from a pagan environment, especially those brought into the Christian fold by Paul's preaching. He had declared to them salvation by grace through faith, free from legalistic entanglements (5:1–6). Since his visit with them some troublemakers had been among them, insisting that the Gentiles strictly adhere to an observance of the Mosaic law, including circumcision. Virtually they were maintaining that the door to Christianity was Judaism, with all its legalistic requirements. To Paul, the Galatians were falling away from the true gospel, with its faith in the sufficiency of Christ alone, and were following the advice of the agitators who demanded Judaism *and* faith. The heretical belief was a faith-and-works combination, not faith alone. These agitators became known as Judaizers.

To the apostle this was not a minor issue. His own experience had taught him that salvation is God's gift through faith, to be accepted by faith alone. Therefore the Galatian epistle is a fiery, impassionate epistle in which Paul started out without his usual thanksgiving but with a firm defense of his apostleship instead. The main body of the letter is an exposition of the doctrine of justification by faith alone (3:1 to 4:31). Then he told the Galatians, "For freedom did Christ set us free: stand fast therefore, and be not entangled again in a yoke of bondage" (5:1). This verse starts the practical application of his doctrinal teaching (5:1 to 6:18). Paul made a plea for ethical and moral living. Even though we are saved by grace through faith, we are not to make our freedom an excuse for living after the flesh (5:13).

The epistle bristles with indignation and disgust that the Galatians would fall for such heretical thinking. It is almost warlike in its approach, as Paul protested the corruption of the true gospel of Christ. The Galatians had left their heritage of freedom, which they had found in Paul's preaching, and had exchanged it for a yoke of bondage (5:1). This book has been called the Magna Charta of spiritual freedom. Galatians and Romans were the two books of the New Testament that had the greatest influence on Martin Luther and other reformers.

(4) Romans For quite some time Paul had a great desire to visit Rome and to preach the gospel in the Imperial City. When he wrote the epistle to the Romans, he had never been to this strategic center of the empire; many times he had planned to visit there but had been hindered (1:13). He said to them, "I long to see you, that I may impart unto you some spiritual gifts" (1:11). While at Corinth prior to his return to Jerusalem with his offering for the poor, Paul wrote this weighty epistle, the one that many scholars consider his greatest. Both William Tyndale and Martin Luther advised that the book be learned by rote, so that it could be recited word for word. The theme that pulsates through its pages is justification by faith, a theme found stated in 1:16–17.

This book, one that has had a tremendous influence on the Christian church through the centuries, is Paul's longest and most formal letter. It was not sent with the hope of its meeting an emergency. It was written with deliberation. Here he very systematically presented the essence of his view of the gospel. The book has all the characteristics of a true letter, for it is warm and personal in its approach. Yet at the same time, it is like a doctrinal treatise or a theological essay, presenting in a formal manner a summary of Paul's thinking about man's plight and God's answer. It contains the core of the gospel, that righteousness is the free gift of God and that faith in Jesus Christ is the way it is given. There is very little Christology, very little eschatology, very little ecclesiology. It is all about man's need of salvation and God's offer of saving grace.

Evidently Paul felt compelled to write to the saints at Rome simply because of their strategic location. Rome was the capital of the Roman Empire, and Christians living there, sound in doctrine and beliefs, could have a great influence on the rest of the empire. Therefore he wanted to preach the gospel in Rome (1:15). He wanted them to have a clear grasp of the Christian faith.

In this great epistle Paul showed the sinner moving from self, sin, and slavery to salvation, sanctification, and service. His reason for presenting the gospel was that it is the power of God unto salvation (1:16). He first demonstrated that all men are sinners and in need of God's grace. The Gentile is sinful in a carnal way; the Jew is sinful in spite of his law. All men are sinners and in a desperate plight (1:18 to 3:20). But God has provided a way of righteousness apart from the law, a redemption through faith in Christ, being justified by his grace, and being redeemed through his blood (3:21–26). This leads to joy in living and victory over sin. Life in the Holy Spirit brings no condemnation and no separation (5:1 to 8:39). As a redeemed individual, man has a responsibility to both God and man. His life, committed to Christ, must issue in service (12:1 to 15:33). If Galatians is the Magna Charta of Christian liberty, Romans is the constitution of Christian liberty.

In this epistle we have the sinner's walk from sin to salvation (1—11), followed by the saint's walk from service to glory (12—15). The doctrinal part of the epistle is composed of 1—11; the practical part is composed of 12—15. The sixteenth chapter is composed of salutations from Paul's various companions, followed by a concluding doxology.

The epistle was carried to Rome by Phoebe of the nearby city of Cenchreae (16:1). It was penned by an amanuensis named Tertius (16:22) and is one of two epistles that Paul wrote to a congregation strange to him. (Colossians is the other epistle of this nature.)

8. Prison Correspondence

When Paul finally reached Rome, after a traumatic experience at sea amid storm and shipwreck, he was confined in his own hired dwelling, probably chained to a Roman guard. But he was far from idle those two years, for he taught and preached and wrote. From his prolific pen came four of his most elegant letters: Ephesians, Colossians, Philippians, and Philemon. We have no way of knowing the order in which they were produced, but it seems that each was written to fulfill a particular need in a particular situation. The deity of Christ is a prevailing theme, especially in the first three epistles as listed above.

Not all scholars accept Rome as the origin of all these epistles. Since Paul was also confined in Caesarea, some say he may have written one or two from there. Some even presuppose an Ephesian confinement and contend for one or two having been written in that city. Tradition maintains that they all came from Rome, however. There is no doubt among students of the New Testament that the epistles came from a time of imprisonment, since all four refer to Paul's "bonds" (Eph. 3:1; 4:1; 6:20; Phil. 1:12–13; Col. 1:24; Philem. 1). The question is where the confinement existed for each epistle.

(1) Ephesians   Some students of the New Testament do not think Paul wrote this letter, but the weight of tradition says that he is the author. Paul's name is found in 1:1 and in 3:1. Also, very early in the second century the book was considered as coming from Paul. The very earliest collections of Paul's epistles included the book. Ephesians 1:3–14 is just as magnificent a piece of writing as is 1 Corinthians 13; both are lofty in style and significant in content.

Quite a number of scholars feel that this letter existed originally as a circular letter intended for many churches, with a blank space in the heading so that the name of the intended church, whatever one it might be, could be penned in by the scribe. (Some books say "general," "encyclical," or "cyclical" instead of "circular.") Some authorities believe that Ephesians was intended to be delivered to other churches of Asia through the Ephesian church. The phrase "at Ephesus" is not found in two of the oldest and most respected manuscripts of the Greek New Testament. Also, there are no personal greetings attached to the letter, which one would expect if Paul intended to send it to a church where he had ministered diligently for three years. Therefore, he must have meant for the letter to be read in several churches; and, if Paul had in mind churches in Asia, at least one copy was sent to Ephesus. Since Ephesus was the most important center for that area, this copy would be copied and recopied more than the others. Therefore one with Ephesus in the text got into the canon. The bearer of the letter was Tychicus (Eph. 6:21–22).

Ephesians reveals Paul's view of the church, which is the theme of this rich epistle. Every time the word *church* is used in the letter, it is employed in the universal sense, not the local sense. The church is depicted as the body of Christ, in which there is neither Jew nor Gentile, bond nor free. The church has been founded according to the sovereign will of God, something easily discerned in the first three chapters. The church is a single functioning body or organism, engaged in spiritual conflict. The animating power of the church is the Holy Spirit. The second half of the epistle, chapters 4—6, describes the conduct of the believer, one who walks according to the Spirit. By this walk the Christian manifests his spiritual life in a practical way.

Much of the thought and content of Ephesians can be found in other of Paul's epistles. It is especially similar to Colossians, which might stem from the fact that the two epistles were written at about the same time, perhaps with different amanuenses.

This book of Ephesians, one of the most exalted of the documents of the

New Testament, is very much like a sermon meditation. Paul was not endeavoring to smooth over any "sticky" situation in any church or to rectify any dangerous heresy. The members constitute the church, which is likened to the temple of God (2:20–22), the body of Christ (1:22–23), and the bride of Christ (5:23–32). The first half of the letter is doctrinal, and the blessings of redemption are displayed in glowing colors (1:1 to 3:21); the second half is a sermon, beseeching the Christian to walk worthily of his high calling (4:1 to 6:24). The believers are not to walk in the Gentile way (4:17–19) but to walk in love as beloved children of God (5:1–2). The aim of the Christian should be "the stature of the fulness of Christ" (4:13). Paul presented two of his prayers that he offered to God in behalf of the Christians: 1:15–23 and 3:14–19. The famous passage urging the reader to put on the armor of God is a unique one (6:11–17).

(2) *Colossians* Colossae was located in the Lycus River Valley about one hundred miles east of Ephesus. It was in the eastern part of the province of Asia not far from Hierapolis and Laodicea. During the time of the Persian Wars (fifth century B.C.), Colossae was the most prominent city in the valley; but in Paul's day it had been surpassed commercially by the two neighboring cities. As far as we know, Paul did not visit Colossae, so it must have been evangelized by fellow workers of Paul, such as Epaphras (Col. 1:7). However, the church may have been founded by others, with Paul merely commissioning Epaphras to minister there. It could be that Paul was in contact with the church during his long Ephesian ministry. At any rate, the apostle mentioned that they had not seen his face (2:1).

Paul wrote the letter to the Colossians to correct an error that had arisen concerning the person of Christ. The Colossians were from an area known as Phrygia, a territory that had been noted for emotional, ecstatic, and mystical religion. A strange philosophy had sprung up among the people, brought in by false teachers who were instructing the people in beliefs similar to the Gnosticism that became quite prevalent a century or two later. This philosophical teaching was tending to destroy the concept of the divinity and supremacy of Christ held by the Colossians. The teaching of false teachers was a heresy that was syncretistic in nature; that is, it was composed of elements drawn from Jewish ritualism, pagan mythology, and Greek philosophy.

Paul warned the Colossians not to be led astray by "philosophy and vain deceit, after the tradition of men, after the rudiments of the world" (2:8). The phrase "the rudiments of the world" can very well be translated "the elemental spirits of the universe." The Colossians were being falsely taught that these "elemental spirits" not only exercised power over men but were superior to Jesus. They were the essence of ultimate reality. Therefore, the Colossians should worship these angelic beings right along with Jesus. Believing in Jesus alone would lead to an incomplete religion. Also, the mundane world was considered evil, so there was to be no association with the world. Instead, men should be introduced and initiated into something higher, where true wisdom was to be found. This was to be accomplished by self-abasement and ascetic living.

Christianity, therefore, was in danger of being turned into Gnostic speculation. The preeminence of Jesus, as one in whom the fullness of God dwells, was in danger of being dethroned. Paul's great passage, one in which he presented Jesus as preeminent and as the only Mediator and Redeemer, is Colossians 1:15–20. In this passage Paul dwelled upon the uniqueness of Christ, one who has the preeminence in all things (v. 18). It was the Father's pleasure that in Christ all the fullness of divinity should dwell (v. 19), who is also "the image of the invisible God" (v. 15). All things were created "through him and unto him" (v. 16). Only through him can we be delivered "out of the power of darkness" and "into the kingdom of the Son of his love" (v. 13).

This letter, as many other letters of Paul, falls into two parts, the doctrinal (1:1 to 3:4) and the practical (3:5 to 4:18). Paul gave his clearest picture of Christ's person in his preexistent state, his state prior to the incarnation. Ephesians and Colossians are strikingly similar in language, style, and contents. At the very end of the letter Paul took the pen himself and wrote, "The salutation of me Paul with mine own hand. Remember my bonds. Grace be with you" (4:18).

(3) Philippians   Paul had an abiding love for the people in the church at Philippi, and they had just as great a love for him. The Philippian church was the first congregation that Paul established on European soil. He called them his "joy and crown" (4:1). Of all his letters not written to an individual, this letter is the most personal in nature. This Macedonian church had meant so much to him and had been so loyal in its affection for him that he felt free to unburden to them his inmost thoughts, desires, and ambitions. The epistle fairly overflows with words such as "I," "my," "mine," and "me." Right after Paul left them, after his first visit and ministry in Philippi, they had supported him; then they apparently neglected him for several years. Hearing of his confinement in Rome evidently revived their interest in their apostolic friend (4:10–16); they sent him a contribution for his need by one of their ministers named Epaphroditus (4:18). This one became very ill, "sick nigh unto death" (2:27), and it was "for the work of Christ he came nigh unto death" (2:30). Paul

sent him back with the letter he wrote to the Philippians, thanking them for their generosity (2:28–29). It was probably near the end of Paul's two-year confinement in Rome that he wrote this letter of Christian appreciation; certain things that he said made it appear that way. That he wrote the epistle from Roman surroundings is highly suggested by the mention of the praetorian guard (1:13) and Caesar's household (4:22). However, some scholars believe the epistle to have come from Ephesus.

Paul hoped to be in their presence yet again (1:23–24), coming to them shortly (2:24). Throughout the book he mentioned no rift-making division in the Philippian church. Instead of having to remonstrate with them over a schism, he could bask in joy and rejoicing as he contemplated their graciousness. Since Paul went from one item to another in his personal reflections, the book is difficult to outline. He warned at least once against the Judaizers, whom he called dogs (3:2), but this remark seems to have been made with the future in mind. Even though he seemed to expect release (1:19), he talked as though death might not be far off (1:20–24). He interpreted his suffering and his imprisonment to be to "the progress of the gospel" (1:12).

The word *gospel* is a key word in the epistle, for he used the term nine times. By this term Paul denoted the story of Christ's ministry, death, and resurrection and the significance of his whole atoning act. Another key word is *joy*, with its cognate verb *rejoice;* even though Paul's confinement would carry with it many frustrations, he rejoiced in every thought of the Philippians (1:3). In spite of the forebodings of the future, there is an aura of brilliant faith in Christ permeating the epistle. As the great apostle sang in a dark and dismal Philippian jail at midnight, he fairly sang of joy and hope in this epistle, though surrounded by the distressing aspects of a Roman confinement. His whole attitude was summed up in the phrase "For me to live is Christ, and to die is gain" (1:21).

When Paul defined what he called "the mind of Christ" (2:5–11), he rose to the height of eloquence. There is nothing more sublime in all his writings, for it constitutes Paul's view of Christ expressed in a poetical style. Paul turned to the practical when he admonished the Philippians to live the life worthy of children of God (1:27–30). The basis for judging the Christian life is the example of Christ himself (2:5).

(4)   Philemon   In this short (one chapter) epistle Paul gave his view on Christian brotherhood. Being the shortest of Paul's letters (twenty-five verses), it was placed last in the arrangement of his writings in the New Testament. The epistle is related to the Colossian epistle, since the names of several people are mentioned in both letters, since both letters were

carried by Tychicus, and since both were sent to Colossae at the same time. A situation arose that concerned Paul and Philemon, one that called for a brief letter to Philemon at Colossae. Onesimus, running away from his master Philemon, probably even stealing some money from Philemon, had come into contact with Paul—a meeting that resulted in the slave's conversion. At the time of the writing of this letter, Paul was sending Onesimus back to his master with the fervent request that Philemon receive him "as a brother beloved" and "no longer as a servant" (v. 16). Paul informed Philemon that he desired to keep Onesimus with him, that he might serve him in his imprisonment, but that he would do nothing without Philemon's consent (vv. 13–14). Most scholars believe that this is a hint for Philemon to send Onesimus back to Paul that he might help him.

In this epistle Paul was talking about Christian brotherhood and not about slavery *per se*. Paul mentioned slavery in 1 Corinthians 7:20–24 and also in Colossians 3:22 to 4:1. He never openly pleaded for abolition of slavery; but all the passages rest upon Christian principles which, if put into practical application, would ultimately call for the banishing of all slavery. When Paul stated his belief that Philemon will do even beyond what Paul asked, he may have been referring to his desire to see Onesimus set free. Paul also told Philemon to prepare for him a lodging place, so he evidently planned to visit Philemon in Colossae before very long (v. 22).

9. Pastoral Correspondence

It has been the custom through the years to term 1 Timothy, 2 Timothy, and Titus as the pastoral epistles because they deal with the problems faced by pastors as they endeavor to lead their congregations. These letters warn of heresies and false teachings and show forth guidelines in the administering of local churches. The traditional view is that Paul wrote all three letters. Many modern scholars believe that he did, while many more believe that they were written by another who used Paul's name, who wrote according to the teachings of Paul, and who did his work after the turn of the century. They maintain that the language, style, and content of the epistles is unlike the style of those definitely written by the great apostle. The view of this author is that these three epistles are Pauline in origin. Paul's style of writing and use of words could very well vary with age and with the circumstances found in the churches. They also have the name Paul embedded in the text.

The material in the three epistles seems to assume that Paul was acquitted of the charges that placed him in confinement at Rome, that he was free for some time to travel and to minister as he chose. The movements of travel sporadically mentioned in the three epistles cannot be correlated with the account described in Acts, a fact which leads us to the conclusion that Paul was traveling again after his two-year Roman imprisonment. However, the exact itinerary cannot be ascertained, just surmised. The information in the epistles is too brief and too sporadic to present a definite route for his journeys.

(1) First Timothy We assume that Paul was acquitted at Rome in 61, that he was free to resume his missionary activities, and that he revisited the churches of the Aegean area. Evidently Paul discovered a straying from the orthodox way, for he advised Timothy, his young co-worker, to "charge certain men not to teach a different doctrine, neither to give heed to fables and endless genealogies, which minister questionings" (1 Tim. 1:3-4). These same men desired to be "teachers of the law," but they had no understanding of what they were saying or affirming (1:7). Some men had become such moral derelicts that Paul committed them to Satan (1:20).

Church organization had become more fixed in the sixties than it was when Paul began his Asia Minor and Aegean area campaigns. Bishops, elders, and deacons are mentioned in this epistle, with the first two offices probably being the same in nature (3:1,8; 5:1,17). The term "bishop" means overseer, while the term "deacon" means servant. "Elder" means presbyter. It seems that bishops and elders performed the duties of a pastor, while deacons looked to the physical needs of the orphans, widows, and the poor. The qualifications for a bishop (3:1-7) and qualifications for a deacon (3:8-13) are quite similar. Paul also advised about care for widows in the church (5:1-16).

Timothy served as pastor of the church at Ephesus (1:3) at a time when the Gnostic philosophy was trying to make an inroad into Christianity. It is believed by some that Paul visited Timothy at Ephesus, helped him in his work, and then wrote 1 Timothy after he departed the city in order to give additional advice to the young pastor.

The growing menace at this time was Gnosticism, which manifested itself in Christianity as Docetism. Paul had fought with the Judaizers and had made a significant victory over that heresy. At this time he began to fight Docetism through his young pastor friends Timothy and Titus. He expected them to carry on his work for him (6:20-21).

He admonished Timothy wisely when he said, "Let no man despise thy youth; but be thou an example to them that believe, in word, in manner of life, in love, in faith, in purity. . . . Give heed to reading, to exhortation, to teaching" (4:12-13). He also advised him to "follow after righteousness, godliness, faith, love, patience, meekness" and to "fight the good fight of the faith'' (6:11–12). Frequently he reminded Timothy of his calling and of the need to feel the responsibility of that call.

(2) *Titus*   The epistle named Titus followed in time the one named 1 Timothy. Paul probably left Ephesus, went north to the province of Macedonia, and then south to Crete, where he had stopped previously on his way to Rome. After spending some time ministering on the island, he departed, leaving Titus to carry on the work of establishing the church in that area. He planned to go to Nicopolis and winter there (Titus 3:12).

The situation in the church in Crete was not what it should have been, by any means. Paul said of the Cretans, ''They profess that they know God; but by their works they deny him, being abominable, and disobedient, and unto every good work reprobate'' (1:16). Six times he urged the Christians to resort to good works (1:16; 2:7,14; 3:1,8,14), even though he stated that salvation could not be received merely by good works (3:5). We are saved due to the mercy of God (3:5). It is in this epistle that Paul presented one of the clearest and most potent statements about the full import of salvation that he set forth in any of his documents. ''For the grace of God hath appeared, bringing salvation to all men, instructing us, to the intent that, denying ungodliness and worldly lusts, we should live soberly and righteously and godly in this present world; looking for the blessed hope and appearing of the glory of the great God and our Saviour Jesus Christ; who gave himself for us, that he might redeem us from all iniquity, and purify unto himself a people for his own possession, zealous of good works'' (2:11–14). In this statement Paul ran the gamut theologically from the preexistence of Christ to the final product that he expected from every Christian life, not only in this age but in the hope and glory of the future.

Both of the first two pastoral epistles, 1 Timothy and Titus, were written to give counsel and admonition to two young pastors. Paul wanted these two ''sons in the ministry'' to be well equipped, doctrinally and spiritually, for the trying days of a difficult pastorate. The early church was experiencing growing pains; much counseling was needed. Paul called Titus ''my true child after a common faith'' (1:4), so he must have had great confidence in the young man.

(3) *Second Timothy*   Clement of Rome, in one of his epistles (about 75), said that Paul ''reached the limits of the west,'' by which he probably meant Spain. From the pastoral epistle of 2 Timothy we glean the information that Paul at some time or other went to Corinth (4:20), to Miletus (4:20), and to Troas (4:13). He left his books, parchments, and cloak at Troas. At some place or other he seems to have been arrested and carried to Rome. The place of his

arrest can only be surmised, for there is insufficient scriptural evidence to speak with any degree of certainty. One wonders concerning Paul's remark, "Alexander the coppersmith did me much evil: the Lord will render to him according to his works: of whom do thou also beware; for he greatly withstood our words" (4:14–15).

Is there in this remark a foreboding of a future misfortune, a disastrous event, caused by the malicious coppersmith? Did the Christian cause, extended and enhanced by the great apostle himself, lead to such a diminution of the idol business in the Aegean territory that an incident similar to that instigated at Ephesus years before by Demetrius and his fellow craftsmen took place (Acts 19:23–41)? It could very well have occurred again at Ephesus, for Paul in his address to the Ephesian elders at Miletus spoke of "the plots of the Jews" at Ephesus (Acts 21:19). The fact that Paul told Timothy to beware of Alexander the coppersmith indicates that Timothy was aware of his movements and that Alexander must have been operating in Timothy's territory, which was Ephesus (2 Tim. 4:15). All through the pastoral epistles we observe indications of a jealous Judaism and a frustrated paganism. Paul, the veteran emissary for Christ, showed in these letters that he was throwing his crusading torch to his more youthful assistants, along with much wise counseling that he wished them to heed.

The purpose of 2 Timothy was Paul's desire to bolster Timothy for the strenuous task lying before him. He reminded Timothy of his holy calling, which was also Paul's calling, and that the call was according to the purpose and grace of God (1:9). He wanted Timothy to suffer "as a good soldier of Jesus Christ" (2:3). As a good soldier, he was not to entangle himself in the affairs of this life but to have as his aim to please the one who enrolled him as a soldier (2:4). Paul advised Timothy to "follow after righteousness, faith, love, peace, with them that call on the Lord out of a pure heart" (2:22). Timothy "must not strive, but be gentle towards all, apt to teach, forbearing, in meekness correcting them that oppose themselves" (2:24–25). Paul warned Timothy that all who endeavor to live godly lives in Christ Jesus will suffer persecution (3:12) and that Timothy should abide in his knowledge of the Scriptures, which he has known from the time he was a babe (3:14–15). In this connection Paul presented one of the greatest passages on the inspiration of the Scriptures that we possess. "Every scripture inspired of God is also profitable for teaching, for reproof, for correction, for instruction which is in righteousness" (3:16). The Greek phrase translated "inspired of God" means "God breathed."

Paul's final charge to Timothy (4:1–6) was the apex of the whole book.

Here he asked his young friend to preach the word urgently, when it is opportune and when it is not opportune, and to "reprove, rebuke, exhort, with all long-suffering" (4:2). He wanted Timothy to do the work of an evangelist (4:5). Here Paul gave what has become known as his "swan song." "I have fought the good fight, I have finished the course, I have kept the faith: henceforth there is laid up for me the crown of righteousness, which the Lord, the righteous judge, shall give me at that day; and not to me only, but also to all them that have loved his appearing" (4:7–8). This epistle is not quite so personal in nature as 1 Timothy. Paul had Timothy and his work more in mind, for he wanted him to train others to carry on the ministry also. He warned of evil days to come (3:1) and desired Timothy to be faithful (3:14).

It is the consensus of most scholars that 1 Timothy and Titus were written while Paul was at large, but that 2 Timothy was written during his last confinement at Rome just prior to his death. The epistle was evidently penned in the cold and desolate Mamertine dungeon just opposite a forum in Rome. Tourists today are shown this prison as the traditional one where Paul and Peter were confined. Second Timothy reveals a degree of loneliness on Paul's part. Demas had forsaken him (4:10), and many of his companions were in other parts. Only Luke was with him (4:11). Tradition says that Paul was beheaded on the Appian Way south of Rome.

24.
General Correspondence

1. The General Letters

The New Testament contains eight epistles that are known as General Epistles, Catholic Epistles, or Non-Pauline Epistles. The term *catholic* as employed here has nothing to do with either the Roman Catholic or the Greek Catholic church. The word means universal and as used here designates the "universal letters." These books of the Bible are Hebrews, James, 1 Peter, 2 Peter, 1 John, 2 John, 3 John, and Jude. They are known as general epistles because they are addressed, for the most part, to general groups of readers. In contrast, Paul addressed his to specific churches or individuals—Ephesians, the cyclical letter, being a possible exception. As a whole Paul's letters are more personal in their outlook than the eight general epistles.

2. Summary of the General Letters

(1) Hebrews   In the King James Version the book of Hebrews bears the heading "The Epistle of Paul the Apostle to the Hebrews." All English versions succeeding the King James omit the name Paul. The book has no salutation or conclusion containing his name. Also, there is nothing in the body of the letter that can be associated with Paul except one thing, the mention of Timothy in 13:23; and many people were associated with Paul's young ministerial friend by that name. The letter is anonymous and is rightfully included in the non-Pauline group. The epistle to the Hebrews immediately follows the Pauline letters and at the same time heads the non-Pauline letters. The Pauline letters are arranged according to decreasing length, with Philemon, the shortest, falling last. Hebrews comes next; so, if it is Pauline, it is out of place. The ones responsible for arranging the order of the books in the New Testament canon evidently considered the book non-Pauline in origin; else they would have placed it in another position. Also, when we compare this epistle with those that are definitely from Paul, many phrases, words, ideas, and expressions are quite differ-

ent. The Greek in which the epistle was penned is excellent Greek, eloquent and majestic in style.

If Paul did not write the epistle, then who composed this splendid work? Many guesses have been set forth, including Barnabas, Apollos, Luke, Aquila, Priscilla, Clement of Rome, Silas, and others. Luther thought Apollos wrote it, and Calvin thought Luke wrote it; therefore, these key figures from the Reformation era at least considered it non-Pauline. The recipients of the letter were Jewish Christians, but we cannot ascertain if they lived in Palestine, Rome, Alexandria, Jerusalem, or elsewhere. Most scholars pick Rome or somewhere in that vicinity.

The time of writing has also been disputed. It could have been written anywhere between 60 and 95. Some students of the New Testament argue for a writing date prior to the destruction of the Temple in 70. Others place it amid the days of extreme persecution during the reign of Domitian, 81–96. Each side has its points of argument in support of its particular view. Therefore, the date of writing is debated almost as much as the identity of the author. There are even no clues in the book as to the place of writing, so this is also a point of variance. Even the form of the letter presents a problem; it starts out as would a treatise, formal in nature, but ends as would an epistle. Since some of it consists of exhortations, very persuasive in nature; it is like a sermon. There is no wonder that this book has been called "the riddle of the New Testament."

The theme of the book, found in its prologue, is that the revelation of God brought by the Son is final and complete. "God, having of old time spoken unto the fathers in the prophets by divers portions and in divers manners, hath at the end of these days spoken unto us in his Son" (1:1–2).

The law and the prophets contain a revelation in times past; but the Son, sharing the very nature of God himself, has presented to man the final revelation. The superiority of the revelation brought by the Son is the foundation for superiority of Christianity over Judaism in area after area. This is why the word *better* appears recurrently in the book. It has been called the "book of betters." Jesus is better than the angels (1:4); there are better things pertaining to the salvation of Christians (6:9); Christians have a better hope (7:19); they enjoy a better covenant (7:22; 8:6); Jesus offered a better sacrifice (9:23); Christians have a better possession (10:34); they desire a better country, a heavenly country (11:16); those suffering persecution for their faith have a better resurrection (11:35); God has provided better for the Christians (11:40). As the writer proceeded from comparison to comparison, he also interjected exhortations and warnings for his readers.

The superiority of the Son is one of the main arguments of the epistle. He is not only superior to the angels; he is also superior to Moses. Both the angels and Moses were servants; Jesus is the Son. The readers are to hold fast their confidence in Christ, for he will establish the true household of God (1:1 to 4:13). Another main argument of the epistle is that of the high priesthood of Christ. Since we have "a great high priest . . . Jesus the Son of God," we are to "hold fast our confession." This high priest is approachable; he knows our weaknesses, for he has been tempted just as we have. Here we see an emphasis upon the present ministry of Christ, the present benefits of his atoning act. Where other New Testament books deal with the cross, resurrection, and ascension of Jesus, Hebrews tells what he is doing now. He is ministering every moment through a heavenly intercession, all a part of his priestly office.

In comparison with the Levitical priests Jesus is far superior, a fact that the writer substantiated with many contrasting points. He even resorted to the order of priesthood derived from Melchizedek in order to demonstrate Christ's superiority (4:14 to 7:28). Due to the superiority of the Son's priesthood, he also has a superior sanctuary, a superior covenant, and a superior sacrifice. His sanctuary is the "true tent," "the heavenly sanctuary." The earthly sanctuary is merely a shadow of the one to come for the Christian. Jesus' better covenant is the fulfillment of the one prophesied by Jeremiah centuries before (Jer. 31:31–34). Jesus' sacrifice is the fulfillment of all sacrifices found in the Levitical sacrificial system (8:1 to 10:39).

Chapter 11 of Hebrews is one of the New Testament masterpieces. It is the roll call of Old Testament heroes whose lives epitomize faith. Now that the superiority of Christ's revelation has been firmly established (1:1 to 10:39), how does one appropriate it in a saving relationship? It is by faith, a faith that has been exemplified in the sterling character of Old Testament saints. Abel, Enoch, Noah, Sarah, Abraham (example supreme), Moses, Gideon, Barak, David, and many others are passed in review, constituting a great "cloud of witnesses." But they did not receive the promise (11:4–40). Jesus is "the author and perfecter of our faith." We need to lay aside every weight and sin that would hold us down so that we can run the race set before us (12:1–2).

One of the great characteristics of this book is that it contains a progressive list of warnings and a progressive list of exhortations. The former constitutes the negative and the latter the positive. The warnings are against perils that beset the Christian on every side: the peril of indifference, the peril of unbelief, the peril of disobedience, and many others. The exhortations, on the other hand, start out with the phrase "Let us." "Let us hold fast our confession" (4:14). "Let us draw near" (10:22). "Let us consider one another" (10:24). There are thirteen in all, scattered throughout the book. If this work can be called the "book of betters," it can also be called the "book of 'let us.' "

Chapter 13, which reads like an epistle, contains a series of admonitions for the reader. Hebrews 13:20–21 is one of the most beautiful benedictions in the entire Bible. It is tragic that Hebrews, due to its logical procedure and lengthy discussions of priesthood, sacrifice, and ritual, is one of the least read of the New Testament documents.

There are three main theories about the purpose of the book. For centuries the theory held sway that the author wrote to dissuade Jewish Christians from reverting to their Judaism, the old, well-settled religion of their fathers. They were to be faithful to Christ rather than go back to the synagogue. As Jews left the ranks of Judaism for Christianity, there was a tendency on the part of Jews loyal to the Jewish fold to win back the converts. Therefore, they would ridicule a faith without law, prophets, priesthood, temple, sacrifices, or covenant. The writer of Hebrews endeavored to show that Christianity not only possesses these things, but possesses them to a superior degree. This theory is commensurate with the view of an early writing of Hebrews, before the Temple was destroyed.

Another theory of purpose is that Hebrews was written in a time of persecution and addressed to a community threatened to resort to apostasy. This theory is commensurate with a late writing of the book, since one of the worst persecutions was during the days of Domitian (81–96). The writer, therefore, wrote to bolster up the faith of his readers, a faith they were tempted to renounce in order to avoid suffering and torture. To show faith rather than to defect and fall away would add great weight to the missionary enterprise. But, we may ask, why does the author make no mention of martyrs?

A third theory and a very plausible one is that the book was meant to combat a growing lethargy on the part of the Jewish Christians. The writer was challenging them to add zeal and dedication to their sluggish and dull spiritual condition by their realizing anew the superiority of Christ and the finality of his revelation.

(2) James   Much dispute and controversy has surrounded the letter of James for a long time. Authorship, date, and setting have all been questioned. The epistle starts with the phrase "James, a servant of God and of the Lord Jesus Christ"; and tradition maintains that this James was the brother of our Lord. Some have tried to maintain that the author was

James, the son of Zebedee, while others have maintained he was James, the son of Alphaeus. Most scholars of today agree with tradition that he was the brother of Jesus (Mark 6:3) and the son of Joseph and Mary. The epistle is surrounded by a Jewish aura, containing many Old Testament phrases and allusions. Also, the work is addressed "to the twelve tribes which are of the Dispersion" (1:1). These factors add weight to the brother-of-Jesus theory.

This James, though he, along with his brothers, did not become a Christian till after Jesus' resurrection, became the leader of the church in Jerusalem and presided over the great Jerusalem Council (Acts 15:13). Tradition says he was known as "The Righteous." (The name *James* is the same as the Hebrew name *Jacob.*) Since this James was martyred about 62, the book was probably written sometime between 50 and 62. Those who favor the position that someone else wrote the book generally favor a late date, sometime between 80 and 100.

Though this document of the New Testament is considered a letter, it has many of the characteristics of a sermon. It abounds in admonitions and exhortations. There are about sixty verbs in the imperative, with only 108 verses in the entire letter. It is a very practical book, having very little of the nature of Christian doctrine or of the nature of the person of Christ and his atoning act. The name of Jesus occurs only twice. The incarnation and the resurrection are not mentioned. Christology in the book takes a minor role. Various topics are discussed; there is very little unity throughout the book. No one theme seems to run throughout its brief pages, unless it be that of Christian conduct.

The book reminds the reader of the wisdom literature that was very popular during the intertestamental period, but it also contains many passages that remind us of the teachings of Jesus as found in the four Gospels, especially the Sermon on the Mount (Matt. 5—7). The writer set forth the requirements for the conduct of the Christian living in a secular world. Admonitions to good behavior are also found in the Gospels and in Paul's correspondence, for the Christian faith considers man's outward performance as very important. All through the New Testament we see that salvation by grace through faith is paramount, but there can be no genuine Christian life without an ethical response in daily living. The book of James endeavors to present a code of Christian ethics for practical, daily living. As a result, it turns out to be an essay of exhortations, injunctions, and imperatives.

Sometimes the charge has been made that James is in conflict with Paul concerning faith and works, that Paul advocates salvation through faith and

James salvation through works. This is not true, however. They are in perfect agreement, which is easily discerned after a definition of terms. Evidently some students have failed to realize this. Martin Luther called the book of James "an epistle of straw" because he thought it negated the teaching of Romans and Galatians that one is justified by faith alone. James said, "Even so faith, if it have not works, is dead in itself" (2:17). He also asserted, "Ye see that by works a man is justified, and not only by faith" (2:24). Paul affirmed, "We reckon therefore that a man is justified by faith apart from the works of the law" (Rom. 3:28). He also said, "For by grace have ye been saved through faith; and that not of yourselves, it is the gift of God; not of works, that no man should glory" (Eph. 2:8–9). Again he maintained, "But if it is by grace, it is no more of works: otherwise grace is no more grace" (Rom. 11:6). On the surface these passages by Paul seem to refute those by James, but deeper study proves otherwise.

James seems to have been one who advocated action, deeds that prove one's faith. It could well be that James knew persons who said they had faith in Christ but whose lives were lived in lethargy and ease. He called such faith a "dead faith" and asserted that it would not save (2:17). This kind of faith is intellectual only—a dogmatic faith, as faith in a creed. It is not the creative, dynamic faith that Paul envisioned when he said that a person is "saved through faith." Such a faith involves not merely the head, but the heart and will also—in short, one's whole being. Paul also agreed that this type of faith issues in works; he said we are "created in Christ Jesus for good works, which God afore prepared that we should walk in them" (Eph. 2:10).

The matter can be summed up very simply. Paul said we are saved by faith. James defined the faith that saves, a working faith, not a dead faith. Paul himself defined the term *faith* in a passage in Galatians; it is "faith working through love" (5:6). Love is the dynamic element in faith that makes the difference. All through the New Testament, ethics, moral responsibility, and Christian deeds are derived from faith. The man of faith has a dynamic that issues *from* the transforming grace of God *to* the outward works of a Christian nature.

The practicality of the teachings of the book of James is abundantly evident. He championed the cause of the poor over that of the rich. Christians are to avoid showing partiality (2:1–9). The "royal law" of the Scriptures is to love one's neighbor as one's self (2:8), based on Leviticus 19:18. The man who endures temptation will receive the crown of life (1:12). The tongue, though little, is a fire, being able to defile the whole body. No man can tame it (3:6–8). "Draw nigh to God, and he will draw nigh to you'' (4:8). Christians are to be patient until the return of Jesus (5:7). The writer made a statement about the sins of omission: "To him therefore that knoweth to do good, and doeth it not, to him it is sin" (4:17). His final word was "that he who converteth a sinner from the error of his way shall save a soul from death, and shall cover a multitude of sins" (5:20).

(3)   First Peter   This letter was written to the Christians living in five provinces in the northern and western parts of Asia Minor (1:1). It probably originated in Rome; there is a slight clue to this effect in 5:13: "She that is in Babylon . . . saluteth you." The "she" refers to the church from which the epistle was sent, and "Babylon" was a symbolic name for Rome. The term *Babylon* is used repeatedly for Rome in the book of Revelation (14:8; 18:2,10,21).

The author introduced himself in the first verse: "Peter, an apostle of Jesus Christ." Silvanus, whom the writer termed a "faithful brother," aided in the production of the document (5:12), either in composing it or delivering it. For centuries tradition stated that Simon Peter wrote the epistle. Not only does his name appear in 1:1; in 5:1 the author stated that he was a witness of the sufferings of Christ. Many modern New Testament scholars hold to this view also. However, some scholars of today do not believe that the book is genuinely a work of the "prophet-of-denial" fame. They base their reasoning on several observations.

First, they ask, how could an Aramaic-speaking fisherman of Galilee write some of the finest Greek to be found in the New Testament? *Second,* they also believe that there would be more of the incidents in the life and ministry of Christ and more of his teaching, since Peter was so closely associated with him. *Third,* they point out that there are passages that reflect highly the teachings of Paul, as found in Romans and Ephesians. How could this be if Peter died in Rome in the Neronian persecution of the sixties? *Fourth,* they point out that persecution of the church in Asia Minor by Roman authority did not begin till the last of the first century or the beginning of the second, too late for Peter's penning of the epistle. Those who believe that Peter wrote the epistle counter each of these contentions with answers that the people who do not accept Petrine authorship reject. And so the academic battle continues over who really penned 1 Peter.

The date of writing is highly involved in the authorship problem. To accept Peter as the author places the writing early in the sixties. Nero's fire was in 64, and the Neronian persecution followed soon after. To accept the non-Petrine authorship is to favor a later date of writing, perhaps at the close of the first century or the start of the second century. This would be during the days of Trajan, 98–117. There was a larger and more extended persecution at this time; Christianity was considered an illegal religion and worship of Christ a crime against the state. The view of this book is that Peter himself wrote the epistle sometime prior to the persecution under Nero.

There is a definite break in thought between 4:11 and 4:12, making two main divisions for the book. So there are four parts in all: salutation, 1:1–2; first part, 1:3 to 4:11; second part, 4:12 to 5:11; benediction, 5:12–14. At the end of the first division there is a doxology and an amen. The suffering of the addressee in the first part seems to be potential, or what might be; the suffering of the reader in the second part seems to be actual, a "fiery trial" among them (4:12). Some scholars think that two letters may have become fused into one and that the combined result is what we now have as 1 Peter.

The author wrote of many exhortations, urging his readers to be "holy in all manner of living"; for they have been redeemed with a costly price, "with precious blood, as of a lamb without blemish and without spot, even the blood of Christ" (1:19). Christians have "been begotten again, not of corruptible seed, but of incorruptible, through the word of God, which liveth and abideth" (1:23). They are to put away all ungodly things and live as newborn babes, longing for the "spiritual milk" (2:2) and are "to abstain from fleshly lusts, which war against the soul" (2:11). At times the writer interjected a series of short imperative sentences: "Honor all men. Love the brotherhood. Fear God. Honor the king" (2:17). He had special messages for servants, for wives, and for husbands (2:18 to 3:7). He also advised that Christians obey governmental authority. As Jesus advised paying tribute to Caesar, and as Paul counseled about being subject to rulers and magistrates, so this writer stated, "Be subject to every ordinance of man for the Lord's sake: whether to the king . . . or unto governors" (2:13–14).

We have already seen that to the writer of this epistle, the main concern is ethically living a righteous life, though surrounded by pagan influences. Yet there is a decided emphasis on the tribulations of the children of God. They should rejoice at their approaching "fiery trial," for they are "partakers of Christ's sufferings." Being reproached for the sake of Christ brings with it great blessing. The Spirit of God rests upon such. The devil stalks the earth as a roaring lion, "seeking whom he may devour"; they are to withstand him in a steadfast manner (4:12 to 5:11).

(4) Second Peter Tradition maintains that Simon Peter, the famous apostle, wrote this book just as he did 1 Peter. He called himself "Simon

Peter, a servant and apostle of Jesus Christ'' (1:1); he alluded to Jesus' prediction of his martyrdom (1:14); and he also stated that he was present at the transfiguration of Jesus on the holy mount (1:17–18). He even alluded to the fact that he wrote a previous letter, obviously referring to 1 Peter (3:1). However, more scholars have attacked the traditional authorship of this book than any other of the New Testament. The majority of modern New Testament scholars regard the book as coming from an unknown author of the early part of the second century. Some place the date of writing as late as 150.

Those who believe that Peter did not write the book present several lines of evidence. They state that it is not definitely quoted by any of the early church writers, though there are slight points of similarity in some early writings that may possibly refer to statements made in 2 Peter. The first definite reference to this book by an early writer was made by Origen (217–251), and we surmise from his statement that the book was not universally received by all the churches throughout the empire. A second line of reasoning is that the style and vocabulary of 2 Peter is vastly different from that of 1 Peter. The Greek of 1 Peter is beautiful Greek, while that of 2 Peter is less fluent and more labored.

A third line of argument is that there appear to be certain passages in 2 Peter that refer to incidents occurring long after Peter's death. One of these passages refers to Paul's epistles as though they were collected and regarded as Scripture along with the ''other scriptures'' (3:15–16). Paul's epistles were not considered canonical until long after Peter's death. Also, the second chapter of 2 Peter contains almost all of the book of Jude (nineteen out of twenty-six verses, in whole or in part), and Jude is considered by most scholars a late book.

All of these arguments are met in some way or another by those who favor the view that the great apostle from Capernaum wrote the book. They point to tradition and also to the fact that everything mentioned in the book accords with Peter's life as we see it in the Gospels. They attribute the difference in style and word usage to a different amanuensis or to Peter's personal transcription of the letter. In regard to the author's reference to Paul's epistles as Scripture, they point to the fact that the author employed the phrase ''our beloved brother Paul'' (3:15), thus implying the apostle from Tarsus to be both equal and contemporary.

Two key words in 2 Peter are *knowledge* and *know*. One or the other of these words is used sixteen times. What the author was trying to show his readers was the true knowledge that comes through Christ as placed against the knowledge set forth by the heretics. God's power brings to the Christian "all things that pertain unto life and godliness" (1:3). God has also granted to us "his precious and exceeding great promises" (1:4). The author listed seven moral qualities that the Christian should possess: virtue, knowledge, self-control, patience, godliness, brotherly kindness, and love (1:5–7). To lack these things is to be "blind, seeing only what is near" (1:9). Christians are to give diligence to make their "calling and election sure" (1:10). The author expected his death soon, as Jesus signified to him (1:14). He was with Jesus on the mount of transfiguration and heard the voice of divine approval from heaven (1:17–18).

The author makes a strong statement about the inspiration of the Scriptures: "Knowing this first, that no prophecy of scripture is of private interpretation. For no prophecy ever came by the will of man: but men spake from God, being moved by the Holy Spirit" (1:20–21). He also warned of false teachers who will come in among his readers, bringing in "destructive heresies" and "denying even the Master that bought them" (2:1). He stated that this is the second epistle he had written to his readers (3:1). The Lord will be long-suffering to his readers, "not wishing that any should perish, but that all should come to repentance" (3:9). His final admonition was that they grow in the "grace and knowledge of our Lord and Saviour Jesus Christ" (3:18).

(5) *First John*   There are four writings in the New Testament that are extremely similar in style and vocabulary: the Gospel of John, 1 John, 2 John, and 3 John. This is virtually to say that whoever wrote the Gospel wrote the three epistles as well, an opinion that is practically unanimous among students of the New Testament. Further study reveals that all four writings appear to have been penned about the same time and in the same locale. Even the purposes of the Gospel and 1 John are related. John 20:31 reads, "These are written, that ye may believe that Jesus is the Christ, the Son of God; and that believing ye may have life in his name." First John 5:13 reads, "These things have I written unto you, that ye may know that ye have eternal life, even unto you that believe on the name of the Son of God." The purpose of the Gospel is that people may believe and have spiritual life; the purpose of the letter is that the believing ones may have assurance that they have this life. The epistle presupposes the Gospel, looking back and building upon it. The Gospel leads to life; the epistle leads to certainty.

Tradition says that these four books of the New Testament and one other, the book of Revelation, were written by one of Jesus' disciples, John, the son of Zebedee; it was this very note of apostolic authority that gave the five books the weight that helped them to become a part of the

New Testament canon. Irenaeus, bishop of Lyons, stated that John lived and worked at Ephesus until the time of Trajan. The Gospel of John and 1 John are anonymous. Second John and 3 John were written by a man called "the elder." Revelation is earmarked as having been written by one named John. The Fourth Gospel, 1 John, and Revelation were accepted into the canon quite readily; 2 John and 3 John were accepted somewhat later. There is a strong tradition associating these five writings with a church or churches in Asia Minor. First John and 2 John were written to a general church situation, while 3 John was intended to be a private letter to an individual.

Both the Fourth Gospel and 1 John deal in contrasts: light and darkness, love and hate, Christ and the evil one, truth and falsehood, life and death, believing and not believing, sin and righteousness, God and the world. This dual nature found in both of these writings becomes immediately apparent to even the casual reader. There are also certain phrases that are noticeably recurrent in the two documents: "bears witness," "life," "eternal life," "of the world," "of the truth," "of God," "do the truth," "Logos," "love," and others. On the other hand, there are a few concepts that 1 John stresses more than the Gospel. This book talks of Jesus' death as being an expiation necessary for the forgiveness of sin. It speaks of the anti-christ, a term not found in the Gospel. It also very seldom refers to the Old Testament, unlike the Gospel.

Tradition says that John the apostle, son of Zebedee, wrote 1 John sometime in the last third of the first century. It also maintains that this John settled in Ephesus after the fall of Jerusalem (70), where he became the leader of the churches in that significant province. What the writer maintained in his prologue couples with John the apostle's being the author: "That which was from the beginning, that which we have heard, that which we have seen with our eyes, that which we beheld, and our hands handled, concerning the Word of life . . . declare we unto you also" (1:1–3). The writer said that he knew, saw, heard, and felt the Christ while he was here on the earth, which would certainly be the case with the beloved apostle.

Yet, as in several other New Testament books, some scholars question the traditional view of authorship. Much of what was said previously in regard to the authorship of the Fourth Gospel applies here; so it will not be completely reviewed. Suffice it to say that some scholars believe 1 John to have been penned by a John the Elder who lived in Ephesus during the last of the first century or the beginning of the second. This prominent church leader is mentioned by Eusebius, the church historian (*Ecclesiastical His-*

tory, III, 39, 3–7). Other scholars believe that the epistle was written by a disciple of the beloved apostle, who might very well have been named John, also. The view maintained in this book is that John, the son of Zebedee and brother of James, wrote the epistle known as 1 John.

There are three additional characteristics of 1 John that need to be set forth. One is that the style is very simple, easy enough for a child to read; but in many places the book is puzzling for even the wisest to comprehend. The Greek is simple, and the words are easily grasped, but the author explored theological and spiritual depths. The book is more of a flowing symphony than a logical debate. There is a central theme with many variations or tributary themes recurring here and there. The book tends to defy being neatly outlined. Simple—yet complex; this is 1 John!

The second characteristic that needs mentioning is that 1 John was composed to combat a heresy, a doctrinal error. This heretical belief seems to have been Gnosticism in an early stage, for Gnosticism made its greatest impact later on, in the second century A.D. When Gnosticism was combined with Christianity, it affected most the view of the person of Christ; it maintained that a pure, spiritual God could not come in a physical, materialistic body, since all matter was considered evil. Therefore, Christ was not really human. He just seemed to be. This type of Christianity was called Docetism; it made Jesus a phantom Christ. He was all divine and not human. The writer of 1 John started out by forcefully maintaining that the Christ he knew came to earth audibly, visibly, and concretely (1:1). He maintained that "every spirit that confesseth that Jesus Christ is come in the flesh is of God" (4:2). Jesus is the one "that came by water and blood" (5:6). Docetic Gnosticism must go, for false teaching of this nature would be fatal to the true gospel.

A third characteristic is the emphasis upon certainty that comes through personal experience. The writer stated, "These things have I written unto you, that ye may know that ye have eternal life, even unto you that believe on the name of the Son of God" (5:13). The term *know* as used in this passage is an experiential term, not just an intellectual one. It concerns the whole personal being—mind, heart, will, body, spirit—and not just the mental faculty. It correlates well with the verb *believe*, an active, dynamic assent to the person of Christ. The writer employed the verb form of believe in this epistle and very seldom the noun *faith*. He wished his readers to avoid a static concept of believing in Jesus, as assent to a creed or a dogma. The dynamic assent to Christ brings not only eternal life but a certainty of that life.

There are several outstanding passages in this epistle. The introduction

(1:1–4), with its emphasis on the true humanity of Christ, has already been mentioned, as well as the purpose passage (5:13), with its emphasis on the God-given certainty conferred upon the believer. There is a marvelous passage on love (4:7–21), in which the writer stressed the fact that those who have experienced God's love in Christ Jesus also extend that love to others. "He that loveth not knoweth not God; for God is love" (4:8). "Beloved, if God so loved us, we also ought to love one another" (4:11). "We love, because he first loved us" (4:19). Docetism tended to produce "super" Christians, a "better-than-thou" Christianity. Since love cannot exist in such an environment, the writer wanted to rectify the situation. This is why stress is placed on loving one's brother (4:20–21).

There are several passages on sin, both concerning the forgiveness of sin and the proper Christian concept of sin. "Whosoever abideth in him sinneth not: whosoever sinneth hath not seen him, neither knoweth him" (3:6). "Whosoever is begotten of God, doeth no sin" (3:9). The terms *sinneth not* and *doeth no sin* should be translated from the Greek "does not continue in sin," meaning "does not make it habitual" or "does not make it a way of life." Since the writer in another place used the phrase "if any man sin," he would have been the last to advocate the possibility of sinless perfection in this life.

(6) Second John   The background of this short epistle is very similar to 1 John. Since it is directed to "the elect lady and her children," it is less general and more personal in nature. There is disagreement among scholars about whom the letter was intended for. Was there an actual individual in whose home a community of believers met, a group known as her "children"? Or does the term *lady* figuratively designate a church, with the members its children?

The emphases in this epistle are much the same as in the first epistle. The writer, who called himself the elder (or presbyter) again stressed the true humanity of Christ, avowing "that Jesus Christ cometh in the flesh" (v. 7). He again stressed the new commandment, "that we love one another" (v. 5). The false teachers, with their false doctrines, are again his objects of warning (vv. 7–10). Even the term "anti-christ" is again mentioned (v. 7). The addressees are to walk in the truth and to abide in the teaching (vv. 4,10).

(7) Third John   This short epistle, also personal in nature, was written by the elder to "Gaius the beloved." Since Gaius seems to have been a church leader, the general emphasis of this letter switches from the doctrinal point of view to that of the administration of a church. The writer wanted the traveling missionary brethren to be entertained and encouraged

on their journeys (vv. 5–8). He also reprimanded Diotrephes, "who loveth to have the preeminence" (v. 9). He was evidently one who was controlled by a self-serving motive—quite the opposite of Demetrius, whom the author commended (v. 12).

(8) Jude Again, as with 2 and 3 John, we have a one-chapter book of the New Testament. It occupies the last place among the general, or catholic, epistles of the New Testament canon; in many ways it is more like a tract than a true letter. The author identified himself as "Jude, a servant of Jesus Christ, and brother of James" (1:1), which would in turn make him a brother of Jesus. The half brothers of Jesus are mentioned in Matthew 13:55 and Mark 6:3; of the four brothers listed, one is named Judas. (*Jude* is merely an anglicized form of *Judas.*) Though there are several men with the name Judas mentioned in the New Testament, the brother of Jesus was probably the only one who would have set himself apart by merely referring to his brother as James. Therefore tradition states that Judas, the half brother of Jesus, wrote this epistle.

However, again, as with other books of the New Testament, many scholars do not accept the traditional view. They believe that the book was written by another author, probably between 125 and 150. Both the identity of the author and the date of writing are tied up with the fact that most of Jude is contained in the second chapter of 2 Peter. Therefore, some relationship exists between these two epistles of the New Testament canon; but what is that relationship? Did the writer of 2 Peter use the book of Jude? Did the writer of Jude use 2 Peter? Or did both of these books have a common source?

It would seem reasonable for the larger epistle to have utilized the smaller. However, all do not accept this reasoning. The traditional view of the authorship of one epistle agrees with the traditional view of the authorship of the other, with an early date of writing for both books. The acceptance of a late date of writing for one book is commensurate with a late date for the other. If a late date is accepted for the books, Peter and Judas are ruled out as the authors. The place of origin of the book and the location of the people for whom it was intended are difficult to ascertain; there is insufficient evidence supplied by the author.

The writer wanted his readers to defend "the faith which was once for all delivered to the saints," but he did not describe the nature of that faith. He assumed that they knew of it (v. 3). He also warned about the men who had privately crept in, perverting the gospel of the Lord Jesus into a libertine and immoral manner of life; but he did not describe their false teaching. He merely stated that they had denied the Lord Jesus Christ

(v. 4). He used three examples from the Old Testament to show how God places his condemnation upon people who, once spiritually blessed, have fallen into sin (vv. 5–16). The readers are asked to pray in the Holy Spirit, to keep themselves in the love of God, and to look forward to the mercy of Jesus unto eternal life (vv. 20–21). The majestic benediction found at the end of this brief book is one of the most beautiful and sublime of all those in the New Testament (vv. 24–25).

PART SIX

The Apocalypse:
God Fulfilling the Church

25.
Christ in Triumph

The book of Revelation is the last book in the arrangement of the canon of the New Testament, whether or not it is the last one to have been written. It displays the expectation of the church in the consummation of the ages and is, therefore, highly predictive in nature. It is called the Apocalypse as well as Revelation, since the former term is the Greek correspondence to the Latin term *Revelation,* or that which is uncovered. Due to the imagery and the symbolical terms employed by the writer, this book presents difficulty in regard to interpretation, a fact that has led to more bizarre and fantastic concepts than those set forth for any other book of the Bible.

1. The Author and Date of Writing

The author identified himself as ''John'' (1:4; 22:8) and called himself ''brother'' (1:9) and ''prophet'' (22:9). He claimed that he received his vision on the isle of Patmos while in exile there. Patmos is a small, rocky island in the Mediterranean about sixty miles southwest of Ephesus. Justin Martyr, writing about the middle of the second century, stated that John, the famous apostle, wrote the book (*Dialogue With Trypho,* 81).

Even such a late date for the writing of the book as the reign of Domitian (81–96) would permit the aged John to be the one who penned it. Therefore, the date of 95 is judged by many as the date of composition. Irenaeus said that John received his vision ''almost in our day, towards the end of Domitian's reign'' (*Against Heresies,* V, XXX, 3).

Some think the book was written during the reign of Nero (54–68), when the burning of Rome in 64 set off a great persecution of the Christians in the Imperial City. This view would favor a date of writing around 65–70. An argument for this early date used by some scholars is that the difference in the Greek style and vocabulary in Revelation, as opposed to that in the Fourth Gospel and the three Johannine epistles, is due to an earlier effort at writing on John's part, before his ability to write had fully matured. The reigns of other emperors have also been suggested by various scholars as the time of composition of the book.

Some present-day students of the New Testament do not believe that John the apostle was the author of Revelation. They say he did not claim to be the beloved apostle; nor did he claim apostolic authority. He also did not claim to have seen Jesus in the flesh, much less to have been associated with him in his ministry. There is also some evidence that John, as well as his brother James, suffered an early martyrdom. These scholars believe that a John wrote the book, but not John the apostle. Other possibilities are John the Elder or a disciple of John who was also named John.

2. The Apocalyptic

Much of this misunderstanding concerning the book of Revelation stems from a failure to recognize the true nature of the document. It is an apocalyptic writing. In such writing a seer, a man of God, has a vision of the unfolding of future events, which he in turn writes down. This vision is couched in highly figurative or symbolic terms, a form of imagery readily understood by the addressees of that age, even though much of the key to the cryptic language is lost to the modern world. *Apocalyptic* (a term not to be confused with *apocryphal,* or that which pertains to the Apocrypha, the fourteen books not included in the evangelical canon of the Bible) literature was generally produced during times of persecution to encourage those being oppressed because of their faith. There is the belief that God will intervene in history, overthrow Satan and the whole demonic order, and bring in the new, blessed, and eternal age for the believing ones, the righteous. Therefore, the apocalyptic is *religious* in nature more than *political,* a fact which a lot of interpreters of the Bible have failed to understand.

Many people confuse the apocalyptic with the prophetic. In prophecy a man of God speaks the message of God to the people. He is God's spokesman. Most of what he declares has to do with the age in which he lives. Some has to do with the future; but when it does, it is purely incidental. Foretelling the future is *not* a requisite of prophecy. In apocalyptic, a man of God receives a vision unfolding the future, a vision set forth in imagery. The first half of Daniel is prophetic; the second half is apocalyptic. The first half of Zechariah is prophetic; the second half is apocalyptic. Isaiah 24–27 is apocalyptic, and the remainder is prophetic. Some of Joel is apocalyptic, as well as much of Ezekiel. Matthew 24:3–51 is called the Little Apocalypse to differentiate it from the book of Revelation, the Apocalypse. Certain sections of 1 and 2 Thessalonians are apocalyptic. During the interbiblical period and into the Christian era, much Jewish apocalyptic writing was produced. In fact, the period rich in apocalyptic writings extended from 165 B.C. to A.D. 135. Some extracanonical apocalyptic writings are Enoch, 2 Esdras, the Apocalypse of Peter, and the Shepherd of Hermas.

3. Interpretation of Revelation

Many highly imaginative interpretations of this book have been set forth through the ages. The work is very unusual, posing quite a different structure and style from most of the biblical books. It is drama, much of which is set in poetic style. There is both prose and poetry. It is intended to be read to a congregation (1:3). At the same time it can be considered a letter, a letter addressed to seven churches. It abounds in very unusual symbolism. The language of the book is cryptic and is therefore puzzling to the reader of today, though the meaning may have been quite apparent to the reader of the era in which the book was penned.

We know that the Lamb is Christ, that Babylon refers to Rome, and that the dragon is Satan. Many other terms are also readily apparent, but the meaning of some of the word pictures and the actions of the book have become lost in antiquity. Scores of people through the years have assured us that they have the key to the entire symbolism of the book. These self-appointed voices of authority produce their charts and enunciate their carefully designed plan for the entire book, many times breaking off Christian fellowship with those who do not completely agree with their detailed interpretations. They become so engrossed with details that they fail to discern that the overall picture is much clearer than many of the details. As a result, they turn the book into sheer nonsense. The ironical thing is that, even though each of these persons speaks authoritatively, there are as many interpretations as there are interpreters.

However, the problem presented by the hidden nature of the writing should not deter us from seeking the central message that this inspired book poses for the Christian of today. It depicts a cosmic struggle between the saints and their persecutors and between God and Satan. There is a beauty and forcefulness in this document that is found nowhere else. It reveals God's righteous dealings with his people, now and for eternity. It assures us of the final and complete overthrow of the forces of evil and of God's blessed and eternal reign through the ages in the company of all the saints and angelic powers. The total picture is the important thing, and this total scene is a magnificent one.

Nothing new about the doctrine of Christ is presented; nothing is set forth not found elsewhere in the New Testament. It is the familiar gospel story and the complete triumph of Christ presented in a striking manner. The dazzling array of cosmic movements, set in the context of cryptic metaphors, strengthens the faith of the believer. He senses anew the might, power, righteousness, and wisdom of God; regardless of the sufferings and presecutions of this life, his faith and supreme trust are placed in the hands of the one who will be completely triumphant some great day. The apparent dualism in the world will be resolved, and the forces of righteousness will emerge in an all-encompassing victory.

4. The Preliminary Message of Revelation (1:1 to 3:22)

In a formal preface (1:1–3), John stated that God is the source of the contents of the book, for the revelation is that which "God gave him to show unto his servants." He also stated that these things "must shortly come to pass." In fact, "the time is at hand" (1:1–3). John was informed that his visions were "the things which are, and the things which shall come to pass hereafter" (1:19) and that he was to send the message to "the seven churches that are in Asia" (1:4). This phrase refers to the province of Asia in western Asia Minor, and the seven churches are in the cities of Ephesus, Smyrna, Pergamum, Thyatira, Sardis, Philadelphia, and Laodicea.

Each letter is individually composed to suit the needs of the church to which it is addressed. The main ideas in each letter are as follows:

(1) Ephesus (2:1–7)

After praising the saints at Ephesus for resisting evil men and false apostles, the writer remontrated with them: "But I have this against thee, that thou didst leave thy first love." They opposed error, but they forgot to love.

(2) Smyrna (2:8–11)

Christ, who died and rose again, understands their tribulation. He knows of their poverty and that they are bothered by Jews of the "synagogue of Satan." If they are faithful in the coming persecution, they will be rewarded.

(3) Pergamum (2:12–17)

Christians here dwell where "Satan's throne is," referring to the city as the center in the East for emperor worship. Christ knows that they hold fast his name and do not deny the faith. Since he also knows of the erring ways of some of the Christians, he begs the sinning ones to repent; else he will come quickly.

(4) Thyatira (2:18–29)

The Son of God knows of their works, love, faith, ministry, and patience. However, he rebukes them for putting up with the "woman Jezebel," a self-named prophetess, who teaches the Christians "to commit fornication, and to eat things sacrificed to idols." This probably refers to the idolatrous feasts sponsored by the trade guilds of idol makers. Since Jezebel and those who have resorted to her ways have not repented, he has a punishment allotted for her. Other Christians have been drawn to "the deep things of Satan," probably referring to Gnosticism.

(5) Sardis (3:1–6)

This church is located in a city noted for its licentiousness. Christ is evidently warning them of the danger of spiritual death, of being outwardly alive but spiritually dead. They should be watchful and should repent.

(6) Philadelphia (3:7–13)

This church, like Smyrna, is troubled by the opposition of the Jews, those of "the synagogue of Satan." Christ will verify his love for the saints of this city before the eyes of the Jews and will keep them from the hour of trial. They are to hold fast to their convictions.

(7) Laodicea (3:14–22)

This is a wealthy city near Colossae. Christ rebukes the city because of its apathy, for they are "neither cold nor hot." The people are affluent but indifferent. Therefore, they are to be rejected. Thinking themselves to be rich and in need of nothing, they are really destitute—wretched, miserable, poor, blind, and naked. They are admonished to be zealous and to repent. Christ desires communion with his people. He knocks, patiently waiting for the response that will make fellowship a reality. The word to this church ends with the same statement of exhortation used at the ending for the other six churches: "He that hath an ear, let him hear what the Spirit saith to the churches."

5. The Principal Message of Revelation 4:1 to 22:21

When the reader goes from the third chapter to the fourth chapter he finds himself in a different setting. The first three chapters picture Jesus as judge and protector of Christian communities, asking the saints to be faithful at all costs. It is a picture of Christ, the Living One, amidst the churches. The last nineteen chapters set forth quite a different aspect, for they present Jesus in dramatic fashion as the consummation of the present era and the ushering in of the future one. John wrote of Christ in true prophetic style. He used many of the phrases and figures of speech employed by the prophets of Israel of old. In fact, he borrowed constantly from the Old Testament—words, phrases, imagery. Yet he never directly quoted from its pages.

John wrote with the firm conviction that history moves under a sovereign God to a planned destiny; and with this conviction in mind he brought comfort to people facing martyrdom. Even though the plight of the churches facing the power of Rome might be grim, the Christians should realize that they are partners with God in a struggle in which God will be victorious. The outcome of the struggle is sure, and the church will share in the triumph. To suffer, even to endure martyrdom, will ultimately bring its reward.

John wrote to people who might be viewed with suspicion if they were to be discovered reading a document that is seemingly disloyal to the emperor or to the empire he represented. Therefore, suspicion is suppressed by the use of highly figurative terms, cryptic symbols, and elaborate imagery. Christians will understand that Babylon means Rome and that the Lamb signifies Christ; they will comprehend the intricate symbolism in its every detail, though this might be hidden from pagan understanding. Domitian viewed himself as *Dominus et Deus* (Lord and God); therefore, he required that he be worshiped. For John God alone is to be worshiped—not men, nor angels, but God alone (22:9). In view of a pagan demand for the Christians to enter into the idolatrous practice of emperor worship, John asked them to resort to civil disobedience, even though this might result in martyrdom.

The last nineteen chapters contain three parts: a scene in heaven, seven visions (each in turn containing seven visions), and an epilogue. These will be briefly surveyed.

John described a scene in heaven that was given to him as he was "in the Spirit" (4:1 to 5:14). He was granted a vision of God on his "throne set in heaven," with a rainbow surrounding the throne. According to his vision, there are twenty-four lesser thrones with as many elders sitting on them; all of the elders wear gold crowns. Out of God's throne proceed "lightnings and voices and thunders." To these are added the "seven Spirits of God" and the "four living creatures." The creatures sing, "Holy, holy, holy, is the Lord/God, the Almighty, who was/and who is and who is to come" (v. 8). The elders sing, "Worthy art thou, our Lord/ and our God, to receive the/glory and the honor and the/power: for thou didst create all/things, and because of thy will/they were, and were created" (v. 11).

To this picture of God's receiving homage from the representatives of all creation is presented a similar magnificent view of Christ, the Lamb of God, the only one worthy to unloose the seven seals of the book of life. He is not only the "Lamb standing, as though it had been slain"; he is also "the Lion that is of the tribe of Judah, the Root of David." He is both suffering servant and reigning king at one and the same time. He is the only one worthy to read the sealed scroll containing the divine destinies of all created ones. A multitude of angels, living creatures, and elders declare with a loud voice, "Worthy is the Lamb that hath/been slain to receive the power,/and riches, and wisdom, and/might, and honor, and glory,/and blessing" (v. 11).

All creation gives homage and worship (5:1–14). The picture of worship here in heaven is at it should be on earth. John was exhorting his readers to worship God—not Caesar, idols, the world, or the state.

Thus, one of the most significant features of the book of Revelation is its Christology, its view of Christ. Any declaration of the destiny of man, present or future, rests on the exalted and sublime picture of the Redeemer, Christ Jesus. Eschatology rests on Christology. The opening phrase of the book bears this in mind: "The Revelation of Jesus Christ." The central theme is the person of Christ as he unfolds the future. Many false interpretations of the book could be avoided if the centrality of the person of Christ were only kept foremost in the mind of the interpreter. Martin Luther, back in 1522, wrote of his lack of esteem for the book of Revelation, stating that in his opinion Christ was neither taught nor recognized in the book. Luther could be no further from the truth, for the person of Christ is the central and crowning glory of the book.

The main body of the book consists of seven visions, each of which has seven visions of its own. These are apocalyptic in nature, extremely rich in imagery and symbolism, and extremely hard to comprehend. The book many times mentions the number seven, a number implying completion in the mind of the Jew. Seven is complete, and anything less than seven is incomplete.

(1) Seven seals (6:1 to 8:1)

The Lamb, who is Jesus Christ, is the only one worthy to open the seven-sealed scroll. When each one is opened, disastrous things occur on earth. The white horse brings war (6:2); the red horse brings civil turmoil (6:3–4); the black horse brings famine (6:5–6); and the pale horse brings death (6:8). The breaking of the fifth seal reveals the martyrs who died for their faith, crying out for vengeance on their persecutors. John probably thought of all the saints as martyrs. Even though they cry out to be avenged, they are told they will have to wait. They are safe under God's altar. The breaking of the sixth seal produces great cosmic disturbances, all involving earth, sun, moon, and stars. The scene then shifts to the future, showing a multitude around the throne of God serving him night and day, all in a state of blessedness and heavenly bliss. The breaking of the seventh seal brings silence in heaven for half an hour.

(2)   Seven trumpets (8:2 to 11:29)

Seven angels initiate another series of seven woes. Their trumpets blast forth one after another, and with each blast a new horror hits the world. Some of these horrors remind the reader of the plagues in Egypt during the days of Moses. The writer is told to eat the little book the angel is to give him, which he does. It is sweet to his mouth and bitter to his stomach. Great voices in heaven sing, ''The kingdom of the world is/become the kingdom of our/Lord, and of his Christ: and he/shall reign for ever and for ever'' (11:15).

(3)   Seven visions of the dragon's kingdom (12:1 to 13:18)

The heavenly woman gives birth to a child but has great suffering. The child is the preexistent Messiah. The ''great red dragon,'' who is Satan, shows great hostility to the child, wanting to destroy the child and the woman. The rest of the seed of the woman is the church. The dragon, Satan, persecutes the church, but the church is not harmed. It is nourished by God instead, a great sign to the persecuted Christians of their ultimate security in God (12:1–17).

John gave visions of two beasts (13:1–18), which are related to his visions of the dragon (12:1–17). The first beast resembles the dragon in that he has ''ten horns and seven heads''; he even receives his power, throne, and authority from the dragon, Satan. The ''ten horns'' represent the ten Roman emperors ruling from the public ministry of Jesus until the writing of the book. These are Tiberius, Caligula, Claudius, Nero, Galba, Otho, Vitellius, Vespasian, Titus, and Domitian. Galba, Otho, and Vitellius had extremely brief reigns. When these three are subtracted from the ten, seven are left—the seven strong emperors represented by the seven heads of the beast. The ''names of blasphemy'' on the heads of the beast stand in contrast to God's marks on the foreheads of the martyrs (14:1) and probably represent the divine titles the emperors claimed for themselves.

The first beast comes from the sea (13:1); the second beast comes from the earth (13:11). The second has two horns, like a lamb, but speaks as a dragon. Therefore, his appearance is deceptive; he looks like Christ, but is really satanic. He makes the people worship the first beast. This second beast represents the pagan priesthood of the empire that pushes emperor worship. Where the first beast is political, the second beast is religious. This is a case of religion making overtures to the state. The second beast tries to get all the people to accept the ''mark'' of the first beast, which will result in their security and prosperity (right "to buy or to sell"). All of this symbolism would be very apparent to a first-century reader of John's document. John gave to the second beast the number 666 (13:18), and this number has been applied by interpreters to almost every infamous character in history.

(4) Seven visions of worshipers of the Lamb and worshipers of the beast (14:1–20).

The Lamb, Christ, stands on Mount Zion with the martyrs (14:1–5). Angels proclaim the worship of God (14:6–7), predict the fall of Babylon, which is Rome (14:8), and condemn those who worship the beast (14:9–12). The martyrs are praised (14:13). Christ executes judgment (14:14–16). There is a vision of the winepress of God (14:17–20).

(5) Seven bowls (15:1 to 16:21)

There is a magnificent hymn to God extolling his holiness (15:3–4), after which John gave the visions of seven golden bowls filled with the wrath of God (15:7). These are poured out on the earth, each one producing a plague (15:5 to 16:21), very similar in purpose to the plagues caused by the seven seals (6:1 to 8:6) and by the seven trumpets (8:7 to 11:19). Again the judgment of God is very vividly depicted. Here there is one distinction, however; the seven bowls are "the last, for in them is finished the wrath of God" (15:1). The seals, trumpets, and bowls do not necessarily follow each other in sequence. They might overlap.

(6) Seven visions of the fall of Babylon (17:1 to 19:10)

Babylon is a name depicting Rome, which John also termed "the great harlot" (17:1). She is dressed in purple and scarlet, showing her regal power, and adorned with gold and precious stones, showing her extreme wealth. In her hand, however, is a "golden cup full of abominations, even the unclean things of her fornication" (17:4). John depicted her as a prostitute endeavoring to beguile the world into the worship of the emperor. (The prophets of the Old Testament also pictured idolatry and apostasy as adultery.) John called the Christian to "come forth . . . out of her" and to have no fellowship with her sins (18:4).

(7) Seven visions of the end of Satan's age and the beginning of God's age (19:11 to 22:5)

Christ comes on a white horse with his heavenly army (19:11–16), quite a contrast to his first humble coming in Bethlehem when he was born of the virgin Mary. He defeats the beast and the kings of the earth arrayed with their armies, after which the beast and the false prophet are cast into the lake of fire and brimstone (19:19–21). There is a thousand-year reign of the martyrs with Christ, with Satan bound. After this, he is unbound (20:1–6).

The "nations which are in the four corners of the earth" are defeated, finally devoured by fire; and the devil is cast into the lake of fire and brimstone, in company with the beast and false prophet. Satan's age is over (20:7–10). There is a judgment before the throne of God. Death and Hades are thrown into the lake of fire (20:11–15). John pictured the consummation of the age, with the passing away of the first earth and the first heaven and the ushering in of the new earth and the new heaven. God's perfect and eternal age begins (21:1 to 22:5).

John very fittingly completed his great document by an epilogue: a final testimony, invitation, warning, and the promise of the Lord Jesus to come quickly (22:6–20). He concluded with a benediction: "The grace of the Lord Jesus be with the saints. Amen" (22:21).

Index